Predicting Politics

Predicting Politics

Essays in Empirical Public Choice

W. Mark Crain and
Robert D. Tollison,
Editors

Ann Arbor
The University of Michigan Press

Copyright © by The University of Michigan 1990
All rights reserved
Published in the United States of America by
The University of Michigan Press
Manufactured in the United States of America

1993   1992   1991   1990   4   3   2   1

Library of Congress Cataloging-in-Publication Data

Predicting politics : essays in empirical public choice / W. Mark
   Crain and Robert D. Tollison, editors.
        p.   cm.
   Includes bibliographical references.
   ISBN 0-472-10167-6
   1. Social choice.   2. Political science—Decision making.
3. Political science—Forecasting.   I. Crain, W. Mark (William
Mark), 1951–   .   II. Tollison, Robert D.
HB846.8.P74   1990
320'.01'132—dc20   90-10767
                                                              CIP

Contents

Part 8. Institutions and Attenuated Property Rights

Part 1
Toward a Positive Public Choice

Empirical Public Choice

W. Mark Crain and Robert D. Tollison

Normally, a collection such as this one would open with a long essay arguing for the importance of the work that follows and for its distinctiveness in the literature. We do not offer such an essay here for a functional reason—the second chapter in the volume more or less fulfills this purpose. We confine ourselves in this introductory essay to some relatively brief remarks about the nature of the research represented by the chapters in the volume and its relationship to the literature, as well as the obligatory short survey of the contents. Moreover, since one or both of us participated in a number of the chapters, we felt that the essays themselves are the best examples of the approach that we follow and the type of problems that attract our interest, and that the bibliographies in each essay reflect the relevant literature from which this research draws inspiration. In essence, we prefer to have the volume judged by the creativity shown in the individual essays, without a lot of prior advertising by us.

To begin, what is meant by public choice? Put simply, it is the application of the principles of economic analysis to political behavior and institutions. At the most basic level public choice is founded on the idea that human behavior in governmental settings is motivated by the same self-interested forces that guide human behavior in private settings. This does not mean that behavior is the same in the two environments—the constraints on self-interest will differ between government and the private sector. But the people acting in both sectors are the same sort of people, whatever the context in which they work, and public choice hypothesizes that private interest will dominate decision making in a large number of cases. It should be stressed that this is not a dogmatic assertion that politicians and other political actors are self-interested; rather, it is a pragmatic analytical convention. The usefulness of the public

We would like to thank William C. Mitchell of the University of Oregon for his encouragement, past and present, of this project. We also thank Thomas D. Willett for his comments on this introductory essay and the contents of the volume generally. The usual caveat applies.

choice approach lies in its ability to generate testable hypotheses and predictions about political behavior. These have been found to hold in a variety of cases, and the appeal of the approach has grown steadily in the past twenty-five years. The collection of essays is presented in the tradition of exploring the explanatory power of public choice theories; hence, the volume is called *Predicting Politics*.

A considerable part of the modern development of public choice theory consisted in transporting the toolkit that economists had evolved for the study of the private sector to the study of the public sector. We do not mean to imply that it was easy to do this, but only that it was a natural line of intellectual development. One can go back through the papers in the 1972 collection of articles entitled *The Theory of Public Choice* by Buchanan and Tollison, and its 1984 sequel, *The Theory of Public Choice—II*, to trace this period in the development of public choice thought. Outside of the Virginia School and its associated journal, *Public Choice*, the extension of economic theory to politics was occurring at other places, such as Chicago and Rochester, and appearing more regularly in standard economics journals such as the *Journal of Political Economy*, *Journal of Law and Economics*, and *Journal of Legal Studies*. The essays in this volume follow in the footsteps of this rich tradition. Concepts, such as team production, which have been found to be useful in analyzing private sector institutions, are carried over to a political setting and applied in what we think are productive ways, productive not only in bettering our understanding of political processes, but in bettering our grasp of the economic principles being applied.

The distinctiveness of the volume is based upon the two basic principles around which it is organized. The first principle is to take the public choice revolution in economics seriously. These essays apply the economic paradigm to politics with a relish. The point is to take the basic economic theory of the firm, labor supply, cartels, long-run contracting, advertising, team production, regulation, and so on, and to apply it to legislatures, politicians, parties, pressure groups, and whatever else one might discover in the universe of political behavior. The essays in this volume attempt to push the economic approach to politics to the limit, for it is at the limit that one can tell whether or not the approach has any merit. This procedure comports with the modern expansion of economic theory to explain other realms of human interaction, such as crime, marriage, sports, and the family. The economic explanation of politics has been an important part of this process, and the essays in this volume hopefully illustrate the usefulness of bringing economic concepts to bear on politics.

The second principle around which the volume is organized is that the proof is in the pudding. Virtually every essay in the volume follows the approach of positive economics. An economic model of politics is presented in a testable form, and the model is then tested. In other words, evidence is brought to bear on the accuracy of specifying economic models of politics. This principle goes hand-in-hand with the first principle in that it is incumbent on those who use economic analysis to explain politics to show that such an interpretation can explain actual behavior better than or in a strongly complementary manner to alternative approaches. This is a challenge that must be met if public choice is to become a truly explanatory theory. In this regard many of the essays take advantage of the existence of a natural empirical laboratory in the form of the cross-section of U.S. state governments. James Bryce (1917, 451) made a similar observation, only more eloquently: ". . . state constitutions . . . are a mine of instruction for the natural history of democratic communities." Differences in political institutions across the states allow a positive economist to test many of his predictions about political behavior and institutions. How, for example, do different sizes of legislatures influence legislative output (for example, bills passed) or the formation of interest groups? Empirical testing is not, however, confined to the level of U.S. state governments. Other essays in the volume present tests based on extensive and original microeconomic data sets on the U.S. Congress. But the basic point is that these authors pursue empirical work on politics with a vengeance, so much so that the volume is given the subtitle *Essays in Empirical Public Choice*. The emphasis is strictly on theories that explain something about the real world. How do individuals in legislatures, regulatory agencies, the judiciary, the executive branch, and so on actually behave?

The two organizing principles of the volume, then, are the use of economics to explain politics and a belief that public choice theories should be tested. These emphases come at a time when the general drift in public choice scholarship is toward highly mathematical theories, theories that are not empirically testable, and indeed some rejection of the idea that economics can be used successfully to explain or predict politics. Perhaps this volume will serve as an antidote to some degree for these trends, and help to refocus attention on what the public choice revolution was all about and what its explanatory promise is. However, none of this is intended as breast-beating. Naturally, we think the approach represented in this volume is useful, but that is ultimately for the reader to judge.

It should also be clear that the essays in this volume derive from the classic literature of public choice, which includes such authors as Duncan Black, Kenneth Arrow, Anthony Downs, Mancur Olson, James Buchanan, Gordon Tullock, William Riker, and George Stigler. Other important influences are reflected in the footnotes and references of the individual chapters. There, one will see listed the above names along with others such as Sam Peltzman, Gary Becker, Armen Alchian, Harold Demsetz, Richard Posner, William Landes, Dennis Mueller, and still others too numerous to mention.

Moreover, this collection of essays is not exhaustive. There were articles that clearly would have been included except for the constraints of space and a desire by the editors to provide a roughly equal number of previously published and unpublished works. What the collection of essays hopefully illustrates is some of the best and most creative work in the area of empirical public choice. We stress that we do not claim to be the only ones working on problems of empirical public choice. Many able scholars from various disciplines have worked and continue to work on such problems. There are differences in approach and emphasis among the various scholars, but there is also a unity of purpose in explaining political behavior and institutions. An altogether too brief survey of related literature follows.

Chicago Political Economy, as typified in a recent volume by that title edited by Stigler (1989), focuses on problems similar to those of empirical public choice, but at an arguably much broader level of analytical discourse. Chicago Political Economy emphasizes the impact of political and regulatory decision making on resource allocation and prices, and in the process more or less assumes that political institutions accommodate the effects of competition among pressure groups. The public choice approach stresses the role and impact of institutions and the transactional nature of politics. Chicago Political Economy, for example, might focus on the impact of economic regulation on the level of a politically determined price; empirical public choice might, by contrast, add to such an analysis an investigation of how the number of regulators affects the political price. In fact, the two problems are not conceptually distinct, though the former level of analysis is somewhat broader in context than the latter.

Other scholars, such as Kenneth Shepsle, Barry Weingast, and Joseph Kalt, have employed economic analogies in their work, just as the essays in this volume do. Weingast, for example, pioneered the use of agency theory to explain the congressional oversight of bureaucratic behavior (Weingast and Moran 1983), and, more recently, has drawn parallels between fundamental aspects of legislative organization and industrial organization (Weingast and Marshall 1988). Shepsle (1978) spearheaded the structure-induced equilibrium approach to understanding legislative organization. Kalt has analyzed legislator voting behavior in terms of the economic theory of team production and shirking (Kalt and Zupan 1984). All of these are important contributions to the literature in basically the same spirit as the chapters in this volume.

Another important group of scholars working in empirical public choice might be labeled the Zurich School. This group is headed by Bruno Frey of the University of Zurich, and over recent years Frey, in collaboration with colleagues and former students, such as Friedrich Schneider, has made fundamental contributions to empirical public choice, most especially in the area of the relationship between macroeconomic conditions, voting behavior, and election outcomes (Frey and Schneider 1978a, 1978b). These are, however, only a few of the many papers and books produced by this group, with no sign of abatement in sight. Like the approach by the authors in this book, the Zurich Group basically seeks to understand how real world public choice processes actually work.

Other contributions to the literature of empirical public choice are more scattered in nature and are hard to group into any particular category. A small sampler of this work follows. Dating from the early 1970s, investigation of the possibility of a political business cycle has attracted various empirical analyses, including Kramer (1971) and Tufte (1978). Many public choice scholars have written about voting behavior and the incentive of individuals to participate in the political process. An early paper by Barzel and Silberburg (1973) about voting in gubernatorial elections notably comes to mind. McCormick and Tollison (1981) have written extensively about legislator pay and other aspects of legislative organization, as well as the economic theory of interest groups and their impact on the economy. There has been a heated debate with respect to the issue of the degree to which ideology or the personal preferences of a representative, as opposed to economic interest group pressures, determine voting behavior. Kau and Rubin (1979) have been important participants in this debate. International political economy is a relatively new area for the application of public choice methodology (Frey 1984; Tollison and Willett 1979), and an earlier contribution in this area is the work of Pincus (1975) on tariffs. Wagner has done basic empirical work on the public choice approach to public finance, including such issues as fiscal illusion and competition among governments (Wagner 1976; Martin and Wagner 1978). Lindsay and Maloney (1987) have recently discussed the nature of political parties in empirical public choice terms. Jacobson (1980) has produced a substantial amount of work on the effects of campaign spending on election outcomes. Gray (1973) and Shughart and Tollison (1984) have studied the process by which laws are diffused across U.S. states. Fenno (1973), Ferejohn (1974), and Fiorina (1974) have published important empirical studies of congressional organization and behavior. Mueller and Murrell (1986) have studied the determinants and impacts of interest groups on economic activity. We could go on, but the point is not to review the literature on empirical public choice exhaustively. We are clearly not the only ones working in this area, but we think that this volume represents a unique contribution to this literature.

As to the organization and contents of the volume, we conclude with a short survey of the sections and individual chapters. The introductory section includes one other chapter by Tollison which, as noted above, is an overview of the literature of which this volume is representative. In addition to outlining the general approach and method used in the volume, many of the articles that could not be included are reviewed and cited in the Tollison chapter.

Part 2 introduces the general principles that inform the empirical approach to the supply of legislation. Crain, Leavens, and Tollison offer and test a theory of floor voting in the U.S. House of Representatives. The theory is based upon team production principles and the idea of controlling shirking in final voting trials by legislators. The construct of team production has effectively revolutionized the standard economist's approach to the organization of economic activity, and the authors apply the same underlying approach to the organization of legislatures. The empirical test of the theory consists in explaining which legislator's bills are voted upon first in final voting on the floor of the House. The results confirm that a major implication of the theory, that more senior legislators have their bills voted upon first, generally holds for a large sample of House bills and legislator characteristics. The second paper in this section analyzes how legislative time horizons are related to the probability of bill passage. Crain, Tollison, and Leavens posit the thesis that a political party will not allocate political benefits strictly by seniority, but will take into account such factors as the probability of reelection and retirement, in other words, the present value of the future benefits of the legislation to the party. Why pass a bill that may result in benefits flowing to a district after the tenure of the current member has ended? Using data on bill passage for the U.S. House of Representatives, strong support is found for the theory. This essay illustrates the principle of party control over the allocation of political benefits to its members. It also suggests that simple-minded theories (for example, that only legislator tenure matters) of logrolling are likely to generate incorrect predictions. In the final chapter in this section, Crain and Goff analyze the interdependence between two constitutional variables, the length and the expiration dates of legislator terms, and their impact on the output of legislatures. In the U.S. Constitution, for example, the Framers determined that senators would have six-year terms and that one-third of the Senate would be elected every two years, in other words, that there were to be three expiration dates. In this essay Crain and Goff examine the effects of this constitutional requirement. Specifically, they find that while an equal number of seats expire each term, the size of the population represented by each of the three Senate classes has become more skewed over time. The importance of the population imbalance across the three classes is linked to the bicameral legislature. Every two years the national elections involve a different number of House and Senate races that "overlap" on the same ballot. The authors use the standard theory of externalities to develop and test propositions about the effects of this constitutional structure on the output of U.S. public laws.

Part 3 examines the impact of political institutions on the demand for legislative outcomes. The broad theme is that institutions which might be considered to separate and balance power among the branches of government can serve a cartelizing function. Anderson, Martin, Shughart, and Tollison apply the Landes and Posner (1975) theory of the independent judiciary to explain the rate of constitutional change across U.S. states. The idea is that constitutional amendments are a more durable form of interest-group legislation, which will be sought when the independence of the judiciary is less pronounced (independent judges are long-run contract enforcers in the Landes-Posner theory). In their test using data for U.S. state constitutions, they find an inverse relationship between the rate of constitutional amendment and the level of judicial independence, which is precisely what the Landes-Posner theory predicts. Crain and Tollison then analyze the executive veto as a mechanism by which the executive can enforce long-run political contracts with interest groups when transient majorities seek to overturn them. They find empirical support for this interpretation of the executive veto in tests using data for U.S. states. In the final chapter in Part 3, Crain, Shughart, and Tollison apply the long-run contracting theory to analyze the sizes of legislative majorities across U.S. states. Legislative majorities are viewed as an asset, in this case serving as an implicit contract which is an alternative to an explicit or third-party contract enforced by the judicial system. Larger majorities mean that interest groups can rely on normal legislation for securing benefits rather than having to take recourse to the more costly constitutional route. Again, a test using legislative majority sizes across U.S. states supports the basic implications of the long-run contracting theory.

Part 4 contains two papers about the internal organization of legislatures. Leibowitz and Tollison offer and test a theory of why committees exist in a legislature. The basic point is that the legislature faces a time constraint on passing its agenda, and in this setting the use of committees allows the legislature to consider and pass more of its agenda than would be the case if the whole legislature debated each bill in detail. They find some limited support for their theory in a series of empirical tests. Crain develops a party loyalty theory of the committee system in the next chapter. One of the most important functions of the committee system—namely, to provide the leadership with a mechanism to control legislator behavior—has been ignored almost totally in the literature. In the conventional view, committees are seen as a way to let legislators specialize in subjects of interest to their constituents, for example, members from farm districts serve on the agriculture committee and urban members join the housing committee. This view has overshadowed a more critical function of the committee system, which is to prevent legislators who are not aligned with party leaders from obtaining positions of prominence. By analogy to the organization of professional baseball, the committee system contains "minor league" and "major league" teams. Legislators must demonstrate their loyalty to party leaders before receiving an assignment to the more influential committees. Evidence on the loyalty theory is provided using data on committee assignments in the U.S. House of Representatives.

Part 5 is about legislative districts and redistricting. The essay by Crain offers a theory of legislative turnover as a function of types of legislative districts. The single-member district, as opposed to a multi-member district, is modeled as analogous to the division of territories in a cartel with consequent restricted entry and lower turnover. Using data on state legislative districts, Crain finds support for this approach to explaining legislative turnover. The essay by Crain, Davis, and Tollison is an effort to analyze redistricting using a microeconomic framework. They theorize that judge-mandated redistricting will be less respectful of incumbent legislators than will legislatively mandated redistricting. They test and find support for their theory using data pertaining to the sizes of state legislative majorities and incumbent turnover under the two types of redistricting schemes.

Part 6 is about nonelected actors in the political process—bureaucrats and regulators—and examines their roles in the economic approach to politics. First, Shughart, Tollison, and Goff discuss the origins of commission government. Running a bureaucracy by a committee rather than by a single actor is, in effect, a way to control variability in agency decision making. This feature of commission governance gives a legislative oversight committee more effective control over their bureaucratic dominion, a feature which might be attractive when the legislature is setting out in new regulatory waters. These authors test their theory on data for the Federal Trade Commission and the Antitrust Division of the Department of Justice, and find it strongly supported. Higgins, Shughart, and Tollison extend the theory of economic regulation to the case of mergers of regulated firms (for example, public utilities). They test their theory using data on state gas and electric utilities and on state regulatory environments, and find that a political wealth-maximization model offers a good explanation of public utility commissioner decision making on mergers between regulated firms.

In Part 7, the focus is on voter behavior and campaign finance. Faith and Tollison test the idea, called expressive voting, that voting is like responding to a pollster. Nothing is supposed to be at stake, so behavior does not reflect the opportunity cost of a choice; hence, the voter can indulge his moral sentiments in the ballot box. The alternative hypothesis is that opportunity costs matter in voting and that voters vote economically, heeding the connection between expected costs and expected benefits. The authors test their theory on data for state welfare spending for U.S. states, and find uniform and strong support for economic as opposed to expressive voting. The effect of campaign spending on election outcomes has been the subject of numerous articles in both the political science and the economic literature. The prevailing view is that spending matters for challengers but not for incumbents. The essay by Thomas revisits this controversy and offers a critique of the theoretical and empirical models that have been used to estimate these relationships. Thomas develops a theory that assumes candidates only spend money on negative advertisement and rebuttals to negative advertisements. Based on an alternative specification to the standard model, Thomas finds that spending matters for incumbents as well as for challengers. In the final chapter in Part 7, Crain, Tollison and Leavens attempt to go beyond the standard issues addressed in the campaign finance literature; specifically, they examine the impact of laws that limit campaign contributions on the size of government. They argue that when legal restrictions are imposed on campaign financing, such as ceilings on the amounts that contributors can contribute, politicians are more inclined to impose tax increases on citizens who are nonconstituents. The authors examine two empirical implications of the analysis using state data on districts, campaign finance laws, the size of state governments, and the enactment of state statutes.

The essays in Part 8 look at the impact of rules and constraints on political activity. In the first chapter, Anderson and Tollison model the role of an appropriations monopoly for the lower house of a legislature and its impact on the size of the lower house. They find support for the idea that the appropriations monopoly leads to a larger lower house size in a test using data for the U.S. states. In the second chapter Anderson and Tollison address the historical development of the secret ballot, concentrating on the circumstances in the United States and the United Kingdom. They argue that prior to secret ballot laws and regulations, votes were fairly openly bought and sold. In such a regime the upper class was able to protect itself from wealth redistributions by the lower class, since the lower class generally found it propitious to sell its votes. Secret ballot laws closed the vote market and made it more difficult for vote-buyers to enforce agreements with voter-sellers. Hence, wealth redistribution from rich to poor and the corresponding size of government increased. Anderson and Tollison test this idea using data on U.S. states for the early 1900s and find larger state governments in those states with open ballot laws at the time, all else equal.

We close by emphasizing that the essays in this book are not presented as the products of a completed research agenda. We can think of many useful projects and data sets to be worked on in the future. There is more to be done about the internal organization of legislatures, the behavior of regulatory bureaus, the nature of cooperation and competition among the branches of government, constitutional change, the behavior of incumbent politicians in erecting entry barriers into politics, judicial behavior, the political economy of deficit finance, legislative oversight of bureaucracy, the much neglected role of the executive branch in public choice theory, international political economy, and so on. Each of these areas contains interesting research projects. Our point is simply that empirical public choice, as presented in this volume and its related literature, provides a challenge to any economist who wants to put his tools to creative use. The following essays hopefully raise this challenge well.

Indeed, although public choice has had a tremendous impact on the way scholars think about and analyze government, it seems fair to argue that it has not yet achieved the status of anything like a paradigm. The subdiscipline is, after all, only about forty years old (dating its origin from Duncan Black's early work of the theory of committees and voting). Moreover, practitioners of public choice are marching off in a variety of directions, not all of which are heartening to us. In this setting an approach based on positive economics and empirical testing of theories represents a way out of the bog of competing theories and claims, and a way to show the power of public choice ideas. This volume is dedicated to such purposes.

REFERENCES

Alchian, A. A., and H. Demsetz. 1972. "Production, Information Costs, and Economic Organization." *American Economic Review* 62 (December): 777–96.
Arrow, K. J. 1951. *Social Choice and Individual Values*. New York: John Wiley.
Barzel, Y., and E. Silberberg. 1973. "Is the Act of Voting Rational?" *Public Choice* 16 (Fall): 51–58.
Becker, G. S. 1983. "A Theory of Competition Among Pressure Groups for Influence." *Quarterly Journal of Economics* 98 (August): 371–400.
Black, D. 1958. *The Theory of Committees and Elections*. Cambridge: Cambridge University Press.
Bryce, James. 1917. *The American Commonwealth*. New York: Macmillan.
Buchanan, J. M., and R. D. Tollison, eds. 1972. *Theory of Public Choice*. Ann Arbor: University of Michigan Press.
———, eds. 1984. *The Theory of Public Choice—II*. Ann Arbor: University of Michigan Press.
Buchanan, J. M., and G. Tullock. 1962. *The Calculus of Consent*. Ann Arbor: University of Michigan Press.
Downs, A. 1957. *An Economic Theory of Democracy*. New York: Harper and Row.
Fenno, R. 1973. *Congressmen in Committees*. Boston: Little Brown.
Ferejohn, J. 1974. *Pork Barrel Politics: Rivers and Harbors Legislation 1947–1968*. Stanford: Stanford University Press.
Fiorina, M. P. 1974. *Representatives, Roll Calls, and Constituencies*. Lexington: D. C. Heath.
Frey, Bruno S. 1984. *International Political Economy*. Oxford: Blackwell.
Frey, Bruno S., and Fritz Schneider. 1978a. "An Empirical Study of Politico-Economic Interaction in the U.S." *Review of Economics and Statistics* 60 (May): 174–83.
———. 1978b. "A Politico-Economic Model of the United Kingdom." *Economic Journal* 88 (June): 243–53.
Gray, Virginia. 1973. "Innovation in the States: A Diffusion Study." *American Political Science Review* 67 (December): 1174–85.
Jacobson, G. 1980. *Money in Congressional Elections*. New Haven: Yale University Press.
Kalt, Joseph P., and Mark A. Zupan. 1984. "Capture and Ideology in the Economic Theory of Politics." *American Economic Review* 74 (June): 279–300.

Kau, J., and P. Rubin. 1979. "Self-Interest, Ideology, and Logrolling in Congressional Voting." *Journal of Law and Economics* 22 (October): 365–84.

Kramer, G. 1971. "Short-Term Fluctuations in U.S. Voting Behavior, 1896–1964." *American Political Science Review* 65 (March): 131–43.

Landes, W. M., and R. A. Posner. 1975. "The Independent Judiciary in an Interest-Group Perspective." *Journal of Law and Economics* 18 (December): 875–901.

Lindsay, C. M., and M. T. Maloney. 1988. "Party Politics and the Price of Payola." *Economic Inquiry* 26 (April): 203–21.

McCormick, R. E., and R. D. Tollison. 1981. *Politicians, Legislation, and the Economy: An Inquiry into the Interest-Group Theory of Government*. Boston: Martinus Nijhoff.

Martin, D. T., and R. E. Wagner. "The Institutional Framework for Municipal Incorporation: An Economic Analysis of Local Agency Formation Commissions in California." *Journal of Law and Economics* 21 (October): 409–26.

Mueller, D. C. 1979. *Public Choice*. Cambridge: Cambridge University Press.

Mueller, D. C., and P. Murrell. 1986. "Interest Groups and the Size of Government." *Public Choice* 48 (February): 125–45.

Olson, M. 1965. *The Logic of Collective Action*. Cambridge: Harvard University Press.

Peltzman, S. 1976. "Toward a More General Theory of Regulation." *Journal of Law and Economics* 19 (August): 211–40.

Pincus, J. J. 1975. "Pressure Groups and the Pattern of Tariffs." *Journal of Political Economy* 83 (July/August): 757–78.

Riker, W. H. 1962. *The Theory of Political Coalitions*. New Haven: Yale University Press.

Shepsle, K. A. 1978. *The Giant Jigsaw Puzzle: Democratic Committee Assignments in the Modern House*. Chicago: University of Chicago Press.

Shughart, W. F., II, and R. D. Tollison. 1985. "Corporate Chartering: An Exploration in the Economics of Legal Change." *Economic Inquiry* 23: 585–99.

Stigler, G. J. 1971. "The Theory of Economic Regulation." *Bell Journal of Economics and Management Science* 2 (Spring): 3–21.

———, ed. 1989. *Studies in Chicago Political Economy*. Chicago: University of Chicago Press.

Tollison, R. D., and T. D. Willett. 1979. "An Economic Theory of Mutually Advantageous Issue Linkages in International Negotiations." *International Organization* 33 (Autumn): 425–50.

Tufte, E. 1978. *Political Control of the Economy*. Princeton: Princeton University Press.

Wagner, R. E. 1976. "Revenue Structure, Fiscal Illusion and Budgetary Choice." *Public Choice* 25 (Spring): 45–61.

Weingast, B. R., and W. J. Marshall. 1988. "The Industrial Organization of Congress; or Why Legislatures, Like Firms, Are Not Organized as Markets." *Journal of Political Economy* 96 (February): 132–63.

Weingast, B. R., and M. J. Moran. 1983. "Bureaucratic Discretion or Congressional Control? Regulatory Policymaking by the Federal Trade Commission." *Journal of Political Economy* 91 (October): 765–800.

Public Choice and Legislation

Robert D. Tollison

The purpose of this essay is to survey what might loosely be called the economic theory of legislation. Its emphasis is on elucidating main principles and results and not on the copious citation and review of literature. Moreover, the piece is primarily concerned with the positive, and not the normative, economics of legislation. Thus the essay emphasizes testable propositions at the expense of normative evaluations of democratic decision-making processes. The issues considered are therefore not whether a given law is "good" or "bad," but rather such questions as why the law was passed, how the law was passed, or why it has not been repealed.

The economic theory of legislation refers to the awakening of economists to the importance of understanding the legislative process. Political scientists have long recognized that the legislature is an important institution in a democratic society and have done a great deal of useful research on legislatures. The comparative advantage of economists in this endeavor consists of their ability to formalize and test theories about legislatures. (Political scientists would say, perhaps with some justification, that economists are good at re-inventing certain wheels.) Economists have worked on a variety of issues in this area that are surveyed in this essay. A brief review of the classic contributions to public choice theory is useful at the outset because these form the fountainhead of later contributions to the economic theory of legislation.

1. Basic Research in Public Choice

Duncan Black's early research on committee decision making[1] was the genesis of modern public choice research. Black formulated the median voter

Reprinted from *Virginia Law Review* 74 (March 1988): 339–71. Thanks go to W. Mark Crain and William F. Shughart II for helpful comments. The usual disclaimer applies.

1. See Black and Newing 1951; Black 1948. This work was later extended and summarized in Black 1958.

theory (presented as a descendent of that first proposed by Harold Hotelling)[2] and a rich, microanalytic framework for studying the behavior of committees and candidates in elections. Kenneth Arrow's famous book on social choice and democracy evaluated majority rule institutions in a social welfare setting.[3] To the extent that one can draw a positive principle from Arrow, it is that democracy should yield capricious and unstable outcomes.

Next in the lineage is Anthony Downs's *An Economic Theory of Democracy*.[4] In this book Downs applied the Hotelling-Black model to a wider scale of political institutions and settings (such as proportional representation and the evolution of the British Labor Party).[5] Moreover, he was the first scholar to articulate the inchoate role of the voter in public choice theory by presenting a testable theory of voter choice and voter participation in elections.[6] From Downs and later writers, such as Gordon Tullock, the individual's decision to vote has come to be viewed as an act of consumption rather than as rationally self-interested, investment-type behavior.[7] Tullock also made an important early contribution to the theory of legislation when he presented a theory of logrolling or vote trading in the context of geographic representation,[8] which forms the basis for a prediction that democratic structures will tend to exhibit an over-expansion of public spending.[9]

In 1962, *The Theory of Political Coalitions* by William Riker[10] and *The Calculus of Consent* by James Buchanan and Tullock[11] made fundamental contributions to the economic theory of legislation. Riker postulated and offered evidence for his famous minimum winning coalition principle.[12] Buchanan and Tullock ranged over various topics from logrolling[13] to different structures and bases of representation[14] in a *tour de force* of public choice analysis. Finally, 1971 saw the appearance of William Niskanen's *Bureau-*

---

2. See Hotelling 1929.
3. See Arrow 1951.
4. See Downs 1957.
5. See Downs 1957, 114–41.
6. See Downs 1957, 295–300.
7. See, for example, Tullock 1976.
8. See Tullock 1959, 571. Logrolling is the trading of votes on one issue for desired votes on other issues. It usually occurs in situations where individual votes represent a significant percentage of the total electorate and where compliance with trading arrangements can be observed easily.
9. See Tullock 1959, 571–79.
10. Riker 1962.
11. Buchanan and Tullock 1962.
12. See Riker 1962, 40, 47–76. A minimum winning coalition is one that can be rendered not large enough to win by the subtraction of any member.
13. See Buchanan and Tullock 1962, 265–81.
14. See Buchanan and Tullock 1962, 43–62.

cracy and Representative Government,[15] which presented an economic theory of bureaucratic behavior suggesting the domination of bureaus over the legislature in the budgetary process, and of George Stigler's paper on *The Theory of Economic Regulation,*[16] which formalized the longstanding capture or interest-group theory of regulation.

These books and articles represent the bedrock contributions to the economic theory of legislation, and they are all, in one way or another, intimately connected with modern developments in this area of public choice research. The quality and importance of these contributions is highlighted by the fact that Arrow, Stigler, and Buchanan won the Nobel Prize in Economics partly for their work in public choice theory. The remainder of this article surveys the literature on legislation and legislatures that has been stimulated by these basic books and articles.

2. The Demand and Supply of Legislation: An Overview

One way to think about legislation is in terms of the interest-group theory of government.[17] Keep in mind that the use of "interest group" as a modifier in this context is not meant to be pejorative. Individual citizens can want or demand laws for any reason—for example, the law makes the world a better place, the law promotes the production of a public good, and so forth—but they will generally act in some group context to obtain the passage of a desired law or the defeat of an undesired law.

A basic principle as well as a basic conundrum underlies the demand for legislation. The principle is that groups who can organize for less than one dollar in order to obtain one dollar of benefits from legislation will be the effective demanders of laws. The conundrum is that economists have little idea of how successful, cost-effective interest groups are formed. That is, how do groups overcome free-rider problems and organize for collective action so as to be able to seek one dollar for less than one dollar?[18] The plain truth is that economists know very little about the dynamics of group formation and action.

One theory that attempts to answer the conundrum is the byproduct

---

15. Niskanen 1971.
16. Stigler 1971.
17. See, for example, McCormick and Tollison 1981.
18. The free-rider problem refers to the issue of why an individual should join the group seeking government benefits if he cannot be excluded from the benefits once the law is passed. If all group members reason this way, no group action would be forthcoming; therefore, one object of the group is to spend resources to deter such behavior.

theory of group collective action.[19] According to this theory, an association provides a private service to its members that cannot be purchased competitively elsewhere. By pricing the service in a monopolistic fashion, the association can raise money for lobbying.[20] Political action becomes a cost-effective byproduct of the organization because start-up costs have already been borne in forming the association for some other purpose. Stigler suggested that an asymmetry of firm sizes, products, and interests in an "industry" tends to promote more effective collective action by the industry (for example, a larger association budget).[21] He argued that participation is mandated by the desire to protect specialized industry interests.[22] These are interesting and useful arguments, but they only begin to solve the difficult analytical problem of group formation and the demand for legislation. At best, one can take the existing array of interest groups and associations in the economy as an expression of such a demand function. Somehow, these groups have become organized as demanders of legislation and other types of government action.[23]

Indeed, for whatever reason organization is undertaken, lobbying for special legislation becomes a relatively low-cost byproduct of being organized. For example, a firm is an example of an organization that can be used for lobbying purposes (not necessarily in the context of an industry lobbying effort). Laborers may organize to bargain collectively and then find it relatively easy to set up a Washington office to advocate increased minimum wages. Lawyers may agree collectively to a code of ethics to address such matters as attorney-client privilege and then proceed to adopt provisions in their code that restrict competition among lawyers. Thus the term "interest group" refers to the use of any organizational form to lobby for or against legislation and not simply to registered groups and associations.

In the interest-group theory, the supply of legislation is an inverse demand curve. Those who "supply" wealth transfers are individuals who do not find it cost effective to resist having their wealth taken away. In other words, it costs them more than one dollar to resist having one dollar taken away.[24] This concept of a supply curve of legislation or regulation suggests that the costs of

---

19. See Olson 1971, 132–41; Moore 1961, 93, 114.

20. This analysis, however, ignores a potentially troubling question: What about rival associations with lower prices?

21. See Stigler 1974, 359.

22. See Stigler 1974, 362.

23. This discussion masks important issues. For example, to how many interest groups does an individual belong? How do interest groups compete? How do they cooperate?

24. "Supply" as used in this context is not the ordinary concept of voluntary supply at higher prices. It is voluntary in the sense that giving up $1 is cheaper than spending $10 to resist giving up $1. It is not voluntary in the sense that the state is a coercive mechanism.

political activity to some individuals exceed the potential gains (or avoided losses). The supply of legislation is, therefore, grounded in the unorganized or relatively less-organized members of society.

Who runs this supply-demand process? The individuals who monitor the supply-demand process are politicians, bureaucrats, and other political actors. These individuals may be conceived of as brokers of legislation, and they essentially act like brokers in a private context—they pair demanders and suppliers of legislation. That is, they seek to pair those who want a law or a transfer the most with those who object the least. In the usual logic of the interest-group theory, brokers will concentrate on legal arrangements that benefit well-organized and concentrated groups for whom the pro rata benefits are high at the expense of diffuse interests, each of which is taxed a little bit to fund the transfer or legislation. By efficiently pairing demanders and suppliers of legislation, the political brokers establish an equilibrium in the market for legislation. Obviously, mistakes can be made in this process. If "too much" legislation is passed, some parties will find it cost effective to organize and to remove inefficient and overreaching brokers in the next election. Equilibrium now!

The political brokers are at the heart of the study of legislation and legislative processes, and the remainder of this article focuses a great deal of attention on their behavior and characteristics. Also, depending on the particular structure of the legislature (total size, number of committees, voting rules, and so on), the brokerage process will operate at different levels of "costs."[25] Stricter voting rules, for example, raise the cost to legislators of finding diffuse minorities to "supply" taxes and transfers. In effect, a legislative production function will impact on the rate of passage of legislation. This production function undergirds the process by which legislation is supplied and is itself an integral part of the study of the supply of legislation.

Finally, the linkage between the legislative production function and the supply of legislation should be clear. Different combinations of legislative inputs—minority size, length of session, bases of representation, and so on—will translate into different rates of legislative output. This process, in turn, explains why there will be a different supply curve of legislation for each configuration of legislative inputs. This point partially explains what some scholars mean by "constitutional economics."[26] Different rules of the game (read legislative production functions) lead to different outcomes in the supply of legislation, both in the aggregate and with respect to what type of legislation is passed. The relevant supply curve of laws, then, is a function of how

---

25. Crain 1979, 607, 608–16.
26. See, for example, Buchanan 1984.

the political process is governed by explicit and implicit constitutional constraints.[27]

3. The Demand for Legislation

Perhaps the most basic issue related to the demand for legislation is how to explain why laws persist over time. That is, why is the work of one legislature not overturned by the next legislature? William Landes and Richard Posner sought to answer this question by addressing the role of the independent judiciary in promoting durable legislation.[28] In the process they offered an interesting and empirically rich theory of the demand for legislation.

Their analysis is framed in terms of the interest-group theory of government. Obviously, an interest group would not bid very much for a protective statute if it lasted only for the current legislative session and was repealed in the next. To be worth anything to the interest group, a law must be durable— that is, it must have a present value of benefits that exceeds the costs of obtaining it. Interest groups and legislatures thus have an incentive to promote institutional arrangements that enhance the durability of laws.[29]

Landes and Posner focused on the role of the independent judiciary in this regard.[30] They posited that the institutional arrangements surrounding judgeships lead judges to behave so as to resolve legal disputes in terms of what the *propounding legislature* actually intended.[31] Given that independent judges actually behave in this manner, the present value demand curve for legislation rotates to the right, and laws become more valuable because they endure longer. The acting legislature's intent is upheld in this theory of the independent judiciary, making each legislature's actions more durable and worth more to interest groups. As I shortly show, this is a testable theory.[32]

Why do judges behave as enforcers of long-term contracts between legislators and interest groups? Landes and Posner did not address this issue. They discussed the institutional arrangements surrounding judges, such as life tenure,[33] but they never specified in a testable fashion why judges promote more durable laws. Indeed, it is hard to explain the behavior of any workers with life tenure contracts, judges being no exception. They should shirk their responsibilities and play a lot of golf.

---

27. The demand curve for legislation can also shift as changes in the costs of organizing interest groups occur. Lower organization costs, for example, will shift the demand curve for legislation to the right.

28. See Landes and Posner 1975, 875.

29. See Landes and Posner 1975, 877–82.

30. See Landes and Posner 1975, 877–79.

31. See Landes and Posner 1975, 885–87.

32. See infra text accompanying notes 38–42.

33. See Landes and Posner 1975, 885–87.

The answer is relatively straightforward, but it has yet to be addressed in the literature. Namely, the judicial branch receives its budget from the legislative branch. Where the judicial branch acts to increase and sustain the durability of legislation, its budget and judicial salaries increase. This is the link that is missing in Landes and Posner. Moreover, the theory is a testable proposition, and the data do not refute its implications for judicial salaries and judicial budgets across states.[34] So, basically, judges behave in a Landes-Posner fashion because to do so is in their self-interest.

Landes and Posner suggested a second route or margin along which the durability of legislation can be increased. The constitutive rules of the legislature itself (regarding committees, voting rules, rules of order, and so forth) can restrain subsequent legislatures from undoing the work of the present one.[35] Moreover, legislators serve for more than one term; hence, as members of subsequent legislatures, they can keep legislative benefits flowing to their interest groups. So the legislature itself can promote the durability of legislation and long-term contracts with interest groups.[36]

Landes and Posner saw constitutional provisions as legislation of a higher order.[37] Constitutional provisions are worth more than normal legislation to interest groups because they are more durable (that is, harder to repeal), but they are also more costly to obtain because of stricter procedures required for passage (for example, higher voting rules and a public referendum).

This difference between normal and constitutional legislation provided the basis for the first empirical test of the Landes-Posner theory. Mark Crain and Robert Tollison put the Landes-Posner theory into the following context.[38] Where judicial independence is higher, interest groups need only procure normal legislation; independent judges will maintain the long-term security of such deals. Where judges are less independent, the more costly route of constitutional protection is more worthwhile. Thus, at the margin, interest groups will demand normal or constitutional legislation as a function of the degree of judicial independence, all other factors being equal.

The states, offering a range of settings in which such behavior can be observed, represent a natural cross-sectional laboratory for testing this theory. State constitutions are changed and amended at different rates, and state judicial systems exhibit varying degrees of independence (measured, for example, in terms of judge tenure and pay). The Landes-Posner theory suggests that these two processes will trade off in a predictable way. Holding other factors constant, this is precisely what Crain and Tollison found.[39] The rate of con-

---

34. See Anderson, Shughart, and Tollison 1987.
35. See Landes and Posner 1975, 877–79.
36. See Landes and Posner 1975.
37. See Landes and Posner 1975, 876.
38. See Crain and Tollison 1979.
39. Crain and Tollison 1979, 172–75.

stitutional amendment is higher where judicial independence is lower, ceteris paribus. Later research on more recent state-by-state data showed the same pattern.[40]

Other variables work in a predictable direction as well. For example, as legislator tenure increases, demand for constitutional protection decreases because legislators are members of subsequent legislatures and can protect normal legislation. The Landes-Posner theory has also been applied to executive vetoes[41] and to the sizes of legislative majorities.[42]

The Landes-Posner theory of durable legislation is an important contribution to the economic theory of legislation. It explains why laws persist over time and how legal environments differ across jurisdictions. Although originally addressed to issues of an independent judiciary, it is also a general theory of the demand for legislation.[43]

4. The Production and Supply of Legislation

There are various ways to approach the issues surrounding the production and supply of legislation. As such, the public choice literature has mingled considerations of production with considerations of supply in what might loosely be called a "reduced-form" approach. This means that aspects of the legislature's productive process, such as legislature size, are commingled with aspects of the political and economic environment, such as population and income, that reflect factors underlying the supply of legislation, transfers, and regulation. This reduced-form approach is adopted in this part. It should be remembered, however, that the slope of the supply curve of legislation is a function of the organizational costs facing voters, whereas the position of the supply curve of legislation is a function of the "technical proficiency" of any given legislative process. A given supply curve will shift depending on the degree of technical proficiency.

Consider the following stylized model of legislation:

$$L = f(POP, \ INC, \ ASSOC, \ SIZE, \ RATIO, \ MAJ),$$

where L is legislation passed per session (a function [f] of the other variables); POP is population; INC is real income; $ASSOC$ is the number of trade associa-

---

40. See Anderson, Martin, Shughart, and Tollison 1986, 13–15.
41. See Crain and Tollison 1979, 555.
42. See Crain, Shughart, and Tollison 1986.
43. Some readers will be put off by thinking of constitutions as repositories of interest-group protection. A way to overcome these qualms is for the reader to obtain a copy of his or her state constitution and read it.

tions; *SIZE* is legislative size; *RATIO* is the ratio of the size of the House to the size of the Senate; and *MAJ* is the size of the legislative majority. Suppose that this model is set to the task of explaining the cross-sectional differences in legislative activities across the states. What would one expect? The variable *L* is simply a measure of the output of legislation over time, the object to be explained. Why does one state pass more laws than another?[44]

The variables *POP* and *INC* are independent variables that proxy the potential supply of legislation. A higher value for *POP* means that each voter has less incentive to be concerned about legislation that transfers wealth away from him. A larger *POP* leads to more acquiescence by voters in legislation because the per capita costs of laws and transfers are lower. In contrast, *INC* is ambiguous in that it cannot be signed as positive or negative; in other words, it cannot be characterized as having a clear positive or negative impact on legislative output. As *INC* goes up, the opportunity costs to voters of monitoring and controlling the political process rise (that is, market time becomes valuable); hence, transfers and legislation should rise. This is a substitution effect. On the other hand, political participation is generally found to be an income-elastic consumption good. This income effect predicts that higher *INC* leads to less and less legislation because greater political participation leads to less acquiescence. Thus, either a positive or negative sign is possible here.[45]

The variable *ASSOC* controls for the demand for transfers. This is an imperfect measure of groups who have organized to seek legislation. It is imperfect because, as noted above, registered groups understate the number of relevant interest groups. In any event, having more interest groups results in more legislation.[46]

The variables *SIZE, RATIO,* and *MAJ* are technical aspects of the legislature's productive process. *SIZE* is ambiguous. A larger legislature generally means that reaching decisions about passing laws is harder. However, larger legislatures also mean that each vote in the legislature is worth less; for a given expenditure, a lobbying group can purchase more influence (that is, votes).

---

44. Laws are by no means homogeneous like grades of wheat. Presumably, this problem could be overcome in principle by denominating laws in terms of dollars of transfers or some such metric. The difficulties for empirical work are apparent.

45. The substitution effect normally dominates in empirical tests.

46. This statement oversimplifies interest-group competition. Some interest groups are organized to compete with other groups in struggles over legislation, transfers, and taxes. This appears to be what one theorist meant by "pressure-group competition." See Becker 1983, 371, 395. Presumably, then, for Becker more associations (*ASSOC*) imply less legislation and regulation. Unfortunately, most empirical results in this area show that having more associations—a higher value for *ASSOC*—causes more legislation. McCormick and Tollison 1980, 293, 306–7. In the aggregate, at least, more interest groups are related to more transfers.

Thus *SIZE* cuts both ways and can be either positively or negatively related to the passage of laws.

An interesting variable is *RATIO*. For a given value of *SIZE*, a larger value for *RATIO* of House to Senate size will reduce the passage of legislation. In other words, a larger *RATIO* leads to a more costly lobbying environment. Suppose that a law requires a simple majority in two houses that have 100 legislators in total. If they are equally split, House and Senate size will equal 50. Passing a law requires the agreement of 26 voters in each house. Let the House expand to 64 and the Senate contract to 36. Passing a law now requires 33, or 7 more, votes in the House, and 19, or 7 less, votes in the Senate.

If the costs of purchasing votes rise at an increasing rate in each house, the fall in costs of purchasing 7 more votes in the Senate will be more than offset by the rise in costs of purchasing 7 more votes in the House. An important result emerges—other things the same, a more unequal chamber size will reduce the supply of legislation because the costs of purchasing votes or, more generally, legislative influence, are higher.

A higher *MAJ* will lead to more legislative output, and this is generally what one would expect. Nonetheless, other considerations operate here. Larger majorities are more difficult to organize as team production processes;[47] hence, an "optimal" majority size will exist beyond which organization and passage of legislation become more cumbersome and costly. This assumes, of course, that there is not straight party line voting, making a larger-than-minimum winning coalition unnecessary.

This "reduced-form" supply of legislation function is for purposes of illustration. Several studies have used this general approach and illustrated its explanatory power. Crain presented a theory and test of legislative production in which he found an early version of the *RATIO* effect.[48] McCormick and Tollison applied the basic skeletal model given above to explain the differences across states in regulation, transfers, and legislation.[49] They found that variables such as *INC, POP, RATIO,* and *SIZE* (with a negative sign) offer a robust and predictable explanation for these legislative outputs across

---

47. See infra text accompanying notes 84–90.

48. See Crain 1979, 616. Crain posited the following testable theories: (1) increases in majority proportions should have a positive but diminishing effect on rates of legislative output; (2) longer legislative sessions should be positively associated with legislative output, assuming the decline in start-up costs dominates the costs resulting from legislator shirking and outside earnings, but longer sessions should be negatively associated with output if the reverse is true; and (3) the absolute size of a legislature should reduce output rates, assuming the impact of size on decision-making costs dominates the gains from increased labor specialization, but absolute size should increase output rates if the reverse is true. Id.

49. See McCormick and Tollison 1981; McCormick and Tollison 1980.

states.[50] Shughart and Tollison used this basic framework to explain the time-series of legislation passed by the United States Congress from 1789 to 1980.[51] Variables such as *RATIO* and *SIZE* (with a positive sign) played a strong role in explaining the behavior of the time-series.[52]

Finally, Shughart and Tollison adapted the supply of legislation model to a unique historical problem—the liberalization of corporate chartering laws across states in the nineteenth and early twentieth centuries.[53] The idea was simple: liberalized chartering should be passed first where the benefits of passage exceed the cost of passage by the largest amount. Measuring the benefits of passage by local manufacturing characteristics and the cost of passage by such factors as contemporaneous *SIZE* and *RATIO,* Shughart and Tollison encountered a robust and interesting demonstration of the way liberalized chartering emerged over time.[54] For example, in states where *RATIO* was larger, liberal chartering laws came later because the cost of legislative change was higher, all else the same.[55] In states with more concentrated manufacturing interests, liberal chartering came sooner, all else the same.[56]

The basic point is that the supply-demand model of legislation is useful and relevant. The model works, and it offers insights into the process by which legislation is produced across legislatures and over time. Moreover, it can be employed to explain specific episodes of legislative change.

5. Issues Related to the Supply-Demand Process

The preceding framework for the discussion of the demand and supply of legislation omits certain specialized topics that build upon and strengthen the conclusions of the economic model of legislative production. A nonexhaustive list of these topics is briefly considered in this part.

Broker Preferences

The public choice literature contains a great deal of discussion about the degree to which ideology affects the voting behavior of elected representatives. In simple terms, does the politician exercise his or her personal value judgments in voting, as opposed to voting strictly in terms of constituents'

---

50. See McCormick and Tollison 1981, 123–25; McCormick and Tollison 1980, 305–11.
51. See Shughart and Tollison 1986, 111.
52. See Shughart and Tollison 1986, 120–24.
53. See Shughart and Tollison 1985, 585, 592.
54. See Shughart and Tollison 1985, 590–98.
55. Shughart and Tollison 1985, 593.
56. Shughart and Tollison 1985, 594.

interests? The answer is obviously yes to some degree, and the debate in the literature is over the degree.

The general form of the debate goes as follows. A model of representative voting behavior is specified, including constituent interest and ideological measures (such as the Americans for Democratic Action [ADA] or the American Conservative Union [ACU] ratings). If the ideological measures prove to have a statistically significant impact on the test, ideology is held to influence the behavior of politicians (at the margin).[57] Sam Peltzman challenged this conclusion with the argument that the inclusion of better measures of the "economic" variables affecting voting behavior in the models that are being tested would reduce the statistical significance of the ideological variables.[58]

The whole issue is mired in difficulties. A simple example suffices to illustrate. Representative *A* is from an oil district and yet votes "no" on an oil import fee bill. The "no" vote gives the representative a higher ACU rating. Did the representative express his ideological preferences in this case? Yes if he voted "no" for free; no if he did not vote "no" for free. Because his voting "no" in exchange for votes on other issues is entirely probable, it is not at all clear that he voted "no" on ideological grounds. Vote trading or logrolling obscures the role of ideological voting on *single* issues. Many post offices and dams are built on such principles, and, in some cases, the post office or the dam generates more local political benefits for the representative than the oil import fee.

On the broader scale of voting across all issues, it seems reasonable to predict that ideology plays an economically rational role in such behavior. Douglas Nelson and Eugene Silberberg put the matter nicely.[59] Narrowly focused bills where the final destination and distribution of funds are well known make ideological voting more costly; hence, less is observed. More general bills where effects are unknown or unpredictable make ideological voting less costly; hence, more such behavior is observed.[60] Ideological voting obeys the law of demand—more is observed where engaging in such behavior is cheaper. Nelson and Silberberg presented evidence from voting on defense appropriations bills to suggest that this approach to ideology and voting is a useful one.[61]

---

57. The studies most representative of this approach are presented in Kalt and Zupan 1984, 279, and Kau and Rubin 1979, 365.

58. See Peltzman 1985, 656, 674–75.

59. See Nelson and Silberberg 1987, 15.

60. Nelson and Silberberg 1987, 16–17.

61. See Nelson and Silberberg 1987, 18–21. Nelson and Silberberg used ADA ratings, as well as several other variables, including the per capita value of defense contracts, as indicators of legislator ideology and measurements of constituent interests. The authors compared individual senators' voting records to their constituents' interests for twelve roll call votes in the United States Senate during the 97th Congress. See id.

Broker preferences also play a role in voting behavior. The degree to which they play a role will be a function of the institutional arrangements that bind political agents to their constituents: the tighter the arrangements, the less pronounced the ideological voting. For example, suppose voters erect residence requirements for local representatives to ensure that only individuals with significant local property holdings will be elected.[62] Legislator shirking will be less of a problem in this setting for an obvious reason—voting for local benefits increases the value of the legislator's local property holdings. The issue, then, is not whether ideology matters at all to political behavior, but how much and under what conditions.

Seniority

Representatives are not homogeneous, which means that their influence is not homogeneous either. They will differ in their natural abilities as politicians, and they will differ in terms of their institutional status in the legislature. A measurable way in which representatives are different is in their length of service or tenure in the legislature. Seniority leads to heterogeneous political influence. Seniority assumes this role because rank and influence in the legislature (for example, committee assignments) increase with legislator tenure.

Of course, this whole discussion is just a hypothesis. Stigler was among the first to show empirically that representation in terms of raw numbers of representatives matters to political outcomes (for example, federal spending in a state or congressional district).[63] Crain and Tollison added seniority weights to Stigler's empirics and found that the seniority of a state's House and Senate delegates was an important variable in explaining the state's receipt of federal programs and expenditures.[64]

The reasons for this conclusion are mostly a priori at present, but nonetheless convincing. The legislature is organized, in many dimensions, like a prototype labor union with a strong form of monopoly power.[65] The increase of legislator influence over political outcomes as a function of seniority is just

---

62. See Faith and Tollison 1983, 211, 215–23.

63. See Stigler 1976, 17, 26–31 (political influence is positively correlated to the number of representatives, based on comparisons between the number of representatives and the percentage of federal grants, the percentage of federal nondefense expenditures, and federal employment for the fifty states in 1970).

64. Crain and Tollison 1977, 355, 355–61. Kenneth Greene and Vincent Munley later questioned this result. They argued that the conclusions of the Crain and Tollison model were flawed because the model failed to account for several important factors, including relative population. When these factors are considered, the correlation between seniority and political influence is nominal. Green and Munley 1981, 207. The drift of the literature, however, is to treat seniority as begetting more political influence.

65. See McCormick and Tollison, 1978, 63, 67–68.

one part of the union analogy, but it suffices to illustrate the basic point.[66] To predict policy outcomes such as the economic impact of government programs across representative districts, one must control for seniority and related differences of legislators; all representatives are not created equal.

Geographic Representation and Logrolling

Since the publication of Tullock's *Problems of Majority Voting*,[67] economists have better understood the problem of vote trading or logrolling. At first, analogies were drawn to normal economic exchanges in which trading clearly makes all relevant parties better off.[68] Vote trading, however, takes place within the institutional context of the legislature, and this context will have a powerful effect on the impact of vote trading on the economy.

Combine, for example, geographic representation and vote trading. The result is that representatives who are proficient at obtaining programs and benefits for their districts will tend to be reelected. The revenue side of the budget is roughly taken as given; hence, the tax consequences of a particular program for a particular district are borne mostly by individuals outside the district. Obviously, if all representatives behave in this way, the expenditure side of the budget will become bloated with local programs ("you vote for my dam, I'll vote for your port"), which, taken to an extreme, will promote inefficient public investments[69] and government deficits.[70] As positive predictions, these do not seem far from the reality of American politics today. In effect, vote trading becomes a gigantic negative-sum game for the whole economy, fueled by local and geographically concentrated economic interests. Legislative history and government budgets are replete with such results.

Not all districts necessarily win in this competition, as the voting rule in the legislature will preclude some clearly inefficient deals. The stricter the voting rule, the more these negative-sum deals will fail to pass muster. The important lesson from public choice theory is that the proverbial pork barrel is not something that is independent of the institutional incentives facing vote-maximizing legislators.[71]

---

66. The literature on agenda control and structure-induced equilibrium provides a strong theoretical rationale for the importance of institutional features of the legislature such as seniority in predicting legislative outcomes. See, for example, Plott and Levine 1978, 146 (within a range of circumstances, controlling a group's decisions by controlling only the agenda appears possible); Shepsle and Weingast 1981, 503 (stability of legislative outcomes is strongly influenced by institutional features such as the committee system).

67. See supra note 8 and accompanying text.

68. Coleman 1966, 1105, 1106.

69. See Buchanan and Tullock 1962, 276–77.

70. See Buchanan and Wagner 1977, 93–105.

71. The point is a general one. In the context of comparative legislatures, systems of representation not based on geography are perhaps not so loaded toward local programs.

Committees

Economists have produced a significant amount of work on legislative committees in terms of theoretical studies of voting behavior à la Black.[72] Less work has been done on the positive problem of why committees exist in a legislature and what their functions are.

One body of literature, pioneered by Kenneth Shepsle, focuses on the role of committees in determining "structure-induced equilibria."[73] In other words, rather than cycling about endlessly as predicted by Arrow,[74] legislatures actually reach decisions and produce laws. In Shepsle's approach, outcomes are induced, indeed predicted and controlled, by the structural characteristics of the legislature, including committees, committee assignments, and so forth.[75]

Shepsle focused especially on the committee appointment process, arguing that farm committees are dominated by farm district representatives and urban committees are dominated by city representatives.[76] This seems like an obvious division of labor in the legislature, with representatives specializing in the economic base of their districts. The algorithm of committee assignment is more complex than this, however; for example, there are not enough farm seats to go around. Moreover, the Shepsle view of committee assignment omits some interesting features of the process.[77] The most important committees (Ways and Means, Rules, and Appropriations) are not issue-specific or large enough to accommodate all the farmers or urban types in the legislature. Thus, such factors as party loyalty in prior voting trials are an alternative way to understand the committee assignment process.[78]

A second major issue in the literature is the control by the committee over its relevant bureaucratic dominion. William Niskanen's theory of bureaucracy set the stage for this debate. In *Bureaucracy and Representative Government,* Niskanen argued that because of its superior information, a bureau had greater bargaining power with regard to its budget than did the bureau's oversight committee.[79] Subsequent work on the economic theory of bureaucracy has been largely in this tradition. Recently, however, Barry Weingast and Mark Moran offered an alternative principal-agent theory, which predicts that the oversight committee (the principal) has most of the relevant bargaining power, including the ability to remove or to hamper the career of the

---

72. See supra text accompanying notes 1–2.
73. See Shepsle 1978, 107–12.
74. See Arrow 1951, 46–60.
75. See Shepsle 1978, 231–61.
76. See Shepsle 1978, 63–93.
77. See Crain 1986.
78. See Crain 1986, 4–7.
79. See Niskanen 1971, 24–35.

bureau head (the agent).[80] They tested this theory with data concerning the Federal Trade Commission (FTC).[81]

The issue raised in this debate is an important one. Are government bureaus out of control or are they merely docile agents following the commands of voters as expressed through their elected representatives on the relevant committees? The Weingast approach suggests that political incentives should be compatible as between the legislature and the bureaucrat. The legislator observes a particular political trade-off in the election. Imposing that trade-off on his bureaucratic agent is in the legislator's self-interest. That is, the bureaucrat's role is to transfer wealth or to implement legislation and policy in the direction of the legislator's preferred trade-off. In this approach bureaucracy is not out of control but is closely monitored and controlled by Congress. Bureaucrats who cannot be made to behave in accordance with the legislature's wishes are moved out of power.[82]

A final issue concerning committees is the question of why committees exist in a legislature. They do not exist in all legislatures, but they predominate in United States legislatures. A natural way to think about legislative committees is that they represent an efficient division of legislative labor.[83] Each legislature faces certain constraints. It must search for efficient pairings of demanders and suppliers of legislation, that is, what do people want and who will pay for it? It faces a time constraint. It cannot meet forever, and it must decide what to vote on within a given session length. Moreover, in the United States, legislators do not always vote along straight party lines.

To control for these various matters, the legislature can specialize by forming committees that hold both hearings to determine what to do and

---

80. See Weingast and Moran 1983, 765.

81. See Weingast and Moran 1983, 775–92. Using ADA ratings for the individual senators on the FTC oversight committees (the Committee on Commerce and the Subcommittee on Consumer Affairs), the authors compared changes in the senators' preferences to changes in FTC policy.

82. The Weingast approach has recently been extended by William Shugart, Robert Tollison, and Brian Goff. See Shugart, Tollison, and Goff 1986, 962. In their article, they compared and contrasted independent agencies or commissions with bureaus that are headed by a single actor (for example, the FTC versus the Antitrust Division of the Department of Justice). They derived the result that the former type of agency headed by a committee should exhibit less variability of output (for example, the number of cases brought) over time than the single-actor case. Id., 968. Their empirical results strongly support this hypothesis. See id. 965–68.

One way to view this point is that independent agencies are often set up with broad mandates in uncharted political waters. In the principal-agent approach, less variability means more control by the oversight committee and less chance for things to get out of hand. A commission-type bureaucracy can be seen, therefore, as deriving from the problem of legislative control over bureaucratic behavior.

83. See Leibowitz and Tollison 1980, 261, 261–64, 268.

voting trials. If the full House accepts the voting trial result of the committee (a very common pattern of behavior), committees will act like Adam Smith's pin factory—they will expand the amount of a party's agenda that can be passed in a given legislative session. For a given party majority in the overall legislature, which is mapped into committee majorities by a rule of proportional representation, the legislative productivity of a party is enhanced by committees.

Committees have other functions and roles than those discussed here. But in the economic theory of legislation, their role is seen as promoting the passage of legislation. They are engines for finding out what laws people want and who will pay for them, conducting preliminary votes, screening and controlling bureaucratic appointments, and so on.

Team Production

A feature of legislative production that has not received much attention until recently is team production.[84] The term refers to a situation where the combined costs of identifying the marginal products of individual workers and compensating them accordingly are high. The work effort is joint, as on an assembly line, and team members work as a unit to achieve productive outcomes. In this setting problems of individual team member shirking will be paramount because shirking members can free ride on the work of others and not be penalized appropriately. To the extent that all team members behave similarly, team productivity falls. Armen Alchian and Harold Demsetz exposit the team production argument in the setting of a private firm where the role of the manager is invoked to monitor and to discipline the team production process.[85]

Voting in a legislature is exactly analogous to team production. A majority vote on a bill requires the cooperation of at least $N/2 + 1$ legislators. Thus, the team production theory can be applied to analyze legislative behavior.

Crain, Donald Leavens, and Tollison proposed a theory of party control and discipline based on team production principles.[86] They applied the theory to the following issue: in final votes on bills in a legislature, whose bills get voted on first? They argued that the bills of more senior legislators will be voted on first because these legislators can be counted on to participate in subsequent votes on the party's bills to carry out their legislative *quid pro quos* and because this arrangement is a reward for party loyalty in previous voting

---

84. See, for example, Crain, Leavens, and Tollison 1986, 833.
85. See Alchian and Demsetz 1972, 777, 779–81.
86. See Crain, Leavens, & Tollison 1986, 833–35.

trials.[87] Essentially, less senior and less tested legislators are less trustworthy with regard to their voting behavior, so their bills are voted on last.[88]

Crain, Leavens, and Tollison then conducted a test of voting on final bills on an extensive data set for the United States House of Representatives.[89] Their findings strongly support the application of the team production theory to legislatures. Indeed, they were able to explain and to predict the queue of final votes in the House, that is, the order in which final bills were voted on.[90]

The team production theory is a totally new way of thinking about legislative behavior. It has the potential for integrating many aspects of legislative behavior, such as party leadership and the process by which coalitions are formed and managed in voting trials. Indeed, other theories of the legislature that emphasize the independence and power of committees, for example, can be seen as special cases of the more general team production theory.

Legislators

The literature on legislators reveals several basic results. First, Crain modeled the tenure of legislators as a function of the type of district they represent, all else the same.[91] His argument focused on entry barriers in politics. At-large districts are viewed as representing the case of competitive entry into politics, whereas single-member districts are seen as analogous to barred or more restricted entry conditions.[92] Legislator turnover is thus higher in at-large districts.[93] This research suggests the structural importance of bases of representation in politics and casts new light on the incentives of aspiring politicians who seek to erect various bases of representation as a way to gain entry into the political arena and to hold onto their seats. Should minorities, for example, prefer single-member or at-large districts?

Second, McCormick and Tollison wrote about legislator pay.[94] With regard to the legal pay of legislators, they analyzed the legislature as analogous to a union or wage cartel. In some states legislator pay is set by the state constitution; in others it is set by the legislature. The latter case amounts to a very strong form of wagesetting power because few, if any, substitutes for legislator services exist in a given state. McCormick and Tollison found that legislator wages in the "union" states (wages set by the legislatures) are much

---

87. Crain, Leavens, and Tollison 1986, 834.
88. Crain, Leavens, and Tollison 1986, 834.
89. Crain, Leavens, and Tollison 1986, 835, 836.
90. Crain, Leavens, and Tollison 1986, 838–40.
91. See Crain 1977, 829.
92. Crain 1977, 831, 832.
93. Crain 1977, 836, 838.
94. See McCormick and Tollison 1981, 61–75; McCormick and Tollison 1978, 71–74.

higher (100 to 200 percent) than in the "non-union" states (wages set by the state constitutions), all else the same.[95]

Not all legislator pay is above the table. Outside-the-legislature pay comes in a variety of legal, quasi-legal, and illegal forms. McCormick and Tollison developed a theory of outside legislator pay that is based upon the occupational composition of a legislature.[96] Imagine the following scenario: an auctioneer starts to call out legislator wages to elicit a labor supply curve for legislators. The first group to volunteer to run for and to serve in the legislature is composed of lawyers. They are the most effective at combining service in the legislature with making outside income. The lawyer who is also a legislator has a particular appeal for certain potential clients: in effect, the derived demand for the services of a lawyer *qua* legislator is more inelastic than the derived demand for plain old lawyers. Thus, low pay results in a greater number of lawyers in the legislature. As legislator pay rises, businesspeople will sign up next for legislative service. They sign up for the same reason as lawyers, only they are not as proficient as lawyers at earning outside income. Finally, at high levels of legislator pay, people are drawn to run for office who are attracted by the high level of pay per se because they are not adept at combining legislative service with procuring outside income.

McCormick and Tollison tested this theory using data on the occupational composition of state legislatures and found its implications strongly supported.[97] Lawyers and business-types dominate low-pay legislatures; farmers dominate high-pay legislatures.

Finally, Fred McChesney recently expanded the concept of the politician's role in the interest-group theory of government in a sensible and significant way.[98] He stressed that in the traditional interest-group theory, the role of the politician is to create rents and returns that interest groups in turn compete to capture. In this case the politician is a passive broker.[99] McChesney went on to argue that the politician cannot only create rents, he can also extract them.[100] Individuals and firms in the economy develop specific and expropriable capital in certain lines of endeavor.[101] Politicians can force side payments from these individuals by threatening them with taxes and/or regulation designed to expropriate their specific capital.

Building on this insight, McChesney developed a very interesting theory of rent extraction by politicians: legislators introduce a bill that threatens an

---

95. McCormick and Tollison 1978, 73–74.
96. See McCormick and Tollison 1978, 77.
97. See McCormick and Tollison 1978, 75–76.
98. See McChesney 1987, 101.
99. McChesney 1987, 102–4.
100. McChesney 1987, 102–6.
101. McChesney 1987, 106–9.

industry's return on capital unless the industry contributes to their legislative campaigns.[102] His theory provides insights into a range of government gestures in the direction of industry: for example, committee investigations and hearings, political speeches mapping out new legislative proposals, and governmental commissions to study "problems." In effect, his work explains how government "trolls" the economy looking for ways to propose regulations and taxation, not so much to correct social problems but to fill up the campaign coffers.

All of these papers examine specific aspects of legislator behavior. As such, they are pieces of a larger puzzle. Looking at the economic incentives that fuel the supply of political labor promotes an understanding of the political process as a rational, self-interested environment. Moreover, it helps to dampen romantic notions of politicians as servants of the public interest. Politicians are like the rest of us; their personal, private interests are their fundamental concerns.

Campaign Spending

The literature on campaign spending can be easily summarized—campaign spending is a means of entry into politics. A challenger's advertising expenditures perform the important function of introducing the unknown candidate to the electorate; the incumbent's cannot do much more than remind his constituency of his virtues. The empirical literature that examines the impact of campaign spending shows that the advertising elasticity of challenger spending with respect to votes is larger than that for incumbent spending.[103] The moral of this body of work is simple—campaign spending laws are incumbent protection laws.

In a larger context, campaign spending laws may have an impact on the size and composition of government budgets.[104] If individual representatives seek to tax voters in other districts to finance benefits for their district, unfettered campaign finance will send money across political geography to defeat such politicians. Unfettered campaign finance should, therefore, yield fewer on-budget transfers—that is, transfers that are specifically set out in the

---

102. McChesney 1987, 106–8.

103. See Grier 1987, 9–11. At low expenditure levels, challenger spending has a relatively larger effect on gaining votes than incumbent spending; therefore, incumbents must significantly outspend challengers to win elections. This explains incumbent resistance to campaign finance limitations. See id.

104. Crain, Tollison, and Leavens 1987, 6–12 (campaign finance regulation will yield a substantial net increase in on-budget legislative activity because, at the margin, passing laws will become a less productive tool for reelection).

legislature's budget itself. On the other hand, unfettered campaign finance means that off-budget government actions, such as favorable regulation, are up for bid; thus, such an environment should be related to more off-budget actions by the legislature. Empirical evidence suggests that unfettered campaign finance is associated with such a pattern—fewer on-budget transfers and more off-budget regulation—across state legislatures.[105]

The important point here, however, is that the economic issue of campaign spending goes beyond the usual incumbent protection result. Campaign finance regulation has an impact on the market for politicians on both the demand and supply sides, and thus, indirectly, affects government programs and policies.

Voters

Voters in the economic theory of legislation have been discussed previously.[106] They are suppliers and demanders of legislation, regulation, and transfers. Their behavior, as such, is always couched in terms of being organized or unorganized. This contrasts with the conventional treatment of voters in public choice theory.

Economists customarily discuss voting behavior in terms of the paradox of voting.[107] That is, on straight economic grounds voting is not worthwhile; yet turnouts in most elections are nontrivial. Hence, voting behavior is rationalized as consumption-type, rather than investment-type, behavior. People vote, for example, to express their patriotic duty rather than to express their self-interest in legislation. In contrast with other parts of public choice theory in which behavior is modeled with maximizing, self-interested agents at the helm, the role of voters is comparatively unarticulated in the conventional wisdom of public choice theory.

Stigler, in particular, questioned this approach to understanding voter behavior.[108] He argued that in politics a little more or a little less plurality matters. In this world votes will matter to politicians and parties at the margin, and they will invest rationally in a supply of votes to have an impact on political and legislative outcomes.[109] In such an instance the paradox of voting is a moot issue. Interest groups will invest in a supply of votes for politicians in exchange for a higher probability of seeing a favorite bill passed.

---

105. See Crain, Tollison, and Leavens 1987, 12–16.
106. See supra text accompanying notes 6–9.
107. Downs 1957, 36–50, 260–76.
108. See Stigler 1972, 91.
109. See Stigler 1972, 100–204.

Such investments will be made on cost-benefit grounds—for example, if it takes one percent more plurality to ensure the power to put a bill through, the interest group will compare the costs of turning out voters in this amount with the benefits of the legislation.[110]

In such a way voting behavior can be incorporated into the interest-group theory of government. In other words, the management of votes supplied by interest groups provides an alternative way to view the voting process, a way that is consistent with the general drift of the economic theory of legislation.

Legislation and the Growth of Government

Few doubt that at least since World War I, government at all levels has absorbed increasing proportions of domestic wealth. The causes and consequences of this trend, which accelerated in the post–World War II era, have been the subject of much scholarly debate. Several hypotheses about governmental growth have been advanced in the public choice literature.[111] First, exogenous events, such as war, are offered as the causes of once-and-for-all increases in the size of the public sector. Second, some version of Wagner's "Law"—that the demand for government services is an increasing function of income—is supposed to operate in the context of an explicit or implicit market for public goods wherein demand and cost conditions determine the level of spending.[112] Other explanations center on the expansionist motives of politicians and bureaucrats, on "unbalanced growth" by a labor-intensive public sector, and on the information costs faced by voters.[113]

Recent contributions emphasize the redistributive elements in governmental activity. For example, Peltzman found wide empirical support for the proposition that "the *leveling* of income differences across a large part of the population—the growth of the 'middle class'—has in fact been a major source of the growth of government in the developed world over the last fifty years."[114] In contrast, Allan Meltzer and Scott Richard developed a theo-

---

110. Crain, Shughart, and Tollison 1987, 10–11.

111. See, for example, Bennett and Johnson 1980.

112. See Buchanan and Wagner 1977, 69–71, 93–124 (criticizing Keynesian theory for fueling constant government expansion by failing to recognize the disincentives of politicians to restrain spending during periods of budget surpluses).

113. See, for example, Buchanan and Tullock 1962, 97–116 (delegation of decision-making power to the government bureaucracy reduces the information costs to citizens); Downs 1957, 201–4 (same); Tullock 1967, 134–36 (bureaucracies expand because government leaders reward politicians for increasing the number of people that they supervise); Baumol 1967, 415, 415–20 (attributing government growth to a labor-intensive public sector that is not responsive to cost-saving technologies).

114. Peltzman 1980, 209, 285.

retical model that suggests that an increase in income differences, because of the extension of voting power to groups with relatively low incomes, raised the demand for redistribution and, hence, led to more government.[115]

In the main, the growth-of-government literature used either public employment or government spending as a percentage of gross domestic product as a proxy for the size of the public sector. This approach does not, however, capture the full scope of governmental activity. Many of the government's intrusions into economic life (for example, minimum wage laws, nonprice trade barriers, antitrust exemptions, and price-entry regulations, to name a few) are off-budget. That is, taxing and spending activities are just the tip of the government iceberg.

In a recent paper, Shughart and Tollison attempted to link the growth of government to the supply of legislation over time.[116] They investigated the growth of government by examining the event necessary to generate a public sector of a given size—the enactment of a body of laws. Specifically, they analyzed the legislative output of the Congress from its first session in 1789 through its ninety-sixth assembly, which ended in 1980.[117]

In relating the legislative output series to the growth of government spending per capita, they found that the factors that tend to raise the output of laws also tend to increase the size of government, and vice versa.[118] More importantly, however, they found that not all governmental activities are a monotone transformation of budgetary expenditures.[119] A significant category of wealth transfers—those put into operation by the passage of private bills—are off-budget, and these laws apparently substitute for on-budget spending.[120] Explanations of the growth of government that focus solely on taxing and spending thus tell only a part of the story.

Shughart and Tollison then went behind the legislative output series to estimate a production function for enacted laws.[121] Basing this work on the interest-group theory of government, they found evidence that the enactment of bills over time depends on factors influencing the demand for and supply of legislation.[122] For example, an increase in the degree of bicameralism re-

---

115. See Meltzer and Richard 1981, 914, 920–25.
116. See Shughart and Tollison 1986, 114–20.
117. See Shughart and Tollison 1986, 114–24.
118. See Shughart and Tollison 1986, 120–25.
119. Shughart and Tollison 1986, 120.
120. Private legislation includes those measures passed for the relief of individual persons or firms. Illustrative private bill categories are refunds of payments made to the government or waivers of such indebtedness, the payment of tort claims, and private immigration and naturalization bills.
121. See Shughart and Tollison 1986, 120–24.
122. Shughart and Tollison 1986, 124–25.

duced the output of laws. That is, as the sizes of the House of Representatives and Senate became more disparate, the cost to individuals and groups of obtaining a majority in both chambers rose.[123]

These results, in total, carry a message for growth-of-government theorists. First, government does not grow uniformly across the board. An effective constraint on wealth transfers makes political trade-offs imperative. To argue that one captures the essence of off-budget developments by looking only at on-budget empirical proxies is to commit a fallacy of composition. Second, government in a democracy grows because the legislature passes laws and the executive signs them. Spending and taxes are ultimately a reflection of legislation. A theory of what drives legislation over time *is* a theory of the growth of government. Thus the proper focus of a theory of governmental growth is one stage removed from a focus on spending and taxes. Moreover, the ability of individuals and groups to use the legislative process to attain their ends, noble or otherwise, causes government to grow or decline.

6. Two Clarifications

At this point, two clarifications should be made. First, the economic theory of legislation is not a Marxist theory in the following sense. Simple Marxism pits Capital against Labor. An interest-group theory just stresses the relative costs of organizing for effective political action. Any group from any part of society can be a demander or supplier of legislation under the postulated conditions.

Indeed, one of the more interesting examples of the interest-group theory in the literature pits high-cost firms against low-cost firms in an industry. The latter firms seek cost-increasing regulations that drive some of the former firms out of the industry, raise industry price, and increase the quasi-rents accruing to the low-cost firms. Such a model has been used to analyze environmental regulation,[124] the British factory acts,[125] and industrial safety regulation.[126]

Second, one should not think of the economic theory of legislation strictly in terms of the legislature passing more laws and regulations. The process can operate in the opposite direction, and the theory is general so that it can explain the repeal of laws and deregulation. As discussed above, Shughart and Tollison used the theory to explain the deregulation of corporate

---

123. Shughart and Tollison 1986, 121.
124. See Buchanan and Tullock 1975, 139.
125. See Marvel 1977, 379.
126. See Maloney and McCormick 1982, 99.

chartering laws in the United States.[127] Moreover, Gary Anderson and Tollison used a similar approach to explain the repeal of the Corn Laws in mid-nineteenth-century England.[128]

7. Concluding Remarks

This essay is not written from the arrogance of a finished research agenda. Rather, the general sketchiness of much of the piece is sufficient in itself to suggest that more work remains to be done before the role of the legislature and all its attendant institutions in the economy and society is well understood.

An approach based on an economic theory of legislation nonetheless offers rich scientific and empirical opportunities to study legislatures. It is by no means the only approach to legislatures, but it is provocative to think of the legislature as an institution guided by private interests. After all, no man is safe when the legislature is in session. Of course, notwithstanding the capacity of the approach described here to puncture complacency or conventional pieties, democracy is still better than the alternatives.

REFERENCES

Alchian, Armen A., and Harold Demsetz. 1972. "Production, Information Costs, and Economic Organization." *Am. Econ. Rev.* 62:777.
Anderson, Gary M., Delores T. Martin, William F. Shughart II, and Robert D. Tollison. 1986. "Behind the Veil: The Political Economy of Constitutional Change." Manuscript.
Anderson, Gary M., William F. Shughart II, and Robert D. Tollison. 1987. "There's No Such Thing as a Free Judge" (Aug.) Manuscript.
Anderson, Gary M., and Robert D. Tollison. 1985. "Ideology, Interest Groups, and the Repeal of the Corn Laws." *J. Institutional & Theoretical Econ.* 141:197.
Arrow, Kenneth J. 1951. *Social Choice and Individual Values.* New York: John Wiley.
Baumol, W. J. 1967. "Macroeconomics of Unbalanced Growth: The Anatomy of Urban Crisis." *Am. Econ. Rev.* 57:415.
Becker, Gary S. 1983. "A Theory of Competition Among Pressure Groups for Political Influence." *Q. J. Econ.* 98:371.
Bennett, J. T., and M. Johnson. 1980. *The Political Economy of Federal Government Growth: 1959–1978.* College Station, Tex.: Center for Education and Research in Free Enterprise.

---

127. See supra text accompanying notes 53–56.
128. See Anderson and Tollison 1985, 197.

Black, Duncan. 1958. *The Theory of Committees and Elections.* Cambridge: Cambridge University Press.

———. 1948. "On the Rationale of Group Decision-Making." *J. Pol. Econ.* 56:23.

Black, Duncan, and R. A. Newing. 1951. *Committee Decisions with Complementary Valuation.* Cambridge: Cambridge University Press.

Buchanan, James M. 1984. "Sources of Opposition to Constitutional Reform." In *Constitutional Economics,* ed. R. B. McKenzie, p. 21. Lexington, Mass.: Lexington Books.

Buchanan, James M., and Gorgon Tullock. 1962. *The Calculus of Consent.*

———. 1975. "Polluters' Profits and Political Response: Direct Controls Versus Taxes." *Am. Econ. Rev.* 65:139.

Buchanan, James M., and Richard Wagner. 1977. *Democracy in Deficit.* New York: Academic Press.

Coleman, James S. 1966. "The Possibility of a Social Welfare Function." *Am. Econ. Rev.* 56:1105.

Crain, W. Mark. 1976. "Legislative Committees: A Filtering Theory." Manuscript.

———. 1977. "On the Structure and Stability of Political Markets." *J. Pol. Econ.* 85:829.

———. 1979. "Cost and Output in the Legislative Firm." *J. Legal Stud.* 8:607.

Crain, W. Mark, Donald R. Leavens, and Robert D. Tollison. 1986. "Final Voting in Legislatures." *Am. Econ. Rev.* 76:833.

Crain, W. Mark, William F. Shughart II, and Robert D. Tollison. 1986. "Legislative Majorities as Nonsalvageable Assets." Manuscript.

———. N.d. "Voters as Investors." In *The Political Economy of Rent Seeking,* ed. C. Rowley, R. Tollison, and G. Tullock. Forthcoming.

Crain, W. Mark, and Robert D. Tollison. 1977. "The Influence of Representation on Public Policy." *J. Legal Stud.* 6:355.

———. 1979a. "Constitutional Change in an Interest-Group Perspective." *J. Legal Stud.* 8:165.

———. 1979b. "The Executive Branch in the Interest-Group Theory of Government." *J. Legal Stud.* 8:555.

Crain, W. Mark, Robert D. Tollison, and Donald R. Leavens. 1988. "Laissez Faire in Campaign Finance." *Pub. Choice* 56 (June):201–12.

Downs, Anthony. 1957. *An Economic Theory of Democracy.*

Faith, Roger L., and Robert D. Tollison. 1983. "Voter Search for Efficient Representation." *Res. L. & Econ.* 5:211.

Greene, Kenneth V., and Vincent G. Munley. 1981. "The Productivity of Legislators' Tenure: A Case Lacking in Evidence." *J. Legal Stud.* 10:207.

Grier, Kevin. 1987. "Campaign Spending and Senate Elections, 1978–1984." Manuscript.

Hotelling, Harold. 1929. "Stability in Competition." *Econ. J.* 39:41.

Kalt, Joseph P., and Mark A. Zupan. 1984. "Capture and Ideology in the Economic Theory of Politics." *Am. Econ. Rev.* 74:279.

Kau, James B., and Paul H. Rubin. 1979. "Self-Interest, Ideology and Logrolling in Congressional Voting." *J. L. & Econ.* 22:365.

Landes, William, and Richard A. Posner. 1975. "The Independent Judiciary in an Interest-Group Perspective." *J. L. & Econ.* 18:875.

Leibowitz, Arleen, and Robert D. Tollison. 1980. "A Theory of Legislative Organization: Making the Most of Your Majority." *Q. J. Econ.* 94:261.

McChesney, Fred S. 1987. "Rent Extraction and Rent Creation in the Economic Theory of Regulation." *J. Legal Stud.* 16:101.

McCormick, Robert E., and Robert D. Tollison. 1978. "Legislatures as Unions." *J. Pol. Econ.* 86:63.

————. 1980. "Wealth Transfers in a Representative Democracy." In *Toward a Theory of the Rent-Seeking Society,* ed. J. Buchanan, R. Tollison, and G. Tullock, 293.

————. 1981. *Politicians, Legislation, and the Economy: An Inquiry into the Interest-Group Theory of Government.*

Maloney, Michael T., and Robert E. McCormick. 1982. "A Positive Theory of Environmental Quality Regulation." *J. L. & Econ.* 25:99.

Marvel, Howard P. 1977. "Factory Regulation: A Reinterpretation of Early English Experience." *J. L. & Econ.* 20:329.

Meltzer, Allan H., and Scott F. Richard. 1981. "A Rational Theory of the Size of Government." *J. Pol. Econ.* 89:914.

Moore, Thomas G. 1961. "The Purpose of Licensing." *J. L. & Econ.* 4:93.

Nelson, Douglas, and Eugene Silberberg. 1987. "Ideology and Legislator Shirking." *Econ. Inquiry* 25:15.

Niskanen, William A., Jr. 1971. *Bureaucracy and Representative Government.*

Olson, Mancur. 1965. *The Logic of Collective Action.*

Peltzman, Sam. 1980. "The Growth of Government." *J. L. & Econ.* 23:209.

————. 1985. "An Economic Interpretation of the History of Congressional Voting in the Twentieth Century." *Am. Econ. Rev.* 75:656.

Plott, Charles R., and Michael E. Levine. 1978. "A Model of Agenda Influence on Committee Decisions." *Am. Econ. Rev.* 68:146.

Riker, William. 1962. *The Theory of Political Coalitions.*

Shepsle, Kenneth A. 1978. *The Giant Jigsaw Puzzle: Democratic Committee Assignments in the Modern House.*

Shepsle, Kenneth A., and Barry R. Weingast. 1981. "Structure-Induced Equilibrium and Legislative Choice." *Pub. Choice* 37:503.

Shughart, William F. II, and Robert D. Tollison. 1985. "Corporate Chartering: An Exploration in the Economics of Legal Change." *Econ. Inquiry* 23:585.

————. 1986. "On the Growth of Government and the Political Economy of Legislation." *Res. L. & Econ.* 9:111.

Shughart, William F. II, Robert D. Tollison, and Brian L. Goff. 1986. "Bureaucratic Structure and Congressional Control." *S. Econ. J.* 52:962.

Stigler, George J. 1971. "The Theory of Economic Regulation." *Bell J. Econ. & Mgmt. Sci.* 2:3.

————. 1972. "Economic Competition and Political Competition." *Pub. Choice.* 13:91.

————. 1974. "Free Riders and Collective Action: An Appendix to Theories of Economic Regulation." *Bell J. Econ. & Mgmt. Sci.* 5:359.

———. 1976. "The Sizes of Legislatures." *J. Legal Stud.* 5:17.
Tullock, Gordon. 1959. "Problems of Majority Voting." *J. Pol. Econ.* 67:571.
———. 1967. *The Politics of Bureaucracy.*
———. 1976. *The Vote Motive.*
Weingast, Barry R., and Mark J. Moran. 1983. "Bureaucratic Discretion or Congressional Control? Regulatory Policymaking by the Federal Trade Commission." *J. Pol. Econ.* 91:765.

Part 2
The Supply of Legislation

Final Voting in Legislatures

W. Mark Crain, Donald R. Leavens, and
Robert D. Tollison

In representative democracies, such as the United States, legislatures provide
the transmission mechanism through which pressure from private interests
becomes public policy. Considerable attention has been given in the literature
to explanations of the relevant forces that appear to be driving the legislative
process. For example, much research has focused on the relative impact of
economic versus ideological influences on congressional voting behavior. In
this approach, the way that legislators vote on proposed legislation is modeled
as a function of the preferences of various economic and ideological interest
groups, including the legislator's own preferences for wealth and ideology
(Kau and Rubin 1979; Kalt and Zupan 1984; Peltzman 1985).

Missing from this approach is the idea that when legislatures are the
transmission mechanism, they are costly and imperfect organizations for generating political influence (Becker 1983). As such, rules and institutions will
emerge that are related to problems of internal control within the organization
of a legislature. In this paper, we focus on the role of floor voting from the
standpoint of legislator organization and control. We seek to expand the interpretation of the meaning of floor voting activity by examining the timing,
sequence, and outcomes of such votes. Specifically, we look at final floor
voting in the U.S. Congress. The patterns described in the analysis below
suggest that a broader analytical perspective on the economic function of floor
voting is required. The findings also suggest that to identify more precisely the
forces that are driving legislator voting behavior, it is important to recognize
the role of legislative transactional costs and institutional constraints.

In section 1, the conceptual framework for the empirical results is discussed in more detail. The purpose is not to develop a full-blown theory of
legislative organization; rather, it is to focus the reader's attention on several

Reprinted from *American Economic Review* 76, no. 4 (September 1986): 833–41. We are
grateful to the referees and to Robert Haveman for useful comments. The usual caveat applies.

hypotheses about the function of final floor voting as a device for controlling legislator behavior within the legislature. Empirical results, including an explanation of the timing and sequence of final votes on bills, are reported in section 2. The data for these tests are drawn from legislative activities in the U.S. House of Representatives during the 96th and 98th Congresses. Some concluding remarks are offered in section 3.

1. Voting and Legislative Organization: Some Economic Principles

Our purpose in this section is simply to prepare the groundwork for the empirical analysis presented in the following section. This discussion is in no sense a formal model of legislative behavior. It is rather an application of some principles of economic organization to derive some empirical inferences about legislative voting patterns. We suggest several explanations for the role of floor voting, other than the usual view that voting represents the final tallying of legislator preferences on public policy.

We begin the discussion with the concept that the nature of collective decision making, per se, makes the familiar principles of team production applicable to legislative behavior (Alchian and Demsetz 1972). By virtue of the requirement of a majority vote to pass legislation, the actions of individual legislators are linked, and the usual implications of team production follow (Crain and Tollison 1980, 1982; Leibowitz and Tollison 1980). In other words, shirking by individual legislators will be a problem, and the monitoring and management of legislator behavior will be an important aspect of the legislature and its organization. We can illustrate the team production argument with respect to how bills are selected for final approval by the legislature.

Final voting on legislation could take place at any time during the legislative session, from the first day on. But the principles of team production imply that final voting will occur primarily at the *end* of the session. This follows because of the potential for legislator shirking. Deals are negotiated during the legislative session among legislators, the leadership, and interest groups. Once it is clear that these "markets" have cleared, the leadership must arrange final votes to consummate each deal. Deals could be voted upon as soon as it was clear what was wanted, but, in a team production setting, this leads to the potential for reneging. A simple way to think about the problem of reneging is that once a legislator gets his bill passed, he goes home without sticking around to carry out the quid pro quos that led to the passage of his bill. Alternative ways to renege are simply to change one's vote on subsequent bills, or not to work as hard for the passage of other bills. Hence, the first testable implication is that most final votes will be taken at the end of the legislative session in marathon, widely publicized meetings, where the opportunities for reneging are low.

The legislature will be a more effective organization the more closely rewards are tailored to individual legislator productivity. The latter can take a variety of forms, but for the purpose of analyzing final votes, individual legislator productivity is defined as the propensity of a legislator to keep his political bargains. Those legislators who can be counted on to keep their bargains receive differentially higher rewards from the leadership. Solutions to the problem of differential rewards for differential productivity can be found in many areas of economic theory. For example, an hypothesis from the screening literature is that legislators, like employees in certain types of job settings, are screened for quality by the employers within the organization. In the legislative context, information about the qualities of party loyalty and trustworthiness is important to the party leaders. Institutions like the committee system and seniority rules are examples of loyalty filters in legislative organizations (Akerlof 1983). The party leadership can influence voting by using votes as a criterion for making superior committee assignments.[1] There are two implications that follow from applying the filtering framework: (a) in the scheduling of final votes, bills sponsored by more trustworthy legislators will stand higher in the floor voting queue, and (b) these same legislators will have a higher probability of obtaining the passage of their bills in committee and floor voting.

We proxy trustworthiness by measures of legislator seniority and influence. The members of the legislature who exhibit more loyalty to the leadership have their bills passed first because the leadership knows from experience that they can be relied upon to carry through on the bargains they made with other legislators. In other words, earlier and more certain passage of bills is a premium paid to those legislators who have passed through a party loyalty filter. Their differential reward is a higher expected present value for the laws they sponsor (they are more likely to be passed and to be passed sooner in final voting), with the accompanying implication of better reelection prospects and so forth.[2]

There are other competing explanations for why the pattern of voting on bills will be influenced by political considerations that stem from the internal organization of the legislature. A theme in political science literature is that more politically powerful legislators get their bills passed sooner and more easily. The basis of their power may not be seniority but, for example, a charismatic personality or the fact that they represent an influential constitu-

---

1. See Charles Bullock (1985) and the references therein for a summary of the political science literature on this thesis. These studies examine congressional committee assignments as a function of past voting behavior.

2. A more complete theory of bill passage would include a framework to explain the date of introduction as well as passage. We make a preliminary effort to come to grips with this problem empirically in the next section by using the loyalty/legislative capital model to explain a bill's success at the stage of committee voting.

ency. The fact, however, that power and seniority have a natural affinity means that a political power theory carries many of the same implications as the above discussion for final voting on bills.[3] The intricacies and sources of power are driven in this type of framework by the concept of accumulating political capital. Since expertness and legislative capital are built over time, legislative competence will also naturally be related to seniority. More senior legislators have been able to acquire larger stocks of legislative capital, and hence we would expect them to get their bills passed sooner. Thus, a legislative capital framework also leads to an implication that floor voting activity depends on elements related to legislative organization.[4]

There is one final approach that we can suggest. It is the idea that voting on the most important bills will occur at the end of the legislative term, so legislators can squeeze the highest return from these transactions. In this view, the passage of legislation is analogous to the holdout problem—the longer you wait, the more rents you can squeeze. This bargaining approach also predicts that final votes will be at the end of the session. There is, however, a way to distinguish this hypothesis from the team production and loyalty filtering hypotheses. The bargaining power theory suggests that returns are greatest by waiting the longest, and if this is so, the bills of the most senior and powerful legislators should be voted on last. The earlier arguments, in contrast, suggest that the control of individual legislator incentives is paramount to producing final bills, and that for this reason the bills of the most senior legislators are voted on first in the queue of final votes.

There are undoubtedly other examples in this spirit. Our point is to stress the importance of political institutions and their possible effects on floor voting behavior. The key to understanding and interpreting the information embodied in voting outcomes requires more focus on these organizational problems.

2. Empirical Analysis: Voting on U.S. House Bills

The Timing and Sequence of Final Votes

The empirical analysis of final floor voting is based on data on the U.S. House of Representatives. First, we examine the timing of final voting on the House

---

3. See Fenno (1973), Fiorina (1974), and Ferejohn (1974) for contributions to this literature.

4. The legislative capital argument embodies a simultaneity problem as do the other frameworks outlined. That is, effective legislators introduce good bills, good bills pass, passage of one's bills increases reelection prospects, reelection means more seniority, and so on. Our approach in the empirical section is somewhat more limited in scope than this. For a given Congress, we seek to explain the order of final votes by legislator characteristics. We recognize, in general, however, that the simultaneity issue is not trivial.

floor. In this case the data are from U.S. Congressional Research Service (1981).

The 96th Congress commenced on January 15, 1979, and adjourned on December 16, 1980. A total of 8,455 House bills were introduced in the 96th Congress. Of these, 6,232 (74 percent) were introduced in the first session and 2,223 (26 percent) in the second session. Most bills were introduced early, and were around to be debated and voted on at an early stage. Yet most voting took place at the end of the available legislative work time. Of the 8,455 bills introduced, 560 (6.7 percent) made it through the chamber and passed on the House floor. Of the 560 bills passed, 250 (45 percent) were passed in the first session and 310 (55 percent) in the second session.

The 96th Congress worked a total of 322 days, excluding holidays and other days not in session such as Fridays and weekends, so a bill that was passed on the first day would have had 322 legislative days remaining. As a crude conversion formula, a legislative work day was equivalent to about 2.3 calendar days in this Congress.

The median for all bills passed by the House in the 96th Congress was legislative work day 207, with 116 legislative days remaining. On either side of this day, 280 bills were passed. Thus, roughly one-half of the successful bills were passed in the final one-third of the working days. The mean number of days remaining for all bills passed is 129, with a standard deviation of 85 days. Although this mean is not significantly different from the end of the legislative term (zero days remaining), it is significantly different from the beginning of the term (322 days remaining).

This overview of the raw data suggests that the timing of final votes is skewed toward the end of the legislative term. However, there is considerable variation in the timing of final votes. Not all votes occur at the end, nor would this pattern be possible due to a time constraint. Some bills have to be voted on before others.

The burden of our effort to apply some economic principles to legislative organization is to explain the order of the final votes that we observe. For this purpose we use the following model:

*LEGISLATIVE DAYS REMAINING AFTER A BILL PASSES =
f(SPONSOR CHARACTERISTICS, NUMBER OF COMMITTEES
THAT CONSIDERED A BILL, LEGISLATIVE DAY BILL
INTRODUCED)*

The dependent variable, *LEGISLATIVE DAYS REMAINING*, measures how close to the end of a legislative term a bill passes. As *LEGISLATIVE DAYS REMAINING* declines, a bill is passed later in the Congress.

The *SPONSOR CHARACTERISTICS* variable is central to our analysis. Several of the hypotheses discussed above suggest that bills sponsored by more senior and well-positioned legislators will be passed earlier in the term. In the filtering approach, earlier passage is expected because it is less likely that more trustworthy members will stop being productive after their deals are consummated. In the team production approach, earlier passage is a greater reward to more productive members because the present value of a bill is higher the earlier it passes. By these same two arguments, bills sponsored by members whose seniority and committee positions are low will be passed later in order to make sure that the work gets done before rewards are handed out. In contrast, the holdout hypothesis predicts that bills sponsored by the more powerful members will be passed later. We proxy *SPONSOR CHARAC-TERISTICS* in several ways, including simple legislator tenure, party affiliation, subcommittee chairmanship, and an index of legislator seniority based on the importance of committee assignments and rank within those committee assignments.[5]

The *NUMBER OF COMMITTEES* variable controls for the problem of overlapping jurisdictions. A bill that must be considered in more than one committee will naturally reach the stage of final voting later. The *DAY IN-TRODUCED* variable functions as a time index for the analysis. Obviously, a bill must be introduced before it can be voted on, and bills that are introduced late in a session cannot be voted on until late.

In table 1, the model is estimated on the 560 bills passed by the House in the 96th Congress.[6] We present results for five specifications of the model. Keep in mind that as a bill is passed closer to the end of the session, the dependent variable gets smaller; a larger value means earlier passage. The *DAY INTRODUCED* variable appears in the expected direction and is strongly significant. The later a bill is introduced, the later it is passed. The coefficient values are calibrated in days. If a bill is introduced 10 legislative days earlier, its date of passage will be moved ahead 7 days. The gain is not day-for-day.[7] The *NUMBER OF COMMITTEES* variable appears in the predicted direction, and approaches a reasonable level of statistical significance in all models.

---

5. The seniority index for an individual legislator is computed as follows:

$$\sum_{j=1}^{n} \{1 - [(RANK_j - 1)/NOFMEMB_j]\} \times [3 - (2MINOR_j/MAJOR_j)],$$

where $RANK_j$ is the sponsor's rank on committee j, $NOFMEMB_j$ is the number of members on committee j, $MINOR_j$ is the number of minority members on committee j, $MAJOR_j$ is the number of majority members on committee j, and n is number of committee assignments for the sponsor. See Crain and Tollison (1981) and Leavens (1984) for other applications of this approach to assessing the influence of legislator seniority.

6. In our approach, a bill is a bill, when surely not all bills are created equally. Bill content is an important issue, but one that is beyond the scope of this paper to address.

7. This variable is obviously a highly significant explainer of the date of bill passage. Yet the seniority variables, as reviewed below, also perform well and have pronounced marginal impacts on the timing of final passage.

Each additional committee to which a bill is referred delays final passage by about 10 days (roughly three weeks of calendar time).

The variables employed to proxy sponsor loyalty and legislative capital appear in the expected direction. Simple legislator tenure (*SPONSOR'S TEN-URE*), included in models A and B, has a positive and highly significant sign. The bills sponsored by more senior legislators are passed sooner. The estimates indicate that for every year of past legislative service, a legislator's bill is passed 2 days sooner (see the coefficients in models A and B in table 1). Thus, a five-term congressman would have his bills passed 20 working days sooner than a freshman legislator, on average.

Party affiliation of the sponsor does not seem to matter at the stage of final floor voting. Indeed model A suggests that minority sponsors obtain earlier passage. This result is an artifact of the legislative process. Few minority bills make it beyond committee for a final vote, and those that do obviously have wide bipartisan support. In the 96th Congress, 47 bills sponsored by minority party House members were cleared by committees for a final vote. Out of these, 46 passed on the House floor.

TABLE 1. OLS Regression Results for Legislative Days Remaining After a Bill Passes, All Bills Passed

Independent Variables	Coefficients[a]				
	Model A	Model B	Model C	Model D	Model E
Constant	213	207	212	209	213
	(23)	(22)	(21)	(20)	(21)
LEGISLATIVE DAY BILL INTRODUCED	−.71	−.71	−.71	−.71	−.71
	(28)	(28)	(27)	(27)	(27)
NUMBER OF COMMITTEES THAT CONSIDERED BILL	−11.08	−10.84	−9.73	−9.89	−9.68
	(1.80)	(1.76)	(1.56)	(1.60)	(1.56)
SPONSOR'S TENURE	2.02	1.57	—	—	—
	(3.73)	(2.72)			
SPONSOR A MEMBER OF MAJORITY PARTY	−9.79	−1.9	—	−3.40	—
	(1.19)	(.22)		(.38)	
SPONSOR A SUBCOMMITTEE CHAIRMAN	—	13.10	—	16.37	—
		(2.24)		(2.80)	
SPONSOR'S SENIORITY INDEX	—	—	5.57	2.87	−.18
			(2.41)	(1.17)	(.04)
Interaction of *SPONSOR'S SENIORITY INDEX* and *MAJORITY PARTY*	—	—	—	—	6.02
					(1.72)
Adjusted R Square	.58	.59	.58	.58	.58
$F_{(d.f.)}$	198	161	255	158	193
	(4.555)	(5.554)	(3.556)	(5.554)	(4.555)

Source: U.S. Congressional Research Service 1981.

[a]The *t*-statistics are shown in parentheses.

The variable *SUBCOMMITTEE CHAIRMAN* exerts a powerful influence over the timing of passage. The estimates presented in table 1 (models B and D) suggest that subcommittee chairmen have their bills passed on average about 14 legislative days sooner than their colleagues. This finding is consistent with several arguments. Committee chairmanships are typically awarded to members who have established the best reputations for party loyalty and who have accumulated considerable legislative capital as well.

Finally, the coefficients on the *SPONSOR'S SENIORITY INDEX* (models D and E) suggest that relative committee rank and committee assignments are important determinants of the earlier passage of legislation. In model C, when this variable is included without the other proxies for *SPONSOR CHARAC-TERISTICS*, it is positive and highly significant. The magnitude of the effect of the seniority index is more difficult to summarize since the coefficient can reflect the importance of different committee assignments as well as different seniority rankings on a given committee.[8]

In model E we enter the *SENIORITY INDEX* for majority party members separately from minority party members. In this case we find that there is a difference between the two parties. For minority party members, there does not appear to be an ordering of final passage dates based on sponsor seniority. However, for majority party members, the *SENIORITY INDEX* retains its statistical significance, and the magnitude of the coefficient is slightly bigger than the estimated coefficient in model C.

Overall, the models in table 1 are highly significant, and explain about three-fifths of the variation in the timing of passage of bills.[9] It should be stressed before proceeding that the bargaining power, or holdout theory, does not fare well in these results; more legislator influence leads to earlier, not later, passage of a bill.

Predicting Outcomes on Final Votes

Not all bills that clear committees pass in final voting. In the 96th Congress, 597 House bills were reported from committee for consideration on the floor.

---

8. For example, the tenth ranking member on the Energy and Commerce Committee could expect his bill to be passed about 3 working days sooner than the tenth ranking member of the Post Office and Civil Service Committee. Moreover, bills sponsored by the tenth ranking member on Energy and Commerce will be passed more than 4 days earlier than the lowest ranking member (twenty-seventh) on this committee.

9. We replicated the results in table 1 on a slightly different data base. We included in the five regressions only bills that were reported from committees for floor action. Out of the 560 bills that passed, 65 were not reported from a committee. Using this set of 495 bills, the results are unchanged. In particular, *SPONSOR'S TENURE* continues to perform as expected, as do the *SUBCOMMITTEE CHAIRMAN* and the *SENIORITY INDEX* variables.

Only 13 of these bills (2 percent) failed to muster a majority vote. However, 89 bills (15 percent) were never brought to a floor vote by the leadership.

These data provide a basis for another application of the economic hypotheses discussed above. Since not all the bills that reach the floor pass or get voted on, the hypotheses should be useful for analyzing the characteristics of the bills that are less likely to pass. For example, when a bill does not pass or is tabled, it can be thought of as resulting from a contractual breakdown of some sort in the legislative marketplace. The sponsor and other supporters of a bill may have engaged in reneging or other noncooperative behavior in carrying through on their commitments. The leadership needs to limit such behavior, and one way to discipline reneging is to refuse to call up a member's bill for a final vote or not to support such bills when the floor vote is held. In other words, when shirking takes place, payoffs are withheld by not passing a member's bill. Our approach should be able to *predict* which legislator's bills will suffer this fate.

Our experiment is the following. We took model A from table 1, and reestimated the coefficients using discriminant analysis.[10] Three ways of classifying the dependent variable were examined, and the results are summarized in table 2. Class 1 divides outcomes in terms of whether bills were passed, rejected, or not considered; class 2 divides outcomes in terms of whether bills were considered or not considered; and class 3 divides outcomes in terms of whether a bill passed or did not pass. This experiment allows us to evaluate the potential of the model to explain the outcomes of final floor voting.[11]

We adopt a classification strategy in table 2 that is naive and biased against the model. We assume that the prior probability that a bill will land in any of the selected categories is the same. This is obviously not so, and we know that we could achieve stronger results by using additional information to weight prior probabilities, for example, the proportion of bills that passed in recent Congresses. The naive approach reported in table 2 is sufficient, how-

---

10. We used model A for this purpose because it was the simplest approach in table 1. It, for example, has the most straightforward definition of legislator tenure. The classification results using models B–E are highly similar to those obtained using model A, and do not change the results in table 2 in any meaningful way. For example, comparing models B–E to the results for model A, the percent of predicted outcomes correctly classified is, respectively, 61, 61, 60, and 61 percent. Moreover, we obtain slightly better results in our ability to identify those bills that were not passed using models C and E. Model C correctly identifies 63 of the 102 bills not passed, and model E identifies 64 of these bills. Models B and D correctly identify 61 and 62 of the 102 bills not passed. We would be happy to provide these results on request.

11. The results of the discriminant analysis using model A can be summarized as follows. The F-significance level for each of the three classifications was 1 percent, and the Wilks *lambda* statistics were well within the acceptable range. These results and the standardized coefficients and the univariate F-statistics for the individual coefficients are available on request.

TABLE 2. Classification Results on Predicted Floor Outcomes

Actual Floor Outcome	No. of Cases	Predicted Floor Outcome[a]		
Class 1		Not Considered	Rejected	Passed
Not considered	89	48	20	21
		(54)	(22)	(24)
Rejected	13	5	2	6
		(39)	(15)	(46)
Passed	495	179	98	218
		(36)	(20)	(44)
Percentage of predicted outcomes correctly classified = 45 percent				
Class 2		Not Considered		Considered
Not considered	89	54		35
		(61)		(39)
Considered	508	196		312
		(39)		(61)
Percentage of predicted outcomes correctly classified = 61 percent				
Class 3		Not Passed		Passed
Not passed	102	61		41
		(60)		(40)
Passed	495	187		308
		(38)		(62)
Percentage of predicted outcomes correctly classified = 62 percent				

Source: U.S. Congressional Research Service, 1981.
[a]Percentage correct of cases predicted is shown in parentheses.

ever, to illustrate the potential of this analytical framework to classify correctly the fate of bills in floor votes.

In class 1, where the categories are tripartite, the model correctly identifies 54 percent of the bills that were not considered. In class 2, the model identifies 61 percent of the bills that were not considered, where a binary classification is used to divide bills into those that were considered (passed or failed) versus those not considered (tabled). In class 3, the division is between bills that passed versus bills that did not pass (failed or not considered). We are able to identify bills in the not-passed category 60 percent of the time. This means that our model correctly identifies 61 of the 102 bills that did not pass. By comparison, a random model (50–50) would predict that 298 of the bills would fail.

Why is this an important result? It is important because we are dealing with the exception rather than the rule. Clearly, once reported from committee, most bills pass. But the 17 percent that did not pass puts an explanatory burden on the economic arguments. That is, can the alternative hypotheses derived from economic theory be applied to predict which bills will fall into this rare category of legislative behavior? (Yes.)

Predicting Outcomes in Committees

The hypotheses discussed in Section 1 also suggest a way to identify which bills will succeed through the committee process. Essentially, the same factors that explain the organization of final voting should explain the fate of bills as they are introduced and referred to committees. More senior and more trustworthy legislators' bills will be more likely to clear the committee stage for final votes on the House floor. Just as earlier passage is a way to reward legislator loyalty and performance, so too is favorable treatment of a legislator's proposals by the committee system.

To examine this implication and to provide more generalized evidence on our approach, we selected a random sample of bills introduced in the 98th Congress. The source for the second data set is Legi-Slate (1985). There were 6,444 House bills introduced in this Congress, out of which we drew a random sample of 2000 bills. We excluded 107 private bills. Thus, our final sample consists of 1,893 bills that were referred to House committees.

Our procedure with this second data set is straightforward. Again, we take model A from table 1, update the right-hand side variables to the 98th Congress, and recast the dependent variable in discrete terms, in this case, in terms of whether a bill passes or fails at the committee stage.[12] A bill can be voted down at the committee stage or simply never be acted upon.

The ability of the model to classify bills according to passed versus not passed in committee is summarized in table 3. We do not have to dwell upon the results. The legislator loyalty/legislator capital arguments offer statistically useful approaches to the problem of identifying which bills survive committees. To illustrate, there are 162 bills (8 percent) in the sample that actually passed committee. Model A correctly identifies 106 (65 percent) of those bills, taking again the naive a priori view that every bill in the sample has an even chance of passing committee.

3. Concluding Remarks

The legislature is an important institution in a mixed capitalist economic system, and understanding and predicting its behavior is a central task for

---

12. We use model A from table 1 for the reasons cited in fn. 11. The results of the discriminant analysis for classification of pass/not passed at the committee stage were: the F-significance level was .0001, and the Wilks *lambda* was .968. These results, the univariate F-statistics, and individual coefficients are available on request.

**TABLE 3.   Classification Results on Predicted
Committee Outcomes**

Actual Committee Outcome	No. of Cases	Predicted Committee Outcome[a]	
		Not Passed	Passed
Not passed in committee	1721	1026	695
		(60)	(40)
Passed in committee	162	56	106
		(35)	(65)
Percentage of predicted outcomes correctly classfied = 60 percent			

Source: Legi-Slate 1985.
[a]Percentage correct of cases predicted is shown in parentheses.

economic theory. Our purpose in this essay has been to suggest several alternative ways to proceed in this task. The findings for the U.S. House of Representatives suggest that the timing, sequence, and outcomes of final floor votes are influenced by organizational considerations. While we do not claim to have pinpointed an exact explanation for final voting behavior in legislatures, we think we have provided enough evidence to broaden the debate about how to interpret its meaning.

REFERENCES

Akerlof, George A. 1983. "Loyalty Filters." *American Economic Review* 73 (March): 54–65.

Alchian, Armen A., and Demsetz, Harold. 1972. "Production, Information Costs, and Economic Organization." *American Economic Review* 62 (December): 777–95.

Becker, Gary. 1983. "A Theory of Competition Among Pressure Groups For Political Influence." *Quarterly Journal of Economics* 98 (August): 371–400.

Bullock, Charles S., III. 1985. "U.S. Senate Committee Assignments: Preferences, Motivations, and Success." *American Journal of Political Science* 29 (November): 789–808.

Crain, W. Mark, and Robert D. Tollison. 1980. "The Sizes of Majorities." *Southern Economic Journal* 46 (January): 726–34.

———. 1981. "Representation and Influence: Reply." *Journal of Legal Studies* 10 (January): 215–19.

———. 1982. "Team Production in Political Majorities." *Micropolitics* 3:111–21.

Fenno, Richard. 1973. *Congressmen in Committees.* Boston: Little, Brown.

Ferejohn, John. 1974. *Pork Barrel Politics: Rivers and Harbors Legislation 1947–1968.* Stanford: Stanford University Press.

Fiorina, Morris P. *Representatives, Roll Calls, and Constituencies.* Lexington: D. C. Heath.

Kalt, Joseph, and Zupan, Mark. 1984. "Capture and Ideology in the Economic Theory of Politics." *American Economic Review* 74 (June): 279–300.

Kau, James, and Rubin, Paul. 1979. "Self-Interest, Ideology and Logrolling in Congressional Voting." *Journal of Law and Economics* 22 (October): 365–84.

Leavens, Donald R. 1984. "Legislator Compensation and the Determinants of Committee Action in the U.S. House of Representatives." Ph.D. diss., George Mason University.

Legi-Slate. 1985. On-Line Database. Washington, D.C.

Leibowitz, Arleen A., and Robert D. Tollison. 1980. "A Theory of Legislative Organization: Making the Most of Your Majority." *Quarterly Journal of Economics* 94 (March): 261–77.

Peltzman, Sam. 1985. "An Economic Interpretation of Congressional Voting in the Twentieth Century." *American Economic Review* 75 (September): 656–75.

U.S. Congressional Research Service. 1981. *Digest of Public General Bills and Resolutions,* parts 1 and 2. 96th Congress, 1st and 2d Sess. Washington, D.C.: USGPO.

Pork Barrel Paradox

*W. Mark Crain, Donald R. Leavens, and
Robert D. Tollison*

Logrolling and pork barrel politics are typically analyzed as a function of political geography and legislator seniority. Legislators who have served a long time in the legislature accrue both power and experience in making legislative bargains that redound to the benefit of their districts. This general approach has explanatory power, but it misses a central point about the pork barrel process. A public works program in a given district produces a flow of benefits over time, in other words, a present value. A political party wants those benefits to be identified with its banner and good works in order to make it easier for party members to be reelected over time. The party wants voters to credit the benefits of local public works to one of its own members, not to members of the opposition party. This preference creates a dilemma; a party member who is in trouble with the voters, or simply getting along in years and closer to probable retirement, will represent a more risky logrolling investment, all else the same. The extra risk is that legislation will be enacted that delivers a flow of future benefits to a district that is captured by the opposition party.

Public investments, like private investments, are made at the margin, in this case, at the political margin. Given the local public goods character of public works programs, such investments will not be made in cases where the benefit flow would likely accrue over the tenure of legislators from the opposing party. These externalities are tailored by a political calculus to be party-specific to the extent feasible.

We thus come to a paradox of political behavior. Legislators, even very senior ones, who are in danger at the polls or who are closer to retirement, will have more difficulty getting the party to support their legislation if it confers long-term economic benefits on their constituents. Their productivity in terms of getting legislation enacted and of obtaining federal expenditure projects for their districts will diminish. For example, controlling for seniority, committee positions, and other relevant factors, a legislator who is

vulnerable at the polls is less likely to obtain major projects for his constituents than one who serves a safe district. At the same time, since vulnerable
party members represent marginal or transitory districts, their campaign coffers will be hefty. The former argument follows from the prior discussion
about present value. The latter follows from the fact that marginal races will
attract more campaign funds, both because the outcomes of those races could
go either way and because campaign spending in such districts generates
party-specific externalities (Jacobson 1980; Crain and Laband 1983).

The point of our analysis goes beyond the development of this positive
framework, however. The usual normative conclusion drawn in the pork
barrel literature is that public expenditures are larger than they would be
otherwise due to this type of legislator behavior (Tullock 1959; Buchanan and
Tullock 1962; Ferejohn 1974). Our analysis suggests that spending distortions
can run in the opposite direction as well. A party might prefer to curtail
spending should seats be about to turn over because it would help the rival
party. From a party's point of view, less public spending may be a decision
that is strategically advantageous. This normative part of the analysis can be
used to rationalize such political institutions as committees and the seniority
system. These institutions can be viewed as mechanisms to protect geographically defined political districts from being underfunded, as their incumbent
representatives become too vulnerable or too old for the party to risk supporting their projects. Instead of the usual conclusions that seniority rules and the
committee apparatus create excess government spending, these institutions
can be seen as offsetting the tendency of political parties to neglect districts
that are politically volatile.

The analytical framework for legislative pork barrel decisions is presented in section 1. In section 2, some empirical implications of the analysis
are examined using data on legislative activity in the U.S. House of Representatives for the 98th Congress (1983–84). A political influence function is
estimated which addresses the factors that determine the ability of House
members to get their bills passed. Electoral vulnerability and legislator age are
predicted and shown to bear negative relationships to a legislator's productivity in obtaining the passage of his/her bills. In section 3, some concluding
remarks are offered, including a discussion of the normative implications
about the role of legislative institutions and the level of public spending.

1. Pork Barrel at the Margin

The purpose of this section is to develop a present value model for analyzing
pork barrel decisions. We develop the model for a legislature that has geographic representation and two political parties. We treat political parties as

the basic decision-making units in the legislature, and suppose that all legislators belong to one party or the other. Legislation is assumed to require a simple majority vote for passage. The problem is formulated from the standpoint
of the party, and the choice is whether to support or oppose legislative proposals. Simply put, a party will favor the enactment of a law if it benefits a
member of its own party, and will oppose a law if it benefits a member of the
opposing party, all else the same. Legislative enactment of a law requires a
majority vote, and those laws that confer more benefits on the majority party
and less benefits on the minority party are more likely to be enacted.

Several factors enter into a party's decision to favor or oppose legislation
that confers benefits on the districts of geographically elected representatives.
The central point of our analysis is that laws have multiple-period effects. This
perspective is important because the political effects of the same piece of
legislation can flip-flop from one period to the next. A public project that
might confer benefits to a party in one period can hurt it in another.

To examine the transitory nature of the effects of legislation, we divide
the effects into electoral periods, each of which is equal to the length of a
single term. Suppose legislative outcomes, L, are expected to have effects that
will last for a certain number of terms, T. In any single political term, let L_t
denote the effects of the legislation on a political party. Thus, increases or
decreases in L_t reflect increases or decreases in benefits to the party per term.
These benefits change in direct relation to how the legislation affects constituents and, in turn, to how these constituents behave at the polls in future
elections. The behavioral assumption about voting is that constituents are
more likely to reelect an incumbent representative when the benefits of legislation are flowing into his district.[1] This means that from a party's perspective
the sign of L_t will depend on which party holds the district. We assume that
the effect is symmetrical. When L_t benefits the constituents of a district, the
sign will be positive when a member of its own party holds the seat. It will be
negative when a member of the other party holds the seat.

To illustrate, suppose there are two parties, D and R. Consider the case
where the majority Party D holds a legislative seat in one term, and loses it in
the next term to Party R. Party D might prefer not to pass a law even though it
yields benefits to its holder of a seat in the initial term. Once a Party R member
obtains the seat, the law becomes bad from the standpoint of Party D. Thus, the
decision of Party D to support or oppose a given law depends on which party is
likely to control particular seats in each electoral subperiod of T.

The party's decision to support or oppose legislation will be based on an

---

1. There is an extensive literature on the relationship between economic fluctuations and
voter behavior. See Tufte 1978, for example.

assessment of the net present value of the benefits (that is, the L_t's). This present value (V) is the summation of the effects of the legislation over all T terms, or

$$V = \sum_{t=1}^{T} \frac{L_t}{(1 + r)^t} ,$$ (1)

where r is the discount rate. As this present value rises or falls, the party's support of or opposition to legislation will change accordingly.

The party has a certain probability of losing or gaining a seat in any given electoral cycle, denoted as P_t. This is the probability of the incumbent losing, and it can be thought of as an added risk factor in the party's calculus. This probability can be added to equation (1) as follows:

$$V = \sum_{t=1}^{T} (1 - P_t) \left[\frac{L_t}{(1 + r)^t} \right].$$ (2)

From a given party's perspective, if it holds the seat, L_t is positive, and a low probability of turnover means that the seat is a low-risk investment. This reduces the value of L_t by smaller amounts, and so on. If the party's opponents hold the seat, L_t is negative, and a small chance of turnover will mean that the negative effects on the party will be larger in equation (2) than is the case when there is a higher chance of turnover. As P_t approaches one, V will be reduced by less when the party does not hold a seat since the L_t's are negative. As P_t approaches one, it indicates that the party has a greater chance of capturing a seat. In general, the relationship between P_t and V

$$\frac{\delta V}{\delta P_t} < 0 .$$ (2a)

The inverse relationship between the probability of an electoral turnover and the present value of legislation posited in (2a) is novel in two respects. First, as noted previously, it is the opposite sign of the relationship between election outcomes and private campaign spending. The latter will be larger where the chances of a seat turning over are larger. Second, it complicates a theme in the pork barrel literature which stresses that incumbent politicians use the public purse to buy votes.[2] In a nutshell the difference stems from our

---

2. See the discussion in Lindsay 1980: "Once a district is safe for a particular party, it is more expedient to use the source funds available from the government treasury to attempt to win others" (94).

formulation of the legislative decision-making problem as one that is driven by expected electoral outcomes and that considers the riskiness of the investment in a seat, as opposed to a formulation where the objective of legislative decisions is to influence electoral outcomes. The literature has tended to overlook the risks of the downside effects on a party when it invests legislative outcomes to influence an election and then its candidate loses. This investment is not simply lost (that is, a zero return), but rather it is handed over to the opposition party, which means that the investment produces a negative return. In terms of equation (2), the sign on L_t goes from positive to negative.

From the behavioral assumption about voters, equation (2) can be expanded to include the feedback effect of pork barrel on future elections. The downside effect is that it will be more difficult for a party to recapture a seat in the future if the constituents are prospering while being served by a member of the opposition party. Symmetrically, it will be easier for a party to retain a seat in the future if a current party investment in legislation creates prosperity during the tenure of one of the party's own members. This intertemporal effect is represented in equation (3):

$$P_t = P(L_t) ,$$

(3)

where $\delta P_t / \delta L < 0$. More benefits flowing to a district in the t period reduce the chances that voters will throw out the incumbent. Substituting equation (3) into (2), we obtain:

$$V = \sum_{t=1}^{T} [1 - P(L_t)] \left[\frac{L_t}{(1 + r)^t} \right].$$

(4)

Equation (4) includes the feedback effect of the political investment decision on future election outcomes. For example, suppose that the opposition party takes over a seat in some future period, t, then L_t is negative and P_t becomes smaller as the size of the benefits gets larger. In turn, this further reduces the present value of the investment to the party.

The two perspectives on the pork barrel problem carry alternative empirical implications. If legislative decisions are designed to buy electoral outcomes, the party would allocate more influence to its incumbents in closer races. The political returns to the party would be increased by delivering more benefits to its members in marginal races and less to members in safe races. In contrast, the present value model developed above predicts that legislative outcomes will favor safe incumbents. Vulnerable party members represent more risky investments. These alternative hypotheses are examined empirically in section 2.

While they are not tested in the present essay, we briefly mention two additional implications of this formulation of pork barrel decisions. A straightforward interpretation of equation (4) is that the net benefit of a law (V) depends on the durability of the law (Landes and Posner 1975). This is represented by the variable T, or the number of terms over which a legislative outcome has effects. As T increases, V will increase if the party expects to retain a seat. If a party holds a seat but expects to lose it in a subsequent election, V will decrease as T increases. More durable legislation will have a lower yield to the party in more volatile districts than in safe districts. This implies that there would be lower government spending levels in polities that limit succession rights of office holders. Limits on the number of terms that may be served by U.S. governors, for example, should reduce the present value of the legislative benefits flow over time, thereby reducing public spending in these jurisdictions, ceteris paribus. A second implication is that shorter term lengths will result in lower public spending levels since with more elections there is greater risk that any given seat will turn over.[3]

2. Influence in the U.S. House of Representatives

The present value formulation of the pork barrel problem is examined empirically in this section. The testable implication that we pursue concerns the ability of a legislator to deliver benefits to his constituents. We seek to specify and estimate the key elements in a legislator's political influence function. All else the same, the analysis predicts that the influence of a legislator will be inversely related to the likelihood that his/her seat will be captured by the opposition party. We proxy this effect in two ways—the closeness of the legislator's most recent election and the legislator's age. Chronologically young and electorally safe legislators are predicted to have greater influence over legislative outcomes.

The model for estimating the determinants of legislator influence is specified in equation (5). We estimate this model using data on the U.S. House of Representatives. As the discussion will indicate, some variables are included to tailor the model specifically to this legislative body.

$$INFLUENCE = f \, (ELECTORAL \ VULNERABILITY, \ AGE,$$
$$PARTY \ AFFILIATION, \ TENURE, \ INTENSITY \ OF \ SPONSOR'S$$
$$INTEREST, \ MAJOR \ OR \ NONMAJOR \ COMMITTEE$$
$$REFERRAL, \ TIMING \ OF \ LEGISLATIVE \ PROPOSAL) \, . \qquad (5)$$

---

3. For a discussion of the effect of term lengths and succession rights on the present value of holding a public office, see Crain and Tollison 1977.

Conceptually, the dependent variable, *INFLUENCE*, seeks to measure the influence of a legislator in terms of his/her ability to obtain party support and passage of legislation that he/she proposes. We assume that a legislator's bills will include benefits to his/her constituency, and that legislators will have a comparative advantage in knowledge about what local constituents want from the pork barrel. Allowing individual legislators to author bills is a way for the party to economize on information costs. The ability of a legislator to deliver constituent benefits is measured in two ways. First, we estimate the likelihood that if a legislator writes and introduces a given piece of legislation, it will be passed. Second, we estimate the number of bills sponsored by a legislator that are ultimately enacted.

The definition and measurement of the explanatory variables included in equation (5) are described in turn. As a general way of thinking about the empirical model, there are two broad categories of independent variables: (a) factors that reflect characteristics about the legislator who is sponsoring the legislation, and (b) factors that reflect the content of the legislation itself.

Two variables are central to testing the analytical model presented in section 1—*ELECTORAL VULNERABILITY* and *AGE*. Both variables reflect characteristics about the sponsor of a given legislative proposal. The present value analysis developed previously predicts that legislators representing more volatile districts will have their ability to pass legislation impaired. These legislators represent more risky investments to their party. The value of allocating influence to vulnerable members diminishes because their seats are more likely to be controlled in the future by the other party. The implication is that legislative proposals sponsored by legislators from more volatile districts are less likely to be enacted. District volatility is measured in two ways. *ELECTORAL VULNERABILITY* is the percent of the vote received in the last election by the bill's sponsor. Party members receiving a smaller share of the vote are expected to be less influential because there is a greater chance that they will be defeated the next time around. *AGE* is the year of birth of the legislator who is sponsoring the bill. *AGE* is a proxy for the volatility of the district because older representatives are more likely to retire and leave the seat open. Even if an incumbent candidate is winning reelection by comfortable margins, his/her retirement would render the seat more vulnerable. Open seat races are more susceptible to party reversals than non-open seat races (Crain and Tollison 1976). We expect *AGE* to reflect the likelihood that the district of the bill's sponsor will become open and, hence, more transitory in terms of a given party's control.

The variables, *ELECTORAL VULNERABILITY* and *AGE*, are entered in the empirical model in a manner that seeks to control for qualitative differences in types of legislative proposals. Obviously, a variety of proposals are introduced in the House. The type of legislation that is particularly sensitive to the volatility of the sponsor's district is that which has important multiterm consequences. The present value calculus predicts that members of a party will be much more concerned with the characteristics of sponsors whose bills have long-lasting effects. In contrast, the vulnerability of a sponsor of a legislative proposal that lacks substantive long-term effects will be less important to the party. Two interaction terms are included to reflect qualitative differences in the content of legislative proposals. We sort out and examine separately the legislation sponsored by committee and subcommittee chairmen to control for substantive versus less important bills.

Committee and subcommittee chairmen in the House have the responsibility for writing and managing the major legislative initiatives under their respective jurisdictions. To illustrate the qualitative difference in the legislation sponsored by committee and subcommittee chairmen versus other legislators in the House, we examined bills cleared by the House Public Works and Transportation Committee. In the appendix, we list all the bills passed on the floor of the House in the 98th Congress (1983–84) that were referred to and passed by this committee. We use this particular data as an illustration because the House Public Works Committee is generally considered to be a hotbed for federal pork barrel projects (Ferejohn 1974). To summarize the data in the appendix, there were 65 House public bills that passed on the floor that were first passed by the Public Works committee. Of these bills, 26 were sponsored by a committee or subcommittee chairman; 39 bills were sponsored by a nonchairman. The 65 bills that passed included 42 "designation" bills. For example, H.R. 593 was a bill to designate the name of a building as the "Michael McDermott Bulk and Foreign Mail Center" (see appendix). More than 80 percent of the relatively unimportant designation bills were sponsored by nonchairmen. On the other hand, about 75 percent of the substantive House Public Works bills were sponsored by a committee or a subcommittee chairman. In sum, distinguishing between bills sponsored by a committee or subcommittee chairman versus other bills, controls somewhat for differences in the importance of legislation.

The two interaction terms used to take into account the importance of legislative proposals are computed by multiplying *ELECTORAL VULNERABILITY* and *AGE* by a dummy variable for committee and subcommittee chairmen. The dummy variable is equal to one if the legislative proposal is sponsored by a committee or subcommittee chairman and equal to zero otherwise. We note that of the 526 House public bills that passed on the floor in the 98th Congress better than two-thirds were sponsored by committee and subcommittee chairmen. We expect that the sensitivity of a member's influence to *ELECTORAL VULNERABILITY* and *AGE* will be very pronounced for the type of legislation that is sponsored by committee and subcommittee chairmen. Since committee and subcommittee chairs introduce the major legislative measures, their influence over bill passage will be damaged the most when their districts are more volatile.

The *PARTY AFFILIATION* of a legislator is included as a dummy variable that is equal to one for minority party members and zero for majority party members. This variable controls for the effects of the party system in the House. All House members caucus with one of two parties for important decisions, such as committee assignments and electing the legislative leadership. The majority party has many ways to maintain control over the fate of legislation. For example, it holds the leadership positions and committee chairmanships, and sets party ratios on committees. Majority party members have a greater chance of passing legislation, all else equal. Minority party legislators, lacking control of committees and floor debates, are less likely to obtain passage of their legislation. We expect this variable to have a negative sign.

TENURE measures the number of years of continuous service of a legislator. Legislators with longer service are expected to have greater influence for several reasons. First, there is the familiar human capital argument. Producing legislation is a skill that requires training and specialized knowledge, and legislators who have been around longer have a larger stock of human capital. Second, influence may require an investment in back-scratching or logrolling, and those legislators with longer tenure have simply been able to pile up more chits. Third, legislators who have longer tenure may have been able to secure better committee assignments and party leadership positions, and in this sense tenure is a proxy for the importance of the positions that a legislator holds within the legislative system. We expect a positive sign on *TENURE*.

The final variable in the model that controls for characteristics of the bill's sponsor is *INTENSITY OF SPONSOR'S INTEREST*. This is a dummy variable that is equal to one if the legislative proposal is referred to a committee on which the bill's sponsor is a member, and equal to zero otherwise. This variable is tailored to fit the institutional structure of the House. All legislators in the House are assigned to serve on specific committees (typically two or three). The committees are given jurisdiction over a particular legislative subject area. In the normal flow of the legislative process, each bill is referred to at least one committee to be evaluated and approved prior to being sent to the floor for a vote by the entire House. Committees are the areas of specialization for particular policy subjects. The result is that House members tend to specialize and develop expertise in the legislative subjects pertaining to the committees to which they are assigned. When bills are introduced that get referred to a committee of which the sponsor is a member, it is an indication of a more intense interest in the outcome of the bill. The sponsor has direct involvement and oversight of the bill's fate. For example, the sponsor can arrange committee hearings for bills in his own committee. If the sponsor is not a member of a committee to which the bill is referred, it is a sign of less interest and direct involvement in the outcome. We predict a positive sign on this variable.

MAJOR OR NONMAJOR COMMITTEE REFERRAL is included as an additional control for differences in the importance of legislative proposals. One way to account for these differences is by examining the committees to which legislation is referred. This is a dummy variable that is equal to one if the bill is referred to a nonmajor committee, and equal to zero otherwise. All House committees are classified as either exclusive, major, or nonmajor committees (*Congressional Quarterly* 1983). The issues considered by nonmajor committees are relatively less important than issues considered by other committees. We expect a positive sign on this variable because it is easier to secure passage of legislation that is less important and, hence, less controversial.

Finally, we include a *TIMING OF LEGISLATIVE PROPOSAL* variable. This measures the number of working days into the legislative session that the sponsor introduced the bill. While there are several a priori arguments that can be made for the sign on this variable, based on the findings of Crain, Leavens, and Tollison (1986), we expect a positive sign. In effect, bills that are introduced earlier in the legislative term appear to be less likely to pass. The rationale is twofold: earlier proposals are simply efforts to appease supporters in the previous election, and later proposals have been more carefully thought through and promoted by their sponsors.[4]

The model is estimated using data on the U.S. House of Representatives for the 98th Congress (1983–84), the most recent period for which all data are complete. We first estimate the effects of the various factors on legislator influence using a large random sample of bills. There were 6,444 House bills (that is, H.R.'s) introduced in the 98th Congress, from which we selected 2,000 bills at random. We eliminated from this sample 91 bills that were "private" bills, leaving only House "public" bills in the sample. The dependent variable for each observation in this random sample of bills is a binary variable. The variable is equal to one if the bill passed the House floor, and equal to zero otherwise. The "otherwise" outcome includes bills that failed to receive a majority vote on the House floor and bills that were tabled (that is, not voted on).[5]

---

4. Relatedly, there are many cases where bills go through multiple revisions. A somewhat common practice is for a sponsor to introduce what is known as a "clean bill." A clean bill is introduced later in the session and is given a new bill number, even though it is the culmination of an extensive debate over one or more previously introduced bills.

5. The data sources on the variables are as follows: electoral vulnerability, *Congressional Quarterly* 1982; age and tenure, Barone and Ujifusa 1983; party affiliation, committee assignments, and classifications, *Congressional Quarterly* 1983; bill sponsor, committee referrals, and timing, *Legi-Slate* 1986.

TABLE 1. Discriminant Analysis Results; Dependent Variable: Outcome of Public Bills (Passed or Not) on the House Floor, 98th Congress

Independent Variable	Model A	Model B	Model C
Sponsor's percentage of vote in last election—committee and subcommittee chairmen only	0.35 (.016)	0.38 (.010)	0.31 (.020)
Sponsor's percentage of vote in last election—nonchairmen	−0.11 (0.34)	−0.05 (0.66)	−0.07 (0.480)
Bill sponsor member of minority party (yes or no?)	−0.22 (0.100)	−0.20 (0.129)	−0.16 (0.181)
Sponsor's years of continuous house service	0.25 (0.026)	0.32 (0.005)	0.30 (0.004)
Bill referred to sponsor's committee (yes or no?)	0.50 (0.001)	—	0.42 (0.001)
Bill referred to a nonmajor committee (yes or no?)	0.64 (0.001)	0.53 (0.001)	0.56 (0.001)
Date bill was introduced	—	0.48 (0.001)	0.42 (0.001)
NOBS	1909	1909	1909
Equivalent F-statistic$_{(d.f.)}$	$16.08_{(6,1902)}$	$16.15_{(6,1902)}$	$16.67_{(7,1901)}$
Percentage of cases correctly classified	69.3	66.7	66.8

Note: Values for standardized canonical discriminant function coefficients are listed, with significance levels in parentheses.

In tables 1 and 2, we present results using discriminant analysis, where the dependent variable is defined as described above. Three variations of the basic specification are reported in each table. Table 1 presents the results when the *ELECTORAL VULNERABILITY* variables are included; table 2 presents the results for the *AGE* variables. These two proxies for the volatility of the sponsor's district are not included in the same models due to multicollinearity.[6]

The empirical findings using discriminant analysis strongly support our theory. In table 1, the coefficients on *ELECTORAL VULNERABILITY* are positive and highly significant for committee and subcommittee chairmen in the three specifications. Bills sponsored by committee and subcommittee chairmen have a lower likelihood of passing when these legislators are in

---

6. We regressed *ELECTORAL VULNERABILITY* against *AGE* and the results are as follows:

$$ELECTORAL\ VULNERABILITY = 76.67 - 0.255\ AGE$$
$$(83.93)(-9.20)$$

The *t*-statistics, listed in parentheses, are significant at the 0.001 level. The *F*-statistic is 85, and is also significant at the 0.001 level.

TABLE 2. Discriminant Analysis Results; Dependent Variable: Outcome of Public Bills (Passed or Not) on the House Floor, 98th Congress

Independent Variable	Model A	Model B	Model C
Sponsor's date of birth—committee and subcommittee chairmen only	0.28 (0.030)	0.34 (0.006)	0.261 (0.025)
Sponsor's date of birth—nonchairmen	−0.25 (0.097)	−0.25 (0.097)	−0.260 (0.059)
Bill sponsor member of minority party (yes or no?)	−0.26 (0.032)	−0.23 (0.060)	−0.20 (0.078)
Sponsor's years of continuous house service	0.16 (0.304)	0.24 (0.108)	0.19 (0.170)
Bill referred to sponsor's committee (yes or no?)	0.50 (0.001)	—	0.42 (0.001)
Bill referred to a nonmajor committee (yes or no?)	0.64 (0.001)	0.53 (0.001)	0.56 (0.001)
Date bill was introduced	—	0.51 (0.001)	0.44 (0.001)
NOBS	1909	1909	1909
Equivalent F-statistic$_{(d.f.)}$	$16.13_{(6,1902)}$	$16.48_{(6,1902)}$	$16.92_{(7,1901)}$
Percentage of cases correctly classified	68.5	65.3	67.5

Note: Values for standardized canonical discriminant function coefficients are listed, with significance levels in parentheses.

trouble with the voters. Stated in the reverse, House committee and subcommittee chairs who win reelection by larger margins have a greater chance of having their bills passed. In table 2, where *AGE* is used to proxy district volatility, the results are likewise supportive. Other things equal, bills sponsored by older committee and subcommittee chairs are less likely to pass. In the three specifications in table 2, these coefficients are highly significant.

In sum, we find that the influence of important House members, as measured by the likelihood that their legislation will pass, is related to the volatility of their districts. This result is predicted by our analysis because legislators in volatile districts represent high-risk investments from the point of view of their fellow party members. Finally, note that district volatility does not appear to have an effect on the chances of legislation passing that is introduced by less important House members. For bills sponsored by nonchairs, the likelihood of success is not related at all to election outcomes (table 1) and bears a "weakly" negative relationship to age (table 2). The absence of these effects in the case of nonchairs is explained by the typically minor importance of the legislation they are handling.

The control variables reflecting *PARTY AFFILIATION, TENURE, INTENSITY OF SPONSOR'S INTEREST, MAJOR OR NONMAJOR COMMITTEE REFERRAL,* and *TIMING* all appear in the expected directions and are significant at the 5 percent level, with one exception in each table. In table 1, the exception is *PARTY AFFILIATION,* which is significant at the 10 percent, 12 percent, and 18 percent levels, respectively, in models A, B, and C. In table 2, the *TENURE* variable is the exception; it is significant at the 30 percent, 10 percent, and 17 percent levels, respectively, in models A, B, and C.

The explanatory power of the models presented in tables 1 and 2, measured by the F-statistics, is significant at the 1 percent level. Moreover, the models correctly classify whether or not bills passed almost 70 percent of the time, using a naive assumption that the prior probability of passage is 50-50. When the prior probability is altered to reflect more realistically the odds of a House bill passing, the discriminating power obviously increases. For example, when the prior probability is set at the actual (ex post) success rate of passage, all of the models in tables 1 and 2 correctly classify over 90 percent of the House bills.

We now turn to a slightly different way of estimating the elements of the legislator's influence function. In this second empirical experiment, the dependent variable is the number of bills that a legislator sponsored which were passed. Again, we use the most recent data on the U.S. House of Representatives (1983–84). All 435 members of the House are included in the sample, and the dependent variable on each observation is the number of public bills sponsored by the member that were passed. Since this is a continuous variable, we use ordinary least squares for our estimations in this case. The independent variables that are included are measured as above. We seek to explain the total number of bills passed by each congressman as a function of the volatility of his district while controlling for his party affiliation and length of service. As in the previous models, two proxies for district volatility are used; the congressman's vote percentage in the previous election and his age. Multicollinearity between these two variables again leads us to use separate equations for each proxy. The results are divided into separate tables, as done previously. In each table two variations of the basic specification are provided. In model A of each table, we present the results when a dummy variable is included that controls for whether the House member ran unopposed in his last election. The variable is equal to one if the member was unopposed, and equal to zero otherwise. Model B drops this dummy variable. The concern that leads us to add this variable is that when an incumbent runs unopposed and his vote percentage is 100 percent, his strength is overestimated. That is, any "nobody" opponent could have mustered, say, 10 percent of the vote. The unopposed legislator, who received 100 percent of the vote, may not be much more influential than the legislator receiving 90 percent of the vote with a weak opponent. The dummy variable controls for such an effect. Finally, in our effort to control for differences in bill content, we follow the procedure discussed in detail above. The models in tables 3 and 4 again distinguish between legislation sponsored by committee and subcommittee chairs versus other legislation.

The results of the ordinary least squares regressions are provided in tables 3 and 4. The prediction from our present value analysis is that legislators in more volatile districts will be less influential. In table 3, we find that the number of bills passed by committee and subcommittee chairs is positively related to their vote percentage in the last election. The coefficient on this variable is significant at the 1 percent level. Likewise, in table 4, the number of bills passed that are sponsored by committee and subcommittee chairmen is inversely related to their age. This coefficient is also significant at the 1 percent level.

The number of bills passed by nonchairs is not related to age in either model in table 4. In table 3, bills passed by nonchairs is unrelated to previous election margins in model A and is negatively related to margins in model B. The latter result is readily understandable and of some interest. As discussed above, bills passed that are sponsored by nonchairs are typically less important. The party can therefore buy votes with the public purse in such cases because this is a low-risk method to attempt to help a vulnerable incumbent member. Such legislation does not have important multiperiod effects, so the cost of the seat turning over to the other party is not as high in such cases.

As for the control variables in the regression models, there are no surprising results. The minority party dummy is negative and significant, meaning that

TABLE 3.   OLS Results; Dependent Variable: Number of Public Bills Sponsored by Each U.S. Representative Passed on the House Floor, 98th Congress

Independent Variable	Model A	Model B
Sponsor's percentage of vote in last election—committee and subcommittee chairmen only	0.021 (5.98)	0.03 (5.94)
Sponsor's percentage of vote in last election—nonchairmen	−0.01 (−1.14)	−0.02 (−2.44)
Bill sponsor member of minority party (yes or no?)	−0.53 (−2.48)	−0.56 (−2.67)
Sponsor's years of continuous house service	0.13 (4.99)	0.14 (5.23)
Sponsor's last election unopposed (yes or no?)	0.97 (1.94)	—
Constant	−0.99 (−1.85)	1.47 (3.07)
NOBS	435	435
F-statistic$_{(d.f.)}$	$33.66_{(5,429)}$	$40.88_{(4,430)}$
R^2-adjusted	0.27	0.27

Note: t-statistics are listed in parentheses.

TABLE 4. OLS Results; Dependent Variable: Number of Public Bills Sponsored by Each U.S. Representative Passed on the House Floor, 98th Congress

Independent Variable	Model A	Model B
Sponsor's date of birth—committee and subcommittee chairmen only	0.04	0.04
	(5.59)	(5.40)
Sponsor's date of birth—nonchairmen	−0.003	−0.002
	(−0.29)	(−0.14)
Bill sponsor member of minority party (yes or no?)	−0.62	−0.618
	(−3.01)	(−3.01)
Sponsor's years of continuous house service	0.17	0.17
	(5.23)	(5.31)
Sponsor's last election unopposed (yes or no?)	−1.05	—
	(−2.45)	
Constant	0.48	0.37
	(0.97)	(0.76)
NOBS	435	435
F-statistic$_{(d.f.)}$	$32.63_{(5,429)}$	$38.84_{(4,430)}$
R^2-adjusted	0.27	0.26

Note: *t*-statistics are listed in parentheses.

Republican House members get fewer bills passed than Democrats. House members with longer terms of service get more bills passed; this variable is highly significant in tables 3 and 4. In model A, the dummy variable for unopposed races is negative and significant at the 1 percent level in table 4 and at the 6 percent level in table 3. This suggests that the influence of these unopposed sponsors is not as strong as the 100 percent electoral margin would indicate otherwise. Finally, we note that the regressions have significant F-statistics and explain better than 25 percent of the variation in the number of bills passed by each House member.

3. Concluding Remarks

We return now to some normative aspects of our analysis introduced at the start of the paper. Normally, the pork barrel literature has concluded that vote-trading behavior distorts public spending decisions. Pork barrel is synonymous with overspending. Our analysis and evidence put this traditional view in a different light. We find that the risk of losing seats leads a party to reduce its investments in pork barrel in volatile districts. In other words, the proclivity of politicians to buy votes with the public purse is tempered by long-run political investment considerations. In such circumstances, public spending will be less than the traditional pork barrel model predicts. Funds for projects such as highways, dams, and education will not be spent where such spending does not make sense from the point of view of long-run political strategy.

What, then, protects the volatile districts from being underfunded? In our analysis, the answer is clearly the ceteris paribus effects of such institutions as the seniority and committee system. The length of legislator service variables, reflecting seniority, leadership, and committee positions, is positively related to bill passage, thus countering the effects of district volatility. For example, an older legislator may have his/her influence impaired because he/she represents a more volatile investment. But, he is able to acquire greater influence through the seniority system over time, which provides him with an institutional mechanism to offset the influence he/she loses simply by being old. Viewed in this light, seniority institutions may soften pressures to underfund political districts due to strictly political motives.

Finally, recall that the incumbent in electoral jeopardy is a magnet for private campaign funds. In our approach, the politician buys votes with the public and private purses. If the private side of this trade-off is constrained by campaign finance regulations, the politician will substitute to purchase more votes with the public purse. Thus, across U.S. states, for example, public spending will be greater, all else equal, where limits are placed on private campaign financing (Crain, Leavens, and Tollison 1985).

REFERENCES

Barone, Michael, and Grant Ujifusa. 1982. *The Almanac of American Politics*. Washington, D.C.: National Journal.

Buchanan, James M., and Gordon Tullock. 1962. *The Calculus of Consent*. Ann Arbor: University of Michigan Press.

Congressional Quarterly. 1982. "Election Results." *Congressional Quarterly* 40, no. 42 (November 6): 2817–2925.

Congressional Quarterly Special Report. 1983. "Committees and Subcommittees of the 98th Congress." *Congressional Quarterly* 41, no. 13 (April 2).

Crain, W. Mark, and David N. Laband. 1983. "Is Campaigning Profitable?" *Policy Report*, October, 2–3.

Crain, W. Mark, Donald R. Leavens, and Robert D. Tollison. 1985. "Laissez Faire in Campaign Finance." Manuscript.

———. 1986. "Final Voting in Legislatures." *American Economic Review* 76 (September): 833–41.

Crain, W. Mark, and Robert D. Tollison. 1976. "Campaign Expenditures and Political Competition." *Journal of Law and Economics* 19 (April): 177–88.

———. 1977. "Attenuated Property Rights and the Market for Governors." *Journal of Law and Economics* 20 (April): 205–11.

Ferejohn, John. 1974. *Pork Barrel Politics: Rivers and Harbors Legislation, 1947–1968*. Stanford: Stanford University Press.

Jacobson, Gary C. 1980. *Money in Congressional Elections*. New Haven: Yale University Press.

Landes, William M., and Richard A. Posner. 1975. "The Independent Judiciary in an Interest-Group Perspective." *Journal of Law and Economics* 18 (December): 875–901.

Legi-Slate. 1986. On-Line Database. Washington, D.C.

Lindsay, Cotton M. 1980. *National Health Issues: The British Experience*. Roche Laboratories.

Tufte, Edward R. 1978. *Political Control of the Economy*. Princeton: Princeton University Press.

Tullock, Gordon. 1959. "Problems of Majority Voting." *Journal of Political Economy* 67 (December): 571–79.

APPENDIX: BILLS PASSED FROM THE HOUSE COMMITTEE ON PUBLIC WORKS AND TRANSPORTATION, 98TH CONGRESS

*	H.R.10	BY OBERSTAR (D-MN)—NATIONAL DEVELOPMENT INVESTMENT ACT
#	H.R.593	BY GUARINI (D-NJ)—'MICHAEL MCDERMOTT BULK AND FOREIGN MAIL CENTER', DESIGNATION
*	H.R.1244	BY CLINGER (R-PA)—FEDERAL CAPITAL INVESTMENT PROGRAM INFORMATION ACT OF 1984
#	H.R.1551	BY THOMAS, ROBERT (D-GA)—JULIETTE GORDON LOW FEDERAL BUILDING, DESIGNATION
*	H.R.1572	BY LEVITAS (D-GA)—FEDERAL PUBLIC TRANSPORTATION ACT OF 1982, AMENDMENT (P.L.98-6, APPROVED 3-16-83)
*	H.R.1580	BY MINETA (D-CA)—AVIATION DRUG-TRAFFICKING CONTROL ACT
*	H.R.1707	BY MINETA (D-CA)—INDEPENDENT SAFETY BOARD ACT OF 1974, AMENDMENT
#	H.R.1748	BY WILSON (D-TX)—COL. HOMER GARRISON JR. FEDERAL BUILDING, DESIGNATION
#,*	H.R.1761	BY D'AMOURS (D-NH)—OCEAN DUMPING AMENDMENTS ACT OF 1983
#	H.R.2484	BY LLOYD (D-TN)—HARRY PORTER TOWER, DESIGNATION
*,#	H.R.2895	BY HOWARD (D-NJ)—PHILLIP BURTON FEDERAL BUILDING AND U.S. COURTHOUSE, DESIGNATION (P.L.98-85, APPROVED 8/26/83)

---

*bill sponsored by a committee or a subcommittee chairman
#"designation" bill

\#   H.R.3090 BY MYERS (R-IN)—CHARLES A. HALLECK FEDERAL
               BUILDING, LAFAYETTE, INDIANA, DESIGNATION

*   H.R.3103 BY ANDERSON (D-CA)—SURFACE TRANSPORTATION
               TECHNICAL CORRECTIONS ACT OF 1983

\#   H.R.3151 BY WRIGHT (D-TX)—JACK D. WATSON POST OFFICE
               BUILDING, DESIGNATION

\#   H.R.3162 BY HAMMERSCHMIDT (R-AR)—WILBUR D. MILLS DAM,
               DESIGNATION

\#   H.R.3163 BY HAMMERSCHMIDT (R-AR)—JOE HARDIN LOCK AND
               DAM, DESIGNATION

\#   H.R.3164 BY HAMMERSCHMIDT (R-AR)—JAMES W. TRIMBLE
               LOCK AND DAM, DESIGNATION

\#   H.R.3165 BY HAMMERSCHMIDT (R-AR)—ARTHUR ORMOND LOCK
               AND DAM, DESIGNATION

\#   H.R.3166 BY HAMMERSCHMIDT (R-AR)—WINTHROP ROCKE-
               FELLER RESERVOIR, DESIGNATION

\#   H.R.3167 BY HAMMERSCHMIDT (R-AR)—EMMETT SANDERS LOCK
               AND DAM, DESIGNATION

\#   H.R.3238 BY ACKERMAN (D-NY)—BENJAMIN S. ROSENTHAL POST
               OFFICE BUILDING, DESIGNATION

*   H.R.3282 BY HOWARD (D-NJ)—WATER QUALITY RENEWAL ACT
               OF 1984

\#   H.R.3303 BY MACK (R-FL)—GEORGE W. WHITEHURST FEDERAL
               COURT BUILDING, DESIGNATION

\#   H.R.3308 BY SKEEN (R-NM)—HAROLD L. RUNNELS FEDERAL
               BUILDING, NEW MEXICO, DESIGNATION

\#   H.R.3379 BY WALKER (R-PA)—EDWIN D. ESHLEMAN POST
               OFFICE, DESIGNATION (P.L.98-128, APPROVED
               10/14/83)

\#   H.R.3401 BY DOWDY (D-MS)—JAMES O. EASTLAND FEDERAL
               COURT BUILDING, DESIGNATION (P.L.98-521,
               APPROVED 10/19/84)

\#   H.R.3402 BY DOWDY (D-MS)—DR. A. H. MCCOY FEDERAL
               BUILDING, DESIGNATION (P.L.98-522, APPROVED
               10/19/84)

*,\#   H.R.3576 BY LUKEN (D-OH)—JOHN WELD PECK FEDERAL
               BUILDING, CINCINNATI, OHIO, DESIGNATION

*   H.R.3678 BY ROE (D-NJ)—WATER RESOURCES, CONSERVATION,
               DEVELOPMENT, AND INFRASTRUCTURE IMPROVE-
               MENT AND REHABILITATION ACT OF 1983

*,\#   H.R.3701 BY STARK (D-CA)—JACK D. MALTESTER CHANNEL,
               CALIFORNIA, DESIGNATION

*   H.R.4025 BY YOUNG, ROBERT (D-MO)—GENERAL POST OFFICE
               BUILDING, TRANSFER TO SMITHSONIAN INSTITU-
               TION (P.L.98-523, APPROVED 10/19/84)

\#   H.R.4107 BY DYSON (D-MD)—MAUDE R. TOULSON FEDERAL

BUILDING, DESIGNATION (P.L.98-296, APPROVED 5/24/84)

\# H.R.4202 BY STANGELAND (R-MN)—JOHN G. FARY TOWER, MIDWAY AIRPORT, CHICAGO, DESIGNATION (P.L.98-260, APPROVED 4/13/84)

\# H.R.4210 BY BRITT (D-NC)—L. RICHARDSON PREYER FEDERAL BUILDING, DESIGNATION

\# H.R.4354 BY MACKAY (D-FL)—GOLDEN-COLLUM MEMORIAL FEDERAL BUILDING, OCALA, FLORIDA, DESIGNA-TION (P.L.98-579, APPROVED 10/30/84)

*,\# H.R.4403 BY BIAGGI (D-NY)—PAUL B. RAO COURT OF INTER-NATIONAL TRADE, DESIGNATION

\# H.R.4473 BY LANTOS (D-CA)—LEO J. RYAN MEMORIAL FEDERAL ARCHIVES AND RECORDS CENTER, CALIFORNIA, DESIGNATION (P.L.98-580, APPROVED 10/30/84)

* H.R.4616 BY ANDERSON (D-CA)—SURFACE TRANSPORTATION ASSISTANCE ACT OF 1982, AMENDMENT (P.L.98-363, APPROVED 7/17/84)

\# H.R.4665 BY FOGLIETTA (D-PA)—WILLIAM A. BARRETT SOCIAL SECURITY BUILDING, DESIGNATION

\# H.R.4700 BY STANGELAND (R-MN)—BYRON G. ROGERS FEDERAL BUILDING AND UNITED STATES COURTHOUSE, DESIGNATION (P.L.98-582, APPROVED 10/30/84)

\# H.R.4717 BY REID (D-NV)—FOLEY FEDERAL BUILDING, DESIGNATION (P.L.98-583, APPROVED 10/30/84)

* H.R.4829 BY D'AMOURS (D-NH)—OCEAN DUMPING AMENDMENTS ACT OF 1984

* H.R.4957 BY HOWARD (D-NJ)—NATIONAL SYSTEM OF INTER-STATE AND DEFENSE HIGHWAYS CONSTRUCTION FUNDS, APPORTIONMENT (P.L.98-229, APPROVED 3/9/84)

*,\# H.R.5146 BY BIAGGI (D-NY)—PAUL P. RAO FEDERAL BUILDING, DESIGNATION

* H.R.5297 BY MINETA (D-CA)—CIVIL AERONAUTICS BOARD SUNSET ACT OF 1984 (P.L.98-443, APPROVED 10/4/84)

* H.R.5313 BY SHARP (D-IN)—NATURAL GAS PIPELINE SAFETY ACT OF 1968, AMENDMENT

* H.R.5323 BY BALTASAR CORRADA—CLEMENTE RUIZ NAZARIO COURTHOUSE, DESIGNATION (P.L.98-589, APPROVED 10/30/84)

* H.R.5402 BY BOEHLERT (R-NY)—ALEXANDER PIRNIE FEDERAL BUILDING, UTICA, NEW YORK, DESIGNATION (P.L.98-591, APPROVED 10/30/84)

*,\# H.R.5489 BY SHELBY (D-AL)—ARMISTEAD I. SELDEN LOCK AND DAM, DESIGNATION

* H.R.5504 BY ANDERSON (D-CA)—SURFACE TRANSPORTATION

AND UNIFORM RELOCATION ASSISTANCE ACT OF 1984

H.R.5531 BY HOYER (D-MD)—BALTIMORE-WASHINGTON PARK-WAY CONVEYANCE, REVERSAL

H.R.5568 BY FERRARO (D-NY)—TRUCK SAFETY ACT OF 1984

* H.R.5607 BY YOUNG, ROBERT (D-MO)—LIBRARY OF CONGRESS MASS BOOK DEACIDIFICATION FACILITY, AUTHORIZATION

* H.R.5640 BY FLORIO (D-NJ)—SUPERFUND EXPANSION AND PROTECTION ACT OF 1984

* H.R.5690 BY RODINO (D-NJ)—AIRCRAFT SABOTAGE ACT

\# H.R.5747 BY LLOYD (D-TN)—JOE L. EVINS FEDERAL BUILDING, OAK RIDGE, TENNESSEE, DESIGNATION (P.L.98-593, APPROVED 10/30/84)

\# H.R.5817 BY HAMMERSCHMIDT (R-AR)—H. K. THATCHER LOCK AND DAM, ARKANSAS, DESIGNATION

\# H.R.5945 BY WATKINS (D-OK)—CARL ALBERT FEDERAL BUILDING, DESIGNATION

\# H.R.5997 BY SMITH (R-OR)—JOHN F. KILKENNY UNITED STATES POST OFFICE AND COURTHOUSE, DESIGNATION (P.L.98-492, APPROVED 10/17/84)

\# H.R.6000 BY TAYLOR (R-MO)—DEWEY J. SHORT TABLE ROCK LAKE VISITORS CENTER, DESIGNATION (P.L.98-597, APPROVED 10/30/84)

*,\# H.R.6255 BY NATCHER (D-KY)—CARL D. PERKINS FEDERAL BUILDING AND UNITED STATES COURTHOUSE, DESIGNATION

\# H.R.6324 BY RAHALL (D-WV)—JENNINGS RANDOLPH FEDERAL CENTER, DESIGNATION

H.R.6430 BY BATEMAN (R-VA)—RIVER AND HARBOR ACT OF 1946, AMENDMENT (P.L.98-606, APPROVED 10/30/84)

*,\# H.R.6440 BY ROE (D-NJ)—JACK D. MALTESTER CHANNEL, DESIGNATION

H.R.6441 BY BLILEY (R-VA)—RICHMOND-PETERSON TURNPIKE, VIRGINIA, RESTRICTION ON COLLECTION OF TOLLS (P.L.98-607, APPROVED 10/30/84)

The Three Classes of Senate Seats

W. Mark Crain and Brian L. Goff

1. The Three Senate Classes

As the founding fathers designed it, the U.S. Constitution requires that one-third of the Senate be elected every two years. To satisfy this requirement, each Senate seat is assigned permanently to one of three classes. The class assignment determines the dates on which each term expires.

The stated purpose of setting up the three Senate classes was to mute the effect of the six-year Senate term. With three equally divided election days, a majority of senators can be replaced every four years instead of six. The intended effect of rotating election days is to reduce the time required to make changes if the electorate is unhappy with the Senate.[1] Whatever the more fundamental motivations by the drafters might have been, this is certainly one outcome of three Senate classes.

The three-class Senate structure generates another outcome. Every two years a different percentage of the population is represented by a Senator whose term is expiring. On the face of the problem, the percentage might appear constant because one-third of the Senate is elected every two years. On closer inspection, though, the population represented by each class is not divided equally. In 1985, class 1 senators represented 74 percent of the population, class 2 senators represented 53 percent, and class 3 senators 73 percent. This situation arose from random population shifts among states and the addition of new states. Originally, the percentage of the electorate with senators' terms expiring was nearly constant across elections.

Because the U.S. House is apportioned on the basis of population, the Senate class structure carries over into the overlapping of House and Senate races. The fraction of House races that are on the same ballot with a Senate race varies in the same proportions as the population varies. In 1984, about

---

1. See Crain and Shughart 1989 for a complete discussion of the normative properties of the Senate class system as described in the *Federalist Papers* (1961).

half of the House elections and concurrent Senate elections shared the ballot. In 1986, almost three-fourths of the House races shared a ballot with a Senate race, and so on.

The result of the variation in population represented by the three Senate classes is to amplify cooperation and disagreements between the legislative chambers. When more House races are on the same ballot with a Senate race, the opportunities increase for conflict or cooperation between the two chambers. Reelection may depend on the legislative deals, or lack thereof, struck prior to the election. When there are fewer overlapping House and Senate races, the spillover effects subside. Also, the magnitude of these spillover effects will depend on whether one party controls both chambers. When different parties are in control, more overlapping will enhance conflict between chambers. When identical parties are in control, conflicts will be reduced due to party control mechanisms.

The next section provides an analytical framework for viewing the impact of rotating expiration dates in a bicameral legislature. We more clearly identify and discuss the effects mentioned in the preceding paragraph. Section 3 presents an empirical model that examines the effects of the fluctuations in overlapping House and Senate races on legislation enacted by Congress since 1910. Section 4 offers some concluding remarks.

2. Cycles of Congressional Conflict and Consensus

Legislative measures in the U.S. Congress must be approved by both the House and Senate before being sent to the president to be signed into law. Of course, this cooperation is not always easy because representatives and senators face different constituencies and, therefore, different incentives. At the same time, both sets of legislators have some legislative agenda that is demanded by voters and interest groups. Reelection depends on satisfying some of this demand. These interchamber incentives for conflict and cooperation are well recognized and investigated.

Institutionally, these interchamber spillovers are controlled and constrained by several factors. The joint committees and conference committees of Congress provide formats for deals to be made and bills to be pushed through. Although the Senate, as a body, may desire to reject a bill, they may accept it in lieu of House consideration of another bill. In addition, political parties are institutions that constrain conflict and provide avenues for legislative trades. Also, they provide a mechanism for enforcement of those trades. In effect, these institutions help to minimize the spillovers of the conflicting incentives of representatives and senators.

Moreover, the level of conflict between the House and Senate is heightened when there is more overlapping in the election. The conditions for conflict increase as legislators are pulled in different directions by a larger percentage of the total constituents. In any type of contractual setting, increases in the number of parties that must reach an agreement decrease the probability of successful cooperation. This is true of game theoretic oligopoly theory, cartel theory, and political agreements. Behaviorally, it suggests that as more legislators face conflicting incentives from their constituents, the flow of legislation will subside.

An example helps to clarify this influence. In a nonelection term, Senator X from a populous and diverse state may be willing to vote for diverse and even conflicting projects supported by representatives from his/her state.[2] With this lack of concurrency in elections, the flow of legislation is enhanced. However, during the preelection term such votes by the senator become more costly. The senator may now only vote for projects benefitting a majority of his constituents. In the preelection term, legislation bogs down. Senator Y from a sparsely populated state with one representative faces the same constituency and incentive as the representative. The election cycles will not affect his/her behavior as it did Senator X.

In general, therefore, we expect fewer bills to be passed when the senators and representatives up for election face a larger percentage of the total U.S. constituency. We expect this general result to hold regardless of whether the Congress is controlled by identical or different parties.

In addition to the spillover effects becoming greater with more concurrent elections, party control of chambers will affect the magnitude of the effects. The external effects will be more negative if different parties control the two chambers, that is, conflicts will be enhanced with different parties in control. Not only does different party control allow one chamber to detract from the party reputation of the majority in the other chamber, but more importantly, cooperation mechanisms are weaker. Although trades between chambers in conference and joint committees may still have benefits, they are less likely without the party mechanisms that help to enforce such trades. In contrast, if the same party controls both chambers, some of the potential for conflicting interests will be mitigated by party deal making and enforcement.

The mechanisms that political parties have to enhance cooperation and the enforcing of deals are varied. They have also received much attention in other places, so we mention only a few. For one, party caucuses provide an additional environment for deal making. Secondly, party leadership can steer and enforce deals by control of party campaign funds, committee assignments, and agenda control among others.

In sum, the result of the three permanent classes of Senate seats is that

---

2. Many articles indicate the relative importance of legislative behavior closer to elections. See Crain, Leavens, and Tollison 1986.

the number of overlapping House and Senate races in each national election is cyclical. Variations in the number of concurrent elections produces an external effect between the House and Senate. In general, more overlapping of races will generate more conflicting incentives and less legislation during a term. If the same party controls both chambers, this effect will be partially mitigated due to party deal-making/enforcement mechanisms.

We want to stress that we are not attempting to discover all of the behavioral mechanisms that propogate interchamber conflict and cooperation. Discussions of these spillovers are commonplace in the popular press and are institutionalized through joint and conference committees. Instead, we stress that to the extent such spillovers are present, they will be magnified in the direction we suggest by the concurrency of House and Senate elections.

3. Empirical Model of Electoral Cycles and Legislative Output

The analytical framework discussed in section 2 suggests the following empirical model:

$$BILLS\ PASSED = f(PCTUP,\ PARTY,\ PCTUP*PARTY)$$

where

$PCTUP$ = percent of concurrent House and Senate elections,
$PARTY$ = dichotomous variable equal to 1 if the same party controls both the Senate and House and 0 otherwise, and
$PCTUP*PARTY$ = the interaction of $PCTUP$ and $PARTY$.

The dependent variable, *BILLS PASSED*, measures the number of public bills passed by both the U.S. House and Senate in each Congress 1911–1986. The measure does not include private bills and resolutions. It is an indicator of the degree of cooperation or conflict between the two chambers, as political conditions have evolved over time.[3]

PCTUP simply measures the number of overlapping House and Senate races during a given election. With the inclusion of the interaction term, the coefficient on *PCTUP* will measure the effect of more concurrent elections

---

3. An alternative measure of cooperation would be the number of bills originating in the other chamber that are passed by the House or Senate. However, a bias exists in this measure because legislators in each chamber will form a probability that the other chamber will pass a bill originating in their own chamber. This probability will affect the incentive to pass a bill in the originating chamber.

when different parties control the chambers (that is, *PARTY* = 0). We expect *PCTUP* to have a negative effect on bills passed.

The interaction variable, *PCTUP*PARTY*, gives the effect of more concurrent House and Senate elections when the same party controls both chambers (that is, *PARTY* = 1). The coefficient on *PCTUP*PARTY* must be added to the coefficient on *PCTUP* to obtain the full effect of overlapping elections when the same party is in control. We expect a positive sign on the interaction term, but a negative sign when it is added to the coefficient on *PCTUP* alone. This would indicate that more concurrent elections generate more conflict and fewer bills even with the same party in control. However, it would also show (by a positive sign on the interaction coefficient) that same party control has a marginal effect of mitigating conflict between the two chambers.

Our interest in the empirical model is not to build a full demand and supply of legislation model to explain secular trends in legislative output. Rather, we are interested in the fluctuations due to Senate class structure around whatever trend exists. Because of this we do not present a full model of supply and demand variables to explain levels of legislative output. Instead we have taken out the trend component of the variation in legislative output by employing an ARMA identification and estimation of the bills passed series. This allows us to look directly at cyclical fluctuations (residuals) in bills around the underlying trend that is a function of many variables.

Identification and estimation showed the bills passed series to be most closely and parsimoniously fit by an AR(1) model.[4] The first two specifications in table 1 present the results of estimating the effects of our Senate classes variables on the residual fluctuations around the trend of legislative output. The third specification in table 1 uses actual instead of residual bills passed and places the first-order lag of bills passed on the right-hand side as an explanatory variable.

The first specification in table 1 uses only the variables discussed in our empirical model. The equation explains over 20 percent of the variation in *residual* bills passed. Overall, the *F*-statistic indicates the equation is significant at the 10 percent level. The Durbin-Watson statistic of 1.81 is above the critical upper bound of 1.66, indicating a lack of serial correlation among the residuals of the equation.

The variables in the equation are all significant above the 5 percent level for a one-tailed test. The coefficients on *PCTUP* and the interaction term are

---

4. We chose the AR(1) model because the autocorrelation and partial autocorrelation functions demonstrated the classic AR(1) properties. Also, an *F*-test of the residuals of the AR(1) model indicated a lack of serial correlation. We overfit an AR(2) model, which indicated no significance on the second-order lag. An MA(1) model also fit the data well and yields similar results when used to generate the residuals for bills passed.

TABLE 1. Public Bills Passed, 1911–84

Variable	Coefficient/(t-statistic)		
Dep. Var.	Bills Passed (residual)	Bills Passed (residual)	Bills Passed (actual)
Intercept	1100.21	1100.21	1407.18
	(2.31)*	(2.27)*	(2.91)*
PCTUP	−18.69	−18.69	−19.13
	(2.50)*	(2.46)*	(2.49)*
PCTUP*PARTY	16.34	16.41	16.77
	(1.99)*	(1.97)*	(1.99)*
PARTY	−921.39	−934.10	−948.65
	(1.74)*	(1.72)*	(1.75)*
PRES		11.42	
		(0.18)	
BILLS PASSED (t − 1)			0.61
			(4.52)*
R^2	0.206	0.206	0.455
F-statistic	2.76	2.02	6.46
Durbin-Watson	1.81	1.81	1.89[a]
N	38	38	38

Sources: PCTUP is from *Guide to U.S. Elections* and *Statistical Abstract of U.S.* (1971–87). BILLS PASSED is from *Historical Statistics of the U.S.* and *Statistical Abstract* (1971–87).

*significant at .05 level for one-tailed test
[a]durbin-h statistic = 0.52

two times their standard errors. In addition, the signs are as expected. The variable showing greater concurrency with different party control, *PCTUP*, is strongly negative. The marginal effect of same party control as shown by the interaction term is positive. Also, addition of these two coefficients shows the effects of greater concurrency to be negative even with the same party in control of both chambers. The total effect with same control yields a coefficient of −2.35. Even with the coefficient on *PARTY* included, this amounts to a reduction in the negative effect of more concurrent elections (in the relevant range).

A numerical example is instructive. At the mean of *PCTUP* (66), when different parties control the chambers, about 133 fewer bills are passed given the coefficient on *PCTUP*. Given the total interaction coefficient of −2.35 and the negative coefficient on *PARTY*, about 24 fewer bills are passed with the same party in control (again at the mean of *PCTUP*). The difference is in excess of 400 percent.

Other regressors came to our mind and to others that might explain fluctuations in residual bills passed. Most prominent among them is whether the presidency is of the same party of the House and Senate. *PRES* in the second specification in table 1 equals one if both chambers and the presidency are controlled by the same party and 0 otherwise. As is seen, *PRES* has no additional explanatory ability and does not affect the other variables. Other regressors that fall into this category include presidential versus nonpresidential years, the majority sizes in the chambers, and interactions of these variables.

The third specification is included to show that the results do not disappear when actual instead of residual values of bills passed are used.

4. Concluding Remarks

The purpose of setting up three rotating expiration dates in the U.S. Senate was (at least allegedly) to reduce the time required to turn over a majority of the senators. In this paper we have identified and assessed another result of the Senate class structure. Our study shows an impact of the three Senate classes on the cyclical output of national legislation.

The main finding of the analysis is that the rotation of Senate terms amplifies the potential conflicts between the two chambers. As more House and Senate elections run concurrently, legislative output slows down. This effect is partially offset when the same party controls both chambers. Output still falls with more simultaneous House and Senate races, but it does not fall nearly so dramatically as when different parties control the chambers. A time series of national legislative output from 1911 to 1986 supports these results.

The conclusion we draw from this result is that three Senate classes do not come without a cost. It decreases the time needed to change Senate majorities, but it also adds to the instability of the flow of operations from one Congress to the next.

REFERENCES

Crain, W. M., D. Leavens, and R. D. Tollison. 1986. "Final Voting in a Legislature." *American Economic Review* 76 (September): 833–41.

Crain, W. M., and W. F. Shughart II. 1989. "The Iron Law of Elections." Manuscript. George Mason University.

The Federalists. 1961. Special Edition printed for National Foundation for Education in American Citizenship. Indianapolis.

Congressional Quarterly, Inc. 1986. *Guide to U.S. Elections*. Washington, D.C.: Congressional Quarterly Press.

Department of Commerce. 1957. *Historical Statistics of the United States*. Washington, D.C.: USGPO.

Department of Commerce. 1971–87. *Statistical Abstract of the United States*. Washington, D.C.: USGPO.

Part 3
Constitutions, Legislative Contracts, and the Demand for Legislation

Behind the Veil: The Political Economy of Constitutional Change

Gary M. Anderson, Delores T. Martin,
William F. Shughart II, and Robert D. Tollison

> . . . State Constitutions furnish invaluable materials for history. Their interest is
> all the greater, because the succession of Constitutions and amendments to Con-
> stitutions from 1776 till to-day enables the annals of legislation and political
> sentiment to be read in these documents more easily and succinctly than in any
> similar series of laws in any other country. They are a mine of instruction for the
> natural history of democratic communities.
>
> —James Bryce (1917, 451)

Probably no institution of democratic government is held as being more a
thing apart from the political process than the constitution. Constitutions are
viewed as repositories of basic individual rights, as documents laying down
the "rules of the game," as durable social contracts that are to be amended
only under the most extraordinary of circumstances. To reinforce this durability, constitutional change has been made everywhere more costly than statutory change. Whereas enactment of laws falls under the normal voting rules of
the legislature, necessitating only a simple majority vote in both houses,
constitutional amendment usually falls under more restrictive rules, often
requiring approval by super-majorities in each legislative chamber and subsequent ratification by popular vote. Reverence for constitutions accounts in part
for the reluctance of many to support calls for conventions for extensive
revisions of old constitutions or the writing of new ones. Even those most
strongly in favor of amending the U.S. Constitution for the purpose of ending
abortion or balancing the federal budget, for example, express concerns about
the consequences if the constitutional convention's agenda cannot be limited
to a single issue. In short, the conventional wisdom is that constitutions are—
and, indeed, should be—above the fray of interest-group politics.

This essay examines the process of constitutional change within the
context of the interest-group theory of government (Stigler 1971; Peltzman

89

1976), using data generated in the natural laboratory comprised of the 50 U.S. state constitutions. The main point of departure for the analysis is taken from the model developed by Landes and Posner (1975) to explain the role played by the independent judiciary in an interest-group setting. In brief, Landes and Posner emphasize the institutional mechanisms that impart durability to the redistributive activities of government. Increased durability raises the present value of rents obtained through the political process and, hence, raises the "price" an interest group is willing to pay to secure a wealth transfer in its favor. In this regard, Landes and Posner suggest that by interpreting laws on the basis of legislative intent, the judiciary confers on legislation something of the character of a binding long-term contract. Such strict constructionism, aided by the representative body's own constitutive rules, can prevent a subsequent legislative assembly from amending or repealing the legislation in ways destructive of the original deal made between the interest group and the enacting legislature.

Having the wealth transfer ratified in the constitution is simply another way of doing the same thing. Which route is chosen therefore depends on the relative costs and benefits to interest groups of legislative versus constitutional change. In particular, although amending the constitution is more costly and time-consuming than enacting legislation, a constitutional provision generally provides a more durable form of protection to an interest group than is possible through simple legislative action. Legislation becomes more of a worthwhile alternative the more the judiciary and the legislature can be relied upon to enforce and maintain the statute creating the wealth transfer. Thus, whether or not an interest group seeks rents through legislative action depends in large part on institutional factors influencing the degree to which the judicial and legislative branches of government are able to play the roles assigned to them by Landes and Posner.

The burden of this essay is to provide a rich empirical framework for investigating the process of constitutional change in an interest-group perspective.[1] To do so, we develop and test a model to explain changes in the lengths of state constitutions as a function of variables measuring the salient characteristics of state judiciaries, legislatures, and demographies. Using data from the years 1975 through 1981, we find evidence strongly supportive of the Landes-Posner hypothesis. Indeed, our model is able to explain on the order of 50 percent of the variation in constitutional activity across the 50 states.

Empirical Model and Results

Table 1 provides a summary of state constitutional activity for the years 1981 through 1985. As pointed out earlier, constitutional change is most frequently

---

1. We thus build on the earlier work of Crain and Tollison 1979.

TABLE 1.   State Constitutional Activity, 1981–85

	Number of States with Constitutional Activity	Source of Amendment					
		Legislative Initiative			Popular Initiative		
Year		Proposed	Adopted	Percent	Proposed	Adopted	Percent
1981	11	28	23	76.7	2	0	0.0
1982	44	287	214	74.6	12	4	33.3
1983	10	43	41	86.0	3	0	0.0
1984	43	172	113	65.7	17	8	47.1
1985	11	39	31	76.9	0	0	0.0
total	119	569	422	74.2	34	12	35.3

Source: Council of State Governments, various years.

initiated by the legislature, and such proposals are more frequently adopted than those measures initiated by petition. Constitutional conventions (not shown in the table) generally result in more wide-ranging constitutional change. New Hampshire, which convened its seventeenth convention in 1984, is the leader in this regard, although the states that were members of the Confederacy tend to have completely revised their constitutions more often than most. Louisiana has had 11 separate constitutions since statehood in 1812; Georgia has adopted 10 different constitutions since 1777, including successive revisions in 1976 and again in 1982.

In contrast to the conventional wisdom, U.S. state constitutions are the repositories of a host of pork barrel provisions. A sampling of the constitutional amendments adopted by the states between 1981 and 1985 is shown in table 2. The constitutional activity displayed there neither is meant to be inclusive nor does it represent a random sample of the 434 amendments approved over the period. Rather, the information is presented to underline the point that having a wealth transfer ratified in the constitution is a quite feasible activity for an interest group. We turn to an empirical examination of this process in the following section.

In seeking rents through the political process, interest groups face a trade-off between the benefits and costs of statutory versus constitutional change. On the one hand, although having a wealth transfer ratified in the constitution is relatively time-consuming and costly, a constitutional right provides a more durable form of protection than is available through legislative action. Precisely because constitutional provisions are more difficult to achieve in the first place, they are less likely to be subsequently annulled. On the other hand, being less costly, rent seeking through statutory change becomes more attractive the more the procedural rules of the legislature and the independence of the judicial branch can be relied upon to prevent deals won from being reneged upon by subsequent legislative assemblies.

TABLE 2.   The State Constitutional Pork Barrel, 1981–85

Year	State	Amendment
1981	Kentucky	Extension of the homestead exemption to totally disabled persons, and authorization of tax incentives for real property repair and rehabilitation
	Texas	Inclusion of livestock and poultry with farm products that are exempt from taxation
1982	Alabama	Elimination of the ceiling on assessments that producers of swine and swine products may levy on themselves to fund promotional activities
	Arizona	Authorization for the legislature to provide for the regulation of ambulances and ambulance services
	Delaware	Modification of the provision concerning state contracts to permit application of the statutory preference for Delaware vendors on all items that the state purchases through competitive bidding
	Louisiana	Exemption from ad valorem taxation of materials, boiler fuels, and energy sources used by public utilities to generate electricity
	Nebraska	Prohibition against nonfamily farm corporations purchasing additional farm and ranch land, and against further establishment of nonfamily corporate crop and livestock operations
	Texas	Exemption of agricultural equipment and machinery from ad valorem taxation
1983	Mississippi	Authorization for the lease of not more than three acres of sixteenth-section lands for a term not exceeding 99 years to any church having its place of worship on such lands which has been in continuous operation at that location not less than 25 years
	Texas	Creation of the Veterans' Housing Assistance Program and authorization for the issuance of $800 million in general obligation bonds to finance home mortgage loans
1984	Alabama	Authorization for the legislature, by general law, to provide for the assessment of levies, financing, collecting, distribution, and expenditure of funds by a designated nonprofit organization for the sole purpose of eradicating or controlling the boll weevil
	Florida	Requirement that county court judge candidates be members of the Florida Bar for the preceding five years or, in counties of 40,000 population or less, a member of the bar in good standing
	Missouri	Authorization for the General Assembly to provide by law for medical benefits for dependents of state officers and employees, and dependents of local government employees
	New Jersey	Prohibition of taxation of payments received under Social Security, the Railroad Retirement Act, or any federal law that substantially reenacts the provisions of those laws

TABLE 2—*Continued*

Year	State	Amendment
	Utah	Elimination of the power of the legislature to regulate the right to bear arms, but allowing the legislature to define the lawful use of arms
1985	Oklahoma	Exempt from ad valorem taxes certain new, expanded, or acquired manufacturing facilities for a period of five years, and establish a fund from which the state would reimburse local government subdivisions for revenue lost because of the exemption
	Washington	Authorization for agricultural commodity commissions to use commodity assessments for trade promotion and promotional hosting

Source: Strum, various years.

A testable implication of the Landes-Posner hypothesis is that the extent of constitutional change in a state will depend in part on the institutional factors influencing the independence of the judiciary. Judges who are more "independent" (of the legislature especially, but also of the executive and voters) are more likely to play the role Landes and Posner envision, namely, to impart durability to statutory wealth transfers by interpreting laws on the basis of the intent of the enacting legislature. Less constitutional change would be predicted in states having more independent judiciaries, and vice versa.

To test this hypothesis, we specified a regression equation of the following general form.

$$CHANGE = f(LENGTH, POP, PCY, CJPAY, REMOVE, CJTERM,$$
$$ELECT, SIZE, SMAJ, HMAJ, LV, R, CONVEN,$$
$$COMMIS, e) ;$$

where

$CHANGE$ = change in length of state constitution, measured in words, over the 1975–81 period;

$LENGTH$ = number of words in the state constitution at the beginning of the period;

POP = state population;

PCY = state income per capita;

$CJPAY$ = salary of the chief justice of the state court of last resort;

$REMOVE$ = dummy variable reflecting the security of tenure of judges serving on the state court of last resort;

$CJTERM$ = length of term of chief justice, in years;

$ELECT$ = 1 if justices serving on the state court of last resort are elected by partisan ballot, and equal to zero otherwise;

$SIZE$ = legislature size (house plus senate membership);

$SMAJ$ = percentage of state senate members belonging to the majority party;

$HMAJ$ = percentage of state house members belonging to the majority party;

LV = 1 if constitutional amendments initiated by the legislature require a super-majority vote, and equal to zero if only a simple majority is required;

R = 1 if the terms of state senate members are the same as members elected to the house, and equal to zero otherwise;

$CONVEN$ = 1 if a constitutional convention was in session during the period, and equal to zero otherwise;

$COMMIS$ = 1 if a constitutional commission was in operation during the period, and equal to zero otherwise; and

e = the regression error term.

The dependent variable, CHANGE, represents the number of words added to or deleted from a state's constitution over the 1975–81 interval. (Additions enter as positive numbers; deletions enter negatively.) We chose this particular time period for two reasons. First, the Landes-Posner hypothesis describes the trade-off between statutory versus constitutional change as a problem in long-term contracting. Because it exceeds the maximum term length in state legislatures, a six-year interval should be sufficient to capture this feature of their model. Second, the pace of constitutional activity in the states has slowed markedly since 1981.[2] We also took note of the fact that certain constitutional amendments are of statewide applicability while others, termed "local amendments," have limited purpose and effect. The latter were included in the results we report later because local constitutional amendments have a straightforward, special-interest interpretation.

LENGTH is the number of words in state constitutions at the beginning of the relevant period, 1975. These are net effective lengths, with sections or words that have been superseded or annulled, subtracted from the total word

---

2. Moreover, what little activity actually taking place was dominated by three states that made substantial changes to their constitutions between 1981 and 1983: Alabama added 43,000 words to its organic law, increasing the constitution's estimated length from 129,000 to 172,000 words; Georgia's constitution was reduced in length from 600,000 to 25,000 words; and New York added 33,000 words to its constitution, raising the length of its document from 47,000 to 80,000 words. (All of these figures include local amendments.)

count. For most states, the number of words in the constitution is estimated, but in a few cases, actual word counts are supplied. Of potential importance is the fact that some states switched from estimated to actual numbers of words during our sample period. The differences were relatively minor, however, and accounting for them did not alter the empirical results perceptibly. Constitution length is a scale variable having two possible interpretations. On the one hand, longer constitutions signify the survival of past amendments in the face of nullification attempts, and this may indicate both greater durability of a state's constitutional provisions and a greater degree of success historically on the part of interest groups in obtaining constitutional wealth transfers. If constitutional activity in the past begets constitutional activity in the present, the estimated coefficient on this variable would be expected to be positive. On the other hand, diminishing returns to constitutional change would imply a negative sign on *LENGTH*. The data will speak as to which of these effects dominates.

States with larger populations are expected to exhibit more constitutional activity for two reasons. First, individual voter influence is inversely related to total population. Second, a larger population means that the cost of any wealth transfer placed in the constitution is spread over a larger group. Thus, in states with larger populations, each individual's vote is worth less, and he or she bears a smaller portion of the costs of rent seeking through the constitution. This leads to reduced incentives for voters to become involved in the political process and leads to more constitutional change because individuals do not monitor such activity as closely as they do in less populous states. More constitutional activity is predicted in states having higher per capita incomes. This is a straightforward implication of the interest-group model: higher incomes increase the amount of wealth at stake in the political process and, pari passu, the political payoff from its redistribution (Peltzman 1976, 224–25).

Four variables measure the degree of judicial independence in a state. Less constitutional activity is predicted in states where judges are paid more, have longer terms, and are less easily removed from office. The pay and tenure variables, *CJPAY* and *CJTERM*, apply to the chief justice of the state court of last resort. The state supreme court (Supreme Judicial Court in Maine and Massachusetts, Court of Appeals in New York, and Supreme Court of Appeals in West Virginia) is the ultimate arbitrator of constitutional questions at the state level; the pay and tenure of the chief justice are highly correlated with those of the other court members.[3] *REMOVE* is set equal to unity if the

---

3. The terms of those chief justices not having specified tenures were set as follows: "pleasure of court," one year; "remainder of term as justice," one-half the term length of other court members; and "life" or "to age 70," fifteen years, one year more than the longest specified term length for chief justices in the United States (New York).

justices serving on the state court of last resort are subject to impeachment *and* recall by the voters, or removal by the governor with the approval of the legislature (the concurrence of two-thirds of each house is typically required in such cases); zero if the justices are subject to impeachment but no other form of removal; and -1 if there are no provisions for removing justices. Elected judges are potentially less secure in their offices than those appointed by the governor.[4] We therefore expect a positive sign on this variable.

An additional five variables measure salient characteristics of state legislatures. Legislature size affects the costs of obtaining a legislative majority (Crain 1979; McCormick and Tollison 1981). On the one hand, more constitutional activity will be observed if increases in legislature size result in greater competition between legislators, thereby lowering the "price" of votes. In contrast, if larger legislatures make it more difficult for legislators to reach agreement, less constitutional change will occur. The sign on this variable must be determined empirically. Because legislatures initiate the vast majority of proposals for constitutional change in the states, more of such activity should be forthcoming where the majority party accounts for a greater proportion of the membership.[5] Simply put, larger majorities are more effective in securing approval of their legislative agendas, including proposals for constitutional change. Similarly, the cost of rent seeking through the constitution is lower if only a simple majority vote is required for legislative approval of amendments; the estimated sign on *LV* is therefore expected to be negative. Members elected to U.S. state legislatures serve terms of either 2 or 4 years. Regardless of the specific length, however, when the terms of state senators and representatives are equal, voters have greater control over the legislature in the sense that the majorities in both houses can be dissolved at one time. By contrast, in states where senators serve longer terms than house members, such dissolution is possible only at every other election. Legislative membership exhibits greater continuity in the latter case, and this should reduce the possibility of reneging.[6] We therefore expect more rent seeking through the constitution in states where legislative terms are the same in both houses, that is, the sign on *R* is predicted to be positive.

Finally, two dummy variables control for the operation of constitutional conventions and commissions during the interval over which we examine constitutional change. The signs on these variables will be positive or negative accordingly as these bodies tend to lengthen or shorten state constitutions.

---

4. Chief Justice Rose Bird of the California Supreme Court is a contemporary example.

5. In Nebraska, where the representatives to the unicameral legislature are elected on a nonpartisan ballot, the majority party percentage was arbitrarily set to 100 percent in the upper house and to zero in the nonexistent lower house.

6. For more on the effect of term lengths and election cycles on the power of voters to dissolve legislative majorities, see Crain and Shughart 1986.

TABLE 3.   Summary Statistics for State Constitutional Activity, 1975–81

Variable	Mean	Standard Deviation	Coefficient of Variation
LENGTH (1975)[a]	36,262.52	83,365.86	2.30
LENGTH (1981)[a]	37,338.70	83,553.96	2.24
CHANGE[b]	1,076.18	3,373.93	3.14
POP (1976)[c]	4,279.12	4,495.89	1.05
PCY (1975)[d]	5,621.98	864.91	0.15
CJPAY (1977)[d]	43,957.10	8,192.38	0.19
REMOVE	0.22	0.65	2.95
CJTERM[e]	5.83	3.84	0.66
ELECT (1976)	0.16	0.37	2.31
SIZE (1976)	151.24	63.44	0.42
SMAJ	0.71	0.16	0.23
HMAJ	0.71	0.14	0.20
LV	0.64	0.48	0.75
R	0.34	0.48	1.41
CONVEN	0.12	0.33	2.75
COMMIS	0.22	0.42	1.91

[a]Including local amendments. The mean constitution length excluding local amendments was 25,157.78 words, with a standard deviation 19,038.74 in 1975, and 26,148.70 words, with a standard deviation of 20,013.21 in 1981.

[b]Including local amendments. The mean change in constitution length excluding local amendments was 990.92 words, with a standard deviation of 3,641.12.

[c]thousands

[d]dollars

[e]years

All data were obtained from Council of State Governments (various years). Summary statistics are displayed in table 3.

The results from estimating our regression equation by ordinary least squares are shown in table 4. All of the estimated coefficients are of the expected sign, and most are different from zero at standard levels of statistical significance. Less constitutional change indeed takes place in states where the judiciary is more independent, as signified by higher pay, more difficulty in removal from office, and longer terms. Elected judges are less reliable—more constitutional activity takes place in those states where the justices serving on the court of last resort must present themselves to the voters on a partisan ballot. Similarly, more constitutional change occurs where only a simple majority vote is necessary for the legislature to initiate a constitutional proposal and where the legislature's continuity is weakened by equal term lengths for state senators and house members. Majority party strength does not work in the predicted direction, but the coefficients on these variables are not different from zero. The estimated coefficient on *LENGTH* suggests diminish-

TABLE 4. Dependent Variable: Changes in Lengths of State Constitutions, 1975–81[a]

Intercept	1,903.91	3,453.04	2,764.43	3,521.56
LENGTH	−0.0016	−0.0011	−0.0014	−0.0009
	(−0.27)	(−0.19)	(−0.24)	(−0.16)
POP	0.4406	0.4228	0.4206	0.4398
	(2.95)***	(2.76)***	(2.66)**	(2.70)**
PCY	1.7723	1.6308	1.6931	1.6257
	(2.74)***	(2.37)**	(2.49)**	(2.34)**
CJPAY	−0.2110	−0.1937	−0.1956	−0.2030
	(−2.34)**	(−2.05)**	(−1.99)*	(−2.03)**
REMOVE	−214.36	−285.74	−253.20	−290.30
	(−0.30)	(−0.39)	(−0.35)	(−0.40)
CJTERM	−430.73	−416.76	−428.18	−407.07
	(−3.02)***	(−2.87)***	(−2.97)***	(−2.72)***
ELECT	1,466.44	1,565.31	1,638.27	1,366.08
	(1.10)	(1.15)	(1.16)	(0.91)
SIZE	−6.1696	−7.5069	−6.6754	−7.9789
	(−0.81)	(−0.95)	(−0.86)	(−0.98)
SMAJ		−2,072.79		−4,169.82
		(−0.65)		(−0.59)
HMAJ			−1,515.80	2,639.99
			(−0.42)	(0.33)
LV	−3,099.02	−3,071.33	−3,068.49	−3,096.50
	(−3.51)***	(−3.45)***	(−3.43)***	(−3.42)***
R	3,560.87	3,816.18	3,740.72	3,761.23
	(3.34)***	(3.33)***	(3.22)***	(3.21)***
CONVEN	3,991.75	4,000.63	3,994.32	4,005.12
	(2.82)***	(2.80)***	(2.79)***	(2.77)***
COMMIS	925.72	1,092.86	1,043.45	1,056.90
	(0.75)	(0.86)	(0.82)	(0.82)
R^2	0.499	0.505	0.501	0.506
F	3.07***	2.82***	2.78***	2.56***

Note: t-statistics in parentheses; asterisks denote significance at the 1 percent (***), 5 percent (**), and 10 percent (*) levels.

[a]including local amendments

ing returns to constitutional change. Conventions added a significant number of words to state constitutions during this sample period; commissions did not. Overall, the regression specification explains about half of the variation in the extent of constitutional change across the 50 states between 1975 and 1981.[7,8]

---

7. We also estimated the model for a shorter time interval, 1975–77. The results basically mirrored those shown in table 4; the model explained about 80 percent of the variation in state constitutional change over the two-year period.

8. We obtained data on lengths of state constitutions since 1981, up to and including the end of 1985, figures for which have just recently become available (Council of State Governments 1986). As mentioned in the text, constitutional activity has slowed markedly since 1981. For example, only nine states adopted constitutional amendments between 1983 and 1958 (the mean

Concluding Remarks

In this essay, we have specified and tested a model of constitutional change in the 50 U.S. states within the context of the interest-group theory of government. Our model emphasized the institutional mechanisms that impart durability to the redistributive activities of government. In seeking rents through the political process, interest groups are faced with a trade-off between the benefits and costs of statutory versus constitutional change. Although having a wealth transfer ratified in the constitution is relatively more time consuming and costly, a constitutional right provides a more durable form of protection than is available through simple legislative action. Rent seeking through statutory change becomes more attractive the more the procedural rules of the legislature and the independence of the judiciary can be relied upon to prevent deals made between interest groups and lawmakers from being reneged upon by subsequent legislative assemblies. The empirical results were strongly consistent with the hypothesis that where judges are more independent, less costly legislative passage of special-interest bills will suffice.

Our findings carry three implications about constitutional activity at the federal level. First, the infrequency with which the U.S. Constitution has been amended suggests that the federal judiciary has been quite effective in imparting durability to the deals made between interest groups and the Congress. Second, the experience of the states suggests that there is some justification for the concerns of many about the consequences of not limiting the agenda of a modern-day constitutional convention. Constitutions are not immune from interest-group influence. Indeed, a constitutional right is simply an alternative way for an interest group to obtain a durable wealth transfer. Thus, opening the U.S. Constitution to unrestricted change is likely to degenerate into a special-interest contest for the delegates' favors. Finally, because amendments to constitutions can be explained on the basis of the benefits and costs of constitutional versus statutory change, the origins of constitutions are likely to be understood in those terms as well. We think this to be a worthy topic for future research.

---

change in constitution length for the fifty states during this period was just 118.72 words). We nevertheless used the data to estimate our model of constitutional change for 1981–83, 1983–85, and 1981–85. In all cases, the results were dominated by the radical reduction in the length of Georgia's organic law, along with the substantial number of words added to the Alabama and New York constitutions (see n. 4). Apparently, these changes were generated by factors whose explanation lies outside of the Landes-Posner theory.

REFERENCES

Bryce, James. 1917. *The American Commonwealth*. Vol. 1, *The National Government—The State Governments*, new ed. New York: Macmillan.

Council of State Governments. Various years. *The Book of the States*. Lexington, Ky.: Council of State Governments.

Crain, W. Mark. 1979. "Cost and Output in the Legislative Firm." *Journal of Legal Studies* 8 (June): 607–21.

Crain, W. Mark, and William F. Shughart II. 1986. "The Iron Law of Elections." Center for Study of Public Choice, George Mason University. Manuscript.

Crain, W. Mark, and Robert D. Tollison. 1979. "Constitutional Change in an Interest-Group Perspective." *Journal of Legal Studies* 8 (January): 165–75.

Landes, William M., and Richard A. Posner. 1975. "The Independent Judiciary in an Interest-Group Perspective." *Journal of Law and Economics* 18 (December): 875–901.

McCormick, Robert E., and Robert D. Tollison. 1981. *Politicians, Legislation, and the Economy: An Inquiry into the Interest-Group Theory of Government*. Boston: Martinus-Nijhoff.

Peltzman, Sam. 1976. "Toward a More General Theory of Regulation." *Journal of Law and Economics* 19 (August): 211–40.

Stigler, George J. 1971. "The Theory of Economic Regulation." *Bell Journal of Economics* 2 (Spring): 3–21.

Strum, Albert. Various years. "State Constitutional Developments." *National Civic Review*.

The Executive Branch in an Interest-Group Theory of Government

W. Mark Crain and Robert D. Tollison

As the Federalists designed it, there are two ways in which a bill can become a law in U.S. legislatures. Bills become law that obtain a simple majority in both houses of the legislature and the signature of the chief executive, or that obtain two-thirds majorities in both houses without the consent of the chief executive (in both cases bills are subject to judicial review). The economic approach to politics and regulation has made genuine progress in the analysis of various aspects of this legislative process. For example, the legislature and the independent judiciary have been the subjects of a good deal of the recent attention of scholars in this area.[1] The question, however, of how the agents in the legislative process are interconnected by the rules for passing laws has received only limited attention in the literature. Most particularly, and the issue of concern in this paper, the role of the executive veto in an interest-group theory of government has not been explored. Before turning to our approach of explaining vetoes as a means of enhancing the durability of legislation (by analogy to Landes and Posner's theory of the independent judiciary),[2] we will review briefly the field of alternative hypotheses.

A primarily theoretical approach to the veto centers around applications of the Shapley-Shubik index of voting power.[3] In this approach the voting power of a legislative body is inversely related to its size, and since the veto constitutes the executive branch as a third house of the legislature (subject to provisions for overriding vetoes by the legislature), the chief executive can be seen as possessing a great deal of voting power relative to the other two houses in a tricameral system of legislation. In fact the chief executive embod-

1. See Ehrlich and Posner 1974; Landes and Posner 1975; Stigler 1976; Crain 1977; McCormick and Tollison 1978; and Crain and Tollison 1979.
2. Landes and Posner 1975.
3. Shapley and Shubik 1954.

ies approximately one-sixth of the voting power contained in the three houses. Brams offers an instructive review and interpretation of this literature, to which the reader may refer for additional references and discussion.[4] Our concern with the voting-power approach is that it contains little predictive power. Since we want to devise a predictive theory of the executive veto, this type of approach offers only the grossest type of help in this regard (for example, more power means more vetoes?).

A second approach to the role of the chief executive dates from *The Federalist* and finds its modern incantation in *The Calculus of Consent* by Buchanan and Tullock.[5] Hamilton, for example, observes in *The Federalist No. 73* that

> A man who might be afraid to defeat a law by his single VETO, might not scruple to return it for reconsideration; subject to being finally rejected only in the event of more than one third of each house concurring in the sufficiency of his objections. He would be encouraged by the reflection, that if his opposition should prevail, it would embark in it a very respectable proportion of the legislative body, whose influence would be united with his in supporting the propriety of his conduct in the public opinion. A direct and categorical negative has something in the appearance of it more harsh, and more apt to irritate, than the mere suggestion of argumentative objections to be approved or disapproved by those to whom they are addressed. In proportion as it would be less apt to offend, it would be more apt to be exercised; and for this very reason, it may in practice be found more effectual. It is to be hoped that it will not often happen that improper views will govern so large a proportion as two thirds of both branches of the legislature at the same time; and this, too, in spite of counterpoising weight of the Executive. It is at any rate far less probable that this should be the case, than that such views should taint the resolutions and conduct of a bare majority. A power of this nature in the Executive, will often have a silent and unperceived, though forcible, operation. When men, engaged in unjustifiable pursuits, are aware that obstructions may come from a quarter which they cannot control, they will often be restrained by the bare apprehension of opposition, from doing what they would with eagerness rush into, if no such external impediments were to be feared.[6]

This view essentially rests on a separation-of-powers argument. The veto equips the chief executive with a means of insuring that legislative bargains

---

4. Brams 1975.
5. Buchanan and Tullock 1962.
6. *The Federalist*, no. 73, 480.

which meet the approval of a majority of the voters are the only ones accepted, and the minimum size of logrolling coalitions is thereby raised. The role of the veto is to control the external costs that minority-inspired legislation places on the citizenry. The problem that we find with this normative approach to vetoes is that the chief executive is construed as a vacuous good guy who seeks to protect the interests of the majority. This view flies in the face of the myriad of special-interest measures that are not only passed by both houses and signed by the chief executive, but are also in many cases proposed by the executive branch.

In this essay we will propose a positive theory of the executive branch and its relation to the legislative process as manifested in the casting of vetoes. Our theory builds on the fundamental study of the independent judiciary from an interest-group perspective by Landes and Posner.[7] They argue that granting the judiciary independence with life tenure for judges is a way to increase the durability (and hence the present value) of special-interest legislation. This result follows because judges rarely nullify or hold laws unconstitutional under these circumstances. Indeed, judges exhibit a pronounced tendency to resolve legal disputes in terms of the expressed intentions of the legislature that originally enacted the law. This sort of behavior by an independent judiciary increases the net worth of bargains reached between legislators and special interests, especially by contrast to a situation where each legislature appoints its own slate of judges and attempts to repeal the legislative bargains reached in previous sessions of the legislature.[8]

In their analysis, however, Landes and Posner overlook the analogy between the veto power of the chief executive and the nullification power of the independent judiciary. We will pursue the functional equivalence between these two powers in an interest-group theory of government in this essay. We argue basically that the veto power is a means of enhancing the durability of legislation, just as are the independent judiciary and the procedural rules of the legislature in the Landes-Posner theory. In effect, we will argue that the veto power raises the costs of reneging on previous legislative contracts, and as such we expect to observe more vetoes in cases where attempts are being made to renege or to alter substantively previous legislative contracts with special interests. For example, larger majorities (independently of party) in the two legislative houses reflect a lower cost of reneging on existing legislative contracts with special interests. Somewhat paradoxically, then, from an interest-group perspective we expect to observe more vetoes when a chief executive confronts large majorities, even of his own party, in the legislature.

---

7. Landes and Posner 1975.

8. As we will discuss later, Landes and Posner also stress the role that legislative procedures, such as majority voting, play in enhancing the durability of special-interest legislation by making it more difficult to repeal laws once they are enacted.

We also expect that the veto as a source of durable legislation will be traded off efficiently against other sources of durability. For example, where turnover in the legislature is lower, there will be less need for the veto as a source of durable legislation.[9]

The essay proceeds as follows. A theory of the executive veto from an interest-group perspective is developed and contrasted to the Landes-Posner theory of the independent judiciary. An empirical test of the major implications of the theory using data on vetoes across state governments in the United States is then presented and discussed.

The Executive Branch as an Enforcer of Long-Term Political Contracts

As Samuels points out in his comment on the theory of the independent judiciary offered by Landes-Posner, they do not consider the role of the executive veto in their analysis.[10] The analogy between the executive branch and the independent judiciary in the interest-group theory of government is straightforward, though Samuels does not draw it.

Landes and Posner base their argument on the concept of a market for special-interest legislation (for example, a law that restricts entry into an industry) in which the legislature sells laws and special interests buy them. The price that a winning special-interest group would bid will depend to a large extent on how durable their legislative protection is expected to be. In private sales and contracts, there are legal sanctions to deal with the event of nonperformance by a seller or buyer. There are no similar legal sanctions in politics, which raises the question of how long-term political contracts are enforced. Landes and Posner point to two important sources of durable special-interest legislation.

First, the procedural rules of the legislature can impart durability to a law once it is initially passed. For example, a majority-voting requirement makes the passage of legislation a costly process so that, once a law is on the books, it

---

9. Hamilton, in *The Federalist* no. 73, also recognized the effect of the veto in promoting more durable law, but in the sense of promoting "good" law rather than sustaining "bad" law. It may perhaps be said that the power of preventing bad laws includes that of preventing good ones; and may be used to the one purpose as well as to the other. But this objection will have little weight with those who can properly estimate the mischiefs of that inconstancy and mutability in the laws, which form the greatest blemish in the character and genius of our governments. They will consider every institution calculated to restrain the excess of lawmaking, and to keep things in the same state in which they happen to be at any given period, as much more likely to do good than harm; because it is favorable to greater stability in the system of legislation. The injury that may possibly be done by defeating a few good laws, will be amply compensated by the advantage of preventing a number of bad ones. *The Federalist* 1941, 478.

10. Samuels 1975.

is unlikely that it will be repealed or substantively altered in the near future. Hence, aspects of legislative organization such as majority voting, bicameralism, the committee system, the seniority system, and so on can be seen as increasing the expected lifetime of a special-interest law. In the Landes-Posner theory, higher costs in the legislative process lead to more durable and therefore more valuable special-interest legislation as reflected in a rotation of the demand curve for special-interest legislation to the right.[11]

Second, the independent judiciary is an equally important source of durable law. This follows because (a) judges rarely nullify or hold a law unconstitutional (an empirical observation), and (b) in the event of a legal dispute over the meaning of a law, judicial methodology tends to lead to an interpretation of the law in terms of the intentions of the enacting legislators. On both counts the independent judiciary increases the durability and hence the present value of special-interest legislation. One might think of the contrasting case where each legislature appointed its own slate of judges and proceeded to try to undo the legislative bargains reached by preceding legislatures. In such an environment, demanders of special-interest legislation would not be willing to bid very much (if anything) for protection that was effective only for the term of the existing legislature. The grant of independence and life tenure to judges, then, can also be seen as rotating the demand curve for special-interest legislation to the right by imparting greater durability to legislative contracts with special interests.

Presumably, investments in institutional arrangements in the legislature and the judiciary that give greater durability to political contracts are proximately optimized. For example, a stricter voting rule in the legislature would imply less need for judicial independence at the margin.

Essentially, then, Landes and Posner attack the idea that a separation of powers very accurately describes how our government functions. Rather than acting as a brake on the actions of the legislature or acting to represent minorities that cannot achieve representation elsewhere in the system (as some political scientists argue), the independent judiciary acts to enforce long-term contracts between special interests and legislators.[12]

Landes and Posner took their main task to be the development of a theory of judicial independence, and they consequently do not pursue many of the empirical implications of their model. They do examine factors (such as the age of judges) that should predictably be related to judicial nullification rates, and their findings in this regard make economic sense (older judges, for

---

11. Landes and Posner 1975.

12. The latter, of course, is a form of minority representation, but not of the type envisaged by political scientists. For references to the political science literature, see Landes and Posner 1975.

example, will be more likely to nullify laws). In a recent article we have attempted a more systematic test of their theory.[13] We applied their theory to the task of explaining the process of constitutional change across state governments in the United States and found that the Landes-Posner model has genuinely strong predictive power in this area. Briefly, in the Landes-Posner theory, a constitutional amendment is an especially durable type of special-interest protection because constitutional provisions, once enacted, are typically harder to repeal than normal legislation. This suggests that constitutional amendments across states can be explained as a function of aspects of legislative (for example, the voting rule) and judicial (for example, the tenure of judges) organization. We find that such a model can usefully explain this important and not often analyzed area of governmental activity. Since the elasticity of demand for special-interest legislation at the state level should be relatively high due to the presence of many competing jurisdictions, the fact that we find strong empirical support for the implications of the Landes-Posner theory of the independent judiciary at this level suggests that it possesses great potential in the further development of the interest-group theory of government, the task to which we now turn.

Consider the analogy between the executive veto and the independent judiciary. Nullification of a law by a judge is exactly analogous to the casting of a veto by the chief executive. In both cases, the legislature may try to override the decision but usually with limited success. The economic value of the veto is to be found, as in the case of judicial nullification, in its impact on the durability of legislation. More specifically, the veto power of the chief executive raises the costs of repealing a law, once it is enacted, in the Landes-Posner framework. Given a rational pattern of investment in the durability-enhancing aspects of democratic decision making, the executive veto, along with the constitutive rules of the legislature and the independent judiciary, acts to increase the durability of special-interest legislation. That is, the veto power increases the returns from legislative contracts with special interests, by making these contracts harder to repeal, more than it increases the costs of passing legislation in the first place.

In the next part of the essay, we will present a systematic test of a durability-enhancing theory of the executive veto. For the moment, however, it would be useful to show how a Landes-Posner theory of the executive branch can rationalize observations about vetoes that do not seem to square with common sense. It has been observed that vetoes seem to vary positively with respect to the size of majorities in the U.S. House and Senate.[14] Presidents Franklin Roosevelt and Lyndon Johnson cast a relatively large number of vetoes when confronted with large majorities of their own party in both

---

13. Crain and Tollison 1979.
14. Brams 1975, 211–12.

houses of Congress. Contrary to the normal desire to elect members of their own party, then, presidents seem to have as much to fear from large majorities of their own party as from the opposition party, and this pattern of behavior has not been seen as congruent with common sense. Yet consider the evidence in terms of the durability-enhancing theory of legislation. In this theory a larger majority implies more new legislators and a lower cost of passing legislation. More new legislators and a lower cost of passing legislation in the Landes-Posner model both imply less durability of special-interest laws (one might think of this case in terms of the election of a faction of candidates who ran on a deregulation platform). In such a setting, the relative value of the veto in prohibiting the overturn of existing legislative contracts with special interests is high. In fact, since it can be applied immediately on the threat of repeal of a legislative contract and not after protracted legal proceedings, the veto can be seen as a quite efficient means of promoting long-term political contracts. The fact that vetoes are sometimes overridden provides a rationale for the role of the independent judiciary in serving as a longer term guarantor of legislative bargains.[15]

This view of the executive branch completes the task that Landes and Posner started. It in effect undermines any semblance of a separation-of-powers argument in favor of our tripartite system of government. If our approach and that of Landes and Posner is correct, we have not a separation but a collusion of powers in our governmental system. The legislative-executive-judicial nexus becomes analogous to a vertically integrated seller of long-term legislation to special interests. As we stressed above, we have found impressive support for this theory in the context of explaining constitutional change.[16] We turn now to an equally systematic test of this theory for the case of the executive veto. We will test the theory using data on vetoes across state governments in the United States, and we expect that those factors which decrease the durability of law will in general increase the demand for vetoes.

Empirical Evidence from State Governments in the United States

State legislative systems in the United States tend to be constituted on the pattern of the federal system. Governors possess the veto power, and bills must obtain stricter majorities (usually two-thirds) to become law in the face

---

15. We also note that the executive veto can be bought and sold in presidential elections. Special interests will therefore be observed contributing to candidates in a presidential election even though they seek no current-period legislation. Thus as old legislation is threatened with repeal by the existence of a large majority in the legislature, the relative value of the president's signature will rise. Other things equal we would expect to see this change in relative value reflected in campaign contributions to presidential relative to congressional candidates.

16. Crain and Tollison 1979.

of a gubernatorial veto. The presence of the veto power across state governments thus offers a unique cross-sectional basis for testing the interest-group
theory of vetoes developed above.

Our model for empirical testing is given in equation (1) and explained
below.[17]

$$V = F(LM, LT, PC, JT, GS, LE) ;$$ (1)

where

> V = the number of gubernatorial vetoes,
>
> LM = the proportion of total legislative seats controlled by majority
> parties;
>
> LT = turnover of legislators defined as the proportion of total legisla-
> tive seats held by new members;
>
> PC = party correspondence defined as a dummy variable that is (a)
> equal to -1 if neither house of the legislature is controlled by
> the party of the governor, (b) equal to 0 if one house of the
> legislature is controlled by the party of the governor, and (c)
> equal to $+1$ if both houses of the legislature are controlled by
> the party of the governor;
>
> JT = judicial tenure defined as the length of term of the chief justice
> of the state supreme court;
>
> GS = gubernatorial succession rights defined as a dummy variable
> that is (a) equal to -1 if there is a one-term limit, (b) equal to
> 0 if there is a two-term limit, and (c) equal to $+1$ if these are
> unlimited succession rights; and
>
> LE = a control variable reflecting the number of bills and resolutions
> enacted by the legislature.

Our dependent variable is gubernatorial vetoes, the aspect of executive
branch behavior to be analyzed.

The size of the majority in the legislature is entered to test for the
implication of our argument that the lower the legislative cost of passing
legislation, the less durable laws will be (once enacted). In related work we
have found that the average cost of passing laws declines with larger majorities.[18] Within the context of this essay this result implies that larger majorities
will be associated with less durable legislation, which in turn reduces the value

---

17. The data on all the variables are for the 1973–74 legislative session(s) in each state and
are standardized over a two-year period to control for the existence of annual versus biennial
sessions.

18. Crain and Tollison 1978, Crain 1979. Like all economic relationships, that between
majority size and the costs of passing legislation exhibits diminishing returns. Diminishing

of legislative contracts with special interests. We would thus expect more incentive to rely on the executive veto as a means of restoring or enhancing the present value of laws to special interests as the size of majority increases. This durability-enhancing view of vetoes and political majorities stands in contrast to the conventional wisdom that chief executives have much to gain by working with large majorities of their own party in the legislature (for example, in the sense of passing a party platform).

Turnover in the legislature is a proxy for average legislator tenure. In the durability-enhancing theory of legislation a longer tenure for legislators implies less need for other institutional sources of durability, such as the veto, since legislators can themselves enforce political contracts made in prior sessions when they are in office for longer periods. Stated in reverse, more turnover among legislators will be associated with more attempts in current legislative sessions to undo old legislative transactions, which gives rise to greater need to rely on the executive branch to uphold deals made by special interests with ex-legislators. This effect should be reinforced by the fact that greater turnover is likely to reduce the time required for elected representatives to progress to more important positions of influence in legislative decision making, for example, subcommittee or committee chairmanships. More rapid rises by legislators to such positions would impede the continuity of transactions made with special-interest groups. Legislator turnover should therefore be positively related to vetoes.

The variable reflecting party correspondence is a proxy for whether it is important for the controlling party in the legislature to be the same as the party of the governor. Conventional political wisdom suggests that such a correspondence is important, that is, we should expect more vetoes where there is not such a correspondence. In effect this variable is useful in assessing the separation- versus the collusion-of-powers views of government operations. The former view sees the various branches of government as part of a competitive system of party rivalry and checks and balances. The collusion theory, as outlined in this essay, stresses the role of cooperation among the branches of government in enhancing the present value of transactions with special interests. The party-rivalry approach leads to the implication of more vetoes where the governor is of a different party than that which controls the legislature. In contrast the collusion model predicts that party correspondence across the various branches would become of secondary importance relative to maximizing joint political profits from special-interest deals.

---

returns set in beyond some majority size, for example, because larger majorities become increasingly more difficult to control by the majority leadership. In fact diminishing returns to majority sizes explain why so few vetoes are overridden, as organizing a relatively larger majority to override a veto is more costly than organizing the original passage of legislation under normal voting and quorum rules.

The judicial tenure variable derives from our work on constitutional change.[19] In that article we find that longer judicial tenure implies more interest-group protection in the form of regular legislation rather than constitutional amendments. This follows because judges will be around longer to enforce normal legislative contracts, and there will be less need for special interests to seek the relatively more costly protection offered by a constitutional amendment. Perhaps the appropriate analogy here is to complementary inputs or "jointness" in the production function for durable legislative contracts. Both vetoes and an independent judiciary are durability-enhancing factors in their own right, although because of the nature of the production technology (that is, the available institutional procedures for establishing and enforcing political contracts), the derived demand for vetoes will be influenced by the extent of judicial independence. For example, a more independent judiciary leads to increased reliance on normal legislation (as opposed to constitutional amendments), which in turn implies more reliance on the veto to protect existing legislative contracts. We therefore expect vetoes and judicial tenure to be positively related.

The variable measuring the succession rights of the governor reflects his independence from electoral politics. Following the same logic as Landes and Posner, we expect that where the governor is less independent in the sense of having to stand for reelection (unlimited succession rights), the less likely he is to use the veto to uphold special-interest contracts. We therefore expect a negative sign on this variable as an indication of the indirect impact of consumer-voters on the special-interest proclivities of the governor.

The number of bills and resolutions enacted is entered in equation (1) as a control variable, that is, to control for the fact that vetoes will tend to vary positively with the volume of legislative output across states.

We do not estimate the coefficients in equation (1) by ordinary least squares because of a simultaneous-equations bias between LE and the other right-hand-side variables. This problem is resolved by forming an additional structural equation in which LE is formulated as a function of the other right-hand-side variables, including an additional variable, the number of bills and resolutions introduced. This procedure effectively purges the simultaneity between LE and the other right-hand-side variables. Making this additional specification of a structural equation in the system allows us to estimate the coefficients in equation (1) by the single-equation method of instrumental variables.[20] We estimate equation (1) by this method using logarithmic transformations of all the continuous variables based on a cross section of data for 1973–74 for U.S. state governments.[21] The results are presented in table 1.

19. Crain and Tollison 1979.
20. See Kmenta 1971 for a discussion of this statistical procedure.
21. Our data are available in *The Book of the States 1974–1975* (Council of State Govern-

**TABLE 1.   Regression Results
for Gubernatorial Vetoes, 1973–74**

LM	8.11
	(2.21)
LT	−0.72
	(−2.61)
PC	0.12
	(0.56)
JT	1.31
	(2.19)
GS	−0.41
	(−1.51)
LE	1.02
	(3.67)
R^2	0.54
$F_{(6.34)}$	6.65
N	41

Source: Calculated from Council of State Governments 1975, 20.
Note: t-ratios are in parentheses.

Our expectations are all essentially verified in the results in table 1. The overall regression explains over half of the variation in gubernatorial vetoes across states and is highly significant at the 1 percent level.

Size-of-majority appears with the expected positive sign and is highly significant at the 5 percent level (two-tailed tests are employed throughout). The veto thus appears to vary positively with the ability of the legislature to overturn existing legislative contracts with special interests, and this result cuts against the conventional wisdom that the executive branch necessarily finds it convenient to have a large majority (especially of its own party) in the legislature.[22] Legislative turnover has the expected negative sign and is significant at the 2 percent level. This result indicates that more stability in the composition of the legislature leads to fewer attempts at reneging on previous legislative contracts with special interests. Where average legislator tenure

---

ments 1975) at various pages. Nine states were omitted from our test due to the absence of data on one or more variables. These were Arkansas, Illinois, Kansas, Minnesota, Nebraska, North Carolina, Tennessee, Wisconsin, and Wyoming. Various linear and nonlinear forms of equation (1) were also estimated. There were no theoretical reasons for choosing a particular form, and our analysis proceeded with a logarithmic transformation of equation (1) based on goodness-of-fit grounds. For the most part the other forms that we examined did not alter substantially the signs or significance levels of the results presented in table 1 in the text.

22. We also note that this finding offers an additional rationale for evidence which we presented in an earlier study (Crain and Tollison 1976), that campaign expenditures by the minority party will exceed those of the majority party in races which are likely to alter legislative proportions. In the present context, this result follows because special interests will find it in their self-interest to prevent larger majorities and will allocate their campaign contributions accordingly.

(the inverse of turnover) is longer, legislators can effectively enforce their own contracts with special interests with less need for the veto power or the independent judiciary as sources of contractual durability. Party correspondence between the executive and legislative branches does not seem to matter at all, as the coefficient on this dummy variable carries no statistical credibility. Combined with the result on the size-of-majority variable above, we take these results as evidence that the conventional wisdom about vetoes is wrong. The conventional wisdom would have predicted less vetoes in the presence of a larger majority, especially where the same party controls both the legislature and the governor's office. We find that party does not matter and that vetoes vary positively with size-of-majority, a pattern of evidence that is consistent with a durability-enhancing theory of vetoes and a collusion rather than a separation-of-powers view of how government operates. Judicial tenure has the expected positive sign and is significant at the 5 percent level. Since longer judicial tenure implies more reliance for protection by special interests on normal legislation, we observe relatively more reliance on the veto in this setting to provide durability for political contracts. The succession rights of governors carries the expected negative sign at a weak level of statistical significance (20 percent). We thus see some tentative evidence that the more a governor is subject to electoral sanctions by consumer-voters, the less he will employ the veto to uphold special-interest legislation. Finally, we find the expected positive sign on the number of legislative enactments that was introduced as a control variable.

As in the case of our results on constitutional change,[23] we find these results encouraging for the durability-enhancing theory of special-interest legislation offered by Landes and Posner. Our theory of vetoes says that vetoes should vary positively with aspects of the political environment (for example, size of the majority) that tend to reduce the expected lifetime of a special-interest law. Alternative theories suggest just the opposite result. For example, Buchanan and Tullock's analysis suggests that where vetoes are inspired to protect minorities, we would expect to observe fewer vetoes as the size of the minority shrinks (that is, as the size of the majority increases).[24] The evidence presented in this essay strongly favors the durability-enhancing theory over the protection-of-minorities theory of vetoes and represents another step in the development of a (testable) interest-group theory of government.

Conclusion

We have now found and presented what we think is impressive empirical support for the durability-enhancing theory of the institutional structure of the

23. Crain and Tollison 1979.
24. Buchanan and Tullock 1962.

market for special-interest legislation offered by Landes and Posner. One set of evidence is contained in our study of constitutional change;[25] the other set is the evidence offered on vetoes in this essay.

The broader implications of the work along the lines suggested by Landes and Posner are important and disturbing. As we said earlier, our governmental system seems better characterized as a collusion of rather than a separation of powers. We cannot put the matter better than Hayek does at the outset of the first volume of his trilogy on *Law, Legislation, and Liberty:*

> In the form in which we know this division of power between the legislature, the judiciary, and the administration, it has not achieved what it was meant to achieve. Governments everywhere have obtained by constitutional means powers which those men had meant to deny them. The first attempt to secure individual liberty by constitutions has evidently failed.[26]

REFERENCES

Brams, Steven J. 1975. *Game Theory and Politics.* New York: Free Press.
Buchanan, J. M., and Gordon Tullock. 1962. *The Calculus of Consent.* Ann Arbor: University of Michigan Press.
Council of State Governments. 1975. *Book of the States 1974–1975.* Lexington: Iron Works Pike.
Crain, W. Mark. 1977. "On the Structure and Stability of Political Markets." *Journal of Political Economy* 85 (August): 829–42.
Crain, W. Mark, and Robert D. Tollison. 1976. "Campaign Expenditures and Political Competition." *Journal of Law and Economics* 19 (April): 177–88.
———. N.d. "Constitutional Change in an Interest-Group Perspective." *Journal of Legal Studies.* In press.
———. N.d. "Cost and Output in the Legislative Firm." *Journal of Legal Studies.* In press.
———. 1978a. "Team Productivity in Politics." Manuscript.
———. 1978b. "The Sizes of Majorities." Manuscript.
Ehrlich, Issac, and Richard A. Posner. 1974. "An Economic Analysis of Legal Rule Making." *Journal of Legal Studies* 3 (January): 257–86.
The Federalist. 1961. Special Edition Printed for National Foundation for Education in American Citizenship. Indianapolis.
Hayek, Friedrich A. 1973. *Law, Legislation and Liberty.* Vol. 1: *Rules and Order.* Chicago: University of Chicago Press.
Kmenta, Jan. 1971. *Elements of Econometrics.* New York: Macmillan.
Landes, William M., and Richard A. Posner. 1975. "The Independent Judiciary in an

---

25. Crain and Tollison 1979.
26. Hayek 1973.

Interest-Group Perspective." *Journal of Law and Economics* 18 (December): 875–901.

McCormick, Robert E., and Robert D. Tollison. 1978. "Legislatures as Unions." *Journal of Political Economy* 86 (February): 63–78.

Samuels, Warren J. 1975. "Comment." *Journal of Law and Economics* 18 (December): 907–12.

Shapley, L. S., and Martin Shubik. 1954. "A Method for Evaluating the Distribution of Power in a Committee System." *American Political Science Review* 48 (September): 787–92.

Stigler, George J. 1976. "The Sizes of Legislatures." *Journal of Legal Studies* 5 (January): 17–34.

Legislative Majorities as Nonsalvageable Assets

W. Mark Crain, William F. Shughart II, and Robert D. Tollison

Explicit and Implicit Political Contracts

Without enforcement mechanisms, agreements between interest groups and legislators would be worthless. Political exchanges, like private transactions, require some assurance that agreements will be honored after the terms of trade are reached. Interest groups are not likely to expend resources to secure the passage of legislation if laws once enacted are easily altered or repealed. Mechanisms to maintain political bargains are the central focus of the interest-group theory of the independent judiciary developed by William Landes and Richard Posner (1975). The judicial branch acts as a third-party enforcer of agreements struck between the legislative branch and interest groups. This mechanism for enforcement is analogous to an explicit contract. The Landes-Posner framework and its extensions are reviewed and summarized below. One of our purposes in this essay is to broaden the analysis of the enforcement problems associated with political transactions. Where explicit political contracts are inadequate or expensive, we examine the use of implicit or self-enforcing mechanisms. In contrast to third-party enforcement, implicit contracts are self-enforcing in the sense that they rely on the threat of the termination of an interest group's wealth transfer to maintain the transactional relationship.

The specific type of self-enforcing contract treated in this essay involves investments by voters, interest groups, and political parties in legislative majorities. Control of the legislature by larger-than-minimum majorities, which is analogous to the purchase of a nonsalvageable, firm-specific asset, emerges in political markets as a way for a party to assure interest groups that it will not

We are grateful to Jon Macey, Scott Thomas, and a referee for helpful suggestions. The usual proviso applies. Reprinted from *Southern Economic Journal* 55, no. 2 (October 1988): 303–14.

renege on deals struck in the past. In our view, such investments trade off at the margin in a predictable way with the alternative, third-party method of enforcing political bargains emphasized by Landes and Posner.

Our analysis is rich in positive content as the empirical section of the essay will illustrate. The point we develop is that actual contractual arrangements in politics consist of a mix of explicit and implicit enforcement mechanisms, which is exactly what we observe in private sector contracts. Over time, we expect the mix of explicit and implicit enforcement mechanisms that emerges to reflect the minimum cost set of political institutions for policing political transactions.

In particular, we examine the role of majority size as a self-enforcing mechanism in political transactions. The analysis stresses a fundamental point about public choice models. Namely, Stigler's (1972) argument that large majorities are more valuable is correct, and Riker's (1962) argument that a party should seek a minimum winning coalition is incorrect. The theoretical and empirical bases for this result follow below.

The chapter is organized as follows. We review the Landes-Posner model and expand the notion of political enforcement mechanisms to include implicit, self-enforcing devices. The analysis is applied to explain the sizes of majority party control in legislatures. Then we specify an empirical model and present results on the sizes of majorities across state legislatures in the United States.

The Model

Landes and Posner (1975) propound an interest-group theory of the independent judiciary. Their basic idea is simple. Like private contracts, the value of a legislative transaction depends on its expected durability. More durable legislation implies a larger present value of benefit flows for interest groups.

Landes and Posner address two relevant margins through which the durability of political agreements is promoted. Their primary focus is on the judicial margin which, in our perspective, is analogous to an explicit contract enforced by a third party. The independent judiciary, because of its methodology in reviewing cases, increases the durability of interest-group deals with the legislature. Thus, if a legal dispute arises with respect to the validity or constitutionality of a law or regulation, the independent judiciary resolves the dispute by interpreting the law, basically, in terms of the intent of the enacting legislature. By following this methodology, the promises that interest groups received from one legislature are made to endure beyond the term of elected representatives. The durability of laws and hence the present value of political benefits to interest groups are thus impacted by the structure and the behavior of an independent judiciary.

Note that this is a theory about judicial organization. As such, it does not have to describe any particular reality. Nonetheless, in the Landes and Posner model, judges are conceived of as federal judges who are appointed by the president, who have life tenure, and who cannot have their nominal salaries cut. Across U.S. states, however, there are degrees of Landes-Posner judicial independence. Few states, for example, have life terms for state supreme court judges, and some states have shorter terms than others. Some states provide for elected judges rather than allowing the governor to appoint them, and so on. In this sense, the margin of judicial independence is not constant across states.

This brings us to the other margin in the Landes-Posner theory—the legislature. While Landes and Posner do not dwell on this margin, we can easily expand their analysis in this direction. Whereas the independent judiciary is analogous to an explicit, third-party enforcement mechanism, legislators can adopt implicit or self-enforcing mechanisms to assure durable agreements. (The constitutive rules of the representative body on such matters as majority voting, committee hearings, and floor action are examples in this regard.) As the degree of independence of the judiciary falls, contracts between interest groups and legislatures become more incomplete in the sense of being less enforceable by a third party. In such cases, we would expect greater reliance on implicit mechanisms to maintain a given level of enforcement in the policing of the contract.

In the literature on private contracting, Klein and Leffler (1981) have analyzed the role of implicit contracts when explicit government-enforced contracts are incomplete or too costly to establish. One form of an implicit enforcement mechanism is for the potential defector to make an investment in a firm-specific, nonsalvageable asset. This investment acts as an implicit guarantee that the firm will not cheat the customer because cheating will result in forfeiture of the investment. That is, the firm will lose future business, and the investment in the nonsalvageable asset is lost. The purchase of a nonsalvageable asset is equivalent to posting a bond that assures noncheating behavior. For their part, customers pay a price premium for the product to induce the firm not to cheat. In equilibrium, the value of the investment in the nonsalvageable asset just dissipates the "protection money" offered by buyers so that the firm earns a normal rate of return.

The analogy we draw to political contracts is the investment by a political party in the size of its majority control of a legislature. Larger majority sizes are costly to achieve and to maintain. As such, parties would prefer third-party enforcement of legislative agreements by the judiciary, if the latter mechanism were complete or costless. A larger-than-minimum majority (à la Riker) is analytically equivalent to a nonsalvageable investment that a political party must make to guarantee noncheating. The size of the nonsalvageable investment is related to the extent of incompleteness in enforcement by the independent judiciary (and obviously to other variables discussed below). Where the judiciary is less independent, the analysis predicts that a larger investment will be made on the legislative margin, that is, that a larger legislative majority will be maintained as a means of self-enforcement of political contracts. Thus, if a party has invested in a larger-than-minimum majority size and it subsequently reneges on an agreement it reaches with an interest group, the interest group will turn its future support toward another party. The past expenditure on the party-specific brandname is forfeited.

In essence, the majority party is a supplier of legislative output, and its brandname capital is a function of keeping its word. If it cheats on its commitments to interest groups, this capital is depreciated. This means that in future elections it will be harder for the party to sell its program to prospective supporters. A super-majority is a way that a party signals that it has more to lose by cheating in terms of its investment in brandname capital, that is, cheating would mean that the party would incur losses in excess of short-run gains.

With respect to the demanders of legislation, interest groups are willing to pay the majority party not to renege on deals struck in the past. This "protection money," which may take the form of additional campaign contributions, extra efforts to deliver voters to the polls, and so on, would in turn just be dissipated by the party's investment in a larger legislative majority. In other words, a normal rate of return to contracting would tend to prevail in political equilibrium. The effect, however, is that the possibility of reneging is reduced on both sides. The political party would lose the value of its investment in a larger majority, and a capital loss would also be imposed on the interest groups that have provided a "premium" with their support.

In the above way, control of the legislature, the implicit enforcement device, can be traded off at the margin against the explicit enforcement mechanism offered by the independent judiciary. There will be less investment in larger majority proportions where the degree of independence of the judiciary is strong, and vice versa. As we shall see, this is a testable hypothesis across U.S. states.[1]

The purpose of the empirical application that follows is to offer a more general test of the enforcement theory of political contracts. As stressed previously, the margin of maintaining political contracts by implicit mechanisms will not be as necessary where explicit mechanisms such as judicial independence are stronger. This perspective suggests a theory of legislative

---

1. The Landes-Posner model has been tested previously based on data on constitutional change across states and on gubernatorial vetoes. The relevant works here are Crain and Tollison 1979a, 1979b and Anderson, Martin, Shughart, and Tollison 1986.

majority sizes across U.S. states. Specifically, larger majorities will trade off in a predictable way against measures of judicial independence and other variables across states. Thus, where state judges have longer terms and have more independence, there is less call for the interest group and the political party to be concerned about the size of the latter's majority in the state legislature; states with more judicial independence should exhibit smaller majorities, all else equal. The purpose of the next section is to offer an empirical test of this analysis.

And note again that the "protection money" theory of legislative majorities stresses why "optimal" majorities will be greater than a minimum winning coalition. In effect, this theory offers a richer, testable rationale for Stigler's (1972) conclusion that larger-than-minimum winning coalitions are valuable in the political process.

Empirical Model and Results

A testable implication of the analytical framework developed above is that the size of the legislative majority in a state will depend in part on the institutional factors influencing the independence of the judiciary. Judges who are more "independent" (of the legislature especially, but also of the executive and of the voters) are more likely to play the role of third-party enforcers. As Landes and Posner envision the problem, judges impart durability to statutory laws by interpreting them on the basis of the intent of the enacting legislature. Smaller legislative majorities would be predicted in states having more independent judiciaries because political contracts are more complete and enforceable by explicit means. Of course, as we discuss below, judicial variables are not the only determinants of majority sizes.

Table 1 shows legislative majority party proportions in the fifty states at four selected intervals over the 1960–83 period. The figures are relatively stable for a given state, both as to size of majority and identity of party in power. Investing in stable legislative majorities appears to be a quite feasible activity for political parties.

Moreover, this preliminary observation and the results that follow below are consistent with the literature. For example, Peltzman (1985) and Kau and Rubin (1982) find, among their other basic results, that political preferences matter to political outcomes and that such preferences remain stable for long periods of time. These findings are consistent with the results of this essay that majority sizes are fairly constant over time. Thus, voters and/or interest groups seem to be able to tailor stable legislative majorities.

In this section, however, we are seeking a positive explanation for the considerable variation in majority sizes across state legislatures. That is, the previous literature is useful in understanding the stability of a legislature over

TABLE 1.   State Legislative Majorities, 1960–83

State	Senate				House			
	1960	1970	1980	1983	1960	1970	1980	1983
Alabama	100.0D	100.0D	100.0D	91.4D	100.0D	98.1D	96.2D	92.4D
Alaska	70.0D	52.4D	50.0[b]	55.0R	50.0D[c]	77.5D	55.0D	52.5R
Arizona	85.7D	60.0R	53.3R	60.0R	66.3D	56.7R	71.7R	65.0R
Arkansas	100.0D	97.1D	97.1D	91.4D	99.0D	98.0D	93.0D	93.0D
California	75.0D	52.5D	57.5D	62.5D	58.8D	53.8D	58.8D	60.0D
Colorado	54.3D	60.0R	62.9R	60.0R	50.8D	58.5R	60.0R	61.5R
Connecticut	66.7D	52.8D	63.9D	63.9D	59.9R	55.9D	56.3D	57.6D
Delaware	64.7D	68.4R	57.1D	61.9D	57.1D	59.0R	61.0R	58.5D
Florida	97.4D	68.8D	67.5D	80.0D	92.6D	68.1D	67.5D	70.0D
Georgia	98.1D	89.3D	91.1D	87.5D	99.0D	88.7D	87.2D	86.7D
Hawaii	56.0R	68.0D	68.0D	80.0D	64.7D	66.7D	76.5D	84.3D
Idaho	52.3R	54.3R	65.7R	60.0R	50.8R	58.6R	80.0R	72.9R
Illinois	53.4R	50.8D	50.8D	55.9D	50.3R	50.8R	51.4R	59.3D
Indiana	52.0D	58.0R	70.0R	64.0R	66.0R	54.0R	63.0R	57.0R
Iowa	70.0R	76.0R	58.0R	56.0D	72.2R	63.0R	58.0R	60.0D
Kansas	80.0R	80.0R	60.0R	60.0R	65.6R	67.2R	57.6R	57.6R
Kentucky	78.9D	60.5D	76.3D	73.9D	80.0D	72.0D	75.0D	76.0D
Louisiana	100.0D	97.4D	100.0D	97.4D	100.0D	99.0D	90.5D	88.6D
Maine	90.9R	56.3R	51.5R	69.7D	74.8R	53.0R	55.6D	60.9D
Maryland	89.7D	76.7D	85.1D	87.2D	94.3D	85.2D	88.7D	87.9D
Massachusetts	65.0D	75.0D	80.0D	82.5D	65.0D	74.2D	79.4D	80.6D
Michigan	64.7R	50.0[b]	63.2D	52.6D	50.9R	52.7D	58.2D	57.3D
Minnesota	—[a]	—[a]	67.2D	62.7D	—[a]	—[a]	52.2D	57.4D
Mississippi	100.0D	94.2D	92.3D	94.2D	100.0D	98.4D	95.1D	95.1D
Missouri	82.4D	73.5D	67.6D	64.7D	63.7D	68.7D	68.1D	67.5D
Montana	67.9D	54.5D	54.0R	52.0R	56.4R	52.9R	56.0R	55.0D
Nebraska	—[a]	—[a]	—[a]	—[a]	—[a]	—[a]	—[a]	—[a]
Nevada	58.8R	65.0D	75.0D	81.0D	68.1D	52.5R	65.0D	54.8D
New Hampshire	75.0R	62.5R	58.3R	62.5R	65.0R	63.0R	60.0R	59.2R
New Jersey	52.4R	76.9R	67.5D	57.5D	56.7D	73.8R	55.0D	55.0D
New Mexico	87.5D	66.7D	52.4D	54.8D	90.9D	68.6D	58.0D	65.7D
New York	56.9R	56.1R	58.3R	57.4R	56.0R	52.7R	57.3D	64.7D
North Carolina	96.0D	86.0D	80.0D	88.0D	87.5D	80.8D	80.0D	85.0D
North Dakota	57.1R	75.5R	82.0R	60.4R	61.9R	60.2R	74.0R	51.9D
Ohio	52.6R	60.6R	54.5R	51.5D	60.4R	54.5R	56.6D	62.6D
Oklahoma	90.9D	81.3D	77.1D	70.8D	88.4D	78.8D	72.3D	75.2D
Oregon	66.7D	53.3D	80.0D	70.0D	51.7D	56.7R	55.0D	60.0D
Pennsylvania	50.0[b]	52.0D	51.0R	54.0D	52.4D	55.7D	50.7R	50.7D
Rhode Island	63.6D	82.0D	86.0D	58.0D	80.0D	75.0D	83.7D	85.0D
South Carolina	100.0D	95.5D	89.1D	84.8D	100.0D	91.1D	86.3D	83.1D
South Dakota	62.9D	68.6R	71.4R	74.3R	76.0R	60.0R	70.0R	77.1R
Tennessee	81.8D	57.6D	60.6D	66.7D	80.1D	56.6D	58.6D	60.6D
Texas	100.0D	93.5D	77.4D	83.9D	100.0D	93.3D	76.0D	76.0D
Utah	56.0D	57.1R	75.9R	82.8R	56.3D	53.6D	76.0R	77.3R
Vermont	76.7R	73.3R	53.3R	56.7R	76.0R	64.0R	55.3R	55.3R

TABLE 1—*Continued*

State	Senate				House			
	1960	1970	1980	1983	1960	1970	1980	1983
Virginia	95.0D	80.0D	77.5D	80.0D	96.0D	76.0D	74.0D	65.0D
Washington	73.5D	59.2D	51.0D	53.1D	60.6D	51.5R	57.1R	55.1D
West Virginia	78.1D	65.7D	79.4D	91.3D	82.0D	68.0D	79.0D	87.0D
Wisconsin	60.6R	62.5R	59.4D	57.6D	55.0R	67.0D	59.6D	59.6D
Wyoming	63.0R	63.3R	63.3R	63.3R	62.5R	65.6R	62.9R	59.4R

Sources: 1960—[U.S. 1961, 358] and [Scammon 1962]; 1970 and 1980—[Congressional Quarterly, 22-B]; and 1983—[Council of State Governments 1984, 85].
anonpartisan ballot
bTie-breaking procedure not available.
cDemocrats held twenty seats, Republicans eighteen, and independents two.

time, but does not get us to an explanation of why majorities might be large or small in the first place.

Our empirical model for this purpose is of the following general form.[2]

$$MAJ = f(DENS80, HSR, CS, COMM, AGENDA, SIZE, TERM,$$
$$SESS, FREQ, CLDUM, PARTY, SPLIT, CJTM81,$$
$$ELCT81, REMOVE, JPAY81, e),$$

where

MAJ = number of majority party members in the house, $HMAJ$, or senate, $SMAJ$ (alternatively, majority party members as a percent of total chamber size, $HMPCT$ or $SMPCT$);

$DENS80$ = 1980 state population per square mile;

HSR = ratio of house to senate size;

CS = average size of standing committees;

$COMM$ = number of standing committees;

$AGENDA$ = number of bills introduced in the 1981–82 biennium;

$SIZE$ = total membership of house or senate;

$TERM$ = length of terms of state senators or representatives;

$SESS$ = length of 1981–82 legislative session, in days;

$FREQ$ = frequency of 1981–82 legislative session (set equal to unity if two legislative sessions were convened during the biennium and set equal to zero if only one session was held);

$CLDUM$ = a binary variable set equal to unity if session length is

---

2. This specification represents an extension of the model proposed by Crain and Tollison 1980.

$PARTY$ = measured in calendar days and equal to zero if measured in legislative days;

$PARTY$ = majority party label (set equal to unity if Democrats are in the majority and equal to zero for Republicans);

$SPLIT$ = a binary variable set equal to unity if the house and senate are controlled by different political parties and set equal to zero if the same party holds a majority in both chambers;

$CJTM81$ = length of term of chief justice of state court of last resort, in years:

$ELCT81$ = 1 if justices serving on the state court of last resort are elected by partisan ballot, and equal to zero otherwise;

$REMOVE$ = a binary variable reflecting the security of tenure of judges serving on the state court of last resort;

$JPAY81$ = salary of the chief justice of state court of last resort; and

e = regression error term.

The dependent variable measures the size of the legislative majority party either in terms of absolute numbers or as a percent of chamber size as of August 1983. We ran separate regressions for both the upper and lower houses.[3]

Four variables measure the degree of judicial independence in a state. Optimal majority sizes are predicted to be smaller in states where judges are paid more, have longer terms, and are less easily removed from office. The tenure and pay variables, $CJTM81$ and $JPAY81$, apply to the chief justice of the state court of last resort.[4] $REMOVE$ is set equal to unity if the justices are subject to impeachment *and* recall by the voters, or removal by the governor with the approval of the legislature (the concurrence of two-thirds of each house is typically required in such cases); is set equal to zero if the justices are subject to impeachment but no other form of removal; and is set equal to -1 if there are no specific provisions for removing justices. Elected judges are potentially less secure in their offices than those appointed by the governor. We therefore expect a positive sign on this variable.

Though we stressed judicial variables in our theoretical discussion, the empirical model of majority sizes is richer than this in fact. Judicial variables are therefore only one element in a theory of optimal majority sizes following Stigler (1972) and Landes and Posner (1975).

---

3. Nebraska's unicameral legislature was excluded from the house majority specifications.

4. The terms of those chief justices not having specified tenures were set as follows: "pleasure of court," one year; "remainder of term as justice," one-half the term length of associate justices; and "life" or "to age 70," 15 years (one year more than the longest specified term length for the state chief justice in the United States, 14 years in the state of New York).

State population density in 1980, *DENS80*, controls for voter monitoring costs. Where interest-group member/voters are more spatially concentrated, the costs of organizing coalitions and monitoring the legislature are reduced compared with less densely populated states. We therefore expect the estimated coefficient to be negative—the optimal majority size is smaller where monitoring costs are lower.

HSR reflects the degree of bicameralism in state legislatures. An increase in the disparity of chamber sizes increases the cost of obtaining a majority vote in both houses and causes the constituencies of representatives and senators to become more dissimilar (see Crain 1979 and McCormick and Tollison 1981). Larger majorities help to offset these costs by lowering the value of each majority party member's vote. Because each party member's vote is worth less, for example, defections on any given issue are of less concern to the leadership and to the success of the party's overall legislative agenda. As the size of the house rises relative to the senate, the optimal majority in either chamber is therefore expected to be larger.

Average committee size and number of committees are analogous to the intensive and extensive margins of legislative specialization, respectively. Increases in both are expected to be associated with larger efficient majorities. On the one hand, larger committees, where average committee size is calculated as the ratio of the total number of senators or representatives to the number of their respective chamber's standing committees plus the number of joint standing committees, will be associated with the formation of smaller legislative teams (subcommittees), where legislator productivity can be monitored more closely by subcommittee chairmen. On the other hand, an increase in the number of standing committees in the chamber (we here exclude joint standing committees) means that more special interests can be monitored more closely. Where there are more and larger committees, larger majorities allow the majority party leadership to exercise its influence over committee assignments to better allocate members to their most highly valued uses and to assure party control of important areas of legislative specialization.

AGENDA and *SIZE* are scale variables. The former, measured by the number of bills introduced during regular legislative sessions in the 1981–82 biennium, represents the demand for legislation. Because a larger volume of legislation means that there are more legislative margins to clear, we expect larger efficient majorities to result. This allows more of the various trade-offs necessary to reach a political equilibrium level and pattern of wealth transfers to be internalized within the party. Chamber size is included to control for two effects (see Stigler 1976). On the one hand, larger absolute majorities will be present in larger houses. On the other hand, the cost of obtaining the requisite number of seats to form a majority is obviously higher the larger the total membership of the legislative chamber. The data will speak as to which of these considerations dominates.

Four variables—*TERM, SESS, FREQ,* and *CLDUM*—control for the length and frequency of legislative sessions as well as for legislator continuity. Members elected to U.S. state legislatures generally serve terms of either two or four years. Longer terms, especially in the state senate, are normally associated with the practice of dividing the chamber into classes so that only a portion of the membership is up for election at any one time. Legislative continuity is weakened in such cases, and we therefore expect larger effective majorities to reduce the probability that a party's control will be dissolved by the voters at any given election. Shorter legislative sessions imply higher rates of output for a given party agenda. Larger majorities serve as a substitute for time in shorter sessions. *CLDUM* controls for the units in which legislative session lengths are actually measured. "Legislative days" count only those days on which the legislature meets; "calendar days" include the time over which the legislature is officially in session, whether or not the legislature actually convenes to conduct business. Calendar-day measurements therefore tend to overstate (by about 3 to 1) the amount of time the legislature is in session. We make no a priori prediction about the sign of this variable. *FREQ* denotes those legislatures that held two separate sessions during the 1981–82 biennium. Because binding votes on the party agenda typically take place at the end of the legislative session, the annual legislature is in the position of delivering legislative contracts with interest groups yearly (see Crain, Leavens, and Tollison 1986). By contrast, delivery dates in legislatures that only meet every other year are twice as far in the future, or, put another way, such legislatures produce legislation over a longer period of time. Larger efficient majorities should be observed in the latter case; the coefficient on *FREQ* is expected to be negative.

Finally, *PARTY* and *SPLIT* control for political effects in generating optimal majorities. If the conventional wisdom that the Democrat Party is an amalgam of a greater number and variety of special interests is correct, then larger effective majorities would be required to broker these additional wealth transfers. Furthermore, because legislation must be approved by two houses of a bicameral legislature, the value of a majority in either chamber is reduced when the same party does not control both. We therefore expect a negative sign on *SPLIT*.

In order to take account of the lack of independence between *AGENDA* and the other legislative variables, we regressed *AGENDA* on all other right-hand-side variables plus 1981 state income per capita, *PCY81,* and the relevant majority size measure. The predicted values so obtained were used as an instrument in the legislative majority regressions. All data were obtained from

TABLE 2. Summary Statistics

Variable	Mean	Standard Deviation	Coefficient of Variation
HMAJ	75.8776	37.7666	0.498
SMAJ	27.6600	9.2728	0.335
HMPCT	68.1662	12.9747	0.190
SMPCT	69.7277	14.1039	0.202
DENS80	148.8300	220.9278	1.484
PCY81	10,129.4800	1,413.0407	0.139
HSR	2.9045	2.1971	0.756
HCS	5.9052	3.1083	0.526
SCS	2.6148	0.9839	0.376
HCOMM	18.7143	11.0830	0.592
SCOMM	14.6000	6.7582	0.463
AGENDA	3,777.0400	5,360.6225	1.419
H	111.2653	55.8259	0.502
S	39.7200	10.7229	0.270
HTERM	2.1633	0.5533	0.256
STERM	3.5200	0.8628	0.245
SESS	175.3000	135.3668	0.772
FREQ	0.8000	0.4041	0.505
CLDUM	0.4000	0.4949	1.237
HP	0.7755	0.4216	0.544
SP	0.6800	0.4712	0.693
SPLIT	0.0800	0.2740	3.425
CJTM81	5.7000	3.8132	0.669
ELCT81	0.2200	0.4185	1.902
REMOVE	0.2200	0.6481	2.946
JPAY81	55,586.5200	9,441.3667	0.170

the Council of State Governments (1984). Summary statistics are displayed in table 2.

Separate regression specifications were estimated using absolute majority size and, alternatively, majority party members as a percent of total chamber size as the dependent variable.[5] The results presented in tables 3 and 4 offer strong support for the political contracting hypothesis. Nearly all variables are of the expected sign, and most are significantly different from zero at the 5 percent level or better.

The judicial variables support the idea that interest groups trade off legislative majorities for independence of judges at the margin. Where judges

5. Representatives in Nebraska's legislature are elected on a nonpartisan ballot. We arbitrarily set majority party strength equal to 100 percent of the state's 49 legislators, but the results are not affected perceptively if Nebraska is excluded entirely from our sample.

TABLE 3.   Legislative Majority Sizes, 1983

	House		Senate	
Intercept	115.2953	115.0726	31.2344	34.9843
DENS80	−0.0433	−0.0238	−0.0200	−0.0150
	(−6.16)***	(−3.82)***	(−2.41)**	(−2.11)**
HSR	10.3150	2.8038	0.7105	0.4700
	(5.16)***	(1.72)*	(1.17)	(0.83)
CS	6.8261	5.7216	3.9433	3.7304
	(8.05)***	(7.31)***	(1.63)	(1.58)
COMM	1.1522	0.9302	0.0348	0.1075
	(6.77)***	(5.71)***	(0.15)	(0.45)
AGENDA	0.0098	0.0080	0.0034	0.0031
	(8.97)***	(8.59)***	(2.29)**	(2.11)**
SIZE	−0.0477	0.2562	0.2510	0.3391
	(−0.48)	(3.16)***	(1.00)	(1.47)
TERM	−2.7427	1.4062	6.5210	5.3588
	(−1.21)	(0.67)	(2.08)**	(1.86)*
SESS	−0.0261		−0.0101	
	(−3.01)***		(−1.28)	
FREQ		−25.5261		−6.2537
		(−6.72)***		(−1.61)
CLDUM	−13.6991	−10.9144	−8.7221	−8.2286
	(−4.60)***	(−4.10)***	(−1.77)*	(−1.76)*
PARTY	29.3308	15.3849	5.3583	3.6317
	(7.40)***	(4.62)***	(1.73)*	(1.29)
SPLIT	−67.2799	−69.2981	−20.8969	−22.8670
	(−11.24)***	(−10.97)***	(−3.09)***	(−2.83)***
CJTM81	−4.1690	−3.6244	−0.5931	−0.7294
	(−6.23)***	(−5.73)***	(−1.14)	(−1.19)
ELCT81	1.1464	4.8588	2.0296	2.7303
	(0.38)	(1.72)*	(0.77)	(1.06)
REMOVE	6.0768	3.0516	−0.1224	−0.5186
	(3.38)***	(1.71)*	(−0.07)	(−0.30)
JPAY81	−0.0025	−0.0022	−0.0010	−0.0009
	(−9.23)***	(−8.87)***	(−2.25)**	(−2.13)***
R^2	0.982	0.981	0.744	0.736
F	120.09	115.43	6.60	6.32

Note: t-statistics in parentheses; asterisks denote significance at the 1 percent (***), 5 percent (**), and 10 percent (*) levels.

are more independent, as signified by longer terms and higher salaries especially, but also by more difficulty in removal from office in a few specifications, efficient majority sizes are significantly smaller. However, our conclusions on this score are weakened by the fact that these variables are generally not significant in the senate regressions.

But, as noted above, judicial characteristics are not the only or, indeed,

TABLE 4. Legislative Majority Proportions, 1983

	House		Senate	
Intercept	166.5008	169.6868	148.2527	160.7202
DENS80	−0.0370	−0.0233	−0.0525	−0.0394
	(−4.46)***	(−2.99)***	(−3.47)***	(−2.84)***
HSR	10.0433	4.6023	2.0050	1.4011
	(4.11)***	(2.19)**	(1.73)*	(1.24)
CS	5.6728	5.0957	8.9473	8.9136
	(5.59)***	(4.87)***	(2.01)*	(2.01)*
COMM	0.9667	0.8062	−0.2007	0.0262
	(4.95)***	(3.98)***	(−0.42)	(0.05)
AGENDA	0.0086	0.0073	0.0092	0.0085
	(6.03)***	(5.09)***	(3.68)***	(3.38)***
SIZE	−0.6055	−0.3935	−1.0450	−0.8336
	(−5.02)***	(−3.66)***	(−2.29)**	(−1.91)*
TERM	−2.3310	0.6825	18.1621	15.2471
	(−0.89)	(0.26)	(3.32)***	(2.95)***
SESS	−0.0329		−0.0352	
	(−3.43)***		(−2.18)*	
FREQ		−20.6198		−18.1277
		(−4.06)***		(−2.45)**
CLDUM	−9.9027	−9.7390	−20.8440	−20.9000
	(−2.85)***	(−2.79)***	(−2.40)**	(−2.50)**
PARTY	24.6200	14.3245	14.8548	10.2591
	(5.14)***	(3.39)***	(2.49)**	(1.77)*
SPLIT	−55.0341	−57.1711	−48.8839	−55.0817
	(−7.58)***	(−6.48)***	(−3.94)***	(−3.70)***
CJTM81	−3.5245	−3.2534	−1.6467	−2.0974
	(−4.19)***	(−3.52)***	(−1.75)*	(−1.88)*
ELCT81	0.2746	4.3975	4.4590	6.9739
	(0.08)	(1.30)	(0.82)	(1.29)
REMOVE	4.9949	2.2934	−1.0391	−2.1826
	(2.53)**	(1.10)	(−0.29)	(−0.60)
JPAY81	−0.0022	−0.0020	−0.0025	−0.0024
	(−6.44)***	(−5.61)***	(−3.42)***	(−3.27)***
R^2	0.821	0.785	0.523	0.482
F	10.10	8.04	2.48	2.11

Note: t-statistics in parentheses; asterisks denote significance at the 1 percent (***), 5 percent (**), and 10 percent (*) levels.

the most important determinants of majority size. Majority sizes are larger where the two legislative chambers are more disparate, where there are more and larger standing committees, and where there is a greater demand for legislation. In addition, efficient majority sizes are smaller where monitoring costs are reduced by more spatial concentration of voters and where legislative sessions are shorter and more frequent. The estimated coefficients on chamber size suggest generally that larger majorities are more difficult to obtain in larger houses, and the party effects tend to confirm the conventional wisdom that, all else equal, Democrat majority sizes are larger because of the party's greater diversity of interests.

Overall, our model explains on the order of 80 percent of the variation in majority party sizes and 50 percent of the variation in majority party proportions across the fifty states.

A final word about causation is in order. We have causation running from less stable judges to more stable majorities. It is conceivable that this pattern could be reversed so as to run from less stable majorities to more stable judges. Our postulated pattern of causation seems reasonable since majority size is endogenous and the institutional aspects of the judiciary are largely exogenous (set in the state constitution) across states. Of course, the economic point is that both judges and legislators have an economic interest in making legislative transactions more durable.

Concluding Remarks

Our findings carry a fundamental implication. We are able to offer independent support for Stigler's (1972) observation that political competition is much like economic competition. That is, political success is not an all-or-none proposition in which winning 51 percent of legislative seats is a victory and 49 percent a defeat. Rather, the size of the optimal majority is determined in part by a benefit-cost calculus wherein the value of legislative control trades off against the margin of judicial independence and other relevant variables. In no case is there a unique or pervasive optimal majority, such as a minimum winning coalition. The size of majorities, like other economic goods, is determined by the relevant marginal costs and marginal benefits to voters/interest groups.

Our analysis of the economic value of incremental legislative majorities extends the earlier literature. Stigler and others have argued that the marginal productivity of majority control is in the form of a lower cost of enacting a legislative agenda. Our analysis stresses the economic value of majorities as an implicit contract to enforce political agreements.

REFERENCES

Anderson, Gary M., Delores T. Martin, William F. Shughart II, and Robert D. Tollison. 1986. "Behind the Veil: The Political Economy of Constitutional Change." George Mason University. Manuscript.
Congressional Quarterly. 1970 and 1980. *CQ Alamanac*. Washington, D.C.: Congressional Quarterly Inc.

Council of State Governments. 1984. *The Book of the States 1984–85*. Lexington, Ky: Council of State Governments.

Crain, W. Mark. 1979. "Cost and Output in the Legislative Firm." *Journal of Legal Studies,* June, 607–21.

Crain, W. Mark, Donald R. Leavens, and Robert D. Tollison. 1986. "Final Voting in Legislatures." *American Economic Review,* September, 833–41.

Crain, W. Mark, and Robert D. Tollison. 1979a. "Constitutional Change in an Interest-Group Perspective." *Journal of Legal Studies,* January, 165–75.

———. 1979b. "The Executive Branch in the Interest-Group Theory of Government." *Journal of Legal Studies,* June, 555–87.

———. 1980. "The Sizes of Majorities." *Southern Economic Journal,* January, 726–34.

Kau, James, and Paul Rubin. 1982. *Congressmen, Constituents and Contributors.* Boston: Martinus-Nijhoff.

Klein, Benjamin, and Keith Leffler. 1981. "The Role of Market Forces in Assuring Contractual Performance." *Journal of Political Economy,* August, 615–41.

Landes, William, and Richard A. Posner. 1975. "The Independent Judiciary in an Interest-Group Perspective." *Journal of Law and Economics,* December, 875–901.

McCormick, Robert E., and Robert D. Tollison. 1981. *Politicians, Legislation, and the Economy: An Inquiry into the Interest-Group Theory of Government.* Boston: Martinus-Nijhoff.

Peltzman, Sam. 1985. "An Economic Interpretation of the History of Congressional Voting in the Twentieth Century." *American Economic Review,* September, 656–75.

Riker, William H. 1962. *Theory of Political Coalitions.* New Haven: Yale University Press.

Scammon, Richard, ed. 1962. *America Votes 4.* Pittsburgh: University of Pittsburgh Press.

Stigler, George J. 1972. "Economic Competition and Political Competition." *Public Choice,* 91–106.

———. 1976. "The Sizes of Legislatures." *Journal of Legal Studies,* January, 17–34.

U.S., Department of Commerce, Bureau of the Census. 1981. *Statistical Abstract of the United States.* Washington, D.C.: USGPO.

Part 4
Committees and the
Organization of Legislatures

A Theory of Legislative Organization: Making the Most of Your Majority

Arleen A. Leibowitz and Robert D. Tollison

The theory of committee decision making focuses on the choices made by a single committee under various assumptions about preferences and voting procedures. This is an important problem since many choices are made by a single committee. Well-known results concerning cycling and median voter outcomes dominate this literature (Arrow 1951; Black 1958).

We seek to explain a more preliminary question: why do committees exist, and what is the optimal number and size of committees in a legislature? Our theory is based on the idea that the legislative committees are a "sample" taken from the full house and on the assumption that it is the objective of the majority party to maximize the proportion of its favored bills which are considered and passed in voting trials. We shall show that for a given percentage of votes controlled by the majority party, fewer committees with larger memberships lead to greater passage rates if the members of a party do not always vote the party line. Clearly, if members of the majority party always voted for the party platform, the majority party could win all votes in the main chamber, legislative business could be quickly dispensed with, and there would be no need for committees.

It is generally assumed that committees arise in legislatures because committee expertise is necessary to handle the bureaucracy, find out what is wanted by voters, minimize opposition, draft legislation, and so forth. Yet in England and Canada, where legislators are also confronted by complicated and technical issues, legislative committees are relied upon hardly at all and never as important voting forums (Galloway 1955). We thus seek an alternative explanation of the origin and role of committees.

We are indebted to Nils Peterson for research assistance and to M. Bruce Johnson for an especially perceptive comment on an earlier version of this essay. Phyllis Ellickson, Dennis Mueller, George Stigler, and Thomas Willett also made helpful comments on a previous draft. The usual caveat applies. Reprinted from Arleen A. Leibowitz and Robert D. Tollison, *Quarterly Journal of Economics*, 1980. Copyright © 1980 by the President and Fellows of Harvard College. Reprinted by permission of John Wiley & Sons, Inc.

Where party discipline is high and legislators vote the straight party line, any majority size will suffice in terms of voting on agenda items. There is no need for committees as voting forums (ignoring for the moment complications caused by time constraints in passing legislation). In the United States, however, there is some chance that members of the majority coalition will renege and vote with the minority on a certain number of issues. Thus, even if all votes were held in the full chamber, some of the majority's agenda would not pass.

We show that the majority leader, in order to maximize the number of his agenda items passed under these conditions, will resort to establishing committees. This is not simply because he needs committees to produce legislation, but because he needs specialized forums in which to apply his party's voting advantage.[1] The need for committees thus derives from viewing the legislature as one big committee, which, when broken up into smaller committees, will be able to review and pass more bills. If there are deviations from the party line in voting by both majority and minority members some proportion of the time, the majority leader can arrive at the optimum number of committees and optimum committee size by considering the trade-off between the size of committees and proportion of the agenda covered and passed. Even where there is straight party-line voting, committees may be used to increase the number of issues that can be considered and passed.

These introductory comments give one a simple intuitive feeling for why committees arise in a legislative setting. However, once the step to committees is made, there is a host of problems to be solved. How many committees should there be? How large should committees be? On how many committees should members serve? In this essay we develop a theory, based on viewing voting in a legislature as analogous to sampling from a binomial probability distribution, which shows how these questions can be resolved. We develop and test specific implications about aspects of legislative organization, such as number of committees and committee size as a function of such variables as size of majority, agenda size, and length of session. We also pursue and test some of the broader implications of our theory with respect to such matters as the close adherence to proportional representation on committees.

Section 1 lays out the barebones characteristics of legislative organization with which our theory is concerned. Section 2 presents our theory of legislative organization, which is based on a binomial sampling analogy, along with its testable implications. Section 3 reports the results of an empirical test of the implications of the theory concerning the optimal number of committees for the majority party. Section 4 considers several broader implications of the model that illustrate its usefulness in interpreting the design

---

1. It will be preferable to have committees and not the full chamber consider legislation if the time required for hearing legislative proposals exceeds the length of the session and if the final vote in the full chamber is costless and always seconds the committee vote.

of democratic institutions. Section 5 offers some concluding remarks on the historical development of legislative organization in England and the United States.

1. Aspects of Legislative Organization

We shall now outline the characteristics of legislatures that are important to our theory. Note that we do not seek to describe a particular legislature perfectly, but rather to sketch certain aspects of legislative organization that are employed in subsequent analysis.

(a) Majority leaders or their functional equivalents (for example, steering committees) appear in all legislatures. These individuals, in conjunction with other senior members of their party, have a great deal of power to determine committee assignments, committee size, and other facets of legislative organization.

(b) Majority leaders typically have a legislative agenda that they are interested in passing. As stated previously, we portray the majority leader's function as maximizing the proportion of his party's favored bills that are reviewed and passed in voting trials.[2]

(c) In U.S. legislatures there is not a strict adherence to the party line in voting by representatives. We thus observe the following paradox: majorities never seem to pass their whole agenda, but they typically do better than their proportion of the legislature.

(d) Not all voting is conducted in the whole house, although a disciplined majority could win all votes there. We observe committees serving as "little legislatures" (Woodrow Wilson's term), with proportional representation of parties on committees.[3] We are interested in the impact of committees on the passage rate of the majority's agenda and not in their role as specialized bodies to produce laws or to control bureaucracies. We do not deny that these aspects of committees are important; we just find that such reasons for committee specialization are complementary but not necessary to our theory.

(e) A related reason that committees exist is to economize on a legisla-

---

2. Shepsle (1975) presents a model of committee assignments in which the role of the majority leader in accommodating requests from party members is stressed. People who have a vested interest in an area are thus put on a committee. This is a useful analysis, but the choice of who goes on committees is distinct from how many committees there are and how many party members go on each committee.

3. Consider the following quotation from Niskanen (1976). "Most of the work of Congress is performed in a set of permanent functional committees. . . . In other words, no member of Congress, except under special circumstances, may submit a bill for a floor vote or undertake a major policy or program review without approval of the relevant committee" (87).

On proportional representation on committees, Jewell (1966) stresses that "the leaders usually try to preserve a party balance roughly proportionate to that in the legislature . . ." (41). We provide further discussion of this point in section 4.

tor's time in considering bills. The time of representatives not on the committee is thereby saved, while they delegate the responsibility for decision making to their colleagues on the committee. This is completely analogous to the procedure of sampling for manufacturing defects by testing a small sample of a run. If the sample is large enough, a good estimate of the defect rate can be made without testing every item. When the defect rate is low enough, it can be assumed at a given level of confidence that the defect rate in the entire run will fall within given bounds. A similar process occurs in legislatures—when the committee rejects a bill, it is assumed that the entire chamber would also reject it at a given level of confidence. Bills that pass the committee are then "tested" in the full house. For the most part, however, the chamber merely seconds the committee's vote.

2. Maximizing the Voting Advantage of the Majority Party

The majority leader is the main economic agent in our model. He seeks to maximize the number of bills favored by his party that pass in voting trials. This would be easy(ier) under straight party-line voting, but members of his coalition sometimes vote with the other side. As stressed above, we also assume that committees are used for the relevant voting trials, and the full house always ratifies the committee choice.[4]

We characterize reneging as the probability of not voting for your party's platform. Reneging occurs because we assume that each legislator decides how to vote on a *particular* issue by sampling the opinions of voters in his district. The legislator then votes the majority position from his particular sample, which he obtains by various means, such as the letters and telegrams written to him on the issue, conversations with constituents, public opinion polls, and so forth. The voters in any district are not monolithic, and although they may have elected a liberal representative and would prefer a liberal

---

4. Data given in Fenno (1973) indicate that this is not an unreasonable assumption: This does not mean, however, that a committee action is never reversed. Technically, the larger house can be viewed in our model as a larger committee, and a certain percentage of the time the smaller committees will make a mistake in sampling that the larger committee will overturn. We provide a further discussion of this point in section 4.

Also, note the following argument by Adrian (1976, 297):

The committee system in legislatures works basically the same as it does in Congress. . . . The legislative house as a whole becomes chiefly a ratifying body for the actions of the committees. Even if the house can override a committee recommendation or relieve the committee of further consideration of a bill, these things are not likely to happen, since each legislator—like each congressman—will tacitly agree to allow other legislators to be supreme in their committee areas if they will extend the same privilege to colleagues. The committee is the key group in the legislature.

position on most issues, a majority of voters may favor a conservative position on a particular issue.[5]

In fact, just as each vote is based on a sampling of opinion, each election can be considered as a sampling of opinion, subject to sampling error. All we know about a district that has elected a liberal is that on a given day a majority of the sample (the voters who turned out) voted for the liberal candidate.[6]

To facilitate the sampling analogy, we make the following simplifying assumptions. (a) Districts have not been gerrymandered within states to be homogeneous groupings of one or the other party, and each district has the same percentage of liberals (L) and conservatives (C). (b) A legislator bases his vote on a random sampling of voters' opinions on each issue. We assume that all legislators take the same size sample. The percentage of the samples that favor the liberal position is positively related to the percentage of liberals in the population and to the constant sample size. The best estimate of these percentages is the vote in the previous election. Thus, our estimates of L and C will be the percentages of liberals and conservatives in the legislature.[7]

This outline of legislative procedure can be formalized as follows. It is analogous to a binomial experiment where voting on each issue on the agenda constitutes a binomial experiment and each legislator's vote is a trial. There are four conditions that must be met to qualify this analogy as a binomial experiment. (1) There must be a fixed number of trials, that is, a fixed number of representatives voting. (2) Each trial must yield a yes or no outcome, as in the case of voting. (3) All trials must have identical probabilities of success. (4) Trials must be independent of one another.

The latter two conditions are violated where vote trading is present in legislative voting patterns. In addition to vote trading by legislators, one could argue that the different binomial experiments are related. For example, agenda items may be correlated negatively due to some overall budget constraint.

---

5. We further assume that the legislator's role is to represent public opinion, derived from samples of his district, acting as a barometer of public opinion, rather than as a "statesman," molding public opinion. Legislators, then, will be responsive to the opinions of their constituency both because of their duty to "represent" them, and also because this will increase their probability of reelection.

6. Political scientists implicitly use the sampling analogy when they analyze how such factors as inclement weather will bias the sample on a given election day.

7. We can obtain the results we want (that is, the majority votes for the majority party's position the majority of the time) either by making the assumption in the text or by using other plausible assumptions. We could assume that both majority and minority representatives vote against their own party a given percentage of the time, but less than 50 percent. Or we could assume that they decide how to vote on the basis of hearings and that the people who testify are a sample thrown up from the population at large. It does not affect our model to introduce an assumption that representatives are nonproportional to votes. Such an assumption only makes legislative proportions subject to error as proxies of the true proportions.

Since we cannot do anything about this type of problem, we assume that the outcome of the binomial experiment for any particular agenda item is independent of any other item's outcome. So the expectation of passing the whole agenda is the same as the expectation for any given item.

If the voting rule on committees is majority rule, then we can show with the binomial analogy that the probability of passing a bill is positively related to committee size. With a given percentage of the population in favor of a piece of legislation, the probability of obtaining a majority of affirmative votes in a small sample (that is, a committee) increases with the size of the committee. At the extreme the entire population could be canvassed, and any issue for which there was support by more than 50 percent of the voters would pass. With a smaller sample there is a probability of drawing a sample where issues that are supported by more than 50 percent of the population will be turned down. The cumulative binomial distribution shows, however, that this is less likely to occur, the greater the percentage of support in the population at large. Figure 1, which is derived from the cumulative binomial distribution, illustrates this point.[8]

Committee size is measured along the horizontal axis, and the percentage of majority party agenda passed is measured along the vertical axis. This is the probability of obtaining a majority (for example, at least four yes votes in a committee of seven) on any agenda item. Suppose that there is a 50-50 split in electoral proportions. The expectation of passing a bill in this case would be 50 percent, regardless of committee size. Once a majority party emerges, however, we can trace the expected relationship between committee size and percentage of agenda passed. For a 60-40 split if all committees had one member, 60 percent of the agenda will be passed. But with a committee of seven members where four votes is a majority, slightly better than 70 percent of the agenda will be passed. With a committee of nineteen more than 80 percent of the agenda will be passed. If the split is 70-30, a committee of seven will pass 87 percent of the agenda, and a committee of nineteen would pass 96 percent.

But still the question remains of why, if pass percentages vary positively with committee size for a given party proportion, would not the majority leader seek to hold all votes in the full house? This does not follow so long as each bill on the agenda requires a fixed amount of hearing time. This condition might be thought of as the not unreasonable assumption that each legislator gets to state his position on a bill. This condition allocates valuable legislative time to debating agenda items.

Where the number of bills on the agenda is larger than the available

---

8. In drawing fig. 1, we assume that votes in committees with an even number of members from each party are decided by the toss of a fair coin.

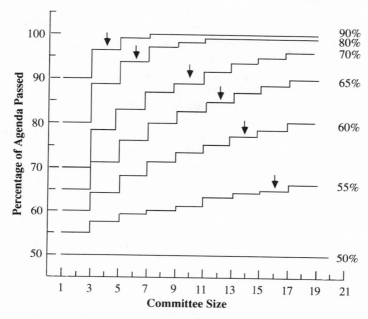

Fig. 1. Committee size and the binomial analogy

hearing time (that is, length of the legislative session), this condition becomes important.[9] Under these conditions where committee decisions are seconded by the full house at no additional cost in terms of hearing time, there is an incentive for the majority party to specialize into committees in order to increase the number of agenda items considered and passed. In this world the trade-offs depicted in figure 1 become quite important, and we now present a formal model of how these trade-offs apply in the presence of a given legislative proportion (M), session length (S), and agenda (A).

Assume that each bill on the majority party agenda requires a fixed number of hearing days (h), and the final vote of the house ratifies the committee choice. At a simple level, if $Ah \leq S$, there is no need for committees. There is no advantage to specialization in voting. If $Ah > S$, the proportion of

9. Remember that the length of the legislative session is fixed in numerous cases and in any event cannot be multiplied indefinitely, since each legislature starts anew after elections. In an age when fewer bills passed and Congress met for shorter periods (roughly prior to 1935), the available hearing time was constrained by the labor supply of the legislators. It is not, however, just the calendar that causes the majority leader to economize; at given levels of pay legislators are willing to spend only so much time at legislating.

bills considered (P_r) with no committees is $P_r = S/Ah < 1$, even if a party has no opposition. If a majority party has opposition and $S/Ah < 1$, then P_r becomes a function of both committee size and size of the majority. That is, $P_r = S/Ah\ P(n,M)$. In order to consider all the items on the agenda, the number of committees (C) would be set equal to Ah/S, but by meeting this condition, the majority party would reduce the number of legislators per committee (that is, trials in the binomial analogy). The majority leader is thus forced to trade off getting more of the agenda covered versus risking lower pass rates through smaller committee sizes. If the majority leader can have enough committees so that all bills on the agenda are considered, then $P_r = P[n(C), M(C)]$. In this case agenda size is not binding, and the pass rate is just a function of size of committee and the majority proportion, as in figure 1.

The discussion to this point assumes that all agenda items are covered and ignores trade-offs between smaller committee sizes and not covering the whole agenda. The majority leader must choose the number of committees and committee size such that the expected rate of passage of favored bills is maximized. This may or may not mean covering his full agenda. He will thus seek to optimize

$$P_r = P(n,M)SC/Ah\ ; \tag{1}$$

where

P_r = the expected pass rate for the party platform,
$P(n,M)$ = the continuous envelope for a majority of M percent connecting points that describe the probability of passing agenda items with committees of size n,
S = length of legislative session,
C = number of committees,
A = agenda, and
h = hearing time per agenda item.

The optimal number of committees can be determined by differentiating (1) with respect to the number of committees, assuming that the passage curve function P is continuous. Since $n = K\alpha/C$, where K = size of the legislature and α = average number of committees served on, we can differentiate (1) to obtain

$$\frac{dP_r}{dC} = \frac{dP}{dC}\frac{SC}{Ah} + \frac{PS}{Ah} = \frac{PS}{Ah}\left(1 - \frac{dP}{dn}\frac{n}{P}\right) = \frac{P_r}{C}(1 - \epsilon), \tag{2}$$

where ϵ = the elasticity of the passage curve with respect to committee size. So the optimum occurs where $\epsilon = 1$ along any passage curve.[10] As can be seen by examining the arrows in figure 1, which point to the segment of the envelope within which unitary elasticity occurs, this optimum point hits at smaller committee sizes the greater the majority.

Some specific implications that can be derived from the model for empirical testing follow.

(a) The greater the size of the majority, the smaller average committee size should be, and the greater the number of committees.

(b) Holding constant the size of the agenda, legislatures with longer sessions should have fewer committees.

(c) The number of committees should be negatively related to committee size.

(d) The larger the agenda, the more committees there will be for a fixed length of the legislative session.

3. Empirical Evidence from U.S. State Legislatures

Our theory can be conveniently summarized in a testable form by equation (3):

$$
\underset{agenda,\ length\ of\ session,\ size\ of\ majority).}{\overset{(-)}{number\ of\ committees} = f(\overset{(-)}{average\ committee\ size},}
$$

(3)

The expected signs are given in parentheses above the independent variables and follow from the above implications of our theory. We estimate equation (3) on data from a cross section of state senates and houses of representatives in 1974. A copy of our data is available upon request.

Although our theory was developed in terms of "conservatives" and "liberals," we are empirically constrained to use the percentage of Democrats or Republicans, whichever is in the majority. We recognize that this introduces error into the independent variables, biasing our coefficients toward zero, because some nominal Democrats are more likely to support the Republican agenda than their own, and vice versa.

Another data problem concerns the agenda variable, for which we use

---

10. Because a passage curve is the envelope of feasible points, the actual optimum will be found by inspection of the end points to determine where the percentage change in passage rate equals the percentage change in committee size.

the number of bills introduced during a legislative session as a proxy. It is not possible to determine how many of the bills actually introduced in state legislatures correspond to the majority party's platform. We removed resolutions from the measure of bills introduced to get away from bipartisan motions (for example, support for Mother's Day), but we cannot control for the strategic introduction of bills by a minority to eat up hearing time and slow down the rate at which the majority can pass its favored legislation.

We follow a bicameral approach and estimate equations for state senates and houses of representatives separately. This is consistent with related work in the area (Stigler 1976). There are no sectional distinctions made in our tests, such as ruling the Deep South or New England states outside the scope of the theory. Three adjustments were necessitated by data sources. Nebraska (which has a unicameral legislature) was dropped because data on party proportions were not available. Michigan was dropped because data on the average number of committees served on, which we need to obtain measures of average committee size, were not given in our data source. Finally, Connecticut and Maine have only joint committees. We assumed in these cases that the number of joint committees equaled the number of committees for both house and senate. For average committee size in these states, we took the maximum number of senate and house members on the average joint committee. This adjustment biases the empirical tests against finding our expected results.

We eliminated observations where there was no plurality party, because as the discussion of figure 1 indicates, the pass rate cannot be increased if there is a 50-50 split between the parties. The senate observations for New Hampshire and Wyoming were eliminated for this reason.

Finally, the regressions are weighted by the square root of the number of legislators to take account of the fact that there would be less sampling variance in larger legislatures.

Table 1 presents the results of estimating equation (3) by ordinary least squares (*t*-values are given in parentheses below the respective coefficients).

In table 1 we see that size of the *agenda* is positively related to the *number of committees*, and this coefficient is significantly different from zero at the 5 percent level in the senate equation and at the 20 percent level in the house equation. Size of majority carries the expected positive sign and is significant at the 20 percent level in the senate equation. Average committee size, while of the expected negative sign, is not very significant. Length of session is not of the expected sign, but the coefficient is not significantly different from zero at generally accepted levels. One rationale for the lack of a negative sign on the *length of session* variable is that both *length* and *number of committees* may be higher in states that have a lot of legislation to enact in a way that we are not capturing in our *agenda* variable.

TABLE 1.   Regression Results for Number of Committees, Standing and Joint, 1974

Independent Variable	Senate	House
Agenda	0.00051**	0.00036
	(2.62)	(1.45)
Days in session	0.003	0.005
	(0.61)	(0.82)
Average committee size squared	−0.008	−0.005
	(0.86)	(0.90)
Size of majority	8.87	9.52
	(1.62)	(1.22)
Intercept	6.345	10.26
R^2 (adjusted)	0.218	0.105
N	46	48

Source: Council of State Governments 1976, 60–63.
**Significant at the 5 percent level.

The empirical evidence is somewhat mixed, but given the difficulty of finding good proxies for the theoretical variables, these results suggest that the number of committees is related to the postulated factors. Additionally, it is probably true that in any given cross section it is unlikely that all units of observation are at equilibrium values since restructuring of the legislative system is not continuous.

4. The Design of Democratic Institutions

In this section we trace five somewhat broader implications of our approach to legislative organization in a democratic setting.

   1. It is generally agreed that because the number of senators per state is not related to population, the senate is a more conservative body than the house due to relatively greater representation of rural, underpopulated areas. Stigler (1976) notes that if upper houses were elected on the same basis as lower houses, the former would be a check on outcomes in the latter only in the sense of controlling for a trivial amount of sampling variability. Our theory complements this point. Even if the basis of representation were the same in both houses (for example, if the number of senators was proportional to population), the smaller size of the senate would lead to more conservative behavior. Facing the same agenda, senators must carry a larger workload in smaller committees. It is thus harder to get legislation through the senate since it takes larger majorities to pass legislation under these conditions. As the Federalists designed it, senates would be less likely to be quickly swayed by sharp changes in public opinion, not only because of the differences in method

of election and differences in length of term, but also because the senate is smaller. For example, if a party has the same size of majority and the same agenda in both houses, and if the house is larger than the Senate, committee size will be larger in the house. This will inevitably lead to the house passing more of the party's agenda than the senate. Even if the number of senators per state were proportional to population, the smaller senate will act as a brake on the house. Therefore, as the ratio of the size of the senate to the size of the house gets smaller, the bottleneck effect in the senate will become more pronounced.[11]

2. A closely related point concerns vetoes. The chief executive can be viewed in our model as a committee of size one that reflects a certain electoral proportion from the most recent election. When the legislature passes a bill that the president refuses to sign, there is essentially a difference of opinion about what the majority of the voters desire. The larger samples of legislators in the house and senate see a majority in favor, but the sample of one—the president—sees a majority opposed. Stricter voting rules are thus required to override vetoes because the chief executive may have made a mistake in sampling public opinion, and to be sure, larger majorities are needed to override.[12]

3. We note that committees bear the same relation to the whole house as the legislature bears to the whole population. If there are economies from voting on bills in committees rather than in the full house, it seems equally clear that it is not efficient to poll the whole population on every issue. The relations of legislative size and population or committee size and legislative size will not therefore be ones of strict proportionality. Since the statistical benefits from expanding a sample beyond 500 or 1,000 persons are trivial, it is not surprising that one would observe an inelastic relation between legislative size and population in a state (Stigler 1976).

4. The growth of subcommittees in the U.S. Congress in recent years can be seen as a way of reducing the effective size of committees in response to the continuing rise of Democratic majorities. The proliferation of subcommittees can also be seen as a response by party leadership to a constantly increasing agenda. In addition to making more efficient use of the party's voting advantage, party leaders may see smaller committees as a method to control productivity in team production (Alchian and Demsetz 1972). That is, the legislative activity of a majority is by virtue of the majority voting rule analogous to a team production process, and an expectation from the theory of

11. Across state governments the proportion of enactments to introductions is positively (0.49) and significantly ($t = 1.98$) related to the ratio of the size of the senate to the size of the house (based on data from Council of State Governments, 1975–76).

12. A similar point holds for legislatures. To control for sampling variability, smaller legislatures will employ more restrictive voting rules.

team production is that larger majorities will exhibit more free riding and shirking among their membership (for example, not showing up for important votes). The formation of smaller teams (that is, subcommittees), on which it is less costly for party leadership to monitor and discipline legislator behavior, can thus be seen as a method of controlling productivity in the party as its majority size increases.

     5. A final implication of the model concerns the close adherence to proportional representation on committees. For one thing, this means that in some cases minority representatives will have to work harder (that is, serve on more committees). Since the majority leader samples for committee choices from the whole house, there will be a tendency for the composition of committees to reflect the whole house.

     In table 2 we provide a test of the strictness with which party proportions on committees adhere to the overall proportions of parties in the full house.

TABLE 2. Committee Sizes and Proportions in the 93d and 94th Congresses

Committee	93d Congress				94th Congress			
	Total Size	Majority Members		*t* Value	Total Size	Majority Members		*t* Value
		Actual	Expected			Actual	Expected	
Agriculture	36	20	19.80	0.07	43	29	28.81	0.23
Appropriations	55	33	30.25	0.74	55	37	36.85	0.06
Armed Services	43	24	23.65	0.11	40	27	26.8	0.15
Banking & Currency	40	24	22.00	0.64	43	29	28.81	0.23
Budget					25	17	16.75	0.16
DC	25	14	13.75	0.10	25	17	16.75	0.16
Education & Labor	38	22	20.90	0.36	40	27	26.80	0.15
Foreign Affairs	40	22	22.00	0.64	37	25	24.79	0.11
Government Operations	41	23	22.55	0.14	43	29	28.81	0.23
House Administration	26	15	14.3	0.28	25	17	16.75	0.16
Interior	41	23	22.55	0.14	43	29	28.81	0.23
Internal Security	9	5	4.95	0.03				
Interstate	43	24	23.65	0.11	43	29	28.81	0.23
Judiciary	38	21	20.90	0.03	34	23	22.78	0.08
Merchant Marine	39	22	21.44	0.18	40	27	26.80	0.15
P.O. and C.S.	26	15	14.30	0.28	28	19	18.76	0.10
Public Works	39	23	21.45	0.50	40	27	26.80	0.15
Rules	15	10	8.25	0.91	16	11	10.72	0.15
Science	30	17	16.5	0.18	37	25	24.79	0.11
Small Business					37	25	24.79	0.11
Standards of Conduct	12	6	6.6	0.35	12	6	8.04	1.25
Veterans Affairs	26	15	14.30	0.28	28	19	18.76	0.10
Ways and Means	25	15	13.75	0.5	37	25	24.79	0.11
Chi-square				1.39				0.56

Data are presented on committee size and number of majority members for house committees in the 93rd and 94th Congresses. We tested whether the observed committee proportions differed significantly from the expected proportions, given that the 93rd Congress was 55 percent Democratic and the 94th was 67 percent Democratic. In none of the twenty-one cases for the 93rd Congress or the twenty-two cases for the 94th Congress are there any significant differences between actual and expected proportions.[13] Chi-square tests also lead to accepting that the actual distributions do not differ from proportional representation on committees.

Although the difference is not significant, there is a slightly greater than proportional representation of Democrats on the Rules Committee in the 93rd Congress. Because this is such a small and important committee, the majority leader may wish to insure his control of the voting trials on this committee at a rate greater than he could with strictly proportional representation. Referring again to figure 1, we observe that for a committee of size fifteen, proportional representation for a majority of 55 percent would provide 65 percent assurance of passage, which is below the point of unitary elasticity. Moving to a committee sharing ratio of 67 percent for a committee of fifteen assures a passage rate of 88 percent, which is beyond the point of unitary elasticity (slight overkill). For the 94th Congress, where the proportion of Democrats goes up to 67 percent, the majority proportion on the Rules Committee was exceptionally close to the expected proportion (eleven out of sixteen places). Thus, when the overall House proportion is low, the majority leader may seek overrepresentation on important and small committees in order to insure passage of agenda items by these committees.

If the purpose of a committee were merely to gather information, we would not expect to see the regularity of proportional representation on committees. Similarly, if representatives with vested interests in certain pieces of legislation were put on committees to buy them off and if vested interests were correlated with parties (farmers are Republicans and Democrats are big city boys), then we would expect to see unequal proportions by party on committees. We argue that the reason proportional representation is insisted on is that committees serve not only as specialized agencies to gather information and so forth, but also as important voting forums.

5. Concluding Remarks on England Versus the United States

Our approach to legislative organization sheds some light on one of the oldest service industries in the United States. At first glance it might seem that there

---

13. Note also that the majority proportion on committees is consistently rounded upward.

has been very little change in the technology of producing legislation since the founding of the country, except for such marginal changes as electric roll call voting. Historically, however, in contrast to typical service industries, there has been very little increase in employment in legislatures in the face of a substantial increase in the demand for legislation. We postulate that these changes have been accommodated mainly by the development of a system of standing committees in the national and state legislatures. For example, Polsby (1968) observes that

> . . . in the beginning the House relied only very slightly upon standing committees. Instead of the present-day system, where bills are introduced in great profusion and automatically shunted to one or another of the committees whose jurisdictions are set forth in the rules, the practice in the first, and early Congresses was for subjects to be debated initially in the whole House and general principles settled upon, before they were parceled out for further action. . . . (153–54)

After splitting from England, a different form of legislative organization evolved in the United States. The difference lies in the legislator's adherence to party-line voting. Where the adherence is strict (England), there is no need for specialized voting forums. Where there is "reneging" (the United States), committees allow the majority leader to maximize the percentage of the votes his party wins. As Polsby suggests, standing committees are no longer controversial in the United States, whereas in the United Kingdom they are still ". . . regarded as a threat to the cohesion of national political parties . . ." (153).

REFERENCES

Adrian, Charles R. 1976. *State and Local Governments*. New York: McGraw-Hill.
Alchian, Armen A., and Harold Demsetz. 1972. "Production, Information Costs, and Economic Organization." *American Economic Review* 42 (December): 777–95.
Arrow, Kenneth J. 1963. *Social Choice and Individual Values*. New Haven: Yale University Press.
Black, Duncan. 1968. *The Theory of Committees and Elections*. Cambridge: Cambridge University Press.
Council of State Governments. 1976. *Book of the States, 1975–76*. Lexington, Ky.: Iron Works Pike.
Fenno, Richard F., Jr. 1973. *Congressmen in Committees*. Boston: Little, Brown and Company.
Galloway, George B. 1955. *Congress and Parliament*. Washington, D.C.: National Planning Association.

Jewell, Malcom E. 1962. *The Stage Legislature*. New York: Random House.

Niskanen, William A. 1976. "Public Policy and the Political Process." In *Governmental Controls and the Free Market: The U.S. Economy in the 1970's*, ed. Svetozar Pejovich, 73–92. College Station: Texas A&M Press.

Polsby, Nelson W. 1968. "The Institutionalization of the U.S. House of Representatives." *American Political Science Review* 42 (March): 144–68.

Shepsle, Kenneth A. 1975. "Congressional Committee Assignments: Optimization Model with Institutional Constraints." *Public Choice* 22 (Summer): 55–78.

Standard Mathematical Tables. 1964. 14th ed. Cleveland: Chemical Rubber Company.

Stigler, George J. 1976. "The Sizes of Legislatures." *Journal of Legal Studies* 5 (January): 17–34.

Legislative Committees: A Filtering Theory

W. Mark Crain

Committees and Farm Teams

In U.S. legislatures most things happen in, or because of, the committee system. Committees are a ubiquitous element of American legislative organization. Yet a central function of the committee system has been largely ignored in the literature. By analogy to sports, committees are to legislatures, what farm teams are to professional baseball organizations. They are mechanisms to discover the quality of labor inputs. This essay models the committee system as a quality filtering mechanism. The main conclusion of the essay is that the committee system biases legislative outcomes away from constituent interests.

The other contribution of the essay concerns the growing economics literature on the determinants of legislator voting decisions. The analyses of economic versus ideological factors in explaining votes are seriously flawed and misleading. These studies have generally ignored the function of voting as a signal of a legislator's qualities to the leadership which, in turn, are used to filter legislators for committee assignments. Instead, the economics literature has focused exclusively on the effect of legislator voting on outside interest groups and constituents.

This essay proceeds as follows. The filtering model of the committee system is presented, and implications of the analysis for the organization of the U.S. House of Representatives are discussed in detail. Finally, proposals for reform of the committee assignment process are briefly discussed.

I am grateful to Lee Culpepper, Rich Grant, Don Leavens, Jim Miller, Mike Munger, Charles Rowley, Bob Tollison, Bruce Yandle, and Asghar Zardkoohi for comments on previous drafts. The usual caveat applies.

Committees as Quality Filters

The Conventional View of Committees: Jurisdiction over Specialized Subject Areas

The conventional view of the purpose of legislative committees is that they allow members to specialize into particular subject areas of public policy. This view is represented in the work of Shepsle (1978), Crain and Tollison (1980), and Weingast and Moran (1983). In the words of the latter:

> . . . the committee system enforces the following trade: each legislator gives up some influence over many areas of policy in return for a much greater influence over the one that, for him, counts the most. Thus, we find that representatives from farming districts dominate Agriculture committees and oversee the provision of benefits to their farm constituents. Members from urban districts dominate banking, urban, and welfare committees overseeing an array of programs that provide benefits to a host of urban constituents. And members from western states dominate interior and public lands committees that provide benefits to their constituents. (Weingast and Moran 1983, 771–72)

In this view, committee assignments are simply the result of a self-selection process, whereby members choose a committee based on the issues relevant to their constituents. The "farmers-on-farm-committees" view obscures the primary purpose of legislative committees. Each legislator necessarily responds to the interests of his/her constituents. This does not mean that the legislator's committee assignment will be improved by heeding these interests in voting. To the contrary, voting his/her constituency may guarantee that a legislator will not be assigned to a personally preferred committee.

Committee Assignments: An Investment Decision Under Uncertainty

A committee assignment is a long-term investment decision on the part of the party leadership. The decision affects the stream of future policies from the committee to which each member is assigned. Once assigned to a committee, party members remain there virtually as long as they desire. They typically rise straight up the committee leadership ladder, as quickly as the seniority system permits. Yet, with few exceptions, when non-incumbents are elected to a legislature, party leaders do not have much information about them. Party leaders have little incentive to acquire information about legislators until after they are elected.

Newly elected party members differ widely in many respects. A key difference across new members is their ability to support their leadership's policy objectives. Party leaders are unsure about the ability of a new member to conform to their preferences on policy votes. This means that most of the time, the leaders will discover this information for themselves. Naturally, the leadership wants to entrust the legislative positions of more responsibility to the more loyal party members. The party members who exhibit the least conformity to the leadership's policies will be most isolated from key positions. The incentive of the leaders to use caution in making committee assignments is straightforward.

The committee system is a filtering mechanism that identifies and sorts party members on the basis of conformity or loyalty to the party policy positions. Some committees are functionally equivalent to observation tanks, (that is, farm teams in the sports analogy), in which the qualities of party members can be identified. In other words, the committee system will contain certain committees whose members have little part in substantive policy decisions. While being held in these tanks, the new members are sorted according to their conformity characteristics, before a long-term investment in a committee assignment is made. The committee system, in this perspective, is a screening mechanism that sends the more loyal party members to the more influential committees.[1] When a loyal party member is discovered, the leadership can create an opening on a key committee for that member. Positions on key policy committees can be eliminated when the leadership cannot find a party member who is loyal enough. Members who do not conform will be left on the farm.

The Voting Record as a Signal of Loyalty to the Leadership

In order to reduce the uncertainty associated with making a committee assignment, party leaders look for signs that identify the loyalty qualities of party members. The voting record of a member is the most important sign in this regard. Voting records are signals of support and loyalty to the leadership's policy goals. A voting record acts as an implicit guarantee of the ability of a member to support "publicly" the leadership's positions, while continuing to get reelected. Obviously, some members do not have this ability. Voting in accord with the leadership would put them at odds with their own constituents and other interest groups, which would make reelection difficult or impossible.

The result of party leaders screening members according to their voting

---

1. See Stiglitz 1975 and Akerlof 1983 for background papers on the theory of screening and filtering.

records is a type of self-selection process. Note that this process is totally different than that suggested in the previous literature (for example, Shepsle 1978; Weingast and Moran 1983). Party members signal their own level of loyalty by choosing their own voting record. In the quality filtering model, there is incentive to select a voting record that signals more conformity to the leadership because it will result in a more influential committee assignment. This choice is subject to the constraint that the voting record is public and, therefore, will have an impact on the behavior of voters and interest groups. The desire to get reelected will not allow some members to conform to the leadership. Those who have disloyal qualities from the leadership's perspective will not be selected for superior committee assignments.[2]

Voting Bias: An Overinvestment in Party Loyalty

The self-selection process whereby each member signals his loyalty to the leadership with his voting record creates a distortion. Each member over-invests in a party loyalty voting record. The distortion occurs because the privately best choice for each member has an effect on the choices of other members. Technically, there is an externality because individual members do not take into account the external effect of their voting behavior. When one member chooses to vote more frequently with the leadership, the benchmark is raised for the more loyal members if they are to signal their even greater loyalty. This shifts the demands on legislators as each weighs the policy interests of his/her constituents against his/her potential to attain an influential committee assignment. The result of this shift is an overinvestment in seeking to establish voting records that signal loyalty to the leadership.

The analogy to education and the job market is useful (Riley 1979). In the absence of full information about productivity levels, education provides employers a means by which individuals of differing talents can be distinguished. If firms base job offers on educational achievements, the result is a self-selection process in which individuals signal their own productivity level. This gives each individual an incentive to spend more time in school than he/she would if productivity levels were costlessly observable. However, as each individual spends more time in school, the education needed by more productive individuals is raised if they are to signal their greater talents to employers.

In the case of voting records, as in the case of education levels, the over-investment or bias results because each individual fails to take into account the external effect of his/her privately best choice. As a party member with a

---

2. See Spence 1973 for the seminal paper in the theory of signaling. Dougan and Munger (1985) discuss Congressional voting as signals to voters. The question they raise is the relative influence of ideological versus economic interests in determining voting patterns. See also Kalt and Zupan 1985, Kau and Rubin 1982, and Peltzman 1984.

given loyalty level seeks a voting record to impress to the leadership, that party member raises the standard to which the more loyal members must conform in their respective voting records.

Summary

The power to set the number of committee positions and to make committee assignments for each party is in the hands of the legislative party leaders. This power is used to open slots on more important committees for more loyal party members. It is used to close positions on important committees for members who cannot (or do not) vote with the leadership. Since party members differ in their ability to conform, party leaders want to discover these differences before assignments to important committees are made.

Some committees are used as holding tanks, or farm teams, to give party leaders the opportunity to identify and sort party members according to their loyalty qualities. Party members who are discovered in this process to be more loyal are selected by the party leaders for service on more influential committees. Less loyal party members are filtered away from key policy committees.

The result of using voting records as a signal of loyalty is a self-selection process. In this process, party members choose their own voting records knowing they are signals of loyalty to the leaders. In selecting a voting pattern, each member has incentive to heed the policy preferences of the leaders of his/ her party in order to secure a more influential committee assignment. The external effect of this decision is to increase the standard to which other party members must conform to be loyal in the eyes of the leadership. The consequence is a bias in public policy outcomes toward the preferences of the party leadership, which comes at the expense of constituent interests. Nonconforming party members can be isolated from committees that make key policy decisions.

Some Observations on Committees in the U.S. House of Representatives

Overview of the House Committee System

The composition of committees in the U.S. House of Representatives is determined in two stages. First, the total number of committee slots that each party will receive is agreed on by the Democratic and Republican leaders.[3] Second, the party leaders independently decide on which of their members

3. An exception is the House Committee on Standards of Official Conduct (formerly known as the Ethics Committee). Its ratio of minority to majority members is dictated specifically by Rule X, clause 6(A)(2) of the Rules of the House. Another exception is that members of the House Budget committee may serve a maximum of three consecutive terms.

TABLE 1.   Democratic Steering and Policy Committee, 99th Congress (31 members)

	Appointed by Speaker (8)	Elected by Region to Serve Two Terms (12)	Ex Officio (11)

New (17)	(6) Breaux (La.)
	Collins (Ill.)
	Fazio (Calif.)[a]
	Jones, J. (Okla.)[w]
	Kennelly (Conn.)[w]
	Kanjorski (Pa.)[f]
		(7) Waxman (Calif.)
		Dicks (Wash.)[a]
		Russo (Ill.)[w]
		Brooks (Tex.)
		Hoyer (Md.)[a]
		Murtha (Pa.)[sa]
		Early (Mass.)[a]
			(4) Gephardt (Mo.)[w]
			    Chairman of Caucus
			Oakar (Ohio)
			    Secretary of Caucus
			Alexander (Ark.)[a]
			    Chief Deputy Whip
			Gray (Pa.)
			    Chairman of Budget

Continuing (14)	(2) Clay (Mo.)
	Fowler (Ga.)[w]
		(5) Sabo (Minn.)[a]
		Daschle (S.Dak.)
		Bennett (Fla.)
		Jenkins (Ga.)[sw]
		Garcia (N.Y.)
			(7) O'Neill (Mass.)
			    Speaker
			Wright (Tex.)
			    Majority Leader
			Foley (Wash.)
			    Whip
			Rostenkowski (Ill.)[w]
			    Chairman of Ways
			    and Means
			Pepper (Fla.)
			    Chairman of Rules
			Whitten (Miss.)[a]
			    Chairman of Appropri-
			    ations
			Coehlo (Calif.)
			    Chairman of Congres-
			    sional Campaign Com-
			    mittee

[f]Freshman class representative
[s]Member of Speaker's Cabinet
[a]Member of Appropriations
[w]Member of Ways and Means

will be assigned to fill each slot. Democratic committee assignments in the House are recommended by the Policy and Steering Committee (table 1) and Republican assignments are recommended by the Executive Committee of the Committee on Committees (table 2). The recommendations must be approved by majority vote in the full party caucuses and finally approved on the House floor.[4]

The party ratios vary for each House committee, and they are rarely

---

4. The only exception is that Democratic members on the Rules committee are appointed by and serve at the pleasure of the Speaker of the House.

TABLE 2.   Republican Executive Committee on Committees, 99th Congress, Representative Robert H. Michel, Chairman

State	Member
1. California	Jerry Lewis
2. New York	Frank Horton
3. Ohio	Del Latta
4. Pennsylvania	Joe McDade
5. Texas	Bill Archer
6. Illinois	Bob Michel
7. Florida	Bill Young
8. Michigan	Bill Broomfield
9. New Jersey	Jim Courter
10. Virginia	William Whitehurst
11. Indiana	John Myers
12. North Carolina	Jim Broyhill
13. 4-Member States	Eldon Rudd
14. 4-Member States	Tom Petri
15. 3-Member States	Bill Frenzel
16. 3-Member States	Floyd Spence
17. 2-Member States	Bill Dickinson
18. 2-Member States	Henson Moore
19. 1-Member States	Don Young
20. 98th Class Rep.	Dan Burton (Ind.)
21. 99th Class Rep.	Tom DeLay (Tex.)
22. Republican Whip	Trent Lott

equal to the ratio that exists between the two political parties in the full chamber. Table 3 lists the party ratios on standing committees in the U.S. House in the 99th Congress (1985–86). For example, in table 3 we find that the Democrats control 69 percent of the seats on the Rules Committee, while they control 58 percent of the seats in the full House. Table 3 also lists the number of party positions and the designations for the House standing committees. The House designates three exclusive committees, eight major committees, and eleven nonmajor committees.

Implications and Evidence of the Filtering Theory of Committees

Table 4 presents some observations on House Committee assignments in the 98th Congress (1983–84).[5] The filtering theory of the committee system

---

5. Observations on the 98th Congress are used in table 4 because it is the most recent Congress for which all the voting data were available.

TABLE 3. Standing Committee Ratios, Sizes, and Designations, U.S. House, 99th Congress

Committee Name	Democratic Members	Percentage of Total Seats	Republican Members	Committee Designation
Agriculture	26	60.5	17	Major
Appropriations	35	61.4	22	Exclusive
Armed Services	27	58.7	19	Major
Banking	28	59.6	19	Major
Budget	20	60.6	13	Nonmajor
District of Columbia	7	63.6	4	Nonmajor
Education and Labor	19	59.4	13	Major
Energy and Commerce	25	59.5	17	Major
Foreign Affairs	25	59.5	17	Major
Government Operations	23	59.0	16	Nonmajor
House Administration	12	63.2	7	Nonmajor
Interior and Insular Affiars	22	59.5	15	Nonmajor
Judiciary	21	60.0	14	Major
Merchant Marine and Fisheries	25	59.5	17	Nonmajor
Post Office and Civil Service	13	61.9	8	Nonmajor
Public Works and Transportation	27	58.7	19	Major
Rules	9	69.2	4	Exclusive
Science and Technology	24	58.5	17	Nonmajor
Small Business	25	59.5	17	Nonmajor
Standards of Official Conduct	6	50.0	6	Nonmajor
Veterans' Affairs	20	58.8	14	Nonmajor
Ways and Means	23	63.9	13	Exclusive
Total	462	60.0	308	

Note: In the full House there are 253 Democrats (58 percent) and 182 Republicans.

suggests that party members who conform in their voting habits to the party leadership will be assigned to positions on the more important committees. To accomplish this, freshman members rarely will be assigned to important committees in order to give the leadership time to observe voting records.

The second column of table 4 lists the total number Democrats added to each standing committee. The third column lists the number of nonfreshman Democrats added. For example, five Democrats were added to the Appropriations committee, an exclusive committee, and four were nonfreshmen. In the 99th Congress (1985–86), two Democrats were added to Appropriations and neither is a freshman. On the Rules Committee, another exclusive committee, only one Democrat was added in the 98th Congress. This was a freshman, which runs against the filtering concept. This freshman, however, was Representative Alan Wheat (MO), who was elected in the District held by the retiring Rules committee chairman, Richard Bolling. Bolling represented this district for 34 years, and as Rules committee chairman was a close ally of the

TABLE 4. Democratic Additions to Standing Committees, 98th Congress

Standing Committee	No. of Democratic Members Added	No. of Nonfreshman Democrats Added	Committee Chairman (ADA Rating)	Name of Nonfreshman Democrats (ADA Rating– Rank in Class)	Year Service Began (No. of Democrats with Equal Length of Service)	Percentage of Time Member Voted Same as Committee Chairman (Rank in Class)	Percentage of Time Member Voted Same as Majority Leader (Rank in Class)
Agriculture	7	0	de la Garza (25)	—	—	—	—
Appropriations	5	4	Whitten (47)	Boner (42-27th)	1979 (35)	89 (1st)	83 (2d)
				Carr[e]	1983	—	—
				Hoyer (75-17th)	1981 (26)	74 (4th)	74 (3d)
				Ratchford (90-6th)	1979 (35)	58 (20th)	58 (22d)
Armed Services	8	1	Price (75)	Bouquard (26-31st)	1975 (37)	47 (30th)	72 (3d)
Banking	9	1	St. Germain (90)	Roemer (15-25th)	1981 (26)	25 (25th)	47 (23d)
Budget	8	8	Jones, Jim (53)	Derrick (50-28th)	1975 (37)	63 (9th)	58 (18th)
				Fazio (80-16th)	1979 (35)	63 (14th)	79 (4th)
				Ferraro (75-18th)	1979 (35)	79 (4th)	68 (10th)
				Frost (70-20th)	1979 (35)	74 (5th)	79 (4th)
				Gray (89-8th)	1979 (35)	50 (31st)	44 (34th)
				Miller, Geo. (95-9th)	1975 (37)	58 (17th)	63 (7th)

(continued)

TABLE 4—*Continued*

Standing Committee	No. of Democratic Members Added	No. of Nonfreshman Democrats Added	Committee Chairman (ADA Rating)	Name of Nonfreshman Democrats (ADA Rating–Rank in Class)	Year Service Began (No. of Democrats with Equal Length of Service)	Percentage of Time Member Voted Same as Committee Chairman (Rank in Class)	Percentage of Time Member Voted Same as Majority Leader (Rank in Class)
				Williams, Pat (85-13th)	1979 (35)	58 (20th)	63 (13th)
				Wolpe (100-1st)	1979 (35)	53 (26th)	58 (22d)
District of Columbia	0	—	Dellums (85)	—	—	—	—
Education and Labor	8	1	Perkins (70)	Martinez[f] (80)	1982	—	—
Energy and Commerce	7	2	Dingell (80)	Dowdy (64)[g]	1981	79	77
				Eckart (74-19th)	1981 (26)	63 (19th)	63 (10th)
Foreign Affairs	10	2	Zablocki (70)	Kostmayer	—	—	—
				Weiss (100-1st)	1977 (32)	67 (18th)	53 (26th)
Government Operations (53)	12	0	Brooks	—	—	—	—
House Administration	4	3	Hawkins (78)	Coehlo (65-23d)	1979 (35)	72 (18th)	84 (1st)
				Foley (68-5th)	1965 (8)	76 (2d)	89 (1st)
				Oakar (82-10th)	1977 (32)	87 (1st)	63 (18th)
Interior and Insular Affairs	9	2	Udall	Kostmayer[h] (85)	—	—	—
				Patman (15-24th)	1981 (26)	20 (19th)	47 (22d)

Committee						
Judiciary	6	Rodino (100)	Schumer (100-1st)	1981 (26)	100 (1st)	56 (17th)
Merchant Marine and Fisheries	9	Jones, Walter (44)	Bennett (40-4th)	1949 (4)	44 (3d)	53 (4th)
Post Office and Civil Service	6	Ford, William (94)	Dymally (81-14th)	1981 (26)	86 (12th)	67 (7th)
			Hall, Katie[i] (100)	1982	—	—
Public Works and Transportation	14	Howard (90)	Hall, Katie[i] (100)	1982	—	—
Rules	1	Pepper (86)	—	—	—	—
Science and Technology	10	Fuqua (26)	Bouquard (26-31st)	1975 (37)	79 (4th)	72 (3d)
			Mineta (80-23d)	1975 (37)	37 (19th)	79 (1st)
			Simon (88-18th)	1975 (37)	38 (18th)	71 (4th)
Small Business	8	Mitchell (95)	—	—	—	—
Standards of Official Conduct	4	Stokes (89)	Coyne, Wm. (90-8th)	1981 (26)	84 (11th)	68 (4th)
			Dixon (85-10th)	1979 (35)	84 (10th)	63 (13th)
			Fazio (80-16th)	1979 (35)	68 (21st)	79 (4th)
			Jenkins (32-25th)	1977 (32)	44 (25th)	56 (25th)
Veterans' Affairs	11	Montgomery (5)	Florio (89-17th)	1975 (37)	5 (35th)	56 (26th)
			Martinez (80-15th)	1982 (26)	—	—

(*continued*)

TABLE 4—Continued

Standing Committee	No. of Democratic Members Added	No. of Nonfreshman Democrats Added	Committee Chairman (ADA Rating)	Name of Nonfreshman Democrats (ADA Rating–Rank in Class)	Year Service Began (No. of Democrats with Equal Length of Service)	Percentage of Time Member Voted Same as Committee Chairman (Rank in Class)	Percentage of Time Member Voted Same as Majority Leader (Rank in Class)
Ways and Means	3	3	Rostenkowski (85)	Dorgan (85-11th)	1981 (26)	80 (7th)	63 (10th)
				Flippo (21-27th)	1977 (32)	37 (27th)	67 (14th)
				Kennelly (95-4th)	1981 (26)	—	—
Total	159	41					

aThe Americans for Democratic Action (ADA) ratings are for 1982, the year preceding the committee assignments to the 98th Congress. Votes on the following twenty measures were used: H.R. 4961, H.R. 5539, H.R. 5922, H.R. 6030 (5 votes), H.R. 6211, H.R. 6214, H.R. 6863, H.R. 6892, H.R. 6957, H.R. 7355, H.C.R. 345, H.C.R. 352, H.J.R. 350, H.J.R. 521, H.J.R. 562, S.C.R. 60.

bRank in class refers to the ordinal rank of the congressman relative to other Democrats elected in the same year. For example, Congressman Boner was elected in 1979, and there was a total of thirty-five Democratic members elected in 1979 with continued service into the 98th Congress. Boner had an ADA rating of 42, the twenty-seventh highest among the thirty-five Democrats in the entering class of 1979.

cThe percentage of the time that the member voted the same way as the Committee Chairman is based on the twenty measures listed in note a above. For example, Boner voted the same way as Appropriations Committee Chairman Whitten 89 percent of the time on the twenty measures. This was the highest of the thirty-five Democrats elected in 1979.

dThe percentage is based on votes on the twenty measures listed in note a above.

eCarr was elected in 1983, although he had served previously in the House from 1975–80.

fMartinez was elected in a special election on July 13, 1982.

gDowdy was elected in a special election on July 7, 1871.

hKostmayer was elected in 1983, although he had served previously in the House from 1977 to 1980.

iHall was elected in a special election on November 2, 1982.

House Speaker. Wheat "inherited" the opening on Rules created by Bolling's retirement. In the 99th Congress, one nonfreshman Democrat was added to Rules, Representative Sala Burton (CA), following the death of Representative Gillis Long (D-LA). On the Ways and Means committee, the third exclusive committee, three Democrats were added in the 98th Congress, all nonfreshmen. Two nonfreshman members were the only Democratic additions to Ways and Means in the 99th Congress.

Table 4 provides data on the voting record for each nonfreshman Democrat who was added to a committee in the 98th Congress. The member's Americans for Democratic Action (ADA) rating and where this rating ranks in relation to the member's class are shown in the fifth column. The sixth column lists the year that member's service began and the number of Democrats with equal tenure. For example, Congressman Boner (D-TN) was elected in 1979, and there were 35 Democrats elected in 1979 with continued service through the 98th Congress. Boner had an ADA rating of 42, the twenty-seventh highest among the 35 Democrats with three terms of continuous service.

The ADA ratings data can be used to compare how closely each member aped the voting record of his/her party leaders. In the seventh column of table 4, the percent of time that the member voted the same as the committee chairman on the ADA bills is shown. Also shown in this column is the rank of this percent in the member's class. Again, using Congressman Boner's data to illustrate, he voted the same way as Appropriations Committee Chairman Whitten (D-MS) 89 percent of the time. Boner's voting record ranked as the most similar to Chairman Whitten's among all Democrats with equal tenure. The pattern implied by the filtering theory is that members added to the more important committees will tend to vote relatively more frequently with the chairman.

The last column in table 4 lists the percent of the time that each member voted the same as the Majority Leader, and the rank in relation to other Democrats with equal tenure.[6] Congressman Boner voted in accord with Majority Leader Wright (D-TX) 83 percent of the time on the ADA votes. Boner ranked second among the 35 Democrats in the Class of 1979. The data tend to support the perspective that committees are a filtering mechanism. Party members who vote relatively more frequently with the leadership are selected for membership on the key committees.

In table 5, six ratings are used to rank the twenty-two House standing committees. The filtering model of the committee system is useful in explaining these rankings.

---

6. The Majority Leader is the second highest position in the House Democratic leadership hierarchy. The Speaker is the highest position, but the Speaker rarely votes and therefore has no record to use for comparison.

TABLE 5. Six Ratings of House Standing Committees, 98th Congress

Standing Committee	Ratio of Democratic to Republican Members	Percentage of Democratic Members Added That Were Nonfreshmen	Average ADA Rating of Committee and Subcommittee Chairmen	Average ADA Rating of All Democratic Members	Uniformity of Democratic Members' ADA Rating	Average Support by Democratic Members for Bills That Failed
Agriculture	14	20	20	19	11	22
Appropriatons	17	5	10	14	10	2
Armed Services	11	15	21	22	20	20
Banking	19	16	8	8	9	8
Budget	4	1	6	10	12	7
District of Columbia	11	4	18	1	1	3
Education and Labor	4	14	9	3	3	15
Energy and Commerce	7	9	1	12	22	16
Foreign Affairs	3	11	3	7	7	9
Government Operations	8	22	16	13	19	11
House Administration	17	6	13	11	5	5
Interior and Insular Affairs	8	10	4	5	13	4

Committee						
Judiciary	4	13	12	6	14	12
Merchant Marine and Fisheries	8	17	19	20	17	14
Post Office and Civil Service	20	7	2	2	2	17
Public Works and Transportation	20	18	11	16	15	10
Rules	1	19	7	4	4	1
Science and Technology	14	8	17	17	16	19
Small Business	14	21	14	15	18	18
Standards of Official Conduct	22	2	15	18	8	13
Veterans' Affairs	11	12	22	21	21	21
Ways and Means	2	3	5	9	6	6

Data Source: LEGI-SLATE

Note: All data reflect committee assignments at the beginning of the 98th Congress.

Committees are given the same rank if the values are identical. For example, the ratio of Democratic to Republican members was 1:75 on Armed Services, Foreign Affairs, and Veterans' Affairs. All three committees are ranked as eleventh and the committee with the next lower ratio, Agriculture, is ranked fourteenth.

Americans for Democratic Action (ADA) ratings are for 1982, the year preceding the committee assignments in the 98th Congress.

Nonfreshmen are defined as members who served in the U.S. House prior to January 3, 1983.

Uniformity is measured as the standard deviation in the committee members' ADA ratings.

Support is measured as the percent of the time that committee members voted in favor of bills that finally failed in House roll call votes.

In the second column, committees are ranked according to the ratio of Democratic to Republican members. This is one indicator of the relative importance of the committees. The third column of table 5 ranks the committees by the percent of Democratic members who were added that were non-freshmen. As discussed above, the filtering model implies that the less important committees will tend to be near the bottom of this ranking. For example, Government Operations, a nonmajor committee, ranks last on this scale. No nonfreshmen were among the eight Democrats that were added (see table 4). Freshman congressmen tend to be assigned to the nonmajor committees while party leaders get to know them better.

In columns four, five, and six of table 5, committees are ranked in three ways based on the ADA ratings of Democratic committee members. In column four, the average ADA rating of the committee and subcommittee chairmen are ranked. Energy and Commerce Chairmen have the highest average ADA rating and Veterans' Affairs Chairmen have the lowest average ADA rating. In column five, committees are ranked according to the average ADA rating of all Democratic members. In this ranking, District of Columbia is highest and Armed Services is lowest. While no further statistical comparison is offered here on these two rankings, the filtering model suggests that the ADA ratings of the more important committees will tend to be closer to the ratings of the leadership.

In column six, committees are ranked according to the uniformity of the ADA ratings of the Democratic members. Uniformity is measured as the standard deviation in the committee members' ADA ratings. The filtering process will tend to create relatively more uniformity on the more important committees. The less important committees will be less uniform because those members representing diverse political viewpoints will tend to be confined there.

Finally, the last column in table 5 ranks committees based on how the Democratic members voted on bills that finally failed in House roll calls. Support for bills that failed is measured as the percent of the time that Democratic committee members voted in favor of these bills. This measure is useful because it examines only those cases in which the party leaders needed each member's support. In contrast, votes on issues that passed the floor are less telling because a member's support might not have been needed for passage. In cases where passage is likely, the party leaders are more lenient in releasing members to vote their constituencies. On issues that failed, however, party leaders are less merciful in letting members off the hook. Each vote is needed to win.

The filtering model implies that members more loyal to the leadership will sit on the more important committees. Party leaders need to be made certain of the support of these committees. This suggests that members of the more important committees will vote more frequently in favor of bills that fail. This principle can be stated in the reverse. Party defections are more likely to occur by members on the less important committees. By this ranking, Rules is the most reliable committee in supporting the leadership, which is consistent with its designated status as an exclusive committee.

Summary

Several observations about the committee system in the U.S. House are presented in this section. The data reveal several patterns that indicate the fundamental importance of the filtering function of House committees.

Eleven House committees are designated as nonmajor committees. From the filtering model perspective, these committees serve a major function. Most freshmen are assigned to these committees, which, the theory suggests, gives the leadership the opportunity to observe their voting habits. More extreme elements of the party, in relation to the leadership, tend to be confined to these committees.

There are eight major and three exclusive committees in the House. Members assigned to these committees tend to have voting records aligned more closely with party leaders, as the filtering model suggests. Finally, the party members on the more important committees exhibit more uniformity in their voting patterns. Greater political diversity tends to be limited to the members of the least influential House committees.

Concluding Remarks on Proposals for Reforming the Committee Assignment Process

The analysis points out a specific target for reform. The power of legislative party leaders to open and shut positions on committees every two years is the source of the bias in voting patterns. The proposed reform is to replace this power with a nondiscretionary rule.

Some proposals have been put forward to specify rules for proportional representation of parties on committees. Indeed, legislation of this type has been introduced into the U.S. House.[7] Proportional representation on committees, however, would not eliminate the problem of voting bias that is stressed in this essay. Party leaders could achieve proportional representation, yet continue to expand or contract the total committee size. For a simple example, to achieve a 60 percent majority, a committee could have twelve D's and eight R's, or nine D's and six R's. A rule of proportional representation

---

7. For example, see the discussion and proposal by Representative Dannemeyer (Dannemeyer 1985).

would not prevent members of a given party from being excluded by their leaders from key committees.

The main aspect of any reform measure is to protect the opportunity of a member to serve on an important committee. This requires that the number of positions for each party be determined outside of the control of the party leaders in each new legislative term. In other words, the rule for reforming committee ratios needs to specify a formula for determining total committee sizes as well.

REFERENCES

Akerlof, G. A. 1983. "Loyalty Filters." *Amer. Econ. Rev.*, March, 54–65.
"Committees and Subcommittees of the 99th Congress." 1985. *Congressional Quarterly Special Report*, April 27.
Crain, W. M., and R. D. Tollison. 1980. "The Sizes of Majorities." *Southern Econ. J.*, no. 46 (January): 726–34.
Dannemeyer, W. E. 1985. "Reforming Committee Ratios." *Congressional Record*, January 3, E103–5.
Dougan, W. R., and M. C. Munger. 1985. "The Rationality of Ideology." Clemson University and University of Texas. Mimeograph.
Kalt, J. P., and M. A. Zupan. 1984. "Capture and Ideology in the Theory of Politics." *Amer. Econ. Rev.*, June, 279–300.
Kau, J. B., and P. B. Rubin. 1982. *Congressmen, Constituents, and Contributors.* Boston: Martinus-Nijhoff.
Leibowitz, A. A., and R. D. Tollison. 1980. "A Theory of Legislative Organization: Making the Most of Your Majority." *Quarterly Journ. of Econ.*, March, 261–77.
Peltzman, S. 1984. "Constituent Interest and Congressional Voting." *Journ. of Law and Econ.*, April, 181–210.
Riley, J. G. 1979. "Testing the Educational Screening Hypothesis." *Journ. of Political Econ.* 87, no. 5, pt. 2, S227–52.
Shepsle, K. A. 1978. *The Giant Jigsaw Puzzle: Democratic Committee Assignments in the Modern House.* Chicago: University of Chicago Press.
Spence, M. A. 1973. "Job Market Signaling." *Quarterly Journ. of Econ.*, May, 356–74.
Stiglitz, J. E. 1975. "The Theory of Screening, Education and the Distribution of Income." *Amer. Econ. Rev.*, June, 283–300.
Weingast, B. R., and M. J. Moran. 1983. "Bureaucratic Discretion on Congressional Control? Regulatory Policymaking by the Federal Trade Commission." *Journ. of Political Econ.* 91, no. 5, 765–800.

Part 5
Districts and Redistricting

On the Structure and Stability of Political Markets

W. Mark Crain

This essay considers an organizational aspect of the market in which votes are exchanged for public-policy outcomes. Specifically, the effect on the stability and behavior of politicians of assigning the demanders of political products (that is, voters) to geographic areas is addressed. Implications concerning the locational division of the "buyers" of political outcomes for collusive efforts by existing officeholders to restrict entry are drawn and tested empirically. The results indicate in effect that the institutional structure of political markets is an important aspect of the degree of rivalry among existing politicians and hence the extent of entry by nonincumbent candidates.

> . . . Machine politicians are simply the response to the fact that the electoral mass is incapable of action other than a stampede, and they constitute an attempt to regulate political competition exactly similar to the corresponding practices of a trade association.[1]
> . . . The conditions appropriate to the assignment of customers will exist in certain industries, and in particular geographical division of the market has often been employed.[2]

Introduction

The policy outcomes supplied through the public sector are demanded ex ante by individuals with their votes. No legal recourse exists for fraudulent product

I wish to thank James Buchanan, Thomas Deaton, Harold Elder, Thomas Saving, and Gordon Tullock for helpful suggestions and encouragement as this paper progressed. The critical comments offered by Roger Sherman, George Stigler, and Robert Tollison warrant special acknowledgment. I am responsible, of course, for any shortcomings that remain. Reprinted from the *Journal of Political Economy* 85, no. 4 (August 1977): 829–42. Copyright © 1977 by the University of Chicago. All rights reserved.

1. Schumpeter 1962, 283.
2. Stigler 1964, 48.

advertising or even for failure of product delivery. Presumably, though no "meeting of minds" has occurred, exchange has.

This essay considers an organizational aspect of the market in which votes are exchanged for public-policy outcomes. Specifically, the effect on the stability and behavior of the "sellers" of assigning the "buyers" of political products to geographic areas is addressed. A conceptual framework for approaching the transactional arrangements between politicians and voters is presented. The following section then draws some observable implications concerning the effects of geographical division of political representation and provides some empirical testing of these implications.

The Functioning of Fixed Political-Market Shares

The rivalry among candidates to obtain (temporary) property rights to operate the production apparatus of the public sector will, in the ideal, serve to protect the sovereignty of individual voter-consumers.[3] The degree of electoral competition among political entrepreneurs will of course vary and as such will result in departures from the ideal. Limitations on this periodic rivalry, then, can be expected to effect the desired functioning of the vote–public policy exchange market.[4]

There are numerous reasons to suspect that the existing "firms" (that is, incumbent officeholders) in the public-policy industry have incentives to restrict electoral competition. For example, the ability to extract rents from those seeking favorable regulatory legislation would be a function of a politician's expected tenure in office. In addition, the politician's influence over legislative outcomes is generally related to his length of service (because of seniority rules) and hence his ability to back promised political benefits to specific interest groups.[5] However, in a more immediate sense, each incumbent candidate for reelection to public office has an incentive to restrict electoral competition due to the presence of scale economies. The scale advantage present at the *individual*-election level is the majority voting rule which provides that the political entrepreneur who obtains half the customers can drive

---

3. For two early discussions of the "ideal" democratic structure, see Schumpeter (1962) and Becker (1958). An important implication of their definitional conception is that "the ultimate aim of each political party may be to acquire political power, but in equilibrium no one, including those 'in power,' has any political power" (Becker 1958, 107).

4. The role played by rivalry in the mitigation of monopoly power in the organization of private economic activity has been discussed by Demsetz (1968, 1971), Telser (1969, 1971), and Crain and Ekelund (1976).

5. For an empirical investigation of the relationship between the seniority power of congressional delegations to the U.S. House and influence over policy outcomes, see Crain and Tollison (1977) and the related study by Stigler (1976).

the other entrepreneur (or entrepreneurs) out of the market.[6] That is, while at an aggregated level elections may not be "won or lost," at an individual level they are.[7] Thus each incumbent entrepreneur has incentives to inhibit electoral rivalry for votes, both from within the field of existing firms and from potential (that is, nonincumbent) entrants.

The rivalry among candidates to obtain (temporary) property rights to operate the representative apparatus takes place within geographic boundaries. The extent of these boundaries establishes the market area in which the exchange between voters and political candidates occurs. In other words, the periodic renewal of political contracts has a spatial element, just as in the case of exchange in private markets. Moreover, again as in the case of the latter, we might expect the degree of electoral competition to be affected by this spatial dimension of exchange.

The locational division of the "buyers" of political outcomes serves a two-fold function in the public-policy industry that may mutually benefit the existing "suppliers." First, it reduces considerably the gains from competition among the existing politicians. That is, the geographical assignment of voters to districts where residency requirements are in effect insures that no political entrepreneur can attract "customers" away from other incumbent politicians. Thus the competition for votes typically will not involve a rivalry between established firms but, rather, between an established firm and a potential (that is, nonincumbent) entrant. The importance of this function of geographic representation, then, is that it virtually prevents an existing political entrepreneur from going into an election contest without an incumbent's advantage. Without such prevention the precampaign advantage of an incumbent would be muted should he have to face another incumbent also seeking reelection.[8] This first aspect is quite analogous to collusive practices in the

---

6. This is essentially the argument made by Tullock (1965); see esp. 464–65.

7. Stigler (1972) has stressed that at an aggregated level (for example, all the seats in a legislative assembly) elections may not be "won or lost" in the sense that the control of a certain percentage of the total number of seats is important even if it is less than a majority. Stigler argues, in effect, that such outcomes can be characterized as more usefully varying continuously because the control of fewer than 50 percent of legislative seats does not exclude an entire coalition or political party (as a group) from influencing public-policy outcomes. For some empirical verification of this argument, see Palda (1975) and Crain and Tollison (1976). The important point to note here is the distinction between election outcomes at the "industry" or aggregated level versus the "firm" or individual level.

8. For some empirical estimates of the preelection advantage attributable to "incumbency," see Welch (1974, 1976) and Jacobson (1976). It should be noted that some incentives would still be present for incumbent politicians to engage in indirect election rivalry. In addition to interparty conflicts, there is some evidence that the competition for campaign funds is not limited to the "home district"; see Dawson and Zinser (1976). The point to be stressed with regard to the present argument is that legally segmented voting districts eliminate direct competition among incumbent candidates for the same voters.

organization of economic activity, where "fixing market shares is probably the most effective of all means of combating secret price reductions" among the existing firms (Stigler 1964, 44).

A second function served by the geographical segmentation of political markets concerns its role in the establishment of barriers to potential entrants. Since incumbents are not likely to be threatened directly in the vote market by other incumbents (as discussed above), incentive to prevent an existing officeholder from enhancing his preelection advantage is reduced. That is, internal resistance to an existing entrepreneur using the powers of incumbency to strengthen his electability is slight because the other officeholders in the industry have the same incentive. For example, to the extent that an incumbent's popularity is increased by his productivity in passing legislative outcomes desirable to a majority of his constituents, his logrolling feats will be enhanced by the fact that other incumbents stand to gain from vote trading for the same reason. In another light, all incumbents are likely to keep the rules of the game in their favor since they only run against nonincumbents.

Legal or constitutional restrictions are generally flexible enough to facilitate collusive measures on the part of incumbents (for example, the passage of legislation providing expense accounts for travel to the home district or for mailing privileges, direct access to media coverage, influence over appointed positions, which can affect positively their brand-name capital and ability to command electoral support.[9] Even in a flexible legal setting, such collusive activity would surely tend to falter if incumbents were subjected to direct rivalry in the vote market. Given the possibility of direct competition, some incentives would be present to hinder the preelection advantage of an incumbent who addresses vote markets that overlap with other incumbents. In effect, incumbents would restrain the subsidized campaign activity of their colleagues, which could reduce further the costs (including information costs) of voting. In sum, the second function served by the locational division of vote markets is to reduce incentive to inhibit use of incumbency powers to establish or strengthen barriers to potential nonincumbent entrants.

The structure of political markets (for example, strict geographic representation versus at-large representation) has perhaps a more profound influence on the conduct of incumbent politicians in establishing entry barriers than do legal or constitutional regulations. In fact many of the latter might be deemed unnecessary under political settings conducive to direct incumbent competition in the vote market.

This discussion has stressed the gains from cooperative behavior among

---

9. Recently several writers have argued convincingly that the passage of laws limiting the contributions and expenditures of campaign funds are nothing but incumbent protection acts. See esp. Kazman (1976) and Jacobson (1976). For an additional discussion of barriers to entry in politics, see Tullock (1965).

the entire class of incumbent politicians in restricting electoral competition. To the extent that affiliations with political parties are for a similar purpose (that is, to coordinate the reelection of incumbent members of the party), it is still in the interest of incumbent officeholders of opposing parties to support agreements which are mutually beneficial in this respect.[10] As mentioned above (n. 9), limitations on campaign expenditures may provide an example of such an agreement.

Willingness to collude across party lines, however, is a function of the particular institutional determinants regarding the relative differential in the political power wielded by an officeholder who is a member of the majority party (for example, committee chairmanships, influence over selecting positions in the executive branch, etc.). That is, at an individual-choice level, incentive to form protective agreements with incumbent members of another party will decline, the greater are the potential gains (or losses) in altering the party proportions of the legislature. In other words, the relevant trade-off facing an incumbent would be to seek to restrict electoral rivalry everywhere (that is, to protect his own "seat" as well as those of the other incumbents) versus risking the entry of nonincumbent candidates in hopes of obtaining incremental proportions for his own party and thus incremental personal influence over legislative outcomes. Of course the "minimax" decision of a risk-averse incumbent would be to collude with other incumbents—regardless of his party's proportion—which suggests that reversals in the majority party controlling the legislative assembly would not be frequent. Party loyalty among the existing entrepreneurs in the public-policy industry, in this perspective, is dependent on individual wealth-maximizing behavior and indeed may be more apparent than real.

Implications and Empirical Findings

Several observable implications follow directly from the operational functions of geographic representation discussed in the preceding section. This section develops some of these implications into falsifiable hypotheses and offers some empirical testing. Implications regarding the impact of specific political-market structures are difficult to test at the federal level, since all direct vote competition for the same office (for example, the Senate or the House of Representatives) generally occurs on a strictly geographic basis. Though the two U.S. senators from each state do confront a common geographic vote

---

10. A dictum by the late Sam Rayburn is illustrative of this role of political parties: "All incumbent Democrats who are in trouble get maximum assistance first. If anything is left over it will then be parcelled out to the best advantage" (quoted in Redding 1958, 303). Indeed the party apparatus may be more important in restricting nonincumbent entry at the level of primary elections than in general elections.

market, they stagger their confrontations temporally. At the state level, however, a fruitful empirical setting is provided since different institutional arrangements concerning representative apportionment are in effect across the different states. Hence, in this latter setting, comparisons can be made across states to isolate different effects where alternative methods of apportionment are employed.

Before presenting the hypotheses, perhaps it is useful to clarify briefly two methodological points. First, the objective is to detect observable consequences attributable to the alternative institutional arrangements as they exist across states. This is in contrast to the separate, albeit interesting, issue of explaining the existing pattern of apportionment institutions. In other words, no theory is offered to explain the underlying differences in districting procedures as they have developed historically. Rather, the approach here is to take the set of institutional rules as given and examine outcomes of these differences. Perhaps the best analogy is to those studies that examine pricing or output behavior in different types of private-market structures, as opposed to studies that seek to explain why some industries tend to be competitively organized while others tend to be monopolized.

The second point concerns the nature of the dependent variable employed in this section. The relative stability of incumbent politicians, as measured by turnover, is examined in various state legislatures in order to obtain evidence on the degree of rivalry among candidates. That is, more stability implies less turnover and thus lower levels of entry by new candidates. While one might argue that high levels of new entry into politics will tend to result in a closer correspondence between ex ante voter preferences and ex post political outcomes, alternative arguments surely could be made to support the benefits of less frequent turnover.[11] This is to say that the effect in principle of free entry is not so clear in a political setting. There are some clear advantages to retaining existing political entrepreneurs because of such factors as start-up costs and on-the-job-training costs and some evidence about the past (versus promised) performance of a candidate.

The electoral process, moreover, can be viewed as an instrument to induce officeholders to behave in accordance with constituency preferences, and thus an increased probability of nonreelection would tend to weaken this effect. That is, in the extreme, if no incumbent were ever reelected, his behavior in the current term would be utterly irresponsible.[12] Hence entry of

---

11. For some discussion of this nature, see Rosenthal (1974, esp. 166–85). Similarly, Crane and Watts contend that the high rate of turnover on standing committees that results from a general legislative instability "reduces the level of performance of both the lawmaking and watchdog functions of a representative body" (1968, 49).

12. For a further theoretical discussion of the impact of succession rights on the behavior of officeholders, see Barro (1973).

new entrepreneurs in a political setting (necessarily implying a turnover of existing suppliers) is not good per se. Frequent (involuntary) turnover does provide an indication, however, of the height of the entry barriers and the degree to which they are surmountable and therefore offers some evidence as to the overall extent of rivalry among candidates. That is, a high rate of turnover suggests that those incumbents who remain in office are likely to do so more because of closeness to voter preferences than because of institutional restrictions on voter alternatives.

We now turn to the presentation of each of the specific hypotheses to be tested empirically.

One fundamental difference in the apportionment procedures across states is the particular agency delegated authority to establish the representative districts. In 1974, for example, six different apportioning agencies held this legal authority across states. Among these agencies were the incumbent members of state legislatures.[13] If the incumbent members of state legislatures have incentives to retain their current property rights, we would expect that when given the power of apportionment they would employ this authority accordingly. Thus one broad implication is that we should observe differences between the stability of the legislative houses in those states allowing the legislature to apportion and in those opting for other apportionment agencies.

A second noticeable difference in apportionment practices across states is the use of multimember districting. This aspect of state representative government renders a rather straightforward implication concerning the specific functioning of fixed political-market shares. In effect, some states employ apportionment rules that place more than one representative in a single district, and in such cases incumbents face incumbents in reelection rivalry. This is in contrast to the arrangements in other states which practice strict geographic representation, that is, one representative per district. Thus a second implication is that we should observe differences between the stability of incumbents in those states where the segmentation of voters does not permit "cheating" or trying to attract voters away from other incumbents (that is, in states employing strict geographic representatives) and in those states where incumbent vote markets overlap (that is, in those states employing multimember districting).[14]

---

13. The six categories of agencies that were responsible for state legislative apportionments in 1974 were boards of commission, federal courts, state courts, governors, legislatures, and secretaries of state (Council of State Governments 1976).

14. Incumbents in the latter type of apportionment setting would still have the same incentives to agree to restrain direct vote rivalry, but in the absence of districting barriers such agreements would be harder to sustain due to the individual gains from cheating. Residency requirements might be viewed more accurately as simply raising the costs of vote rivalry. That is, it is conceivable that a candidate might pay the relocation costs of citizens in exchange for

A third implication to be addressed empirically is the relationship between the number of voters ("potential customers") and the extent of electoral rivalry among political candidates. To draw once more on an analogy from the organization of economic activity, we would expect rivalry for votes (in those institutional settings where this is possible) to be more intense as the number of potential voters per representative decreases. This is because the potential gains from "cheating" or attracting votes away from another incumbent are offset by the potential losses in votes to other incumbents who similarly seek new customers. Moreover, as size of the vote market increases, a given level of cheating activity will achieve smaller percentage increases in vote shares. Thus, where the number of voters in a district is relatively large, we would expect less incentive to "cheat" or to engage in vote rivalry among existing political entrepreneurs.[15]

The fourth and final implication to be investigated in the present essay concerns the influence of political parties on incumbent rivalry. Following the discussion in the previous section, the extent of cooperative effort among all incumbents to restrict entry will depend on the subjective evaluation of each existing officeholder as to the relative gains from altering party proportions versus enhancing the overall stability of the existing seats. The expected benefits from altering party proportions would be a function of the probability that enough candidates are elected from the same party as well as the particular institutional setting, which I discussed previously. Thus the preelection closeness of party percentages might be expected to affect this underlying decision calculus. That is, given a level of benefits attributable to being an incumbent member of the majority party, the fewer seats that are necessary to affect this majority, the higher are the expected returns to rivalry. The logic here in effect is that less collusive activity will occur (implying more entry) as the preelection party proportions approach equality.

The empirical model employed to examine these four implications across states is specified thus:

$$N_i = \beta_0 + \beta_1 A_i + \beta_2 MD_i + \beta_3 ID_i + \beta_4 D_i + \beta_5 V_i + \beta_6 S_i$$
$$+ \beta_7 DP_i + \beta_8 EP_i + \mu_i; \tag{1}$$

promises of future votes. However, the chances of a candidate being double-crossed are high due to ballot secrecy, thus reducing the expected benefits from incurring such transactional costs. This does, however, raise a further implication (which is not tested in the present work) that, where residency requirements for voting are less stringent, geographically divided markets would be less effective in prohibiting candidate rivalry.

15. For a discussion of this point in the context of industrial organization, see Stigler (1964, esp. 49).

where

N_i = the number of nonincumbent candidates elected to the legislative body in state i in 1974,[16]

A_i = a dummy variable denoting the apportioning agency in state i, where $A_i = 0$ if the legislature has this power and $A_i = 1$ otherwise,

D_i = a dummy variable denoting the presence of multimember districting in the legislative body in 1974, where $D_i = 1$ if state i has *any* multimember districts and $D_i = 0$ otherwise;

M_i = the number of multimember districts in the legislative body of state i in 1974;

MD_i = an interaction term, the product of M_i and D_i;

I_i = the average number of incumbents per district running for reelection in state i in 1974;

ID_i = an interaction term, the product of I_i and D_i;

V_i = the average size of a single legislative district in state i in 1974;

S_i = the total number of seats in the legislative body of state i that were up for election in 1974;

P_i = the ratio of the number of seats held by the minority party to those held by the majority party in the legislative body of state i prior to the 1974 elections;

DP_i = an interaction term, the product of P_i and D_i, that differs from zero in those states *with* multimember districts;

EP_i = an interaction term that differs from zero in those states *without* multimember districts (that is, the product of P_i and E_i where $E_i = 1$ in states without multimember districts and $E_i = 0$ elsewhere); and

μ_i = a random-disturbance term.

The eight coefficients defined in equation (1) are estimated from 1974 data on the variables across states in the United States (Council of State Governments 1976). The upper and lower houses of the state legislative assemblies are examined separately since the relevant incentives on the part of incumbent

---

16. If the size of a legislative assembly increased in this election, the election of a nonincumbent candidate would not necessarily imply the defeat of an incumbent. There were three cases in 1974 in which the size of legislatures changed, but in two of these instances the number of seats was reduced. The size of the lower houses in Alabama and Maryland was reduced by one seat each to 105 and 141, respectively. The size of the upper house in Maryland, however, was expanded by four seats to 47. Thus Maryland is excluded from the regression sample for the upper houses.

officeholders are operative primarily with regard to competition for a specific type of office. The results for state lower houses are presented in equation (2) and for state upper houses in equation (3):[17]

$$N_i^L = 11.88 + 7.85A_i + 0.37MD_i + 13.11ID_i - 46.67D_i$$
$$(1.52)\quad(1.81)\quad\ \ (1.98)\qquad\quad(2.62)\qquad(-2.58)$$

$$- 0.62 \times 10^{-4}V_i + 0.29S_i - 6.95DP_i - 13.39EP_i$$
$$(-1.67)\qquad\qquad\ \ (6.43)\ \ (-0.62)\qquad\ (-1.37)$$

$$R^2 = 0.7828, \qquad F_{(8,39)} = 17.57, \qquad N\text{ observed} = 48; \qquad (2)$$

$$N_i^U = -0.72 + 5.59A_i + 0.70MD_i + 2.38ID_i - 16.66D_i$$
$$(-0.25)\quad(3.27)\quad\ \ (1.63)\qquad\quad(0.72)\qquad(-1.16)$$

$$- 0.10 \times 10^{-4}V_i + 0.38S_i + 9.81DP_i + 0.10EP_i$$
$$(-1.43)\qquad\qquad\ \ (6.06)\quad\ (1.25)\qquad\ (0.03)$$

$$R^2 = 0.5943, \qquad F_{(8,34)} = 11.19, \qquad N\text{ observed} = 43. \qquad (3)$$

The results for each independent variable are discussed and interpreted in turn.

The estimated coefficient for the variable denoting the agency responsible for legislative apportionment, A_i, is positive for both the state lower and upper houses, occurring at a 0.05 level of significance in the former case and at a 0.005 level in the latter. The positive sign of this coefficient indicates that the level of nonincumbent entry is lower in those states where the incumbent members of the respective legislative body are delegated apportionment rights. The magnitude of this effect is greater in the case of state lower houses, where the power to apportion (on average) saves the political lives of over seven incumbents per election; while in the case of state upper houses apportionment rights in the hands of incumbents, ceteris paribus, reduces the average turnover per election by about five seats. This initial finding supports the specific contention that, when endowed with legal authority to establish legislative boundaries, incumbents can effectively do so in accordance with their self-interest, for example, to secure an extended tenure in office.

The extent of multimember districting can be varied in two ways, both of which have been accounted for in the empirical specification in equation (1).

---

17. Louisiana and Mississippi were omitted from equation (2) because no elections were held in the lower houses of these states in 1974. Likewise, six states did not hold elections for upper-house members in 1974. The states omitted from equation (3) for this reason were Kansas, Louisiana, Minnesota, Mississippi, South Carolina, and Virginia. In addition, Maryland was omitted from equation (3) for the reason cited in n. 16.

One, states can vary the number of districts that are to be served by more than one representative; or two, they can vary the number of representatives per district.[18] The variable accounting for the former method in equation (1) is MD_i, and for the latter, ID_i. The MD_i and ID_i are interaction variables with D_i, while D_i is included independently in equation (1) as strictly a shift parameter. The independent effect estimated for the number of multimember districts, MD_i, is positive in both equations above. For the lower houses (equation [2]), the estimated coefficient is significant at the 0.05 level; and for the upper houses (equation [3]) it is significant at the 0.10 level. These two estimated results suggest that the entry of new politicians is affected marginally by the number of multimember districts in the legislative body. More specifically, this result can be interpreted to imply that the more incumbents placed into direct vote rivalry, the easier it is for nonincumbent candidates to enter. As discussed previously, the logic here is that collusive agreements to restrain electoral competition will be harder to maintain because of the potential gains in votes, and the ability of incumbents to construct entry barriers will be inhibited.[19]

Similarly, as the number of incumbents per multimember district, ID_i, increases, the entry of new members into state lower houses increases. The estimated coefficient for this effect in state lower houses is positive and significant at the 0.01 level. This variable does not appear at a statistically significant level for state upper houses (equation [3]), which is perhaps due to its rather narrow range in the case of the latter. The sign is, however, also positive. Again, this variable is interpreted here to imply that the increased difficulty of incumbent collusion due to larger numbers per district will result in relatively lower entry barriers and hence the observed pattern of more new entrants.

The coefficient estimated for V_i indicates the relationship between average size of the districts in the legislative body and the rate at which new

---

18. For some further discussion and empirical investigation of institutional factors as variables in the political structure of state governments, see Crain (1976).

19. Rivalry among incumbent politicians also has direct external benefits to nonincumbents seeking election in such situations, because the impact of one incumbent challenging the credibility and past performance of another would carry a larger impact than identical attacks by a nonincumbent challenger. That is, the advantages from brand-name capital and accessibility to media coverage mentioned above can be employed "positively" or "negatively," with roughly similar results. Further, incumbent competition could tend to reduce generally the costs to voters of acquiring information about the past performance of officeholders seeking reelection. Such information would be generated during the rivalry because each incumbent potentially could expand his market share of votes by exposing the foibles of his colleagues. This effect is in addition to the indirect effects discussed in this paper concerning the collective ability of incumbents to create or heighten entry barriers to nonincumbent challengers. These barriers should be generally lower in those settings where incumbents share common vote markets.

political entrepreneurs entered in the 1974 elections. The effect estimated in both equations is negative and significant at the 0.10 level for both types of state legislative assemblies. As suggested earlier in this section, this negative relationship is precisely what we would expect, by analogy to the organization of economic activity. That is, as the total size of the vote market increases, we would expect the gains from "cheating" (that is, seeking to pull voters away from the support base of other incumbent representatives) to be offset by the potential losses from other candidates behaving likewise. As the average size of the constituencies increases, we would expect less incumbent rivalry and thus the observed result of fewer new entrants. Moreover, the shift parameter, D_i, which controls for differences in the two types of districting procedures, is negative and significant in the equation for state lower houses. This negative all-or-none shift indicates that the size of the vote market affects a smaller "base" level of entry in those lower houses with multimember districts.

As one would suspect, the rate of entry by new politicians is positively and significantly related to the number of seats up for election. This variable is included in the specification of equation (1) primarily to control for the absolute size of legislative bodies in examining the other somewhat more interesting institutional variables concerning the structure of political markets. However, one would expect the extent of collusive behavior to diminish as group size increases.

Finally, the results estimated for the effects of the preelection party proportions on nonincumbent entry are somewhat mixed. The estimated coefficient for DP_i (which is nonzero for those legislatures where multimember districting is employed) is positive and significant at the 0.15 level for state upper houses but does not differ significantly from zero when estimated for state lower houses. The estimated coefficient for EP_i (the variable which is nonzero in states employing single-member districting) is negative and significant at the 0.10 level for the lower legislative bodies, but this estimate for the upper houses does not differ significantly from zero.

Thus, following the logic of the decision calculus posited above, in state upper houses we do observe a detectable tendency for incumbents to opt for potential gains from altering party proportions. Only in this case do we find consistent increases in the level of nonincumbent entry as the preelection party proportions approach equality. This suggests that differences in the value of incumbency issuing from institutional aspects of majority control are more pronounced in the case of state upper houses. However, this appears to hold only in state upper houses that employ multimember districting, perhaps because the opportunity cost of partisan rivalry is higher in single-member districting states. That is, if the structural advantages to incumbent cooperation are greater under strict geographic representation, we would expect less partisan rivalry when incumbents calculate the relevant trade-offs in this latter type of setting.

These results concerning the role of political parties in state legislatures indicate that partisan loyalties in general are not sufficient to generate electoral competition among the existing set of incumbents. The institutional structure of vote markets seems to influence party aspects of candidate behavior and, in a broader sense, party control over representatives. While the empirical findings on the role of parties are admittedly tentative, this economic formulation of the choice problem facing incumbent officeholders may provide a useful framework for further investigation.

Concluding Comments

This essay has relied heavily on theories from the organization of economic activity in developing a conceptual framework for viewing the transactional arrangements between politicians and voters. Specifically, I examined the relationships between some aspects of representative apportionment and the conduct of the suppliers of political products. Implications regarding the effects of alternative apportionment institutions on the degree of rivalry among incumbent political entrepreneurs were tested in the context of state governments. The empirical findings supported the contention that the structure of political markets influences the stability of existing members of state legislative bodies and hence the entry of new members.

The role of political parties on electoral competition was examined in the context of a simple wealth-maximizing choice problem. The results in this case indicated that the expected benefits from partisan rivalry were also dependent upon the particular institutional structures employed in state legislative assemblies. In most settings, the gains from party rivalry did not appear to offset the gains from cooperative effort among all incumbents.

The level of new entry has further implications concerning the correspondence between voter preferences and outcomes in the public-policy industry. In addition, the use by over half the states of political-market structures that function to foster incumbent rivalry may provide some clues as to the vast disparity which persists between the rate of nonincumbent entry into politics at the state level as opposed to the federal level.[20]

REFERENCES

Barro, Robert J. 1973. "The Control of Politicians: An Economic Model." *Public Choice* 14 (Spring): 19–42.
Becker, Gary S. 1958. "Competition and Democracy." *J. Law and Econ.* 1 (October): 105–9.

---

20. For an extensive overview of the tenure patterns in the U.S. House of Representatives, see Polsby (1968).

Council of State Governments. 1976. *Book of the States, 1976–1977*. Lexington, Ky.: Iron Works Pike.

Crain, W. Mark. 1976. "Institutional Factors and the Production of Political Products." Virginia Polytechnic Institute and State University. Mimeo.

Crain, W. Mark, and R. B. Ekelund. 1976. "Chadwick and Demsetz on Competition and Regulation." *J. Law and Econ.* 19 (April): 149–62.

Crain, W. Mark, and R. D. Tollison. 1976. "Campaign Expenditures and Political Competition." *J. Law and Econ.* 19 (April): 177–88.

———. 1977. "The Influence of Representation on Public Policy." *J. Legal Studies* 6 (June): 355–61.

Crane, W. W., and M. W. Watts. 1968. *State Legislative Systems*. Englewood Cliffs, N.J.: Prentice-Hall.

Dawson, P. A., and J. E. Zinser. 1976. "Political Finance and Participation in Congressional Elections." *Annals American Acad. Polit. and Soc. Sci.* 425 (May): 59–73.

Demsetz, Harold. 1968. "Why Regulate Utilities?" *J. Law and Econ.* 11 (April): 55–65.

———. 1971. "On the Regulation of Industry: A Reply." *J.P.E.* 79, no. 2 (March): 356–63.

Jacobson, G. 1976. "Practical Consequences of Campaign Finance Reform: An Incumbent Protection Act?" *Public Policy* 24 (Winter): 1–32.

Kazman, S. 1976. "The Economics of the 1974 Federal Election Campaign Act Amendments." *Buffalo Law Rev.* 25, no. 2, 519–43.

Palda, K. S. 1975. "The Effect of Expenditure on Political Success." *J. Law and Econ.* 28 (December): 745–71.

Polsby, N. W. 1968. "The Institutionalization of the U.S. House of Representatives." *American Polit. Sci. Rev.* 62, no. 144, 144–68.

Redding, J. 1958. *Inside the Democratic Party*. Indianapolis: Bobbs-Merrill.

Rosenthal, A. 1974. *Legislative Performance in the States*. New York: Free Press.

Schumpeter, J. A. 1962. *Capitalism, Socialism, and Democracy*. 3d ed. New York: Harper & Row.

Stigler, George J. 1964. "A Theory of Oligopoly." *J.P.E.* 72, no. 1 (February): 44–61.

———. 1972. "Economic Competition and Political Competition." *Public Choice* 13 (Fall): 91–106.

———. 1976. "The Sizes of Legislatures." *J. Legal Studies* 5 (January): 17–34.

Telser, Lester G. 1969. "On the Regulation of Industry: A Note." *J.P.E.* 77, no. 6 (November/December): 937–52.

———. 1971. "On the Regulation of Industry: Rejoinder." *J.P.E.* 79, no. 2 (March/April): 364–65.

Tullock, Gordon. 1965. "Entry Barriers into Politics." *A.E.R.* 55 (May): 458–66.

Welch, W. P. 1974. "The Economics of Campaign Funds." *Public Choice* 20 (Winter): 83–97.

———. 1976. "The Effectiveness of Expenditures in State Legislative Races." *American Polit. Q.* 4 (July): 333–56.

An Economic Theory of Redistricting

W. Mark Crain, Margaret N. Davis, and
Robert D. Tollison

Introduction

In 1964, the Supreme Court ruled that states were required to draw legislative district lines for seats in both houses of a bicameral legislature such that each district within a state would contain the same number of constituents.[1] The constraint that population equality places on the redistricting process leaves many opportunities for drawing legislative boundaries for specific political advantage. In this essay, we examine the institutions and incentives surrounding the redistricting process post *Baker versus Carr,* especially in the 1970s. In a nutshell, the redistricting process is controlled by two different agencies. In some states, the state legislature draws its district boundaries. In other states, the court(s) draws the boundaries for the state legislature. The crux of our analysis of redistricting in this essay is that these two agencies face different cost-reward structures in the task of reapportionment.

We develop a testable theory of the different apportionment incentives faced by the two agencies and test this theory on data for U.S. states.

Redistricting: Theory

The Legislature as the Apportioning Agent

Consider the redistricting problem from the point of view of the incentive of the individual legislator, specifically, an incumbent majority party member. Through redistricting, the majority party member can increase his political

---

1. Reynolds v. Sims, 377 U.S. 533 (1964). In an earlier case, Baker v. Carr, 369 U.S. 186 (1962), the Supreme Court ruled for the first time that apportionment issues are justifiable under the Equal Protection Clause of the Fourteenth Amendment. In Wesberry v. Sanders, 376 U.S. 1 (1963), the Supreme Court required that U.S. Congressional district lines must be drawn on the basis of "one person, one vote."

influence in two ways. He can enhance his reelection prospects by moving more potential supporters within his district. This means that he will not have to campaign as hard to be reelected and that he is more likely to survive the next several elections to reach a higher seniority position in the legislature, for example, a committee chairmanship. Second, redistricting can be used to increase the party's legislative majority by shifting party voters out of previously held districts and into targeted districts. While an increase in the party's proportion comes at the expense of reelection security for previously held seats, it is also a way for an incumbent to increase his/her political influence. A larger legislative majority increases the likelihood that the party will win key floor votes. Thus, those issues and legislation that are favored by the current majority party would be more likely to become law. A larger party majority also means that majority legislator productivity will rise because each member can specialize into more legislative subject areas (Crain and Tollison 1980). Finally, a larger party majority leads to increased proportionate representation on standing committees (Leibowitz and Tollison 1980). These factors suggest that there can be advantages to both the party as a whole and to the individual party member from increasing its proportion in the legislature. Incumbent legislators would support a redistricting plan to enhance their political influence with this sort of possibility frontier in mind.

Given that the size of the house remains constant and one-man-one-vote prevails, if districts are drawn to insure the reelection of all incumbents, the party ratio in the house will remain unchanged. As the majority party seeks control of new seats through redistricting, it becomes necessary to delete voters aligned with the party from one district and to add them to a targeted district. Initially, this will hurt the reelection possibilities of those minority party members who currently hold the targeted seats. But there is a limit to the number of supporters that the majority party can shuffle out of minority-controlled districts: so if the majority party desires large gains in the number of seats it holds, it becomes necessary to draw voters out of an incumbent majority party member's district as well. That is, skewing voters so that the majority party holds a slim majority in many districts decreases the security of incumbent majority party legislators.

Figure 1 illustrates the negative relationship between the number of new seats the majority party seeks to control by redistricting and the security of incumbents. This nonlinear relationship results from the fact that as the majority party seeks to control more districts, it decreases at an increasing rate the security of its own incumbents who will experience smaller margins of victory. Faced with this trade-off between party gains and incumbent reelection security, an incumbent legislator will choose a redistricting plan such as plan A, which maximizes political influence.

The redistricting plan that emerges from this process could be damaging

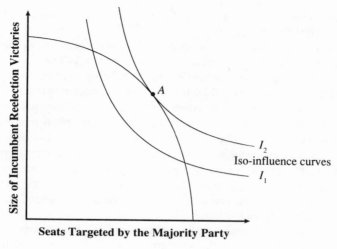

Fig. 1

to long-term political contracts, especially in the case where majority party control changes hands.[2] This could happen if the majority party, seeking a large gain in seats, spreads its supporters so thinly across districts that it ends up with a net loss of seats. Another possibility occurs when an incumbent must vote on alternative redistricting plans. When faced with the choice between giving up majority party status or a higher risk of losing his reelection bid, an incumbent is more likely to favor the former. Being reduced to minority party status is preferable to defeat for most legislators. A change in party control of a legislative house can create difficulties for interest groups in a state. It means, for example, that all leadership positions and committee chairmanships change. In effect, most of the internal mechanisms that parties employ to stabilize long-term legislative policies would be dealt a severe blow. During the 1970s, party reversals occurred in state legislative houses in about 20 percent of the elections immediately following redistricting.

The Court as the Apportioning Agent

Consider the incentive of the courts when they act as the apportioning agent. First, it is expected that the courts will be relatively less sensitive to the reelection prospects of incumbent majority legislators. At the relevant margin, then, we would predict that court plans would be less likely than legislative plans to result in majority party reversals. Again, a casual look at the 1970s redistricting results is interesting if only suggestive. Of the nineteen state

---

2. See Landes and Posner 1975 for a discussion of long-term political contracts.

upper and lower houses where majority party reversals occurred, only three were redistricted by the courts.

Another distinction about the courts serving as apportioning agents is that the outcome of the judicial decision-making process is more likely to be influenced by the value of maintaining past legislative contracts with interest groups (Landes and Posner 1975). Interest groups, concerned that the current legislative majority will pass a redistricting plan that reverses party control, can be expected to devote resources to challenging such plans in court. This means that the courts are likely to end up ruling on redistricting plans when the value of preserving long-term political contracts with interest groups is high, and that in all likelihood, the plan finally approved by the courts will favor the relevant interest groups. This implication follows so long as there is a positive relationship between the resources devoted to a case and the probability of winning (Tullock 1980).

In sum, we are approaching the redistricting issue from the standpoint of the incentive structure facing the alternative apportioning agents. In figure 2, the court will prefer a redistricting plan such as B, which favors the size of the majority party proportion, while an incumbent legislator will choose a plan such as A, which better protects his/her seat.

Redistricting: Empirical Results

Test 1: Majority Sizes

The economic theory of reapportionment, as outlined above, implies that majority party leaders will trade off the size of their majority in exchange for more security for party members. Stated succinctly, when legislative districts are set by majority party leaders, majority sizes will be smaller than when they are set by the judiciary. This hypothesis can be tested at the state level because not all state reapportionment plans are set by legislatures. In the 1970s, roughly 20 percent of state reapportionment plans were drawn by the courts. (See table 1 for the court-apportioned states.) When districts are drawn by independent judges, there is no incentive to exchange majority sizes for the enhancement of incumbent security. In terms of a testable null hypothesis, there should be no systematic difference in the sizes of legislative majorities in states where plans are drawn by the court versus states where plans are drawn by the legislature.

The model to test this proposition is specified in equation (1).

$$size\ of\ majority\ party\ = f(apportionment\ agent,\ size\ of\ majority \\ party\ prior\ to\ election,\ term\ length, \\ multimember\ districts,\ Democratic\ or \\ Republican\ majority)\ . \qquad (1)$$

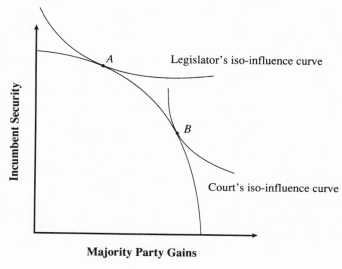

Majority Party Gains

Fig. 2

The dependent variable is the post-election difference between the percentage of seats held by the majority party and 50 percent. It measures the net strength of the post-election majority. If two parties controlled 50 percent of the seats, the dependent variable is equal to zero; if one party controls all of the seats, it equals 50 percent.

The *Apportionment Agent* variable distinguishes between reapportion-

TABLE 1.   States Where the Courts Were the Apportionment Agency in 1970s

State Upper and Lower House	State Upper House Only
Alabama	Kansas
Alaska	Virginia
California	
Iowa	
Maine	
Michigan	
Minnesota	
North Dakota	
Oregon	
Washington	

ment plans that are drawn by the legislature and plans that are drawn by the courts. The variable is equal to one for court-drawn plans, and equal to zero for legislatively drawn plans. The theory predicts a positive coefficient on *Apportionment Agent;* court-drawn plans should result in larger majorities than legislatively drawn plans.

The other variables are control variables. The *Size of the Majority Party Prior to the Election* is a proxy for the level of party competition in a state. It is computed, as above, by subtracting 50 percent from the percentage of seats held by the majority party. The variable controls for two effects. First, it controls for the ease with which the majority can pass its redistricting plan in the legislature. Larger majorities presumably face a lower cost of passage. Second, the variable controls for the extent of partisanship in the polity, for example, the southern states in the U.S. tend to be dominated by large Democratic majorities. Less competitive legislatures will result in larger post-redistricting majorities, all else equal. A positive sign is expected on this variable. The variable that controls for a Democratic or Republican majority is included for the same reason. This variable is equal to one if the Democrats were the majority party, and equal to zero if the Republicans were the majority party.

The *Term Length* variable measures the number of years a legislator in a given house serves during a single term. With longer terms there are more incumbent retirements in any given election. The majority party size will be more volatile with longer terms because open seat races turn over to the other party more often. This suggests that the post-election majority size would be smaller, that is, a negative sign on *Term Length*.

The *Multimember District* variable is equal to one if the redistricting plan creates any multimember districts, and equal to zero otherwise. This variable is included because it affects incumbent security. More incumbents are re-elected when they run in districts that are single member (Crain 1977). This suggests that party leaders face different opportunity sets for exchanging incumbent security for majority sizes with versus without multimember districts. The expectation is that when multimember districts are employed, incumbents are less secure, ceteris paribus. Hence, party leaders will have to pay a higher price in terms of sacrificing additional majority seats. A positive sign is expected on this variable.

The data used to estimate equation (1) are for state governments in the United States.[3] Separate models are estimated using OLS for state senates and state houses of representatives, and the results are presented in tables 2 and 3. Two sets of results are provided in each table. The first column examines the first election held after 1970 redistricting. The second column provides the

---

3. The data are available from the authors on request.

TABLE 2. Determinants of the Size of the Majority Party in State Senates Before and After 1970s Redistricting

Explanatory Variable	Election Held After Redistricting Coefficients	Election Held Before Redistricting Coefficients
Intercept	8.449	−1.573
	(1.96)*	(−0.36)
Apportionment Agent	4.349	−0.296
	(1.96)*	(−0.14)
Term Length	−2.980	−0.150
	(−2.39)*	(−0.12)
Multimember Districts	−2.468	2.958
	(−1.11)***	(1.40)**
Size of Majority Party Prior to Election	0.777	0.817
	(10.85)*	(10.57)*
Majority Party Before Election	8.431	6.022
	(3.87)*	(2.83)*
R^2	0.80	0.81
F (5,41)	33.107	35.67
Number of Observations	47	47

Note: *t*-values are in parentheses. Minnesota and Nebraska are excluded from the data because they did not denominate their legislatures in partisan terms. West Virginia is excluded because it failed to adopt a new plan for the Senate prior to 1975.
*significant at the 5 percent level
**significant at the 20 percent level
***significant at the 30 percent level

results for the last election prior to redistricting.[4] "Before" versus "after" equations are examined separately in order to compare what happened over time. The before-redistricting results provide a benchmark for evaluating the after-redistricting results. For example, if it is found that after redistricting there are differences between the two types of states, the relevant question is whether these differences existed before redistricting.

The results for state senates in table 2 strongly support the theory. Overall, the model explains 80 percent of the variation in senate majority sizes across states after redistricting. The *Apportionment Agent* variable is positive and significant at the 5 percent level. Legislatively drawn reapportionment plans result in smaller majorities when compared to plans drawn by the judiciary. This supports the implication that party leaders sacrifice the size of

---

4. Because not all states redistricted during the same year and not all states held elections during the same year, the dependent variable is based on the election results from the first election after the 1970 redistricting was completed. The independent variables are based on the data gathered for the last legislative session prior to the election examined by the dependent variable. The year redistricting was completed for each observation is provided in the data appendix.

the majority in exchange for increased incumbent security. The coefficient suggests that majority sizes are over 4 percent smaller on average in the legislatively apportioned state senates. The *Term Length* variable is negative and significant at the 5 percent level. In the case of state senates, shorter terms result in large majorities. The *Multimember District* variable is negative and marginally significant. This suggests that larger majorities are being sacrificed in multimember district settings because incumbents are even more vulnerable to begin with as compared to incumbents representing single-member districts. The size and the identity of the majority party variables are both positive and highly significant. These variables control for the level of party competition in a state.

As noted above, these results are subject to the following criticism. Even though the majority sizes are significantly smaller after reapportionment in the legislatively apportioned states, the majority sizes might have been smaller in these states before redistricting. In order to address this issue, the model was estimated using data on the last election before the 1970 redistricting.[5] These results are presented in the second column of table 2 for state senates. All of the variables are defined exactly as before, with one exception. The *Apportionment Agent* variable retains the same values for each state as it has in the post-redistricting estimation. That is, the procedure checks for any difference, prior to redistricting, between the two types of states. The results of estimating the equation using the preredistricting data reinforce the earlier interpretation. To summarize, in the preredistricting equation, the *Apportionment Agent* variable is not significant. While no systematic difference existed between the two groups of states prior to redistricting, there was a significant difference afterward.

The results from estimating equation (1) on data for state houses of representatives are provided in table 3. The first column contains the after-redistricting results, and the second column contains the preredistricting results. The model explains 66 percent of the variation in majority sizes after redistricting and 42 percent of the variation before redistricting. The findings on the *Apportionment Agent* variable again support the theory. In the before-redistricting equation, the *Apportionment Agent* variable is negative and weakly significant. States that had their districts drawn by the legislature had, on average, 8 percent larger majorities prior to redistricting. In the after-redistricting equation, the *Apportionment Agent* variable is not significant. There is no difference in majority sizes between the two groups of states post redistricting. In other words, prior to redistricting, majority sizes were about 8 percent larger in those states where the districts were redrawn by the legislatures. After redistricting, majority sizes in these states were reduced to the

---

5. See Landes 1968 and Crain 1980 for previous applications of this technique.

level of other states. The results for the other variables are generally consistent with the previous discussion.

Test 2: Legislative Turnover

A second and related hypothesis suggested by the analysis is that incumbent legislators will be less vulnerable under redistricting plans that are drawn by the legislature. The analysis implies that increased incumbent security is the benefit that party leaders seek to obtain at the expense of a smaller-sized majority. The empirical model used to examine this implication of the analysis is specified in equation (2).

$$\text{Challenger Wins} = f(\textit{Apportionment Agent, Term Length, Size} \\ \textit{of Majority Party Prior to Election,} \\ \textit{Multimember Districts, Bicameralism,} \\ \textit{Number of Seats Up for Reelection}) \, . \quad (2)$$

TABLE 3. Determinants of the Size of the Majority Party in State Lower Houses: Before and After 1970s Redistricting

Explanatory Variable	Election Held After Redistricting Coefficients	Election Held Before Redistricting Coefficients
Intercept	−9.240	29.240
	(−1.53)**	(2.43)*
Apportionment Agent	−1.669	−8.054
	(−0.59)	(−1.23)***
Term Length	6.422	5.115
	(2.15)*	(0.80)
Multimember Districts	2.780	2.880
	(0.99)	(0.43)
Size of Majority Party Prior to Election	0.554	0.613
	(3.96)*	(2.34)*
Majority Party Before Election	4.158	−28.364
	(1.23)***	(−4.24)*
R^2	0.66	0.41
$F\,(5,42)$	16.512	5.616
Number of Observations	48	48

Note: t-values are in parentheses. Minnesota and Nebraska are excluded from the data because they did not denominate their legislatures in partisan terms.

*significant at the 5 percent level
**significant at the 15 percent level
***significant at the 30 percent level

The dependent variable, *Challenger Wins*, measures the number of non-incumbents elected. More challenger wins means that incumbents are more vulnerable. The *Apportionment Agent, Term Length, Multimember Districts,* and the *Size of the Majority Party Prior to Election* variables are all defined as before.

When districts are drawn by the courts, the *Apportionment Agent* variable is equal to one; it is equal to zero when plans are drawn by the legislature. In the former case, the number of challenger wins is expected to increase. Legislatively drawn districts are more likely to favor incumbents. A positive coefficient on *Apportionment Agent* is expected.

The effect of the *Term Length* variable is unpredictable, a priori. On the one hand, longer terms stagger the years of expiration of incumbent terms, thus reducing turnover. On the other hand, with longer term lengths the value of legislator specialization is greater, which gives party leaders more incentive to expand the majority team size. A byproduct of this expansion is to make incumbents more vulnerable.

The *Size of the Majority Party Prior to Election* is again included to control for the degree of partisan rivalry in a state. The *Multimember Districts* variable is included, as before, because earlier studies find that more challengers win in states that use multimember districts (Crain 1977). The *Bicameralism* variable is the number of seats in the state senate divided by the number of seats in the state house. It is expected that as the two chambers become more equal in size, there will be more consensus about the redistricting plan. That is, when the sizes of the chambers are the same, the underlying bases of representation are more equal.[6] Finally, the model controls for the number of seats up for election, which is self-explanatory.

Equation (2) is estimated using OLS on four separate data sets. The results for state senates are shown in table 4. The model explains 67 percent of the variation in challenger wins in the post-redistricting sample, and 49 percent of the variation in the preredistricting sample. The main variable of interest to the analysis is *Apportionment Agent*. The theory suggests that legislatively drawn plans will result in lower incumbent turnover than court-drawn plans. This is what the evidence shows. The *Apportionment Agent* coefficient is positive and highly significant in the post-redistricting equation. On average, about three more state senate challengers win under court-drawn plans. This is roughly 7 percent of the average state senate size.

The result here is subject to the same objection previously raised. If turnover were already higher before redistricting in the court-drawn states, then the observed differences could not be attributed to the alternative appor-

---

6. See Buchanan and Tullock 1962, Crain 1979, and McCormick and Tollison 1981.

tionment agents. To test for this criticism, the model was estimated on the preredistricting elections. Using the same methodology that was discussed for tables 2 and 3 previously, it is found that prior to the 1970 redistricting there was no significant difference in the number of successful challengers between the two types of states. In other words, there were no systematic differences in turnover prior to redistricting, yet after redistricting, turnover was significantly lower in the states that had legislatively drawn districts. This adds support to the theory that incumbents are safer when redistricting plans are set by the legislature.

Examining the results for state lower houses, presented in table 5, the same pattern emerges. Overall, the empirical model explains approximately 80 percent of the variation in challenger wins across state lower houses. The *Apportionment Agent* variable is positive and, in this case, significant at the 15 percent level. House turnover is lower where districts are established by

TABLE 4. Determinants of the Number of Challenger Wins in State Senates: Before and After 1970s Redistricting

Explanatory Variable	Election Held After Redistricting Coefficients	Election Held Before Redistricting Coefficients
Intercept	−4.790	−0.018
	(−1.38)**	(−0.00)
Apportionment Agent	2.874	1.107
	(2.33)*	(0.79)
Term Length	0.840	0.558
	(1.11)***	(0.63)
Size of Majority Party	0.021	0.035
Prior to Election	(0.47)	(0.70)
Multimember Districts	−0.254	1.868
	(−0.20)	(1.37)**
Bicameralism	5.230	−1.280
	(0.98)	(−0.24)
Number of Seats Up	0.379	0.268
for Election	(7.65)*	(4.72)*
R^2	0.67	0.49
$F (6,40)$	13.832	6.39
Number of Observations	47	47

Note: *t*-values are in parentheses. Minnesota and Nebraska are excluded from the data because they did not denominate their legislatures in partisan terms. West Virginia is excluded because it failed to adopt a new plan for the Senate prior to 1975.
  *significant at the 5 percent level
  **significant at the 20 percent level
  ***significant at the 30 percent level

TABLE 5.   Determinants of the Number of Challenger Wins in State Lower Houses: Before and After 1970s Redistricting

Explanatory Variable	Election Held After Redistricting Coefficients	Election Held Before Redistricting Coefficients
Intercept	−2.557	−18.270
	(−0.14)	(−1.45)***
Apportionment Agent	6.070	0.038
	(1.51)**	(0.01)
Term Length	8.830	9.478
	(2.12)*	(3.29)*
Size of Majority Party	−0.057	0.031
Prior to Election	(−0.35)	(0.28)
Multimember Districts	4.443	4.431
	(1.17)***	(1.52)**
Bicameralism	−27.802	1.242
	(−1.05)***	(0.07)
Number of Seats Up	0.317	0.264
for Election	(5.97)*	(7.10)*
R^2	0.78	0.81
F (6,41)	24.783	29.139
Number of Observations	48	48

Note: t-values are in parentheses. Minnesota and Nebraska are excluded from the data because they did not denominate their legislatures in partisan terms.

*significant at the 5 percent level

**significant at the 15 percent level

***significant at the 30 percent level

the legislature. On average, about six fewer challengers, or 5 percent of the average lower house size, are elected in these states. Once again, no significant difference in turnover is found between the two types of states prior to the 1970 redistricting (see the second column in table 5). The results on the control variables in tables 4 and 5 are mixed. The *Term Length* variable is positive and significant in both the senate and house estimations. Where term lengths are longer, the productivity gains from legislator specialization are greater. This gives party leaders more incentive to increase majority size. The cost of these larger majorities is observed through increased turnover. Not surprisingly, the *Number of Seats Up for Reelection* variable is positive and significant. Nothing noteworthy can be said about the findings for the *Size of the Majority Party Prior to the Election* or the *Bicameralism* variables. The coefficients on the *Multimember Districts* variable are positive and significant in three of the four regressions. This agrees with earlier studies that conclude single-member districts are analogous to a market-sharing cartel arrangement that discourages political entry.

Conclusion

Legislators prefer redistricting plans that protect their seats. This concern for incumbent security can lead legislatures, particularly those where the majority party's advantage is small, to adopt plans that jeopardize the long-term durability of special-interest legislation. However, when the courts become involved in the redistricting process, they are relatively insensitive to incumbent vulnerability, and enact plans assuring the continued success of past legislative agreements. In other words, the courts are more likely than incumbent legislators to choose redistricting plans that maintain or increase the size of the majority party. Moreover, the result is not independent of the preredistricting size of the majority party. The largest gains are for majorities in states that have slim preredistricting margins, and where redistricting is done by the courts. After redistricting, past special-interest contracts will be much more secure than before redistricting.

As the courts continue their recent pattern of becoming more involved with the redistricting process, our analysis predicts that existing majority party control of state houses will continue to strengthen. This will lead to increased stability in state legislatures concerning the party in command. Special-interest groups will be content that their past legislative contracts will remain intact, and new legislative agreements will have even longer-term durability. In sum, returning the control of redistricting to the hands of the legislature, which is more concerned with incumbent security than with the security of special-interest legislation, may lead to less partisan gerrymandering than currently exists.

REFERENCES

Buchanan, James M., and Gordon Tullock. 1962. *The Calculus of Consent*. Ann Arbor: University of Michigan Press.

Council of State Governments. 1964–76. *Book of the States*. Lexington, Ky.: Council of State Governments. Various issues.

———. 1967, 1969, 1971, and 1973. *State Election Officials and the Legislatures*. Lexington, Ky.: Council of State Governments. Various Issues.

———. 1973. *Reapportionment in the Seventies*. Lexington, Ky.: Council of State Governments.

Crain, W. Mark. 1977. "On the Structure and Stability of Political Markets." *Journal of Political Economy*, August, 829–42.

———. "Cost and Output in the Legislative Firm." *Journal of Legal Studies*, June, 607–21.

———. 1980. *Vehicle Safety Inspection System: How Effective?* Washington, D.C.: American Enterprise Institute.

Crain, W. Mark, and Robert D. Tollison. 1976. "Campaign Expenditures and Political Competition." *Journal of Law and Economics,* April, 177–88.

_____. 1979a. "Constitutional Change in an Interest-Group Perspective." *Journal of Legal Studies,* January, 165–75.

_____. 1979b. "The Executive Branch in the Interest-Group Theory of Government." *Journal of Legal Studies,* June, 555–67.

_____. 1980. "The Sizes of Majorities." *Southern Economic Journal,* January, 726–34.

Landes, William M. 1968. "The Economics of Fair Employment Laws." *Journal of Political Economy,* July/August, 507–52.

Landes, William M., and Richard A. Posner. 1975. "The Independent Judiciary in an Interest-Group Perspective." *Journal of Law and Economics,* December, 875–901.

Leibowitz, Arleen, and Robert D. Tollison. 1980. "A Theory of Legislative Organization." *Quarterly Journal of Economics,* March, 261–77.

Tullock, Gordon. 1980. *Trials on Trial.* New York: Columbia University Press.

U.S. Department of Commerce, Bureau of the Census. 1975. *Statistical Abstract of the United States: 1975.* Washington, D.C.: U.S. Government Printing Office.

Part 6
Bureaucrats and Regulators

Bureaucratic Structure and Congressional Control

*William F. Shughart II, Robert D. Tollison, and
Brian L. Goff*

Introduction

The interest-group theory of government (Stigler 1971, Peltzman 1976) has
generated many valuable insights into the workings of the political process.
Although subsequent contributions to this literature (McCormick and Tollison
1981, for example) have extended the theory to explain a wide variety of
government behavior, the discussion of the political process tends to be carried out in terms of the interests of groups within the polity that either demand
or supply wealth, and those of the legislators who broker the transfers. Little
attention is normally paid to the bureaucratic organizations that enforce and,
indeed, often set the policies that the legislature wishes to put in place.
Exceptions are Eckert (1973), who discussed how the personal incentives of
regulators affect policy choices as a function of the costs and rewards of
serving on a commission versus being employed by a bureaucratic agency,
and Ehrlich and Posner (1974), who offered a useful theoretical exposition
based on legislative decision costs of why Congress delegates programs and
policies to bureaus. In addition, Faith, Leavens, and Tollison (1982) and
Weingast and Moran (1983) have shown that the composition of important
oversight committees influences bureaucratic policy-making initiatives.

Our purpose is to examine a further aspect of the principal-agent problem
confronting the legislature. In particular, we develop a model of legislative
control of bureaucratic policy-making that focuses on the differences between
two alternative organizational structures, independent commissions and bureaus administered by a single department head. Our analysis suggests that,
other things equal, the output generated by the former will have a smaller
variance. This reduction in variance facilitates congressional oversight responsibilities by helping assure that the policy decisions of the agency con-

Reprinted from *Southern Economic Journal* 52, no. 4 (April 1986): 962–72.

form to those desired by the legislature. Empirical evidence using data on antitrust enforcement supports the main predictions of the theory. As such, our model provides an explanation for the existence of commission-type agencies, and offers some suggestions as to why a particular agency is organized in one way and not the other.

The plan of the paper is as follows. We outline our model of legislative control, and then present empirical evidence.

A Model of Legislative Control

In this section we present a stylized model of congressional control of bureaucratic policy-making that focuses on the differences in policy outcomes observed under two alternative organizational structures. The bureau is administered by a single agency head in one case and by an independent commission in the other. The question we pose is, how does the institutional structure of the bureaucracy affect the degree to which the policy decisions of the agency conform to the preferences of its congressional "sponsor"?

Although the preferences of each legislator help determine the direction taken on any policy issue, we concentrate on the monitoring problem faced by the members of the legislative oversight committee, which exercises proximate control over agency appointments and funding. By and large, these committees are composed of members to whom the policies established by the agencies they oversee are important electorally. Thus, we normally observe agricultural committees to be dominated by representatives from rural constituencies, maritime committees to be dominated by representatives from coastal areas, and so forth. The position taken by each committee member on a given issue is chosen so as to maximize the political support (votes) from his/her constituency. It is the committee's task to clear as many of these margins as possible, that is, to arrive at a set of policy objectives that is consistent with overall political equilibrium and to see to it that the policies actually undertaken by its bureaucratic agent fall within this equilibrium set.

To simplify, we assume that the agency sets policy over a unidimensional issue, say, antitrust enforcement, and that the preferences of the oversight committee concerning policy outcomes in this area are distributed on the closed interval $[X_L, X_H]$. The endpoints represent the amount of antitrust intervention preferred by the "low" and "high" demanders, respectively. For example, the range X_L to X_H might correspond to increasing numbers of antitrust cases brought annually by the law enforcement agency. We further assume that the policy preferences of the agents are distributed on the interval $[a, b]$, which is a proper subset of $[X_L, X_H]$. That is, because the committee exercises veto power over agency appointments, we expect political appointees to be confirmed only if their preferences fall within the range, $X_L \leq a < b \leq X_H$.

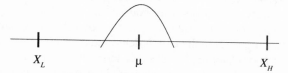

(a) single department head

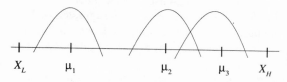

(b) three-member commission

Fig. 1. Agency preferences over antitrust enforcement

The two possible types of bureaucratic organization are contrasted in figure 1. Panel (a) shows a representative preference distribution for an agency operating under a single department head. (In our example, the distribution function corresponds to the preferences over enforcement activity of the Justice Department's Assistant Attorney General for Antitrust.) We require only that the distribution be single-peaked with finite mean and variance, and that the preferences of the department head be decisive in determining agency enforcement activity. If so, then during any one individual's term of office, the number of cases brought annually by the agency will be a draw from his preference distribution. Average annual case output will accordingly be equal to μ, with variance σ^2.

The preferences of three individuals serving on a commission that sets antitrust policy by majority vote are depicted in panel (b). We assume that the commissioners' preferences are independent random variables distributed in the same form with equal variances, $\sigma_i^2 = \sigma^2$, that is, the distributions differ only in their means. If the variances are indeed finite, then we can appeal to the central limit theorem for the result that the mean of the three distributions tends to be distributed about $\mu^* = (\mu_1 + \mu_2 + \mu_3)/3$, with variance $\sigma^2/3$[4, 193]. In general, for commissions composed of n members, expected agency output will center about the mean of the individual μ_1's, with variance equal to σ^2/n.

Our main conclusion therefore is that, holding turnover constant (and assuming that the variances in the preferences of agency heads are the same as the variances in the preferences of commission appointees), the output of commissions tends to be less variable than the output produced by agencies operating under a single department head. Moreover, the variance in commission output is a decreasing function of commission size.[1] This suggests that the cost to congressional oversight committees of monitoring bureaucratic output is less when agency policies are determined by a commission rather than by a single administrator. Put in other terms, lower variance of output means that commission-type bureaucracies are less likely to nullify the political equilibrium set of policy objectives emerging from the oversight committee's struggle to reconcile each member's desire to redistribute wealth in favor of his own constituency. In this sense, "independent" commissions may have come into being for reasons similar to those suggested by Landes and Posner (1975) in explaining the existence of an "independent" judiciary, namely, to enforce with little tolerance for error the legislature's contracts with interest groups.

The reduction in the variance of bureaucratic output associated with commissions comes at a cost, however. In particular, the composition of important congressional oversight committees has been shown to be influential in controlling bureaucratic policy-making initiatives (Faith, Leavens, and Tollison 1982; Weingast and Moran 1983), and when oversight committee membership changes, commissions will be less responsive to any corresponding shift in committee preferences because of the variance effect we have postulated. On the one hand, this serves to reduce the degree of bureaucratic control exercised by new committee members; on the other hand, the contracts with interest groups made by previous committees become more durable. The terms of trade between these considerations may in part explain differences in the sizes of various independent commissions.[2] Larger commissions obviously "sample" oversight committee preferences more accurately in that the variance of outcomes will be lower. An implication of the theory, then, is that more valuable legislative contracts will be protected with larger commissions.

In sum, our model of legislative control of bureaucratic policy-making yields two testable predictions. First, holding the turnover of political appointees constant, the output of commissions will have a smaller variance than the output of agencies operating under a single department head. Second, the variance in commission output will be a decreasing function of commission size. In the following section, we offer empirical evidence on these propositions.

---

1. Both of these results also hold if the output of commissions centers about the median of the n individual preference distributions. In particular, the variance of the commission is $\pi\sigma^2/2n = 1.5708\sigma^2/n$, which is less than the variance of the mean in draws from the preference distribution of the single agency head, σ^2, for $n \geq 2[4, 237]$.

2. To illustrate, the Federal Labor Relations Authority consists of three members, while the American Battle Monuments Commission has eleven members.

Empirical Results

The dual enforcement of American antitrust law supplies the conditions for a natural test of our hypotheses concerning the relationship between bureaucratic structure and the variability of agency output. Authority to enforce the relevant statutes resides in two agencies, the Justice Department's Antitrust Division and the Federal Trade Commission (FTC), having overlapping jurisdictions and differing organizational structures. On the one hand, the Antitrust Division is administered by a single department head, the Assistant Attorney General for Antitrust, who may bring cases under the Sherman Act (1890).[3] On the other hand, the FTC is an independent five-member commission that enforces its own enabling legislation, the FTC Act (1914), and shares with the Antitrust Division authority to initiate suits under the Clayton Act (1914). Subsequent additions to the body of antitrust law, the Robinson-Patman Act (1936) and the Cellar-Kefauver Act (1950), are enforced by both agencies. The Antitrust Division and the FTC thus generate quite similar outputs, making direct comparisons between the two agencies possible.

Our model of legislative control of bureaucratic policy-making suggests that the output of the FTC will be less variable than that of the Antitrust Division. To test this prediction, we obtained a time series of cases for the two antitrust enforcement agencies, and calculated their respective coefficients of variation. (We used this measure of relative dispersion rather than the variances of output because of the large difference in the mean number of cases brought annually by the two agencies.) The results of this exercise, which are presented in table 1, suggest that Antitrust Division output is significantly more variable than that of the FTC. For example, when we compare output variability over the complete time series of cases for both agencies (row 1), the relevant F-statistic implies that we can reject the null hypothesis of equal coefficients of variation at the 1 percent level.[4] Similarly, if we focus on the subperiod, 1915–81, during which both agencies were in existence (row 2), we can again reject the null hypothesis at the 10 percent level of significance.

Our model also predicts a relationship between output variability and turnover of agency heads. To test this proposition, we constructed a time series of coefficients of output variation for overlapping three-year intervals.

---

3. The first Assistant Attorney General for Antitrust was appointed in 1929, and the Antitrust Division did not become a separate line item in the Department of Justice budget until 1932. Prior to these events, Sherman Act (and, later, Clayton Act) enforcement was under the proximate control of the Attorney General.

4. Snedecor and Cochran (1967, 117) give the relevant statistic for testing the equality of two variances. When the estimated variances, s_1^2 and s_2^2, are uncorrelated as they are in our data, the test criterion is $F = s_1^2/s_2^2$, where s_1^2 is the larger mean square. When using coefficients of variation, $F = (CV_1/CV_2)^2$, where CV_1 is again the larger statistic (1967, 197).

TABLE 1. Means, Standard Deviations, and Coefficients of Variation of Cases

Period	Antitrust Division			FTC			F
	Mean	Standard Deviation	Coefficient of Variation	Mean	Standard Deviation	Coefficient of Variation	
1890–1981	25.88	25.19	0.97				2.23***
1915–81	33.27	25.01	0.77	182.30	119.06	0.65	1.40*

Note: Asterisks denote significance at the 1 percent (***) and 10 percent (*) levels.

(The data are listed in the appendix.) For the FTC, for instance, we calculated the means and standard deviations of cases instituted for the years 1915–17, 1916–18, and so on through 1979–81. We then estimated a regression equation of the following form.

$$CV_{t,t-2} = b_0 + b_1 TURN_t + b_2 BGTHAT_t + b_3 DMAJ_t + b_4 CHDUM_t + b_5 DUM48_t + v_t;$$

where

$CV_{t,t-2}$ = coefficient of variation of cases instituted in years t through $t + 2$,

$TURN_t$ = number of commissioners appointed at the beginning of the three-year interval,

$BGTHAT_t$ = percentage change in real budgetary appropriations for the agency,

$DMAJ_t$ = proportion of commissioners affiliated with the Democratic Party,

$CHDUM_t$ = dummy variable denoting party affiliation of the FTC chairman (=1 if Democrat, and zero otherwise),

$DUM48_t$ = liaison agreement dummy variable (=1 for the years 1948 and beyond, and zero otherwise), and

v_t = regression error term.

In addition to commissioner turnover, the regression specification controls for other factors that are expected to influence the variability of FTC case output. Specifically, output is expected to be more variable during periods preceded by a large change in the Commission's budget and, if politics matter, during times when the Commission is dominated by members of the Democratic Party (whose members are normally associated with policy activism).

DUM48 controls for the effects of the liaison agreement between the FTC and the Antitrust Division. Prior to that event, the two agencies com-

TABLE 2. Dependent Variable: Coefficient of Variation of FTC Cases, 1915–81

Intercept	0.2566	0.3192	0.2248	0.3147
TURN	0.0635	0.0757	0.0780	0.0762
	(2.21)**	(2.74)***	(2.81)***	(2.72)***
BGTHAT	0.2497	0.2359	0.2403	0.2362
	(2.42)**	(2.41)**	(2.45)**	(2.39)**
DMAJ			0.1811	
			(0.86)	
CHDUM				0.0075
				(0.15)
DUM48		−0.1427	−0.1493	−0.1422
		(−2.80)***	(−2.89)***	(−2.76)***
R^2	0.132	0.232	0.242	0.233
DW	1.20	1.34	1.34	1.34
F	4.64***	6.05***	4.70***	4.47***

Note: DW is the Durbin-Watson *d*-statistic. Asterisks denote dignificance at the 1 percent (***), 5 percent (**), and 10 percent (*) levels.

peted vigorously in enforcing the antitrust laws, but following the Cement Institute decision, the FTC and Antitrust Division agreed to divide this responsibility according to industry of respondent and, to a lesser extent, according to type of violation.[5] Under the agreement, case allocations are handled through a procedure in which one agency grants "clearance" to the other. By simultaneously limiting and making more predictable each agency's area of enforcement responsibility, we expect the liaison agreement to have reduced output variability, ceteris paribus.

The results shown in table 2 support these predictions. In particular, the variability of FTC case output is increased by increases in the number of new members appointed to the Commission and by large changes in the size of the Commission's budget. Moreover, the 1948 liaison agreement reduced the coefficient of output variation significantly. In contrast, neither the political makeup of the Commission as a whole nor the party affiliation of the chairman appears to be an important determinant of the variability of case output. These latter results suggest that it is the organizational structure of the FTC, and not the political identities of the individual commissioners, which affects the degree of congressional control. Overall, the regression specifications in table 2 explain about 25 percent of the variation in the dispersion of FTC cases over the past 67 years.

5. FTC v. Cement Institute et al., 333 U.S. 683 (1948). The Court held that the Commission could bring cases under Section 5 of the FTC Act against conduct that violates the Sherman Act, and that filing of a Justice Department suit did not require termination of FTC proceedings involving the same respondent.

We also estimated a similar regression for the Antitrust Division. As before, the dependent variable was constructed from observations on the means and standard deviations of cases instituted by the agency during overlapping three-year intervals. In addition, we tracked the turnover of the Attorney General (*AG*) and Assistant Attorney General (*AAG*) separately, and used the percentage change in real gross national product, *RGNPHAT*, in place of the political variables employed in the FTC regressions. Estimates were generated for both the complete Antitrust Division case series, 1890–1981, and for the subperiod, 1932–81, over which observations on the Division's budget and Assistant Attorney General turnover were available.

Although the results reported in table 3 are generally weak, they are supportive of the hypothesis that the variability of agency output depends upon the rate of turnover of the department head. Specifically, an increase in the frequency of new appointments to the post of Assistant Attorney General leads to an increase in the coefficient of variation of Antitrust Division cases. On the other hand, the effect of increases in Attorney General turnover works in the opposite direction, although the estimated coefficient on this variable is significantly different from zero in only one of the regressions. Finally, the 1948 liaison agreement appears to have reduced the variability of Antitrust Division output, at least over the complete time series. In sum, we view the results obtained with the Antitrust Division data set as suggestive, but certainly not conclusive as a test of our hypothesis concerning bureaucratic structure and congressional control.

TABLE 3. Dependent Variable: Coefficient of Variation of Antitrust Division Cases

	1890–1981		1932–81	
Intercept	0.6035	0.3796	0.3830	0.4067
AGTURN	−0.0223	−0.0664	−0.0694	−0.0726
	(−0.57)	(−1.60)	(−1.62)	(−1.70)*
AAGTURN		0.0720	0.0677	0.0668
		(1.81)*	(1.66)*	(1.65)*
RGNPHAT	−0.4000	−0.3236		−0.5059
	(−1.12)	(−0.74)		(−1.03)
BGTHAT			−0.0116	−0.0108
			(−0.17)	(−0.16)
DUM48	−0.2738	−0.1037	−0.1156	−0.1169
	(−1.98)*	(−1.19)	(−1.29)	(−1.29)
$\bar{\rho}$	0.6834	0.4836	0.4805	0.4913
R^2	0.065	0.153	0.146	0.167

Note: $\bar{\rho}$ is the estimated first-order autocorrelation coefficient.
*significant at the 10 percent level.

Concluding Remarks

In this essay we have outlined a model of legislative control of bureaucratic policy-making that focuses on the organizational structure of public agencies. Specifically, holding the turnover of political appointees constant, our model suggests that the output of commissions will have a smaller variance than the output of agencies operating under a single department head, and that the variance in commission output will be a decreasing function of commission size. In tests of these hypotheses using data on antitrust enforcement by the FTC and the Antitrust Division of the Department of Justice, we found that the output generated by the five-member independent commission is indeed less variable than that of its counterpart agency operating under the proximate control of a single administrator. Moreover, the evidence suggests that the variation over time in the dispersion of agency output is in part explained by the frequency with which political appointees are replaced.

To sum up, we offer some observations about the structure of bureaucracy. First, as a general proposition, the policy mandates given to commissions tend to be quite broad. The Federal Trade Commission Act, for example, bans "unfair methods of competition in commerce and unfair or deceptive acts or practices in commerce . . . ," and gives to the Commission authority to investigate, prosecute, and adjudicate such violations. Our analysis suggests that agencies that are given wide-ranging responsibilities are more likely to be set up as commissions than to be placed under the control of a single administrator because such an organizational structure facilitates congressional oversight and control. In a broad sense our theory explains why commission government was invented. As Congress has sought to take initiatives and expand the range of interest-group transfers in the economy, it has written laws of broad, sweeping applicability. So as to control and monitor the application of these laws, commission-led agencies were created to insure bureaucratic compliance with congressional intent. Second, from time to time vacancies on some commissions remain unfilled for extended periods. This may be a signal to the agency that the preferences of the legislature have shifted in favor of more activism in commission policy-making, that is, fewer commissioners lead to a larger variance. A similar signal may be implied when Congress "punishes" an agency by appropriating more funds than the agency has requested. Third, these differences in bureaucratic structure carry over to the executive branch of government. To illustrate, compare the Council on Environmental Quality, the Council of Economic Advisers, or the National Security Council with the Office of the U.S. Trade Representative, the Central Intelligence Agency, or any of the cabinet-level departments. Such differences in organizational structure imply differences in mandates, margins of control, and policy outcomes across agencies reporting to the president similar to those observed in creatures of the Congress. Finally, our results suggest that it is artless to describe an agency as an "independent commission." On the contrary, commissions are less independent of congressional control than other types of bureaucratic organization.

APPENDIX: MEAN, STANDARD DEVIATION, AND COEFFICIENT OF VARIATION OF ANTITRUST CASE OUTPUT FOR OVERLAPPING THREE-YEAR INTERVALS, 1890–1981

	Antitrust Division			FTC		
Year	Mean	Standard Deviation	Coefficient of Variation	Mean	Standard Deviation	Coefficient of Variation
1890	2.00	2.65	1.32500			
1891	2.00	2.65	1.32500			
1892	2.67	2.08	0.77903			
1893	1.33	0.58	0.43609			
1894	2.00	1.00	0.50000			
1895	2.00	1.00	0.50000			
1896	1.67	1.53	0.91617			
1897	1.00	1.00	1.00000			
1898	0.33	0.58	1.75758			
1899	0.33	0.58	0.75758			
1900	1.00	1.73	1.73000			
1901	1.67	1.53	0.91617			
1902	2.00	1.00	0.50000			
1903	2.67	2.08	0.77903			
1904	6.67	6.66	0.99850			
1905	9.67	4.51	0.46639			
1906	10.33	3.51	0.33979			
1907	6.67	3.51	0.52624			
1908	8.33	6.11	0.73349			
1909	13.67	10.07	0.73665			
1910	19.33	4.04	0.20900			
1911	21.67	1.53	0.07060			
1912	17.66	5.86	0.33164			
1913	13.33	7.77	0.58290			
1914	6.67	4.51	0.67616			
1915	10.00	9.85	0.98500	10.00	13.23	1.32300
1916	11.00	9.54	0.86727	78.67	110.73	1.40753
1917	11.33	9.07	0.80053	181.00	145.12	0.80177
1918	7.00	3.61	0.51571	223.33	81.40	0.36448
1919	10.33	8.74	0.84608	208.00	90.16	0.43346
1920	15.00	6.24	0.41600	135.00	36.59	0.27104
1921	15.00	6.24	0.41600	135.67	37.07	0.27324
1922	12.67	4.51	0.35596	131.33	33.38	0.25417

	Antitrust Division			FTC		
Year	Mean	Standard Deviation	Coefficient of Variation	Mean	Standard Deviation	Coefficient of Variation
1923	11.00	2.65	0.24091	135.33	26.50	0.19582
1924	11.33	2.08	0.18358	109.33	35.70	0.32653
1925	11.33	2.08	0.18358	78.67	25.11	0.31918
1926	13.00	4.00	0.30769	64.67	10.60	0.16391
1927	12.67	4.51	0.35596	104.33	78.62	0.75357
1928	10.67	5.51	0.51640	133.00	66.36	0.49895
1929	6.00	2.65	0.44167	145.67	47.17	0.32381
1930	5.00	2.00	0.40000	111.67	25.72	0.23032
1931	5.67	3.06	0.53968	85.00	21.17	0.24906
1932	6.67	2.08	0.31184	95.00	35.04	0.36884
1933	6.33	2.52	0.38910	197.67	179.54	0.90828
1934	5.00	1.00	0.20000	294.33	143.64	0.48802
1935	5.33	1.53	0.28705	338.00	70.41	0.20831
1936	7.33	2.52	0.34379	335.33	66.89	0.19948
1937	16.00	13.08	0.81750	318.33	67.40	0.21173
1938	35.33	27.75	0.78545	384.33	80.35	0.20907
1939	55.67	21.57	0.38746	326.67	122.20	0.37408
1940	60.67	13.05	0.21510	300.67	137.99	0.45894
1941	46.33	24.50	0.52882	222.33	2.52	0.01133
1942	29.00	14.80	0.51034	200.00	40.73	0.20365
1943	20.33	1.53	0.07526	176.00	42.46	0.24125
1944	25.33	10.12	0.39952	122.33	50.54	0.41314
1945	27.33	8.74	0.31979	87.33	54.86	0.62819
1946	35.33	9.61	0.27200	73.00	30.51	0.41795
1947	33.33	9.71	0.29132	84.33	31.79	0.37697
1948	41.00	8.89	0.21682	103.67	4.93	0.04755
1949	40.33	8.62	0.21373	103.00	4.36	0.04233
1950	39.00	10.82	0.27743	115.00	16.46	0.14313
1951	29.00	12.12	0.41793	106.67	26.54	0.24880
1952	23.00	4.58	0.19913	113.67	28.57	0.25134
1953	25.33	8.08	0.31898	135.33	59.55	0.44004
1954	29.33	5.03	0.17149	182.00	49.73	0.27324
1955	34.00	4.00	0.11764	246.67	64.45	0.26128
1956	38.33	8.50	0.22175	288.00	58.04	0.20153
1957	43.67	4.93	0.11289	337.00	26.89	0.07979
1958	42.67	6.66	0.15608	417.00	125.87	0.30185
1959	42.67	6.66	0.15608	389.00	161.53	0.41524
1960	46.00	10.54	0.22913	376.00	165.58	0.44037
1961	43.00	15.39	0.35790	337.67	103.27	0.30583
1962	44.33	16.07	0.36250	338.00	102.80	0.30414
1963	37.33	12.66	0.33913	287.67	139.74	0.48576
1964	40.67	8.96	0.22031	197.33	37.00	0.18570
1965	35.00	1.00	0.02857	169.33	11.72	0.06921

(*continued*)

	Antitrust Division			FTC		
Year	Mean	Standard Deviation	Coefficient of Variation	Mean	Standard Deviation	Coefficient of Variation
1966	39.00	7.00	0.17948	180.33	28.04	0.15549
1967	41.33	6.66	0.16114	197.67	36.86	0.18647
1968	32.67	21.46	0.65687	210.33	16.01	0.07612
1969	35.67	24.83	0.69610	251.00	72.79	0.29000
1970	53.67	44.55	0.83007	257.67	70.23	0.27255
1971	71.00	22.61	0.31845	254.00	75.32	0.29653
1972	76.00	19.00	0.25000	206.67	34.30	0.16596
1973	64.67	5.69	0.08798	198.67	20.60	0.10369
1974	66.33	4.16	0.06271	177.67	52.29	0.29431
1975	62.33	3.06	0.04909	136.67	78.39	0.57320
1976	69.67	13.61	0.19535	76.33	40.15	0.52600
1977	72.00	13.00	0.18055	58.00	14.80	0.25517
1978	91.0	22.61	0.24846	56.33	13.32	0.23646
1979	88.67	23.86	0.26908	48.67	26.58	0.54612
1980	—	—	—	—	—	—
1981	—	—	—	—	—	—

REFERENCES

Eckert, R. D. 1973. "On the Incentives of Regulators: The Case of Taxicabs." *Public Choice*, 83–99.

Ehrlich, I., and R. A. Posner. 1974. "An Economic Analysis of Legal Rulemaking." *Journal of Legal Studies*, June, 257–67.

Faith, R. L., D. R. Leavens, and R. D. Tollison. 1982. "Antitrust Pork Barrel." *Journal of Law and Economics*, October, 329–42.

Kendall, M. G., and A. Stuart. 1963. *The Advanced Theory of Statistics*. Vol. 1, 2d ed. London: Charles Griffin and Co.

Landes, W. M., and R. A. Posner. 1975. "The Independent Judiciary in an Interest-Group Perspective." *Journal of Law and Economics*, December, 875–901.

McCormick, R. E., and R. D. Tollison. 1981. *Politicians, Legislation, and the Economy: An Inquiry into the Interest-Group Theory of Government*. Boston: Martinus-Nijhoff.

Peltzman, S. 1976. "Toward a More General Theory of Regulation." *Journal of Law and Economics*, August, 211–40.

Snedecor, G. W., and W. G. Cochran. 1967. *Statistical Methods*. 6th ed. Ames, Iowa: Iowa State University Press.

Stigler, G. J. 1971. "The Theory of Economic Regulation." *Bell Journal of Economics*, Spring, 3–21.

Weingast, B. R., and M. J. Moran. 1983. "Bureaucratic Discretion or Congressional Control? Regulatory Policy-making by the Federal Trade Commission." *Journal of Political Economy*, October, 765–800.

The Political Economy of Merger between Regulated Firms

Richard S. Higgins, William F. Shughart II, and Robert D. Tollison

1. Introduction

It is not uncommon for regulated firms to compete in portions of their markets. In this instance, as in unregulated markets, merger between firms raises potential antitrust concerns for consumers, state and federal antitrust agencies, and state public service commissions (PSC's) that regulate the firms' activities.[1]

This essay explores the politico-economic dimensions of merger between regulated firms.[2] The conventional wisdom, which treats regulation as mitigating the reduction in consumer surplus associated with natural monopoly, would see the regulators' job as one of weighing the advantages and disadvantages of merger to consumers. On the benefit side, there may be economies of scale or scope from the joint ownership of previously independent firms, and the direct cost of regulation might be reduced. The major disadvantage of merger is likely to stem from a reduction in competition (Primeaux 1986).[3] Given that there will be benefits and costs of merger between regulated firms,

We wish to thank Margaret Davis and Robert McCormick for providing us with some useful data. The usual caveat applies.

1. There are numerous examples along these lines, including mergers between public utilities, hospitals, and banks, all of which may be subject to approval by state regulatory commissions. At the federal level, pipeline mergers provide a case in point.

2. In so doing, we ignore the role of federal and state antitrust enforcement in the merger-approval process. Focusing on the decisions of regulators alone simplifies the analysis at the expense of completeness. Our approach is appropriate where antitrust immunity accompanies regulation. It may also be appropriate absent antitrust immunity if the antitrust authorities defer to regulators' decisions.

3. There would be no disadvantages to consumers if regulation operated entirely in the "public interest" such that any welfare-reducing effects of merger were completely offset at zero cost. This premise is unlikely to hold empirically, however.

one method of predicting merger-approval decisions would be to tally these social benefits and costs on a merger-by-merger basis. Those mergers that provided social benefits, on balance, would be expected to receive the regulators' blessing under the public-interest model.

We adopt a different approach based on the political gains and losses of merger that leads to jurisdiction-specific predictions of merger-approval decisions. We assume that public service commissioners' conduct is described by the theory of economic regulation (Stigler 1971; Peltzman 1976), according to which regulators balance the costs and benefits of political support. Maximizing political support is not identical to maximizing total surplus. With or without merger, regulators can achieve various combinations of producer and consumer surplus by altering the rate of return (ROR) allowed the merged entity or each independent firm. The outcome of the merger decision depends on whether political support (or wealth) is larger with or without merger when for each structural outcome the allowed ROR is chosen to maximize political support.

In section 2 we briefly describe the application of Peltzman's theory of economic regulation to the case of profit maximization subject to ROR constraint. In section 3 we apply the Peltzman framework to a merger and a no-merger environment. We show how political wealth differs between the two environments depending on whether the regulators favor consumers or favor producers. Based on these wealth differences, we predict the outcome of merger decisions. In section 4 we present empirical tests of our predictions based on data about mergers between gas and electric utilities. In section 5 some brief concluding remarks are offered.

2. An Economic Theory of ROR Regulation

Several alternative forms of regulation have been applied when economies of scale or scope are alleged to make laissez-faire entry policy inefficient relative to perfect competition: government ownership, marginal cost pricing with multipart tariffs, contract bidding, ROR regulation, and so on. Presently, among regulation economists, there is considerable doubt whether or not the Averch-Johnson (AJ) (1962) model of ROR regulation realistically describes current public utility regulation (Joskow 1972, 1974). In one view, public-utility regulators have learned from a long line of theoretical and empirical research of the capital bias implicit in ROR regulation, and to mitigate the AJ effect, they have broadened their supervision to include factors other than ROR. Or perhaps the AJ model was always an unrealistic description of average-cost pricing. Economists will correctly reject criticisms of a model that it is an incomplete description of reality; however, they will not overlook repeated refutations of a model's predictions. Since Joskow's paper, economists have sought more realistic models based primarily on regulator price-setting behavior.[4] It remains to be seen whether these new descriptions predict better than the Averch-Johnson model.[5]

We adopt the AJ model in our analysis. In doing so we recognize that recent work suggests that as an empirical matter the model is not entirely satisfactory. However, we note that the problem we set for ourselves—predicting merger decisions—is substantially different from those the AJ model was designed to analyze. It is not unreasonable to expect the AJ model to have predictive power for some purposes and not for others. Furthermore, we do not adapt the AJ model to our purpose wholesale, but we incorporate it into the Stigler-Peltzman theory of economic regulation. Ultimately, of course, the proof of the pudding is in the eating, which comes later in section 4.

In broad outline, our model is as follows. The regulator maximizes political support, which depends on the combination of producer surplus (or profit) and consumer surplus supplied by the regulated firm. The combination of profit and consumer surplus supplied depends on the allowed ROR set by the regulator. The regulator has a locus of profit/consumer surplus opportunities available that depends on the choice of allowed ROR. The regulator chooses the allowed ROR to maximize political support.

Our analysis of merger decisions is based on deriving alternative opportunity curves for a merger and a no-merger environment. For a given political support function, political wealth may be greater or smaller with merger than without merger depending on the relative configuration of these two opportunity curves confronting the regulator.

3. Predicting Merger Approval

In this section we derive profit/consumer surplus opportunity curves for two structural regimes. In one, merger is approved, and the two firms jointly maximize profit subject to a ROR constraint. In the other, merger is not allowed, and the two firms compete, independently maximizing profit subject to a ROR constraint. We make several simplifying assumptions. The merger partners produce identical single products and use identical Cobb-Douglas

---

4. In the model developed by Burness, Montgomery, and Quirk (1980), for example, the regulator sets the price of the firm's output rather than the allowed rate of return.

5. Burness, Montgomery, and Quirk (1980) observe that the empirical case for their approach "has not been established." Perhaps this is the best that can be said in behalf of the AJ model as well. One problem that complicates modeling efforts in this area is that the allowed ROR may not be an effective constraint on the regulated firm. That is, the extent by which the actual ROR diverges from the rate set by the PSC may be a margin of regulatory control. For example, the regulator may establish a relatively low allowed ROR but not penalize the firm for exceeding the "constraint."

technologies. Demand exhibits constant elasticity, which is at least unity. Political support depends on the levels of total profit and consumer surplus supplied by the firms under regulatory constraint. The distribution of profit between the regulated firms and the distribution of surplus among classes of customers is irrelevant to regulators. We will note below the implications of relaxing certain of these assumptions.

Monopoly

The merged firm chooses outputs and capital stocks to maximize

$$\pi(Q_1,Q_2,K_1,K_2) \equiv p(Q_1 + Q_2)(Q_2 + Q_2) - C(Q_1,K_1) \\ - C(Q_2,K_2) - rp_K(K_1 + K_2) \tag{1a}$$

subject to

$$\pi(Q_1,Q_2,K_1,K_2) \leq (s - r)p_K(K_1 + K_2) . \tag{1b}$$

In (1), the Q_1 and K_1 are the outputs produced and capital stocks employed, p is the price of output, p_K is the price of capital, s is the ROR allowed by the regulator, and r is the competitive (zero-profit) ROR.

Assuming the constraint binds and on account of symmetry, the marginal conditions are

$$MR(Q) = MC(Q,K), \tag{2a}$$

$$C_K + rp_K = \lambda(C_K + sp_K), \tag{2b}$$

$$\pi(Q,K) = (s - r)p_K K . \tag{2c}$$

Conditions (2a) and (2c) define for each value of s between r and r^*, the unconstrained ROR, the values of Q and K that solve (1). These functions are denoted $\Theta_Q(s)$ and $\Theta_K(s)$. One can show readily that $d\Theta_Q/ds$ and $d\Theta_K/ds < 0$. At $s = r^*$, $\Theta_Q(r^*)$ and $\Theta_K(r^*)$ are the unconstrained solution values, and as s approaches r, Θ_Q and Θ_K approach the maximum values of K and Q for which profit is zero (see Baumol and Klevorick 1970).

If the functions $\Theta_Q(s)$ and $\Theta_K(s)$ are substituted for Q and K in $\pi(Q,K)$ and in $CS \equiv \int_Q^\infty p(u)\, du - p(Q)\, Q$, we get $\pi = h(s)$ and $CS = f(s)$. Thus, for a given s, constrained profit maximization yields a particular combination of CS and π. As s is altered, a profit/consumer surplus locus is traced out. A graph of the opportunity curve appears in figure 1. The graph is drawn to

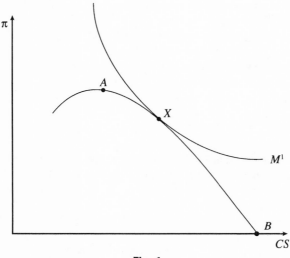

Fig. 1

indicate that π and CS are substitutes, and the marginal cost of CS in terms of π foregone rises as CS increases.[6]

Point A in figure 1 corresponds to unconstrained profit maximization; consumer surplus is minimized at point A. Point B is strictly speaking a limit point of the opportunity locus corresponding to maximum consumer surplus and zero profit, which results as s approaches r.

Political support for the regulator is maximized at point X, where an iso-political support curve is tangent to the π/CS opportunity curve. Implicit at X is an allowed ROR that achieves maximum political support, M^1. In general, s^* will exceed r but fall short of r^*.

Duopoly: Competition

In the absence of merger the two ROR-regulated firms compete in overlapping markets. We assume that the competitive equilibrium is Cournot. That is, we assume that given the output of its competitor, each firm chooses its output and capital stock to maximize profit subject to its ROR constraint. The equilibrium pairs of output and capacity simultaneously satisfy four marginal

---

6. Under general conditions, $d\pi/dCS < 0$. However, $d^2\pi/dCS^2$ is not necessarily negative. It can be shown that constant demand elasticity (of at least unity) and Cobb-Douglas production are sufficient conditions for concavity of the profit/consumer surplus opportunity locus.

conditions.[7] We also assume that the regulator sets the same allowed ROR for each firm.

The equilibrium conditions are ($i = 1,2$)

$$MR_i(Q_1,Q_2) = MC_i(Q_i,K_i), \tag{3a}$$

$$C_{K_i} + rp_K = \lambda_i(C_K + sp_{K_i}), \tag{3b}$$

$$\pi_i(Q_1,Q_2,K_i) = (s - r) \, p_K K_i \,. \tag{3c}$$

Conditions (3a) and (3c) are solved simultaneously for $K_i = \Theta_{K_i}(s)$ and $Q_i = \Theta_{Q_i}(s)$. On account of symmetry, $\Theta_{K_1} \equiv \Theta_{K_2}$ and $\Theta_{Q_2} \equiv \Theta_{Q_2}$. These equilibrium functions are substituted into $\pi_C \equiv 2 \, \pi_i(Q,K)$ and into $CS_c \equiv \int_o^{2Q} p(u) \, du$-$p(2Q) \, 2Q$ to get $\pi_C = h_c(s)$ and $CS_c = f_c(s)$. These last relations are used to define the profit/consumer surplus opportunity curve under competition.

In general, $d\pi_c/dCS_c < 0$ and given the assumptions about constant elasticity demand and identical Cobb-Douglas technologies, $d^2\pi_c/dCS_c^2 < 0$.[8] Thus, as in the merger regime, there is an allowed ROR in the competitive regime that maximizes political support. We presume that in either regime the firms' output and capacities are described by a Stigler-Peltzman regulatory equilibrium.

The Merger-Approval Decision

We are able to predict whether or not merger between ROR-regulated firms would be approved if we can fix the relative configuration of the opportunity curves with and without merger. In this section we prove that for CS levels in the relevant portion of the no-merger opportunity curve, the profits attainable without merger exceed those attainable with merger.

The horizontal sum of Cournot duopolists' marginal revenue curves with identical cost functions and equal capital stocks, MR_C, lies above the monopolist's marginal revenue curve, MR_M. For a given capital stock the monopolist equates $SRMC$ and MR_M. In the case of Cournot competition, MR_C is equal to summed $SRMC$s for the two duopolists. Thus, when the total capacity of the

---

7. The relationship between the optimal values of output and capacity and the allowed ROR are influenced by the maintained equilibrium concept. Thus, the opportunity curve in the competitive regime depends on the type of competition assumed. We have not investigated how our predictions of merger approval would be affected by different equilibrium concepts.

8. An appendix is available from the authors which shows that the π/CS opportunity curves are downward-sloping and concave.

duopolists equals the capacity of the monopolist, total output is greater under duopoly then under monopoly.

Now consider the duopoly equilibrium output when the regulatory constraint does not bind. We know that the duopolists are on their long-run marginal cost curve. We also know that when the monopolist produces this same output (and hence this same consumer surplus) it is subject to regulatory constraint. That is, the monopolist will only produce this output when its *SRMC* equals its *MR* at this output, and thus it will use a larger capital stock than the duopolists to produce this output. Since the duopolists are producing this output at minimum total cost, the monopolist must be incurring greater cost. Thus, at the unconstrained competitive equilibrium output, and at the particular comsumer surplus implied by this output, total profit for the duopolists must exceed that for the monopolist. Moreover, for every output greater than the unconstrained competitive equilibrium output, the duopolists will incur *SRMC* that deviates less from its *LRMC* than the monopolist's *SRMC* deviates from its *LRMC*. And since both the monopolist and the duopolists use too much capital (that is, $SRMC < LRMC$), the cost of producing a given output is always larger for the monopolist than for the duopolists. Thus, for a given output and, hence, given total revenue and consumer surplus, the duopolists earn higher total profit than the monopolist does.[9]

In figure 2, we depict graphs of the π/CS opportunity curves for monopoly and competition. Note that in its relevant range, π_C/CS_C lies above π_M/CS_M. Inspection of the graphs in figure 2 indicates that political wealth will be higher (lower) in the competitive environment when political support derives primarily from consumers (producers). Specifically, if the iso-political support curves in the jurisdiction are relatively flat (steep)—indicating that in general the marginal valuation of consumer surplus in terms of willingness to forego producer surplus is low (high)—the regulatory equilibrium without merger will occur near A_C (B_C). Thus, the maximum political support attainable will be greater (lower) with merger than without merger. For example, if the iso-political support curves in a jurisdiction are described by M^0, M^1, and M^2 in figure 2, we would predict merger approval since Y_C produces less overall political support than Y_M.

Our basis for predicting merger-approval decisions is clear. Factors identified as indicators of the relative importance in a jurisdiction of "consumer protection" and "producer protection" will predict the outcome of merger decisions.

---

9. Even if the opportunity curves are convex, this relative configuration applies provided the technologies are identical. The assumption of identical technologies is not a necessary condition, however. We discuss the role of this assumption at a later point.

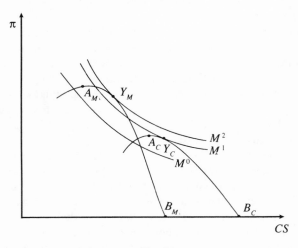

Fig. 2

A Caveat: Nonidentical Technologies

Our analysis concludes that the competitive opportunity curve supplies more consumer surplus over its relevant range per dollar of profit than does the merger opportunity locus. This result is probably not true in general; unfortunately, we do not know the limits of its applicability. To explore these limits, we consider a slight relaxation of our assumption that technologies are identical.

Suppose, for example, that both technologies are Cobb-Douglas, each yields the same long-run marginal cost, but the capital-labor ratio differs between them. With monopoly there are two opportunity curves if we consider the monopolist alternatively using exclusively one or the other technology. We know that both curves attain the same maximum profit at the same level of consumer surplus since $LRMC$ is the same for the two technologies. Moreover, we can show that one of the curves (the one based on the more capital-intensive technology) lies above the other for all relevant π/CS combinations. Thus, in the long run, political support would be maximized by fully depreciating the relatively labor-intensive technology.

Under competition, the π/CS opportunity curve may cross under the monopoly π/CS curve that derives from the sole use of the capital-intensive technology at low profit levels. To see this note that although the π/CS curves under competition that would result from exclusive use of the two alternative technologies lie everywhere above their monopoly counterparts, the actual competitive locus, which is based on the combined use of the two technologies, may not lie everywhere above the most efficient monopoly locus.

A priori, we cannot determine *in general* the relative configuration of the relevant opportunity curves in the merger and no-merger environments. The actual configurations will depend on the applicable production technologies and the degree to which capital in the labor-intensive firm is sunk.

4. Empirical Model and Results

In this section, we test some predictions of our theoretical model. Specifically, we apply our model to the decisions of state regulators to approve combinations of gas and electric utilities, estimating a merger-approval function that includes as arguments salient characteristics of the regulatory environment in each state.

Several caveats are in order at this point. First, in our theoretical discussion we assumed that the potential merger partners produced identical outputs. This assumption is not overly restrictive. In the case at hand, for example, the output of the two utilities can be defined as units of energy (BTUs) to meet the conditions imposed by the model. More importantly, however, we assumed identical production technologies, and our attempts to relax this assumption led to ambiguous conclusions about the relative configuration of the regulator's opportunity curves in the merger and no-merger environments. Ultimately, then, our ability to predict merger-approval decisions based on indices of political support and restrictive assumptions about production technologies is an empirical matter.

Earlier research in this area (see Anderson 1974; Brandon 1971; Collins 1973, 1974; and Owen 1970; for example), which has focused on the relative performance of combination versus straight utilities, has generally concluded that merger leads to higher average prices for gas and electricity. These findings have led to the hypothesis of a so-called combination Averch-Johnson (1962) effect, which suggests that merger provides an incentive for the firm to expand electricity relative to gas output because the more capital-intensive nature of electricity production provides a greater opportunity for building the utility's rate base.

While such results have typically been taken as further evidence of regulation's ineffectiveness, the literature has heretofore ignored the fact that merger is not an event which makes utility regulation more or less difficult, but rather is endogenous to the regulatory process. Indeed, the decision to approve or disapprove a merger represents a political choice by regulators between the interests of consumers and producers, and, as such, is subject to

TABLE 1.   Summary Statistics for Merger and No-Merger States

Variable		Merger	No-Merger	t
Electric Utilities				
PCTC	Percentage combination utilities	50.80	0.00	—
ESALES	Total electricity sales (MKWH)	42,993.50	40,189.30	0.24
ECUST	Total electricity customers	1,919,171.	1,350,260.	1.14
ERES	Percentage of sales to residential customers	34.98	37.64	1.64
EP	Average electricity price (cents per KWH)	6.94	6.57	0.77
PCTGAS	Percentage of electricity generated by gas	7.86	13.54	1.00
FCOST	Average fuel cost (cents per KWH)	2.41	2.95	1.24
LOAD	Load factor (percentage)	39.97	41.64	0.64
INVPCT	Percentage generated by investor-owned utilities	79.86	69.48	1.08
ROR	Allowed rate of return	14.08	14.66	2.08**
NETEXP	Exports as a percentage of electricity generated	7.39	−44.75	1.01
Gas Utilities				
GSALES	Total gas sales (tril. BTU)	319.92	232.69	0.72
GCUST	Total gas customers (thous.)	1,162.16	477.90	2.25**
GRES	Percentage of sales to residential customers	38.55	27.38	3.61***
GASP	Average gas price ($ per MMBTU)	5.29	5.85	0.78
NR	Net gas receipts (MCF)	75,491.30	−114,705.10	0.79

an understandable benefit-cost calculus. It is the purpose of this section to explore empirically the politico-economic dimensions of merger between gas and electric utilities.

The data cover all public and investor-owned gas and electric utilities operating in the fifty states during 1982. (The analysis accordingly excludes municipal electric companies, the Tennessee Valley Authority, rural electric cooperatives, and state-owned power companies.) For the purposes of this essay, a state is considered to be "not merged" if no combination utilities operate there. Correspondingly, a state is considered to be "merged" if at least one electric utility operating in the state has merged with a gas company. Although this definition is somewhat arbitrary, it should be noted that our criterion represents a natural break point in the data. In the states falling into the merger category, 51 percent of the electric utilities own a gas company, on average. Moreover, our definition puts thirty states into the merger category, and twenty states into the no-merger category.[10]

---

10. The merger states are: Arizona, California, Colorado, Connecticut, Delaware, Illinois, Indiana, Iowa, Kansas, Kentucky, Louisiana, Maryland, Massachusetts, Michigan, Minnesota,

TABLE 1. (*Continued*)

Variable		Merger	No-Merger	*t*
Demographic Variables				
POP	State population (thous.)	5,335.17	3,670.53	1.27
INC	State personal income ($ mil.)	61,353.70	37,566.40	1.52
Regulatory Variables				
COMM	Number of public utility commis- sioners	3.93	3.50	1.18
STAFF	Number of commission employees	198.90	119.50	1.79*
SAL	Commissioner's salary ($)	39,332.50	40,306.60	0.33
DEC	Average decision time (mos.)	8.90	8.50	0.35
ELEC	= 1 if commissioners are elected	0.17	0.30	1.11
FADJ	= 1 if automatic fuel cost passthrough prohibited	0.13	0.20	0.62
BIAS	Regulatory bias (1 is most favor- able to investors, 10 is least favorable)	6.73	6.41	0.44
Other				
RELQ	Electricity sales/gas sales	200.84	498.12	1.80*
RELP	Electricity price/gas price	1.33	1.36	0.12

Source: The observations on PCTC were derived from *Moody's Public Utility Manual, 1982,* and those on ROR are from McCormick 1986. The other electric utility and demographic data were taken from the *Statistical Yearbook of the Electric Utility Industry, 1982.* Information on the performance of gas companies is from *Gas Facts—1982 Data,* and the regulatory data are from the *1979 Annual Report on Utility and Carrier Regulation.* Finally, the regulatory commission rankings, BIAS, are from Salomon Brothers 1981.

Note: t is the absolute value of the t-statistic for the test of differences between means.
*significant at the 10 percent level
**significant at the 5 percent level
***significant at the 1 percent level

Comparisons between merger and no-merger states for a menu of polit-ico-economic variables are displayed in table 1. Overall, the data suggest that there are few dimensions on which merger and no-merger states differ signifi-cantly. In general, merger states tend to be net exporters of electricity and net importers of natural gas, while the opposite holds for no-merger states. Fur-thermore, the domestic gas utility industry is of less importance in the no-merger states, serving a significantly smaller number of in-state customers.

Of interest are some of the dimensions on which merger and no-merger states do not differ significantly. First, there is no evidence that efficiency gains are associated with merger. For example, electric utilities in merger states generate a smaller proportion of their output by burning natural gas than

Missouri, Montana, Nevada, New Jersey, New Mexico, New York, North Dakota, Ohio, Penn-sylvania, South Carolina, South Dakota, Vermont, Virginia, Wisconsin, and Wyoming. The classification of states was made on the basis of data in *Moody's Public Utility Manual, 1982.*

do electric companies in no-merger states. Although this no doubt reflects the fact that the combination utilities do not have significantly lower fuel costs, the data suggest that vertical integration is not an important merger motive. Second, there is reason to believe that merger complicates the regulatory process. In particular, even though the time it takes the public utility commission to act on a rate request is not significantly longer in merger states, the commissioners require more complementary inputs (employees) to make their decision. This occurs despite the fact that more of the merger states permit the automatic pass-through of fuel cost increases to electricity customers.

The comparisons displayed in table 1 are somewhat misleading in the sense that the variables are treated as being independent of one another. Accordingly, we tested whether or not division along geographic lines is appropriate by estimating a discriminant function using the merger/no-merger dichotomy as the classification criterion on a subset of the politico-economic variables. The results reported in table 2 suggest that the classification is indeed robust. Specifically, only five, or 10.6 percent, of the forty-seven states are classified incorrectly on the basis of the ten explanatory variables employed in the analysis.[11] Of these, the merger states differ significantly from the no-merger states on two dimensions, namely, the proportion of natural gas sales to residential customers, *GRES*, and the rate of return allowed to electric utilities, *ROR*. Overall, the multivariate *F*-statistic suggests that the classification is significant at the 1 percent level.

If neither vertical integration nor regulatory efficiencies are associated with merger between gas and electric utilities, what factors might explain the merger-approval decision? Our hypothesis is that the decision to approve or disapprove mergers represents a political choice by regulators which involves a trade-off between the interests of consumers and producers. When political support is greater in the merger regulatory equilibrium, the merger is approved; it is denied otherwise. As such, our model predicts that the extent of merger in a state will depend upon the regulators' political support function and upon other measures of the costs and benefits to interest groups of using the regulatory process to obtain their desired outcome.

In order to test some of these propositions, we estimated a merger-approval function of the following general form.

$$MERGE = f(POP, INC, NETEXP, GRES, ERES, ROR, COMM,$$
$$SAL, DEC, ELEC),$$

where *MERGE* is set equal to unity if at least one combination utility operates

---

11. Three states (Alaska, Nebraska, and Tennessee) were omitted from the analysis because observations on allowed rate of return were not available.

TABLE 2. Discriminant Analysis Results for Merger/No-Merger States, 1982

	Univariate Statistics		
Variable	F	Prob $> F$	R^2
POP	1.014	0.319	0.022
INC	1.477	0.230	0.032
NETEXP	1.742	0.193	0.037
GRES	12.188	0.001	0.213
ERES	1.445	0.235	0.031
ROR	4.329	0.043	0.088
COMM	2.293	0.137	0.048
SAL	0.251	0.619	0.006
DEC	0.072	0.790	0.002
ELEC	0.318	0.575	0.007

Multivariate Statistic	
$F(10,36) = 3.626$	PROB $> F = 0.002$

	Classification Results		
From	To No-Merger	To Merger	Total
No-Merger	15	2	17
	(88.24)	(11.76)	(100.00)
Merger	3	27	30
	(10.00)	(90.00)	(100.00)
Total	18	29	47
	(38.30)	(61.70)	(100.00)

in the state and set equal to zero otherwise, and the other variables are as defined in table 1.

In accordance with the predictions of our theoretical model, we expect the estimated coefficients on *INC* and *NETEXP* to be positive. That is, merger approval is more likely in states with higher incomes and in those where a larger proportion of electricity output is sold to out-of-state customers. The former result follows because higher incomes increase the total surplus over which regulators might have control and the political payoff from its redistribution (Peltzman 1976, 224–25); the latter from the fact that more of the costs of regulation are borne by individuals without political voice (Maloney, McCormick, and Tollison 1984).

The sign of the coefficient on *POP* is indeterminant a priori. On the one hand, larger populations give rise to free-rider problems among the group that bears the costs of welfare-reducing regulation. Put another way, consumers face higher costs of organizing to oppose the approval of a proposed merger in more populous states. On the other hand, a larger population means that there are more voters per regulator, and this might lead to improved monitoring by consumers. In a similar vein, *GRES* and *ERES* measure the degree of concentration of interests among two of the groups that would be adversely affected by the approval of a merger. Because of their greater numbers, residential customers would be expected to face higher organizational costs than industrial customers. We therefore expect merger approval to be more likely in states where residential customers account for a larger proportion of sales.[12]

Our theory predicts merger states to be characterized by a regulatory environment that is favorable to producers. We associate regulatory environments more congenial to utilities with higher allowed rates of return. The estimated coefficient on *ROR* is thus expected to be positive.

The empirical model also contains four variables that control for differences in the characteristics of regulatory commissions across states. The salary paid to public utility commissioners, *SAL*, accounts for the trade-off between pecuniary and nonpecuniary rewards in the support function of regulators. That is, money and votes are substitutes. Higher salaries accordingly reduce the value at the margin of the political support forthcoming from producers in exchange for merger approval. On this interpretation, paying higher salaries to regulators is equivalent to consumers offering "protection money" to the commissioners.

As in the case of state population, the expected sign on *COMM* is ambiguous. More commissioners make it more difficult for the commission to reach agreement on a merger-approval decision. This is in part due to the smaller relative influence of each individual regulator. Such considerations reduce the ability of producers to sway the commission in their favor. In contrast, more commissioners mean more competition between the regulators, and this tends to reduce the costs of influence to interest groups. Whether or not larger regulatory commissions lead to the approval of more mergers depends on which of these effects dominate.

DEC represents the average time required for the utility commissioners in a state to act on a rate request. Because longer decision times are costly to producers, we expect the estimated coefficient on this variable to be negative, especially if merger complicates the regulatory process such that regulators take longer to act on the rate requests submitted by combination utilities. Finally, *ELEC* controls for the method of selection of public utility commis-

---

12. Empirically, *ERES* is highly correlated ($r^2 = 0.99$) with *TRES*, a variable we constructed as the average of *GRES* and *ERES*, using either sales or customers as weights.

TABLE 3. Logit Model of Electric-Gas Utility Merger, 1982

Intercept	39.3633	35.0059	33.6576	64.0938
POP	−0.0092	−0.0076	−0.0089	−0.0195
	(−2.64)**	(−2.53)**	(−2.53)**	(−1.79)*
INC	0.00008	0.00007	0.00008	0.00017
	(2.65)**	(2.54)**	(2.54)**	(1.78)*
NETEXP	0.0116	0.0134	0.0139	0.0186
	(1.68)	(1.12)	(1.15)	(1.75)*
GRES	0.2332	0.2193	0.2458	0.4902
	(2.76)***	(2.65)**	(2.67)**	(1.79)*
ERES	−0.2742	−0.2330	−0.2529	−0.5360
	(−2.00)*	(−1.78)*	(−1.87)*	(−1.71)*
ROR	−3.0756	−2.4893	−2.4755	−5.1100
	(−2.58)**	(−2.66)**	(−2.69)**	(−1.96)*
COMM	2.0079	1.6637	1.6938	3.0195
	(2.20)**	(1.92)*	(1.95)*	(1.93)*
SAL	0.0001			0.0002
	(1.32)			(1.51)
DEC		−0.0817		
		(−0.74)		
ELEC			1.8494	5.6821
			(1.13)	(1.33)
LOG LIKELIHOOD	−10.37	−10.93	−10.54	−8.75

Note: Asymptotic t-statistics are in parentheses. Asterisks denote significance at the 1 percent (***), 5 percent (**), and 10 percent (*) levels.

sioners. If elected commissioners ($ELEC = 1$) are more responsive to the polity, fewer welfare-reducing mergers ought to be approved.

We estimated the merger-approval function using a logit regression model.[13] The results reported in table 3 provide broad support for the predictions of our theoretical model. In particular, more mergers between gas and electric utilities have been approved in states where income is higher, where more of the electricity output is sold out of state, and where more of the gas sales are made to residential customers. Moreover, the results suggest that mergers are less likely in states where more of the electricity sales are made to residential customers and where the electric utilities are allowed higher rates of return.

Although the latter two results are not consistent with our a priori predictions, they point to several interesting aspects of the merger-approval calculus. First, the finding that a higher proportion of electricity sales to residential users leads to a lower probability of merger, whereas the opposite holds true for natural gas, suggests that electric customers are better situated (face lower costs of organizing) to prevent welfare-reducing regulation than their

---

13. Quantitatively similar results were obtained with a probit specification.

gas-purchasing counterparts. While this is somewhat surprising in view of their larger numbers, it is also the case that electricity costs generally represent a larger proportion of the average residential customer's budget than do the expenditures on energy made by those using natural gas. On the other hand, this result conflicts with the perception in the literature that the combination Averch-Johnson effect tends to work to the benefit of electricity purchasers. Second, the estimated coefficient on *ROR* implies that higher allowed rates of return are a regulatory substitute for merger approval.[14]

Fewer merger approvals are forthcoming in more populous states. This suggests that the increased monitoring potential associated with larger populations more than offsets the higher costs of organizing to oppose the approval of mergers. Similarly, larger commissions lead to the approval of a larger number of mergers, implying that the cost of influencing commissioners falls enough to offset the higher costs of reaching agreement among more regulators. Finally, the method of commissioner selection, their annual salaries, and the average time taken to act on rate requests do not appear to have an effect on the decision to approve a merger.[15] Overall, however, our empirical model performs quite well in explaining the variation in merger approval across the forty-seven states.[16]

5. Concluding Remarks

In this essay, we have extended the interest-group theory of regulation to explain the occurrence and effects of merger between firms subject to ROR regulation. In so doing, we have treated the approval or disapproval of such mergers as endogenous to the regulatory process, making the outcome a political choice involving a trade-off between the interests of producers and consumers. The regulatory body chooses between various combinations of producer profit and consumer surplus generated by the equilibrium outputs and prices in each of the merger and no-merger regimes, and picks the regime that maximizes political support.

Empirical evidence using data on the prevalence of merger across states in

---

14. Counterintuitive results were also obtained when we used *BIAS* as our proxy for the regulatory environment in a state. The estimated coefficient on this variable, which ranks utility commissions from 1 to 10 in order of decreasing favorability to investors in electricity producers, was positive and significantly different from zero.

15. Crain and McCormick (1984) found that the method of commissioner selection had ambiguous effects on utility pricing. More recently, Costello (1984) found little or no effect of electing commissioners on electric prices.

16. We also estimated the logit model using state income per capita rather than total income as an explanatory variable. The coefficient was positive and significant, and although the coefficient on *POP* remained negative, it was no longer different from zero at standard levels. Importantly, however, the remaining coefficient estimates were essentially unchanged.

1982 provided support for the predictions of our theoretical model. In particular, we found that mergers between gas and electric utilities are more likely to be approved in states where the costs to producers of using the regulatory apparatus to obtain their desired outcome are lower and where the benefits are higher. Moreover, the data were consistent with the idea that the decision to approve merger depends in part on factors entering into the political support function of regulators and is subject to an understandable benefit-cost calculus involving the private interests of producers, consumers, and regulators.

REFERENCES

American Gas Association. 1983. *Gas Facts—1982 Data.* Arlington, Va.: American Gas Association.

Anderson, J. A. 1974. "Comparative Performance of Combinations and Separately Managed Utilities: Comment." *Southern Economic Journal* 41 (October): 317–21.

Averch, H., and L. L. Johnson. 1962. "Behavior of the Firm under Regulatory Constraint." *American Economic Review* 52 (December): 1052–69.

Baumol, W., and A. Klevorick. 1970. "Input Choice and Rate of Return Regulation: Overview of the Discussion." *Bell Journal of Economics* 1 (Autumn): 75–89.

Brandon, P. S. 1971. "The Electric Side of Combination Gas-Electric Utilities." *Bell Journal of Economics* 2 (Autumn): 688–703.

Burness, H. S., W. D. Montgomery, and J. P. Quirk. 1980. "Capital Contracting and the Regulated Firm." *American Economic Review* 70 (June): 342–54.

Collins, W. H. 1973. "Comparative Performance of Combinations and Separately Managed Electric Utilities." *Southern Economic Journal* 40 (July): 80–89.

———. 1974. "Comparative Performance of Combinations and Separately Managed Utilities: Reply." *Southern Economic Journal* 41 (October): 321–24.

Costello, K. W. 1984. "Electing Regulators: The Case of Public Utility Commissioners." *Yale Journal on Regulation* 2:83–105.

Crain, W. M., and R. E. McCormick. 1984. "Regulators as an Interest Group." In *The Theory of Public Choice—II,* ed. J. M. Buchanan and R. D. Tollison, 287–304. Ann Arbor: University of Michigan Press.

Edison Electric Institute. 1983. *Statistical Yearbook of the Electric Utility Industry, 1982.* Washington, D.C.: Edison Electric Institute.

Joskow, P. L. 1972. "The Determination of the Allowed Rate of Return in a Formal Regulatory Hearing." *Bell Journal of Economics* 3 (Autumn): 632–44.

———. 1974. "Inflation and Environmental Concern: Structural Change in the Process of Public Utility Regulation." *Journal of Law and Economics* 17 (October): 291–327.

McCormick, R. E. 1986. "Inflation, Regulation, and Financial Adequacy." In *Electric Power: Deregulation and the Public Interest,* ed. J. C. Moorhouse. Cambridge: Ballinger.

Maloney, M. T., R. E. McCormick, and R. D. Tollison. 1984. "Economic Regulation, Competitive Governments, and Specialized Resources." *Journal of Law and Economics* 27 (October): 329–38.

Moody's Investor Services, Inc. 1982. *Moody's Public Utility Manual, 1982.* New York: Moody's Investor Services Inc.

National Association of Regulatory Utility Commissioners. 1980. *1979 Annual Report on Utility and Carrier Regulation.* Washington, D.C.: National Association of Regulatory Utility Commissioners.

Owen, B. M. 1970. "Monopoly Pricing in Combined Gas and Electric Utilities." *Antitrust Bulletin* 15 (Winter): 713–26.

Peltzman, Sam. 1976. "Toward a More General Theory of Regulation." *Journal of Law and Economics* 19 (August): 211–40.

Primeaux, W. J. 1986. *Direct Electric Utility Competition: The Natural Monopoly Myth.* New York: Praeger.

Salomon Brothers. 1981. *Stock Research, Industry Analysis: Electric Utility Regulation.* New York: Salomon Brothers.

Stigler, G. J. 1971. "The Theory of Economic Regulation." *Bell Journal of Economics* 2 (Spring): 3–21.

Tresch, R. W. 1981. *Public Finance: A Normative Theory.* Plano, Tx.: Business Publications, Inc.

U.S. Department of Energy, Energy Information Administration. 1984. *State Energy Overview—1982.* Washington, D.C.: USGPO.

Part 7
Participation and Elections

Expressive versus Economic Voting

Roger L. Faith and Robert D. Tollison

Introduction

A basic premise in public choice theory is that voting is irrational as an investment activity. This is because voting is costly, and an individual's vote has no effect on the outcome of most elections. Because of the lack of a logical foundation for voting as an investment process, voting as a consumption activity has emerged as the received theory explaining voter participation.

Voting as consumption may explain why people enter the voting booth, but it does not predict how people will choose once they are inside the booth. Recent literature on "expressive voting" suggests that a voter's actual choice reflects the voter's preference for one option over another rather than one voting outcome over another (see, for example, Brennan and Buchanan 1984). Choosing in the voting booth is like responding to a pollster. The voter/respondent, knowing that he/she has no influence over the outcome, treats the opportunity cost of his/her choice as zero. One will express his/her preference for option A over option B regardless of whether his/her choice implies that he/she can have A instead of B or regardless of whether having A instead of B implies giving up other goods. In economic terms the voter considers only the marginal benefits of the implied outcome if that option is selected by a majority of voters. The voter expresses his/her approval without committing his/her dollars.

An alternative model of voting is that the individual behaves in the voting booth the same way he/she does in the marketplace, that is, economically. Choices are made on the basis of marginal value net of opportunity costs. Even though the voter knows that personal choice has no influence over what outcome will, in fact, be selected, his/her vote reveals his/her preference over outcomes. In other words, the predictable effects of relative prices and mar-

We thank Gary Anderson, Stuart Low, and Dennis Hoffman for comments and assistance. The usual caveat applies.

ginal values will characterize individual voting choices and the resultant political outcomes that emerge.

To illustrate further the differences between the two models, consider a vote over two exclusive options, A and B. Option A is a proposal to build a new school, while option B is a proposal not to build. Each proposal, if chosen by a majority of the voters, leads to an outcome, α or β. Outcome α consists of the new school and an increase in taxes to pay for its construction and operation; outcome β consists of no school and no tax increase. Under expressive voting a voter choosing option A over B means that the voter approves of more schools, but this choice does not mean anything about the willingness of the voter to pay for the school. Under economic voting a voter choosing A means the voter is choosing outcome α over β. Because the individual's vote is not decisive in determining the final outcome, both models are expressive in that the voter can only express a preference over alternatives without committing his/her dollars. The empirical question is what are the alternatives over which the voter expresses his/her preference—options or outcomes?[1]

In this essay we test the economic model of voter behavior against the expressive model with respect to state expenditures on welfare. We lay out a model of the demand and supply of welfare and its implications for voter choice, and specify the empirical model. Then we discuss the results, and provide our conclusions.

The Demand and Supply of Welfare

Several authors have modeled charity as a public good from the viewpoint of the donor (Thompson 1967; Tullock 1971). Donors can all agree that transfers to low-income persons are a good thing. Knowing that the poor are better off makes each donor better off. But given the total amount of charity, greater personal contributions to the redistribution effort reduce the donor's welfare. Thus, the best of all possible worlds for the individual donor is for everyone else to contribute while the individual donor contributes zero. The individual benefits from the increase in the recipients' welfare at no personal cost. Even if one suffers some guilt from not giving one's "fair share," the price of avoiding guilt still matters. Because of the pervasive free-rider problem in private charity, publicly provided charity is typically supplied by government and financed through general tax revenues.

In the economic and expressive models of public welfare, the "demand

---

1. If there are no actual or perceived costs, a choice between options is equivalent to a choice between outcomes. An example is the 1982 Nuclear Freeze Referendum (Feigenbaum, Karoly, and Levy 1988). Votes on essentially costless proposals do not provide a good test of the two models.

for public welfare" comes from donors rather than from the recipients of charity. We assume that public charity is a normal good and that the greater the number of "needy" persons, the greater the demand for charitable giving. The per person cost of a given amount of tax-financed charity declines with the number of taxpayers. Thus, the larger the population of taxpayers, the lower the price of exercising one's charitable preferences. If voters behave in an economic fashion, the law of demand predicts that the lower the price of charity, the more will be purchased. So it follows that where the population of taxpayers is larger, more public welfare will be observed, ceteris paribus.[2] Similarily, where the number of welfare recipients is larger, the greater the per voter cost and less welfare will be observed, again, other things equal.

Under the expressive model the marginal value of charity drives voter behavior. Some factors that might be important in determining the amount of welfare demanded in this model are the wealth of the individual and the perceived "neediness" and size of the recipient group. Price or cost, however, should not be a determinant of welfare.

One may argue that welfare spending does not often come up for popular vote. Most welfare spending decisions are made in state legislatures, and thus welfare is not a good issue to test the two models. However, if elected representatives are responsive to their constituents, their choice should be consistent with the demand for public charity by their constituents. If the economic model holds, legislators will respond to larger populations as a lower price of welfare per person. If the expressive model holds, voters do not respond to cost factors, and thus neither should their representatives.[3]

A Proposed Test

A test of the economic model of voting consists of regressing state welfare expenditures on a set of variables that directly measure or proxy the voter's demand for and cost of public welfare. The analysis is conducted on a cross section of states in two different time periods, 1970 and 1980.[4]

---

2. The ceteris paribus condition applies most strongly to the charitable voters because it is their economic status, along with that of recipients, which determines the amount of public welfare provided by the state.

3. An alternative model of welfare spending, based on legislative logrolling, treats public welfare as purely redistributional. The poor, through their representatives in the state legislature, trade their votes on issues of little concern to themselves in return for welfare benefits. In this case the price of the welfare recipients' votes to the voter falls with number of voters. Thus, the price of "buying" welfare to the low-income group falls with the size of the nonpoor population, even if charity does not drive the state's expenditures on public welfare. This interest-group model of public welfare is also an economic model in which price and opportunity cost matter. The difference is that welfare is treated as a pure transfer rather than a public good by the donor.

4. Sander and Giertz (1986) analyzed a state's demographic makeup in terms of religion, race, and education as predictors of state welfare spending. Their measure of welfare was

The dependent variable is *WELFARE*, defined as total spending by a state on public welfare (State Government Finances 1980, 77). *WELFARE* includes both the state's direct spending on welfare, such as aid to families with dependent children, and the state's indirect spending in the form of intergovernmental grants to local governments for welfare purposes. *WELFARE* does not include federal intergovernmental grants to state and local governments. Thus, *WELFARE* is state government expenditures on welfare financed by state government revenues.

In order to arrive at measures for the determinants of the demand and cost of public welfare, we partition state population into two groups, donors and recipients. The size of the recipient group is measured by *POOR*, the number of persons belonging to families designated as having low income by the Social Security Administration. The remaining population, *NONPOOR*, comprises the donor group, which we shall assume finances the state's welfare expenditures.

The price of public welfare is proxied by *NONPOOR*. States with larger nonpoor populations can spread the cost of a given amount of welfare over a larger base, permitting each donor to consume the benefits of charitable giving at a lower cost. The law of demand is expected to work here as it does in private markets. The greater the nonpoor population, the lower is the per person price, and the greater the amount of welfare demanded. However, more populous states may spend more on welfare simply because they have more nonpoor residents, even if the number of potential recipients of charity is the same across states. A larger nonpoor population, ceteris paribus, means a greater aggregate demand for giving at every price.

In order to isolate the price effect of an increase in the nonpoor population from the demand-shift effect, we also use the square of *NONPOOR*, *NONPOOR2*, in our test equation. In a linear model, regressing *WELFARE* on *NONPOOR* and *NONPOOR2* is equivalent to regressing per capita *WELFARE* on *NONPOOR* and a constant term. A positive coefficient on *NONPOOR* in such an equation means that *WELFARE* expenditures increase with the donor population for reasons other than demand shifts.[5] The partial derivative of *WELFARE* with respect to *NONPOOR* is $a_1 + 2a_2 NONPOOR$, where a_1 and a_2 are the estimated coefficients of *NONPOOR* and *NONPOOR2* in a linear regression equation. The economic model of voting predicts that the value of this derivative will be positive somewhere within the range of population values in the sample.

Another determinant of public welfare is the size of the recipient group,

---

restricted to AFDC payments, a much narrower definition of welfare spending than we use in our tests. They also only look at a single cross section (1980).

5. A zero-valued or insignificant coefficient does not provide evidence against the economic model since one cannot tell if the price effect of *POPULATION* or the demand-shift effect is driving the result.

POOR. This variable affects the amount of welfare in two ways. First, the number of poor persons proxies the aggregate amount of "neediness" in the state. By the charity argument greater need should increase the demand for welfare. Further, even if all states had the same percentage of low-income persons, larger states may spend more on welfare than smaller states because more populous states are likely to have more poor persons. As a measure of need or as a reflection of scale, *POOR* should affect welfare expenditures positively.

On the other hand, assuming the degree of individual poverty is the same in all states, the greater the number of low-income persons in a state of a given population, the greater the cost of bringing this group's standard of living up to nonpoverty levels. The greater cost of achieving any level of real income for the poor population is higher the greater the number of poor persons. This implies that donors will demand a lower level of welfare per recipient, and total welfare expenditures may decrease with increases in *POOR.* Thus, the predicted effect of *POOR* on *WELFARE* is ambiguous. While a positive sign on the estimated coefficient of *POOR* does not disprove the economic model, a negative sign supports the economic model and provides evidence against the expressive model. In the event there are either economies or diseconomies of scale in administering public welfare programs, we include the square of *POOR, POOR2,* in our regression equation.

The demand for welfare expenditures is also affected by donor income. Assuming welfare is a normal good to each nonpoor voter, greater state disposable income for a given population (or equivalently higher per capita income) should lead to greater charitable output. The expected sign of the estimated coefficient on *INCOME,* total state personal income, should be positive. By analogy subtractions from gross income should reduce welfare spending. Since taxes come out of personal income either directly or indirectly, higher tax collections imply lower personal disposable income and a lower demand for charity. Because taxes provide some of the revenue with which welfare payments are financed, greater tax revenues may reflect a greater demand for welfare. However, state-financed welfare consumed only between 8 and 9 percent of state-raised revenues in 1970 and 1980, so this effect is probably negligible. The variable we used to measure deletions from personal income is *TAXES,* defined as total state and local tax collections. For either model the expected sign of the estimated coefficient on *TAXES* is negative.

A good deal of a state's expenditures, including welfare, is subsidized by the federal government. In 1980, for example, 55 percent of welfare expenditures made by the states was financed by federal revenues in the form of intergovernmental grants. Grants specifically for public welfare have income and substitution effects on the amount of state-financed welfare. Likewise, a federal grant to states for any other purpose frees state-raised revenue for other expenditures and thus generates an income effect on state-financed welfare. If state revenue is a normal good, the income effect of a federal grant is positive. We use two variables to control for additions to state revenue: *FEDWEL*, the amount of federal grants to a state for public welfare, and *FEDGRANT*, the amount of nonwelfare federal grants. Both *FEDWEL* and *FEDGRANT* exclude federal grants made to local governments, even if administered through the state government. Both variables should impact positively on *WELFARE*.

Data were gathered from two sources, *State Government Finances* and the *Statistical Abstract of the United States*. Exact definitions of all variables used in this study, along with sample means, are listed in tables 1 and 2.

Model Specification

The ordinary least squares (OLS) equation suggested by the previous discussion is:

$$
\begin{aligned}
WELFARE = a_0 &+ a_1 NONPOOR + a_2 NONPOOR2 + a_3 POOR \\
&+ a_4 POOR2 + a_5 INCOME + a_6 TAXES \\
&+ a_7 FEDWEL + a_8 FEDGRANT + \epsilon_1,
\end{aligned}
\tag{1}
$$

where ϵ_1 is an error term with zero mean and variance σ^2.

A potential difficulty with this specification is that some of the variables determining *WELFARE* also are likely determinants of *FEDWEL* and *FEDGRANT*. For example, we expect that federal grants for public welfare, *FEDWEL*, depend on the nonpoor and poor populations, state income, and so on. In addition, during the cross-sectional year 1980, federal revenue sharing was in force. Population (*NONPOOR* + *POOR*), *INCOME*, and *TAXES* are all part of the revenue-sharing formula. And even though revenue sharing is a relatively small fraction of *FEDGRANT*, these same variables may still influence the amount of nonwelfare grants. If so, OLS estimates of equation (1) are subject to simultaneous equations bias. As a consequence, the effect on state welfare spending of a change in a hypothesized independent variable in the OLS equation, such as *NONPOOR*, may actually be due to simultaneous shifts in federal spending.

The possibility of simultaneity between *WELFARE*, *FEDWEL*, and *FEDGRANT* suggests the following structural model:

$$
\begin{aligned}
WELFARE = a_0' &+ a_1' NONPOOR + a_2' NONPOOR2 + a_3' POOR \\
&+ a_4' POOR2 + a_5' INCOME \\
&+ a_6' TAXES + a_7' FEDWEL \\
&+ a_8' FEDGRANT + \epsilon_1' \, ;
\end{aligned}
\tag{1'}
$$

TABLE 1. Variables and Definitions

Variable	Definition
WELFARE[a]	State-financed direct and indirect spending on public welfare (in millions of dollars)
POOR[b]	Number of persons in state below poverty income level (in thousands)[1]
POOR2	POOR squared
NONPOOR[b]	The number of persons in state above poverty income level (in thousands)
NONPOOR2	NONPOOR squared
INCOME[b]	Total state personal income (in millions of dollars)
TAXES[c]	Total state and local tax revenue (in millions of dollars)
INCTAX[a]	State income tax revenue (in millions of dollars)
URBAN[b]	State urban population (in thousands)
FEDWEL[a]	Federal grants to state for welfare purposes (in millions of dollars)
FEDGRANT[c]	Nonwelfare federal grants to state (in millions of dollars)
TOTGRANT	FEDWEL plus FEDGRANT

[1] In the previous year. Thus, *POOR* for 1980 is the number of poor persons in 1979, and likewise for POOR in 1970.

[a] Source is *State Government Finances,* various years.

[b] Source is *Statistical Abstract of the United States,* various years.

[c] Source is *Governmental Finances,* various years.

TABLE 2. Sample Means

Variable	1980	1970
WELFARE	390.7	109.4
NONPOOR	3,958	3,495
POOR	559.4	554
INCOME	24,025	15,877
TAXES	4,446	1,725
INCTAX	741.7	227.7
URBAN	3,328	2,971
FEDWEL	493.6	151.0
FEDGRANT	743.7	237.6
TOTGRANT	1,237	388.6

$$FEDWEL = b_0 + b_1 NONPOOR + b_2 NONPOOR2 + b_3 POOR$$
$$+ b_4 POOR2 + b_5 INCOME + b_6 TAXES$$
$$+ b_7 INCTAX + b_8 URBAN + \epsilon_2 ; \qquad (2)$$

$$FEDGRANT = c_0 + c_1 NONPOOR + c_2 NONPOOR2$$
$$+ c_3 POOR + c_4 POOR2 + c_5 INCOME$$
$$+ c_6 TAXES + c_7 INCTAX + c_8 URBAN$$
$$+ \epsilon_3 . \qquad (3)$$

Total state income tax collections, *INCTAX*, and a state's urban population, *URBAN*, are potential identifiers of equations (2) and (3).

Results

OLS estimates of equation (1) and two-stage (TSLS) estimates of equation (1'), along with the first-stage OLS estimates of equations (2) and (3), with and without *POOR2*, are reported in table 3 for the 1980 cross section. Estimation results for the 1970 cross section are reported in table 4.

1980

Ordinary least square estimates of *FEDWEL* and *FEDGRANT* show that the variables hypothesized to determine state welfare spending also determine either federal welfare or nonwelfare spending. *INCTAX* identifies the *FEDGRANT* equation while *URBAN* identifies the *FEDWEL* equation. However, comparing the OLS and TSLS estimates of *WELFARE*, we find little evidence of simultaneity bias. Estimated coefficients, standard errors, adjusted R-squares, and F-statistics differ only slightly.

The variables of interest to the economic versus the expressive models of state welfare spending are *NONPOOR, NONPOOR2, POOR*, and *POOR2*. In column (2) in table 3, for example, the partial derivative of *WELFARE* with respect to changes in number of donors, $a_1 + a_2 NONPOOR$, evaluated at the sample mean of *NONPOOR*, is 0.060. This estimate likely misstates the true ceteris paribus effect of population on state welfare spending. This is because increasing state population while holding constant other state aggregates, such as personal income and tax collections, effectively changes the economic status of the typical voter as well as lowering the price of charity. For example, the implied decrease in an average donor's income should lower the demand for charitable giving, potentially offsetting the positive effect of a lower price. In order to get an unbiased estimate of the marginal donor population effect, we calculate

TABLE 3. 1980 Estimation Results

Equation Technique Dependent Variable	OLS WELFARE (1)	TSLS WELFARE (2)	OLS FEDWEL (3)	OLS FEDGRANT (4)	OLS WELFARE (5)	TSLS WELFARE (6)	OLS FEDWEL (7)	OLS FEDGRANT (8)
CONSTANT	-95.5	-132.8	-37.4	157.2	-78.8	-64.3	-37.4	149.7
	(1.75)**	(1.68)**	(1.66)*	(5.98)***	(1.98)**	(1.04)	(1.60)*	(5.65)***
NONPOOR	0.032	0.025	0.048	-0.130	-0.246	-0.271	0.049	-0.170
	(0.322)	(0.212)	(0.801)	(2.00)**	(2.88)***	(2.50)***	(0.794)	(2.42)***
NONPOOR2	4.9×10^{-6}	4.5×10^{-6}	1.3×10^{-6}	-7.3×10^{-7}	1.4×10^{-5}	1.5×10^{-5}	1.2×10^{-6}	1.2×10^{-6}
	(3.82)***	(3.24)***	(1.63)*	(0.813)	(8.04)***	(6.47)***	(0.827)	(0.748)
POOR	-1.61	-1.71	0.230	0.715	0.008	0.049	0.224	0.944
	(8.77)***	(7.69)***	(2.34)***	(6.24)***	(0.028)	(0.121)	(1.28)	(4.76)***
POOR2					-0.0006	-0.0006	3.2×10^{-6}	-0.0001
					(6.20)***	(5.14)***	(0.042)	(1.40)
INCOME	0.030	0.033	-0.010	0.031	0.045	0.051	-0.010	0.030
	(1.55)*	(1.15)	(0.826)	(2.15)***	(3.12)***	(2.41)***	(0.816)	(2.14)***
TAXES	-0.201	-0.231	0.207	-0.065	-0.116	-0.139	0.206	-0.046
	(3.42)***	(2.17)***	(10.9)***	(2.94)***	(2.61)***	(1.81)**	(9.16)***	(1.79)**
FEDWEL	0.763	0.869	—	—	0.565	0.679	—	—
	(3.17)***	(1.83)**			(3.18)***	(1.99)***		
FEDGRANT	1.18	1.39	—	—	0.733	0.662	—	—
	(6.16)***	(4.18)***			(4.65)***	(2.13)***		
INCTAX	—	—	0.027	0.222	—	—	0.028	0.190
			(0.732)	(5.10)***			(0.659)	(3.91)***
URBAN	—	—	-1.58	0.035	—	—	-0.158	0.036
			(3.74)***	(0.711)			(3.69)***	(0.738)
Adj R^2	0.952	0.950	0.986	0.980	0.974	0.974	0.986	0.980
F-statistic	140.1	135.7	508.7	350.4	236.6	232.5	434.5	314.1

*significant at 15 percent or better
**significant at 10 percent or better
***significant at 5 percent or better

TABLE 4. 1970 Estimation Results

Equation Technique Dependent Variable	OLS WELFARE (1)	TSLS WELFARE (2)	OLS TOTGRANT (3)	OLS WELFARE (4)	TSLS WELFARE (5)	OLS TOTGRANT (6)
CONSTANT	-14.9	-19.6	81.2	-15.2	-21.0	73.7
	(1.11)*	(1.20)	(2.98)***	(1.10)	(1.31)	(2.76)***
NONPOOR	-0.010	-0.015	0.064	-0.011	-0.017	0.048
	(0.372)	(0.517)	(1.00)	(0.395)	(0.561)	(0.771)
NONPOOR2	-8.3×10^{-8}	3.8×10^{-7}	2.6×10^{-6}	-9.5×10^{-9}	-4.50×10^{-7}	4.6×10^{-6}
	(0.137)	(0.455)	(1.85)**	(0.012)	(0.455)	(2.65)***
POOR	-0.112	-0.121	0.234	-0.104	-0.121	0.409
	(4.00)***	(3.71)***	(3.57)***	(1.91)**	(2.02)***	(3.61)***
POOR2	—	—	—	-3.9×10^{-6}	-1.1×10^{-6}	-0.0001
				(0.156)	(0.040)	(1.86)**
INCOME	0.0008	0.0026	-0.063	0.0009	0.003	-0.071
	(0.099)	(0.298)	(3.09)***	(0.118)	(0.363)	(3.48)***
TAXES	0.060	0.054	0.444	0.059	0.052	0.392
	(2.12)***	(1.75)**	(4.79)***	(2.02)***	(1.66)*	(4.15)***
TOTGRANT	0.279	0.320	—	0.277	0.332	—
	(4.86)***	(3.23)***		(4.75)***	(3.47)***	
INCTAX	—	—	-0.300	—	—	-0.233
			(3.11)***			(2.33)***
URBAN	—	—	0.063	—	—	0.121
			(1.29)			(2.13)***
Adj R^2	0.961	0.960	0.967	0.960	0.959	0.969
F-statistic	202.5	199.9	212.5	169.6	166.1	197.4

*significant at 15 percent or better
**significant at 10 percent or better
***significant at 5 percent or better

$$\hat{a}_1 + 2\hat{a}_2 NONPOOR + \hat{a}_5 (INCOME/X) + \hat{a}_6 (TAXES/X)$$
$$+ \hat{a}_7 (FEDWEL/X) + \hat{a}_8 (FEDGRANT/X) , \tag{4}$$

where X is the relevant population and each variable is evaluated at its sample mean. Since X is measured in thousands of persons and monetary variables are measured in millions of dollars, (4) holds per capita income, taxes, and federal subsidies constant. Setting X equal to total population implies that average nonpoor income equals state per capita income and clearly understates average nonpoor income. It also places a lower bound on the adjustment of income necessary to keep per donor income constant when *NONPOOR* increases. Setting X equal to *NONPOOR* overstates average nonpoor income and places an upper bound on the necessary adjustment. The same holds for adjustments in *TAXES, FEDWEL,* and *FEDGRANT*. Upper and lower bound results of the simulated effects of *NONPOOR* on *WELFARE* for the various estimated equations in table 3 are reported in table 5, panel a. Notice that the effects of an increase in the nonpoor population of 1000 persons is positive. For equation (2), for example, an additional 1000 "average" nonpoor persons in a state increases total state welfare spending by $329,600 to $367,000.

Consider now the effect of adding more low-income persons to a state while holding the nonpoor population constant. The partial derivative of *WELFARE* with respect to *POOR*, $a_3 + 2a_4 POOR$, gives a biased estimate of the effect of neediness on state welfare spending. Holding income constant while increasing the size of the low-income population means that the per capita income of the nonpoor has fallen, reducing their propensity to vote for welfare. Again, to correct for this downward bias in income and the biases created by changes in per capita taxes and federal subsidies, we calculate

$$\hat{a}_3 + 2\hat{a}_4 POOR + \hat{a}_5 (INCOME/X) + \hat{a}_6 (TAXES/X)$$
$$+ \hat{a}_7 (FEDWEL/X) + \hat{a}_8 (FEDGRANT/X) . \tag{5}$$

Upper and lower bound results of these simulations are reported in table 5, panel a.[6] They show a consistently negative effect of increases in the number of poor persons on state welfare spending of around $265,000 to $375,000 in the models using *POOR2* (and over $1 million in the other models). This is consistent with the economic model of voting on welfare.

The remainder of the estimated coefficients are as expected. *INCOME* and *TAXES* have signs consistent with the presumption that public welfare is a

---

6. *F*-tests on the significance of the insignificant coefficients used in the calculation of the *POOR* effect generally indicate that these variables belong in the regression equation. The exception is *POOR* in equations (5) and (6) in table 2. Including the coefficient on *POOR* in our calculation only biases the result against the economic model.

TABLE 5. Estimated Marginal Effects of *NONPOOR* and *POOR* on *WELFARE*

		(a) 1980 (table 3)				(b) 1970 (table 4)			
		(eq. 1)	(eq. 2)	(eq. 5)	(eq. 6)	(eq. 1)	(eq. 2)	(eq. 4)	(eq. 5)
NONPOOR	(L)	0.308	0.329	0.171	0.164	0.043	0.054	0.043	0.045
	(U)	0.341	0.367	0.214	0.205	0.053	0.061	0.053	0.055
POOR	(L)	−1.37	−1.44	−0.374	−0.306	−0.058	−0.066	−0.053	−0.057
	(U)	−1.34	−1.40	−0.331	−0.265	−0.048	−0.048	−0.044	−0.047

Note: L = lower bound estimate; U = upper bound estimate; see text.

normal good. And federal subsidies, both welfare-specific and general, have positive impacts on the level of state welfare spending.

1970

For this cross section *FEDWEL* and *FEDGRANT* have been dropped, and *TOTGRANT* has been added to the regression equations. *TOTGRANT* is *FEDWEL* + *FEDGRANT*. The reason for this change is that first-stage OLS estimates of *FEDWEL* and *FEDGRANT* showed these variables to be identified by the same exogenous regressor. Thus, we could not separately identify both of the first stage equations. Because we are not interested in the breakdown of federal grants between welfare and other programs, using a single variable to measure the effect of federal grants on state welfare spending does not affect the substance of our tests.

Our revised structural model for 1970 is:

$$WELFARE = d_0 + d_1 NONPOOR + d_2 NONPOOR2 \\ + d_3 POOR + d_4 POOR2 \\ + d_5 INCOME + d_6 TAXES \\ + d_7 TOTGRANT + \epsilon_4 ; \tag{6}$$

$$TOTGRANT = e_0 + e_1 NONPOOR + e_2 NONPOOR2 \\ + e_3 POOR + e_4 POOR2 + e_5 INCOME \\ + e_6 TAXES + e_7 INCTAX \\ + e_8 URBAN + \epsilon_5 . \tag{7}$$

TSLS and OLS estimates of equation (6) (see table 4) show little evidence of simultaneous equations bias. Estimated coefficients are about the same in the two regression equations although significance levels are a little higher in the OLS equation. The version of equations (6) and (7) not containing *POOR2* seems to perform worse in terms of individually significant variables than the version with *POOR2*. However, *F*-tests reveal that the insignificant variables, as a group, belong in the various equations.

With respect to the effect of the nonpoor population on state welfare spending, we perform the same simulation as in the 1980 cross section. Simulation results are reported in table 5, panel b. Notice that in each case the nonpoor population effect is positive as hypothesized by the economic model of welfare spending. An increase in the donor population of 1000 persons, holding per capita income, taxes, and outside grants constant, consistently increases total welfare spending by $40,000 to $60,000.

Similar calculations on the effect of increases in the *POOR* population, holding the nonpoor population and per capita taxes, income, and grants constant, show a negative effect of *POOR* on state welfare spending of 0.047 to 0.066. This effect is considerably smaller than that reported in the 1980 cross-section. Making the same calculation from the *TOTGRANT* equation (column 6, table 4), the effect of *POOR* on federal grants to a state is about 0.26. Thus, at the federal level greater "need" implies more welfare, while at the state level "need" is viewed as a cost. Calculations for *POOR* are reported in table 5, panel b.

One reason for running two separate cross sections is our conjecture that the 1970 data would reflect a prerevenue sharing effect in the pattern of federal grants. The formula nature of federal grants under revenue sharing might remove some degrees of freedom from states in making themselves eligible for grants. It is conceivable that federal lawmakers, when having free rein on public giving, might behave as a state would behave. In this way federal legislators could capture some of the rents accruing to state legislators in the market for state public welfare. Further, the federal government would be less constrained in pursuing distributional goals with respect to the states. However, there is little evidence of this occurring. One reason may be that revenue-sharing funds going to state governments are a relatively small fraction of total nonwelfare grants from the federal government to the states (around 6 percent).[7]

---

7. Along with the interest-group model posited earlier, where the poor as a group trade their votes on other issues for welfare, other interest groups may exist that would favor greater welfare spending. Unions, for example, may prefer greater welfare payments in order to reduce the supply of competing labor services. Another interest group may be the welfare bureaucracy that benefits from increased public welfare in terms of a higher derived demand for social workers, administrators, or any other job created by greater welfare spending. To test for these possibilities we also ran regressions of the form in equations (1) and (5), with the additional variables *UNION*, the percentage of the state labor force that is unionized, and *EMPLOYEE*, the number of state employees. Neither variable, when entered into our original specifications, was

Concluding Remarks

The two models of voting behavior which we test in this paper, expressive and economic, are consistent with the idea that an individual's vote is inconsequential. If so, on what does a voter base his/her choice? The simple expressive model argues the voter looks only at the options presented on the ballot, while the economic model argues the voter looks at the outcomes implied by the options. Why the voter behaves in an economic fashion despite his inability to influence the outcome we can only conjecture. Perhaps the voter's lifetime of experience in the market conditions the voter to take both benefit and cost into account in *all* of his/her decisions.

In general, we find support for the economic model of voter behavior when applied to public welfare. The estimated effects of population size (the price of welfare) and the number of welfare recipients (the cost of welfare) are as predicted by the economic model. We conclude that price and costs matter. By the same token we find no support for the simple expressive model of voter choice. Our results reaffirm our belief that the economic approach to politics and collective decision making is an appropriate way to view the world. Despite a constant flow of arguments to the contrary, *homo politicus* can be modeled as *homo economicus*.

REFERENCES

Brennan, Geoffrey, and James M. Buchanan. 1984. "Voter Choice." *American Behavioral Scientist* 28 (November): 185–201.
Feigenbaum, Susan, Lynn Karoly, and David Levy. 1988. "When Votes Are Not Deeds: Some Evidence from the Nuclear Freeze Referendum." *Public Choice* 58 (September): 201–16.
Sander, William, and J. Fred Giertz. 1986. "The Political Economy of State Level Welfare Benefits." *Public Choice* 51, no. 2: 209–19.
Thompson, Earl. 1980. "Charity and Nonprofit Organizations." *Research in Law and Economics,* suppl. 1, 125–38.
Tullock, Gordon. 1983. *Economics of Income Redistribution.* Boston: Kluwer Nijhoff.
U.S. Bureau of the Census. 1969–70, 1979–80. *Governmental Finances.* Washington, D.C.: USGPO.
———. 1970a, 1980a. *State Government Finances.* Washington, D.C.: USGPO.
———. 1970b, 1980b. *Statistical Abstract of the United States.* Washington, D.C.: USGPO.

significant. Finally, we also thought that the ability to sell votes might be greater the more closely contested the election for governor. Entering the variable *CLOSE,* the size of the winning plurality in the race for the state executive, did not change our equations, and the estimated coefficient was small and insignificant.

A Negative Advertising Theory of Campaign Expenditures

Scott J. Thomas

1. Introduction

This essay develops and tests a formal theory of campaign expenditures. A formal theory is needed for two reasons. First, the formal theory will help us empirically estimate the effect of campaign expenditures; the testable predictions can be used to specify a regression model. Second, the formal theory will enable us to learn more about the electoral process. Without a formal theory we really cannot explain how the electoral process works.

None of the studies that previously examined the effect of incumbent campaign expenditures (Glantz, Abramowitz, and Burkhart 1976; Jacobson 1978; Silberman and Yochum 1978; Welch 1981; Jacobson 1985; Thomas n.d.) developed a formal theory. This caused most of the studies to specify implausible regression models. For example, some studies (Welch 1981; Jacobson 1985) specify regression models that require both candidates to spend a positive amount of money. These specifications eliminated approximately 25 percent of the available observations in their samples.

Other studies (Glantz, Abramowitz, and Burkhart 1976; Jacobson 1978) specify regression models that restrict the effectiveness of a candidate's additional campaign expenditures to be independent of how much money the candidate has already spent. Finally, all of the studies but one (Thomas n.d.) specify regression models that restrict the effectiveness of a candidate's additional campaign expenditures to be independent of how much money the opponent has already spent. These implausible specifications lead to results that the authors do not believe (Jacobson 1985).

The formal theory will be developed by assuming that candidates only

I am grateful to Tyler Cowen, Bernard Grofman, and especially to Amihai Glazer for helpful comments. Any errors are my responsibility.

spend their money on political advertisements. This assumption makes it easier to understand how campaign expenditures can affect a voter's behavior, that is, it is easier to conceptualize how an advertisement can affect a voter's behavior than it is to conceptualize how a dollar can affect a voter's behavior. This assumption is realistic since most campaign expenditures are spent for media exposure (Alexander 1984; Goldenberg and Traugott 1984).

The formal theory will be developed by assuming that the candidates only buy negative advertisements and rebuttals to negative advertisements. The formal theory focuses on negative advertisements for three reasons. First, previous empirical work has shown that incumbents are likely to lose if voters form negative opinions of them (Monroe 1979). This implies that negative advertisements will be more effective than positive advertisements. Second, a formal theory should generate plausible results. The results should show that a candidate can increase votes by increasing campaign expenditures, that a candidate's campaign expenditures exhibit diminishing returns, and that the effectiveness of a candidate's additional campaign expenditures depends on how much money the opponent has already spent. Although other theories may generate some of these results, the simplest theory that I could create is the one based on negative advertisements.

Finally, the assumption of negative advertisements accurately describes modern elections. For example, the negative advertising assumption accurately describes the 1988 presidential election. George Bush ran advertisements both attacking Michael Dukakis's record on crime and defending the administration's record on integrity. Likewise, Michael Dukakis ran advertisements both attacking the administration's record on integrity and defending his record on crime.

The negative advertising assumption also accurately describes other 1988 elections. In the California U.S. Senate election, the challenger, Leo McCarthy, ran advertisements attacking the incumbent's voting record on environmental issues, while the incumbent, Pete Wilson, ran advertisements defending his voting record. Likewise, in the Ohio U.S. Senate election, the challenger, George Voinovich, has run advertisements attacking the incumbent's actions on a child-porn bill, while the incumbent, Howard Metzenbaum, has run advertisements defending his actions.

2. Theory for Races Involving Incumbents

Assumptions

Assume that all constituents vote, that there are only two candidates (a challenger and an incumbent) and that the candidates spend their money on two types of advertisements (negative advertisements and rebuttals to negative advertisements). Also assume that only the challenger sends negative advertisements and the incumbent sends rebuttals.[1]

This last assumption recognizes that most challengers have never held public office before; in contrast, incumbents have track records that they are likely to stand on and emphasize. This assumption implies that only the constituents who initially intend to vote for the incumbent will be affected by the advertisements. That is, a constituent who initially intends to vote for the challenger will not be affected by an advertisement that criticizes the incumbent. My results do not change if I generalize this assumption to allow the incumbent to also send negative advertisements.[2]

Assume that if no advertisements are sent, then the constituents will decide who to vote for based on party loyalty, incumbent constituency service, incumbent name recognition, newspaper endorsements, etc. Also assume that if no advertisements are sent, then a fraction (c) of the constituents will vote for the challenger and the remainder $(1 - c)$ of the constituents will vote for the incumbent.

Assume that if a constituent initially intends to vote for the incumbent and if the constituent receives (that is, hears or reads) at least one negative advertisement, then the constituent will vote for the challenger. Also assume that if the constituent receives at least one rebuttal to the negative advertisement, then the constituent will vote for the incumbent.

This last assumption implies that a rebuttal will only affect a constituent if the constituent has already received at least one negative advertisement. That is, if a constituent has not received an advertisement criticizing the incumbent, then a rebuttal addressing the criticism has no effect.

Finally, assume that only two things can happen to each advertisement (it can be received or not received) and that the event of receiving one advertisement is independent of the event of receiving another advertisement. This means the number of received advertisements follows a binomial distribution. To simplify the analysis, I will use a limiting distribution of the binomial, the Poisson distribution.[3]

---

1. This assumption is consistent with the standard Downsian model that candidates simply pick issue positions to maximize vote support (Downs 1957; Davis, Hinich, and Ordeshook 1970; Aldrich 1983), as well as with the neo-Downsian models that recognize that candidates may have to precommit in order to win their primaries (Aldrich 1983) or because they "have specific preferences as well as an interest in winning per se" (Wittman 1983).

2. An additional assumption is needed, that if no advertisements are sent then the incumbent will receive more votes than the challenger.

3. The Poisson distribution is a good approximation of the binomial distribution if the probability of receiving any given advertisement is small (Hogg and Craig 1978).

The Effects of Campaign Expenditures

The probability that a constituent receives x negative advertisements is given by the Poisson distribution as

$$f(x) = \left\{ \frac{(np)^x e^{-(np)}}{x!} \, , \qquad x = 0,1,2, \ldots ,0, \text{elsewhere} \right.$$

where

n is the number of negative advertisements sent by the challenger, and p is the probability that a constituent will receive any given advertisement.

The probability the constituent receives no negative advertisements is e^{-np}; therefore, the probability the constituent receives at least one negative advertisement is $(1 - e^{np})$. Defining r to equal the number of rebuttals that the incumbent sends, the probability the constituent receives no rebuttals is e^{-rp}.

If a constituent who initially intends to vote for the incumbent only receives negative advertisements about the incumbent, then the constituent will vote for the challenger. Since the joint probability of receiving at least one negative advertisement and no rebuttals is $(1 - e^{-np})e^{-rp}$ and since initially a fraction $(1 - c)$ of the constituents intend to vote for the incumbent, the challenger's percentage of the two party vote (CV) is

$$CV = [c + (1 - c)(1 - e^{-np})e^{-rp}]100 \, .$$

The previous subsection postulated that there is a one-to-one relationship between a candidate's campaign expenditures and the number of advertisements that he sends. This means I can determine the effect of the challenger's and incumbent's campaign expenditures (CE and IE, respectively) by differentiating CV with respect to the number of negative advertisements (n) that the challenger sends and to the number of rebuttals (r) that the incumbent sends.

The first partial derivative of CV with respect to n is

$$\frac{\delta CV}{\delta n} = [(1 - c)pe^{-p(n+r)}]100 \, ,$$

which is positive. Intuitively $\delta CV/\delta n$ is positive since there is always a positive probability that a constituent has received no negative advertisements. This implies that a challenger can increase votes by increasing campaign expenditures, that is, $\delta CV/\delta CE > 0$.

The first partial derivative of CV with respect to r is

$$\frac{\delta CV}{\delta r} = -[(1 - c)p(1 - e^{-np})e^{-rp}]100,$$

which is nonpositive. Intuitively $\delta CV/\delta r$ can either be zero or negative depending on whether the challenger has sent any negative advertisements. If the challenger has not sent any negative advertisements, then $\delta CV/\delta r$ will be zero since rebuttals have no effect. If the challenger has sent some negative advertisements, then $\delta CV/\delta r$ will be negative since there is always a positive probability that a constituent has received at least one negative advertisement but has not received any rebuttals. Since most challengers spend money, this implies that an incumbent can usually increase votes by increasing campaign expenditures, that is, $\delta CV/\delta IE \leq 0$.

The second partial derivative of CV with respect to n is

$$\frac{\delta^2 CV}{\delta n^2} = -[(1 - c)p^2 e^{-p(n+r)}]100,$$

which is negative. Intuitively $\delta^2 CV/\delta n^2$ is negative since each negative advertisement has fewer and fewer constituents that it can affect. This implies that the challenger's campaign expenditures exhibit diminishing returns, that is, $\delta^2 CV/\delta CE^2 < 0$.

The second partial derivative of CV with respect to r is

$$\frac{\delta^2 CV}{\delta r^2} = [(1 - c)p^2(1 - e^{-np})e^{-rp}]100,$$

which is nonnegative. Intuitively $\delta^2 CV/\delta r^2$ can either be zero or positive depending on whether the challenger has sent any negative advertisements. If the challenger has sent no negative advertisements, then $\delta^2 CV/\delta r^2$ will be zero since additional rebuttals have no effect. If the challenger has sent some negative advertisements, then $\delta^2 CV/\delta r^2$ will be positive since each additional rebuttal will have fewer and fewer constituents that it can affect. Since most challengers spend money, this implies that the incumbent's campaign expenditures usually exhibit diminishing returns, that is $\delta^2 CV/\delta IE^2 \geq 0$.

The cross partial derivative of CV with respect to r and n is

$$\frac{\delta^2 CV}{\delta r \delta n} = -[(1 - c)p^2 e^{-p(n+r)}]100,$$

which is negative. Intuitively $\delta^2 CV/\delta r \delta n$ is negative since the effectiveness of an additional rebuttal depends on how many constituents have already received at least one negative advertisement: the more negative advertisements that have been sent, the more effective is an additional rebuttal. This implies that the effectiveness of additional incumbent campaign expenditures depends on how much money the challenger has already spent, that is, $\delta^2 CV/\delta IE \delta CE < 0$.

Finally, comparing the absolute values of the first partial derivatives shows that if the probability of receiving any given advertisement (p) is small and if the number of advertisements that the challenger sends is not too large, then the absolute value of the first partial derivative of CV with respect to n is greater than the absolute value of the first partial derivative of CV with respect to r. Intuitively the result occurs because there are more constituents that can be influenced by the challenger's negative advertisements than there are constituents that can be influenced by the incumbent's rebuttals. This implies that, in general, the challenger's campaign expenditures are more effective than the incumbent's campaign expenditures, that is, $|\delta CV/\delta CE| > |\delta CV/\delta IE|$.

3. Regression Model

The theory in section 2 predicts the signs and magnitudes of the partial derivatives of CV with respect to CE and IE. What the theory does not predict is the exact functional form of the relationship. Two reasonable functional forms are:

Model A

$$CV = a_1 + b_{11}CE + b_{12}IE + b_{13}SHARE + b_{14}P + b_{15}CPS + e_1$$

and

Model B

$$CV = a_2 + b_{21}CE + b_{22}IE + b_{23}CECE + b_{24}IEIE + b_{25}CEIE + b_{26}P + b_{27} + e_2;$$

where

CV = the challenger's percentage of the two party vote,[4]
CE = the challenger's spending in ten thousands of dollars,[5]

---

4. Election data come from Scammon and McGilvary 1987.
5. Campaign expenditure data come from the Federal Election Commission 1987.

IE = the incumbent's spending in ten thousands of dollars,
$SHARE$ = the challenger's percentage of total expenditures, that is, (CE/CE + IE)100,
$CECE$ = the challenger's spending in ten thousands of dollars squared,
$IEIE$ = the incumbent's spending in ten thousands of dollars squared,
$CEIE$ = the challenger's spending in ten thousands of dollars times the incumbent's spending in ten thousands of dollars,
P = the challenger's party (1 if Democratic, 0 if Republican),
CPS = the challenger's party strength in the district,[6]

the a_j's are the intercepts, the b_{ji}'s regression coefficients, and the e_j's are the stochastic disturbance terms.[7]

Models A and B are reasonable functional forms since they can be used to test the signs of the partial derivatives. For example, the sign of $\delta CV/\delta CE$ can be evaluated by differentiating the models with respect to CE.

4. Empirical Results

Models A and B were estimated for the 1986 U.S. House of Representative general elections using ordinary least squares.[8,9] The results, listed in table 1, show that the estimated regression coefficients for IE and $SHARE$ in model A and for CE, $CECE$, $IEIE$, and $CEIE$ in model B are statistically significant.[10] The results also show that the estimated regression coefficients for CE in model A and for IE in model B are statistically insignificant.

Although the estimated regression coefficients for some of the expenditure variables are statistically insignificant, these variables should not be dropped from the models. The high R^2s from regressing these variables on the other explanatory variables in each model suggest that a multicollinearity

---

6. The vote of the candidate running under the challenger's party affiliation in the previous election was used as a proxy for this variable.

7. The variables P and CPS are included to be consistent with the previous literature.

8. Following Jacobson (1978 and 1985) I have only included electoral races in which the incumbent faced a major party challenger in the current and in the previous election. I exclude the electoral races in Ohio since new districts were established July 12, 1985.

9. To examine whether the ordinary least squares estimates for model A suffer from a simultaneity problem, I ran a Hausman test (see Kmenta 1986). The instruments that I used for the Hausman test were the ones proposed by Jacobson (1978). The results of the Hausman test do not support the conclusion that the ordinary least squares estimates suffer from a simultaneity problem.

10. The signs of the estimated regression coefficients for $SHARE$ in model A and for CE, $CECE$, $IEIE$, and $CEIE$ in model B are predicted by theory. To test their statistical significance, I used one-tail tests.

TABLE 1.   OLS RESULTS:
Dependent Variable CV

Explanatory Variables	Coefficients/(t-statistics)	
	Model A	Model B
Constant	8.447	12.34
	(5.852)	(8.786)
CE	−0.0524	0.5829
	(−1.623)	(11.89)
IE	0.0699	−0.0280
	(4.276)	(−0.9033)
SHARE	0.2863	—
	(8.189)	
CECE	—	−0.0038
		(−7.799)
IEIE	—	0.0003
		(1.699)
CEIE	—	−0.0013
		(−1.946)
P	4.687	4.271
	(6.957)	(6.483)
CPS	0.4109	0.4007
	(9.632)	(9.302)
R^2	0.6711	0.7022
F-statistic	110.2	90.29
Number of observations	276	276

problem exists.[11] This means the insignificance of the expenditure variables may be due to the multicollinearity problem and not to lack of causality.

To test the estimated signs of the partial derivatives, I proceeded in three steps. First, I calculated a point estimate of the partial derivatives for each and every race. The point estimates were calculated by substituting the actual values of CE and IE into the equations for the partial derivatives.[12] Second, I divided the point estimates of each partial derivative according to sign and calculated an average value for the partial derivative, CE, IE, and SHARE.[13] Third, I calculated a t-statistic for each point estimate that had the predicted

---

11. The R^2 for CE regressed on the other explanatory variables in model A is 0.76, and the R^2 for IE regressed on the other explanatory variables in model B is 0.86. Since these R^2s are greater than the R^2s for the overall regressions, it appears that a multicollinearity problem exists (Klein 1962).

12. The actual values of CE and IE were not used to calculate the point estimates of all of the partial derivatives. For example, the point estimates of $\delta^2 CV/\delta CE^2$, $\delta^2 CV/\delta IE^2$, and $\delta^2 CV/\delta IE\delta CE$ for model B just equal the estimated regression coefficients for CECE, IEIE, and CEIE.

13. The races in which the point estimates for model A do not equal their predicted signs contain all of the races in which the point estimates for model B also do not equal their predicted signs. For this reason, I only used the point estimates for model A to calculate the average values.

TABLE 2. Point Estimates of Partial Derivatives

Point Estimates	Model A[a]		Model B[a]	
	+	−	+	−
$\dfrac{\delta CV}{\delta CE}$	274	2	1	275
	(266)	—	—	(273)
$\dfrac{\delta CV}{\delta IE}$	109	167	2	274
	—	(157)	—	(79)
$\dfrac{\delta^2 CV}{\delta CE^2}$	0	276	0	276[b]
	—	(276)	—	(276)
$\dfrac{\delta^2 CV}{\delta IE^2}$	239[c]	0	276[b]	0
	(239)	—	(276)	—
$\dfrac{\delta^2 CV}{\delta IE \delta CE}$	13	263	0	276[b]
	—	(263)	—	(276)
$\dfrac{\delta CV}{\delta CE} - \dfrac{\delta CV}{\delta IE}$	270	6	272	4
	—	—	—	—

[a]The number of statistically significant point estimates is shown in parentheses.
[b]The estimated regression coefficient is the point estimate.
[c]Thirty-seven of the point estimates are zero.

sign. The *t*-statistics were calculated by dividing each point estimate by its estimated standard error.

The results, listed in tables 2 and 3, support the conclusion that the challenger can increase votes by increasing campaign expenditures. The estimated value of $\delta CV/\delta CE$ is negative (and essentially equal to zero) only in races where the challenger outspends the incumbent by a wide margin. But this is consistent with the theory.[14] Similarly, the results support my claim that an incumbent can usually increase votes by increasing campaign expenditures. The only time the estimated value of $\delta CV/\delta IE$ is not negative and significantly different from zero is in races where the challenger spends either no money or so little money that there are no vote losses among the incumbent's supporters to be offset.[15] This is also consistent with the theory.[16]

The results support the conclusion that challenger and incumbent campaign expenditures exhibit diminishing returns, that is, the estimated sign of $\delta^2 CV/\delta CE^2$ is negative and the estimated sign of $\delta^2 CV/\delta IE^2$ is nonnegative. The results also support my claim that an increase in the challenger's cam-

---

14. The effect of large *CE* and *SHARE* is determined by taking the limit of $\delta CV/\delta n$ as n approaches infinity. Since the limit is zero, this implies that for large *CE* and *SHARE*, the absolute value of $\delta CV/\delta CE$ is very small.

15. Since the multicollinearity problem in model B is much greater than the multicollinearity problem in model A, this may explain why so few of the negative point estimates in model B are significantly different from zero.

16. The effect of large *IE* and small *SHARE* is determined by taking the limit of $\delta CV/\delta r$ as r approaches infinity. Since the limit is zero, this implies that for large *IE* and small *SHARE*, the absolute value of $\delta CV/\delta IE$ is very small.

TABLE 3. Average Values of Estimates

		Average Value[a]		
Point Estimates	Partial Derivative[b]	CE	IE	SHARE
$\dfrac{\delta CV}{\delta CE} > 0$	0.8	13	—	19
$\dfrac{\delta CV}{\delta CE} < 0$	0.01	94	—	79
$\dfrac{\delta CV}{\delta IE} > 0$	0.04	—	54[c]	9[c]
$\dfrac{\delta CV}{\delta IE} < 0$	0.14	—	34	28
$\dfrac{\delta^2 CV}{\delta IE \delta CE} > 0$	0.0008	68	—	58
$\dfrac{\delta^2 CV}{\delta IE \delta CE} < 0$	0.05	11	—	17
$\dfrac{\delta CV}{\delta CE} > \dfrac{\delta CV}{\delta IE}$	—	12	—	18
$\dfrac{\delta CV}{\delta CE} < \dfrac{\delta CV}{\delta IE}$	—	70	—	58

[a]Average values calculated by dividing the point estimates of each partial derivative according to sign.

[b]The table shows the absolute value of the partial derivative.

[c]Average value calculated using only the 72 races where the challenger spent money.

paign expenditures increases the effectiveness of additional incumbent campaign expenditures. The estimated value of $\delta^2 CV/\delta IE \delta CE$ is positive (and essentially equal to zero) only in races where the challenger outspends the incumbent by a wide margin. This is also consistent with the theory.[17]

Finally, the results support the conclusion that, in general, additional challenger campaign expenditures are more effective than additional incumbent campaign expenditures. The estimated value of $|\delta CV/\delta IE|$ is greater than the estimated value of $|\delta CV/\delta CE|$ only in races where the challenger outspends the incumbent by a wide margin.

5. Conclusion

The empirical results support all of the testable predictions of the negative advertising theory. In particular, the empirical results are consistent with my

---

17. The effect of large CE and SHARE is determined by taking the limit of $\delta^2 CV/\delta r \delta n$ as n approaches infinity. Since the limit is zero, this implies that for large CE and SHARE, the absolute value of $\delta^2 CV/\delta IE \delta CE$ is very small.

claim that the principal effect of incumbent campaign expenditures is to win back voters who would have voted for the incumbent in the absence of the receipt of challenger (negative) advertisements.

The empirical results also show the importance of developing a formal theory prior to specifying a regression model. Without a formal theory, most of the previous studies specify regression models that restrict the effectiveness of a candidate's additional campaign expenditures to be independent of how much the candidate or the opponent have already spent. This explains why most of the studies find, in contrast to my findings, that an incumbent cannot increase votes by increasing campaign expenditures.

REFERENCES

Aldrich, John H. 1983. "A Downsian Spatial Model with Party Activism." *American Political Science Review* 77:974–90.

Alexander, Herbert E. 1984. "Making Sense About Dollars in the 1980 Presidential Campaigns." In *Money and Politics in the United States,* ed. Michael J. Malbin. Chatham, N.J.: Chatham House.

Davis, Otto A., Melvin J. Hinich, and Peter C. Ordeshook. 1970. "An Expository Development of a Mathematical Model of the Electoral Process." *American Political Science Review* 64:426–48.

Downs, Anthony. 1957. *An Economic Theory of Democracy.* New York: Harper & Row.

Federal Election Commission. 1987. *FEC Reports On Financial Activity 1985–1986.* Washington, D.C.

Glantz, Stanton A., Alan I. Abramowitz, and Michael P. Burkhart. 1976. "Election Outcomes: Whose Money Matters?" *Journal of Politics* 38:1033–38.

Goldenberg, Edie N., and Michael W. Traugott. 1984. *Campaigning for Congress.* Washington, D.C.: Congressional Quarterly.

Hogg, Robert V., and Allen T. Craig. 1978. *Introduction to Mathematical Statistics.* 3d ed. New York: Macmillan.

Jacobson, Gary C. 1978. "The Effects of Campaign Spending in Congressional Elections." *American Political Science Review* 72:469–91.

———. 1985. "Money and Votes Reconsidered: Congressional Elections, 1972–1982." *Public Choice* 47:7–62.

Klein, Lawrence R. 1962. *An Introduction to Econometrics.* Englewood Cliffs, N.J.: Prentice-Hall.

Kmenta, Jan. 1986. *Elements of Econometrics.* 2d ed. New York: Macmillan.

Monroe, Kristen R. 1979. "Econometric Analysis of Electoral Behavior: A Critical Review." *Political Behavior* 1:137–73.

Scammon, Richard M., and Alice V. McGilvary. 1987. *America Votes 17.* Washington, D.C.: Congressional Quarterly.

Silberman, Jonathan, and Gilbert Yochum. 1978. "The Role of Money in Determining Election Outcomes." *Social Science Quarterly* 58:671–82.

Thomas, Scott J. N.d. "Do Incumbent Campaign Expenditures Matter?" *Journal of Politics*. Forthcoming.

Welch, William P. 1981. "Money and Votes: A Simultaneous Equation Model." *Public Choice* 36:209–34.

Wittman, Donald. 1983. "Candidate Motivation: A Synthesis of Alternative Theories." *American Political Science Review* 77:142–57.

Laissez-Faire in Campaign Finance

*W. Mark Crain, Robert D. Tollison, and
Donald R. Leavens*

1. Introduction

Basic economics teaches that money is a veil over the real economy. The same
axiom applies to the role of money in politics. Campaign contributions are the
money of politics; one must pierce the veil of campaign contributions to
understand their real effects. To date the literature has been focused, with
varying results, on two issues—the impact of campaign finance on election
outcomes, stressing that such laws represent a form of incumbent protection,
and the ability of contributors to 'buy' legislation. These and related issues
have been addressed by analysts working in this area (see, for example,
Jacobson 1980; Welch 1981; Peltzman 1984; and Thomas 1986).[1]

In this essay we take a different tack in analyzing the role of money in
politics. We ask what we think is a more basic question—what is the impact
of campaign contribution limits on controlling government? To address this
issue we present a theory of legislative activity in section 2. The theory, which
is based on the incentives of geographically-based legislators to support
wealth transfers from the polity at large to finance benefits for local constituents, makes a specific prediction. It predicts that laissez-faire in campaign
contributions will lead to less government spending on budgetary redistribution and to a greater output of laws by the legislature. In other words, the rules
governing campaign finance affect the incentives of politicians to redistribute

Reprinted from *Public Choice* 56 (1988): 201–12. © Martinus Nijhoff Publishers, Dor-
drecht. Reprinted by permission of Kluwer Academic Publishers. We are grateful to Kevin Grier,
James C. Miller III, William Miller, Dennis C. Mueller, and Scott Thomas for helpful discussions. The usual caveat applies.

1. Discussions of the relationship between campaign finance and election outcomes are
also in Glants, Abramowitz, and Burkhart 1976; Jacobson 1976 and 1978; Silberman and
Yochum 1978; and Jacobson 1985.

wealth in specific ways (on-budget versus off-budget). We test the implications of the theory in section 3, using data on U.S. state governments. Some concluding remarks are offered in section 4.

2. The Model

Consider the following model of the legislative process. Each legislator seeks reelection using two tools of office, the creation of laws (L) and fiscal transfers to constituents (T). The legislator's production process for reelection is expressed as

$$V = V [L, T] . \tag{1}$$

The vote functions (V) can be thought of as iso-majority curves where L and T are the relevant inputs to achieve given vote margins.

There are two bases for distinguishing between laws and fiscal transfers in the vote-generating function. First, in U.S. legislatures the budgetary process is governed by different procedural rules and committees than other types of legislative measures. Second, the costs and benefits of laws are spread over the whole constituency, while the costs and benefits of fiscal transfers are concentrated within given interest groups or districts.

The passage of additional laws (L) increases votes for two reasons. First, new laws offer direct benefits to voting residents, and second, laws increase receipts from campaign contributors.[2] So,

$$V_L > 0 . \tag{1a}$$

(Throughout the essay subscripts stand for partial or total derivatives, as appropriate.)

Fiscal transfers to constituents (T) increase votes, so in general

$$V_T \geq 0 . \tag{1b}$$

Transfers can be obtained in two ways. Each legislator can generate new wealth transfers to constituents by taxing residents of his/her district (R) or by taxing the residents of some other legislator's district (N). This relationship is expressed as

$$T = T [R,N] , \tag{2}$$

---

2. The importance of campaign expenditures for election outcomes is controversial. The weight of the empirical evidence suggests that spending has an effect on voting outcomes. See the references cited previously.

where

$$T_R \geq 0 \text{ and } T_N \geq 0 , \tag{3}$$

because taxes from either source provide a budget to finance transfers. However, $T_N > T_R$ because nonresidents cannot vote in the legislator's home district. At the margin taxes imposed on "foreigners" have more political appeal and will increase the incentive to generate transfers. Thus, in arranging the supply schedule of potential transfers, those programs that tax residents in other districts and benefit residents in the home district represent one of the lowest cost margins of political action because nonresidents cannot vote in local elections.[3]

The set of opportunities for exporting the cost of a transfer to nonresidents is N, where

$$N = N [D,C] . \tag{4}$$

Legislative districts are represented by D, and C is a vector of other characteristics of the constituents in these districts (age, sex, race, income, and so on). The number of tax exporting opportunities will grow as the number of districts increases.

For the individual legislator,

$$N \text{ (Individual)} = (D - 1) . \tag{5}$$

Each district besides the legislator's own is a potential place to export taxes to finance transfers to constituents. In total, each legislator is in the same position. Thus, the number of aggregate export opportunities is

$$N \text{ (Aggregate)} = (D) (D - 1) . \tag{6}$$

At the lower limit, at-large representation, there is only one legislative district, and there are no nonresidents. When there are two districts, there are two export opportunities—A taxes B and B taxes A. For three districts export opportunities grow to six—A taxes B and C, B taxes A and C, and C taxes A and B. As the number of districts increases, the number of aggregate export opportunities grows exponentially, according to

$$N_D = 2D - 1 . \tag{7}$$

---

3. The process of taxing or passing through price effects to nonvoters has been discussed, from various points of view, in the literature. See especially McLure 1967, Peltzman 1971, Zardkoohi 1977, Easterbrook 1983, and Maloney, McCormick, and Tollison 1984.

The effect of a change in the number of districts on votes is

$$\frac{\delta V}{\delta D} = V_T \cdot T_N \cdot N_D > 0. \tag{8}$$

From (1b), (3), and (7), the second derivative will be nonnegative as well. This implies that an increase in the number of districts will increase budget transfers, and at an increasing rate. Transfers will also be related to the number of districts because the scope of interests within a district will narrow as there are more of them. More homogeneity within districts increases the opportunity for tax exporting. A larger set of tax options becomes politically feasible with more districts because it becomes easier for the legislator to find taxes that avoid his/her own district.[4]

With this model of legislator behavior in hand, we pose a simple question—how do campaign finance laws impact on the process? Campaign contributing laws affect the most productive mix of the two types of reelection tools. The attractiveness of passing another law versus voting another transfer changes when campaign finance money is controlled. The impact of controls on the incentive of the legislator to rely on L versus T is twofold.

First, when campaign contributions are unrestricted, the incentive to produce additional laws is higher, so V_L (restrictions) $< V_L$ (no restrictions). Contributions in any form or amount are legal, and contributors will bid according to the expected market value of legislation. Restrictions on contributions will reduce the return to legislators from passing laws. This part of the model is straightforward—an unregulated contributing environment will produce more output because contributions are relied upon for reelection. When contributions are restricted or banned, passing laws becomes a less productive tool for reelection at the margin.

Second, the impact of fiscal transfers on votes, V_T, depends directly on campaign contribution laws. Votes are not portable across legislative districts; money is. The exportation principle works because residency requirements for voting mean that "foreign" citizens cannot vote in local elections. However, and this is the important point, citizens from outside the district can make campaign contributions to local candidates. The possibility of foreign campaign contributions in local elections means that the incentive of local politicians to export the cost of local programs will be dampened. Thus, V_T (restrictions) $> V_T$ (no restrictions). Foreign money can be used to defeat

---

4. In practical terms the exportation process we discuss is quite feasible. The financing of local benefits with general taxes is perhaps the most common form of this behavior, but there are a myriad of ways in which the exportation of costs can be accomplished. A legislator, for example, can support a tax on farmers and rich people when he represents poor people in an urban district, with the proceeds of the tax going into urban programs.

costly local candidates, and so the tendency of politicians to export costs will be less where campaign money can flow freely across districts.

There are two main testable implications of our theory. Across U.S. states there is a dichotomy in campaign finance laws. Some states provide unregulated environments for campaign contributions by corporations, labor unions, and individuals. Other states ban direct contributions by business enterprises and organized labor, limit the allowable contributions by individuals, and generally make it difficult for organizations and individuals to influence politics with regulations about how and how much money can be given to politicians. Table 1 provides this information in summary form. Our theory suggests that states with bans or constraints on campaign finance will have more on-budget transfers and less legislative activity. We now turn to a test of these predictions.

TABLE 1. Laws Controlling Campaign Contributions to State Legislators

State	Corporations	Unions	Individuals	State	Corporations	Unions	Individuals
AL	Prohibited	—	—	MT	Prohibited	—	Limited
AK	Limited	Limited	Limited	NE	Prohibited	Prohibited	
AZ	Prohibited	Prohibited	—	NV	—	—	—
AR	Limited	Limited	Limited	NH	Prohibited	Prohibited	Limited
CA	—	—	—	NJ	—	—	—
CO	—	—	—	NM	Prohibited[a]	—	—
CT	—	Limited	Limited	NY	Limited	—	Limited
DE	—	—	Limited	NC	Prohibited	Prohibited	Limited
FL	—	—	Limited	ND	Prohibited	—	—
GA	—	—	—	OH	Prohibited	—	Limited
HI	—	—	—	OK	Prohibited	—	Limited
ID	—	—	—	OR	Prohibited[b]	—	—
IL	—	—	—	PA	Prohibited	Prohibited	—
IN	Limited	Limited	—	RI	—	—	—
IA	Prohibited	Prohibited	—	SC	—	—	—
KS	Prohibited	—	Limited	SD	Prohibited	Prohibited	Limited
KY	Prohibited	—	—	TN	Prohibited	—	—
LA	Limited	—	—	TX	Prohibited	Prohibited	—
ME	Limited	Limited	Limited	UT	—	—	—
MD	Limited	Limited	Limited	VT	—	—	Limited
MA	Prohibited	—	Limited	VA	—	—	—
MI	Prohibited	Limited	Limited	WA	—	—	—
MN	Prohibited	—	Limited	WV	Prohibited	—	Limited
MS	Limited	—	—	WI	Prohibited	—	Limited
MO	—	—	Limited	WY	Prohibited	Prohibited	Limited

Source: Book of the States 1980–81, 62–64. The state laws are current as of 1978.
[a]prohibited from insurance companies
[b]prohibited from certain corporations

3. Empirical Evidence

On-Budget Transfers

State budgetary and legislative activities in the U.S. provide a cross-sectional basis for testing the implications of our theory. We begin by looking at the predicted relationship between campaign finance laws and fiscal transfers. To do so we postulate the following model:

$$TRANSFERS/STATE\ BUDGET = f(House\ Districts,\ Senate\ Districts,\ Campaign\ Contribution\ Laws). \qquad (9)$$

We proxy the extent of fiscal redistribution with the proportion of transfers in the state budget.[5] The right-hand side of the model tests our theory in its most basic and simplified form. We enter the number of state house and senate districts to measure the number of transfer-export opportunities, and contribution laws to measure the presence or absence of laissez-faire in campaign finance.[6]

As the number of districts increases, we expect the share of the state budget used for transfer payments to increase, where campaign contributions are restricted. In states with no restrictions on contributions, we predict that campaign contributions will mitigate and forestall the impact of districts on the ability of legislators to export the costs of transfers to voters in other districts. The effect of *Districts* is an interactive one, and should differ in the two types of states, that is, restricted versus nonrestricted in campaign contributing. This calls for dividing the states into two separate samples— laissez-faire states versus states imposing *any* type of legal restrictions on political contributions. (From table 1 we classify California, Colorado, Georgia, Hawaii, Indiana, Illinois, Nevada, New Jersey, New Mexico, Rhode Island, South Carolina, Utah, Virginia, and Washington as laissez-faire states.)

The relevant test is whether the two types of states are different in the sense that our theory predicts. House and senate districts are entered as nonlinear relationships because our theory suggests an exponential growth rate in export opportunities (see equation [7]). We expect diminishing returns

5. The specific items included in our proxy of fiscal transfers are state government expenditures on public welfare, hospitals, health, and employment security administration. See Council of State Governments 1980, 288–89.

6. Note that we enter the number of districts in each house and senate and not the number of representatives. This controls for the fact that some states have multimember districts.

TABLE 2. State Government Transfers as a Share of State Budgets, 1978

	Coefficients/(t-values)		
Independent Variables	Controlled States	Uncontrolled States	Combined Sample (all states)
House districts	0.18×10^{-1}	-0.12×10^{-2}	0.15×10^{-1}
	$(3.49)*$	(-0.08)	$(3.3)*$
(House districts)^2	-0.15×10^{-3}	0.61×10^{-4}	-0.14×10^{-3}
	$(-2.87)*$	(0.34)	$(-2.67)*$
(House districts)^3	0.40×10^{-6}	0.34×10^{-6}	-0.38×10^{-6}
	$(2.54)*$	(-0.51)	$(2.45)*$
Senate districts	-0.72×10^{-1}	-0.26×10^{-1}	-0.17×10^{-1}
	$(-2.89)*$	(-0.85)	(-0.97)
(Senate districts)^2	0.14×10^{-2}	0.82×10^{-2}	0.22×10^{-3}
	$(2.12)*$	(0.80)	(0.43)
(Senate districts)^3	-0.95×10^{-5}	-0.69×10^{-5}	-0.61×10^{-6}
	(-1.63)	(-0.71)	(-0.13)
Constant	0.70	0.34	0.70×10^{-1}
	$(2.29)*$	(1.11)	(0.34)
Adjusted R^2	0.468	0.017	0.19
$F_{(d.f.)}$	$5.99*_{(6,28)}$	$1.04_{(6,7)}$	$2.83*_{(6,42)}$
N of observations	35	14	49
Residual sum of squares	0.27379	0.04201	0.50601

Source: Data are from *Book of the States* 1980–81, 86–87, 282–83, 288–89.
Note: Nebraska is excluded because it has a unicameral legislature.
[a]significant at the 5 percent level

at some point. The results of an OLS estimation of equation (9) on a 1978 cross section of U.S. states are shown in table 2.

In the states where some form of campaign finance regulation exists, we observe that the basic model explains almost half of the variation in the share of government expenditures on transfer payments across states. In contrast, the same model does not work at all in the laissez-faire states. Comparing the separate samples to the combined sample of states, we can reject the null hypothesis that the two types of environments for campaign finance are the same. (A Chow test is statistically significant.) Transfers are lower and unrelated to the number of legislative districts in laissez-faire states. This supports the argument that when it is allowed to flow freely across political geography, money resists exporting behavior by local politicians.[7]

In figure 1, we illustrate the general form of the relationship estimated for the states that control campaign financing. Figure 1 shows the effect of chang-

---

7. We tried various linear and nonlinear specifications of the model, and in no case were we able to find an effect of districts in laissez-faire states.

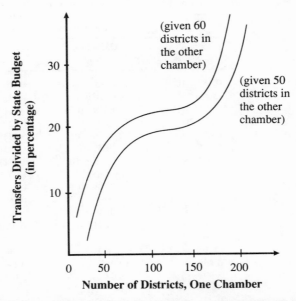

Fig. 1. Effect of geographic districts on budget transfers

ing the number of districts in one chamber for two selected numbers of districts for the other chamber (50 and 60). Using the estimated coefficients from the first column of table 2 as an example, we see a pronounced effect of adding districts on budget transfers. Over the range for state legislatures with up to 100 districts, more districts lead to rapid increases in transfers as a proportion of state budgets. The pattern levels off for the range of 100 to 150 districts, and increases exponentially thereafter.

Consider the magnitude of changes in the number of districts on the share of transfers in state budgets. In moving from 50 to 100 districts, for example, transfers are estimated to rise from about 13 percent to 25 percent of the budget (holding the number of other chamber districts constant at 60). Doubling districts again from 100 to 200 results in a 35 percent share of the budget going to transfer payments. In each case we are observing the effect of exponential growth in the number of export opportunities. When house districts increase from 50 to 100, the number of potential export opportunities rises from 2,450 to 9,900. Moving from 100 to 200 districts, transfer opportunities jump to 39,400.

These results are strong evidence that controls on campaign contributions result in the growth of government transfers, and that the growth is fueled by the incentives of geographically-based legislators. And, notably, a model that focuses directly on political incentives and not on cross-sectional demographic differences yields this result.

Off-Budget Legislative Activity

As a test of the second basic implication of the theory, we examine the output of state legislation in the two types of campaign contributing environments. The form of our statistical model in this case is:

$$RATE\ OF\ BILL\ PASSAGE = f\ (Campaign\ Contributing\ Laws,$$
$$Bills\ Introduced,\ Size\ of$$
$$Majority) \tag{10}$$

Three variants of the dependent variable are examined: bills passed per biennium, bills passed per day, and bills passed as a fraction of bills introduced. The variable for campaign contributing laws is defined as equal to zero in laissez-faire states and equal to one in states that ban or limit contributions (see table 1). *Bills Introduced* is entered into the regression explaining "bills passed per biennium" as the number of bills introduced per biennium. In the "bills passed per day" regression, it is entered as the number of bills introduced per day. In the "bills passed per bills introduced" regression, the number of bills introduced per biennium is entered. In each of the three estimations, we enter an interaction variable, calculated as the product of bills introduced times the campaign contributing law dummy variable. The interaction term allows for the possibility that the effect of contributing laws on legislative output is not independent of the level of legislative activity. Finally, we control for the effect of the size of the majority party in the legislature, which affects the cost of passage of legislation.

The results of estimating equation (10) by OLS for the three measures of legislative output are presented in table 3. All the regressions are significant, and each explains variations in legislative output reasonably well. In all cases legislative output rates are strongly related to the rate of bill input. The variable controlling for majority size is highly significant in two of the three regressions.

We test for the prediction that output is higher in laissez-faire states in two ways. In the third regression, *Bills Passed per Bills Introduced,* we find that passage rates in laissez-faire states are about 21 percent higher than in states with restrictions. (See the third column in table 3.) The interaction term is tentatively significant, which suggests that the difference between laissez-faire and controlled states gets smaller for higher and higher volumes of bills introduced per biennium. In the other two equations (the first and second columns in table 3), we find that the relationship is strictly an interactive one.

TABLE 3. Campaign Contributing Laws and State Legislation, 1977–78

Independent Variables	Coefficients/(t-values)		
	Bills Passed (per biennium)	Bills Passed (per day)	Bills Passed (per introduced)
Bills introduced (per . . .)	0.14	0.22	-0.50×10^{-4}
	(3.12)**	(4.89)**	(−2.11)**
Interaction between bills introduced and	-0.87×10^{-1}	−0.11	0.40×10^{-4}
contribution regulation variable	(−2.02)**	(−2.50)**	(1.66)
Size of the majority party	448	3.60	—
	(1.70)*	(2.38)**	
State campaign finance regulation	—	—	−0.21
(equals 1 if yes, equals 0 otherwise)			(−2.29)**
Constant	296	−0.15	0.52
	(1.51)	(−0.14)	(6.19)**
Adjusted R^2	0.27	0.41	0.20
$F_{(d.f.)}$	$6.77^{**}_{(3,45)}$	$12.07^{**}_{(3,45)}$	$4.90^{*}_{(3,45)}$
N of observations	49	49	49

Source: Data are from *Book of the States* 1980–81, 85, 104–5.
Note: Nebraska is excluded from the data because it does not denominate its legislature in partisan terms.
*significant at the 10 percent level
**significant at the 5 percent level

In each case, for a given number of bills introduced, about 10 percent more bills are passed in states where campaign contributions are unrestricted. One can think of this result in the following way. Over all states in the data, the mean volume of proposed legislation is about 4,000 bills per biennium. So if campaign contributions were "deregulated" to laissez-faire terms across the country, roughly 400 more bills would be passed each biennium in the now regulated states.[8]

4. Conclusion

What can we make of our results? It will come as a surprise to no one that entities such as corporations are better able to resist taxes and general purpose transfers and to obtain the passage of more laws and off-budget wealth transfers where campaign finance is not regulated. Indeed, recognition of this effect is undoubtedly one of the reasons that states have moved to regulate campaign finance. However, our analysis stresses the other side of the coin.

8. This extrapolation of the results assumes that campaign contributing in one state does not depend on contributing in other states. The predicted increase in legislation would be less if some of the money now contributed in laissez-faire states is diverted to deregulated states.

Campaign finance regulation is not a free lunch. While off-budget government may decline in the presence of controls on financing, on-budget government grows rather dramatically. This suggests that the relevant political trade-off in efforts to regulate campaign finance is between corporate and perhaps labor interests on the one hand and the recipients and brokers of fiscal transfers on the other. That incumbent legislators may gain from campaign finance regulation is not new; that there are other major interest groups that may gain, such as political entrepreneurs for the needy, is, to our knowledge, new. Finally, our theory suggests that campaign finance regulation will be more profitable (in the Peltzman sense) in those jurisdictions that offer the greatest opportunity for geographic redistributions. We note that the average number of house districts is 98 in regulated states and 67 in unregulated states. We thus see campaign finance regulation where the gains from regulation are highest.

REFERENCES

Council of State Governments. 1980. *Book of the States,* vol. 23. Lexington, Ky.: Council of State Governments.
Easterbrook, F. H. 1983. "Antitrust and the Economics of Federalism." *Journal of Law and Economics* 26 (April): 23–50.
Glants, J., A. Abramowitz, and M. Burkhart. 1976. "Election Outcomes: Whose Money Matters?" *Journal of Politics* 38: 1033–38.
Jacobson, G. 1976. "Practical Consequences of Campaign Finance Reform: An Incumbent Protection Act?" *Public Policy* 24 (Winter): 1–32.
———. 1978. "The Effects of Campaign Spending in Congressional Elections." *American Political Science Review* 72: 469–91.
———. 1980. *Money in Congressional Elections.* New Haven: Yale University Press.
———. 1985. "Money and Votes Reconsidered: Congressional Elections, 1972–1982." *Public Choice* 47: 7–62.
McLure, C. E. 1967. "Tax Exporting in the United States: Estimates for 1962." *National Tax Journal* 20 (March): 49–77.
Maloney, M. T., R. E. McCormick, and R. D. Tollison. 1984. "Economic Regulation, Competitive Governments, and Specialized Resources." *Journal of Law and Economics* 27 (October): 329–38.
Peltzman, S. 1971. "Pricing in Public Enterprises." *Journal of Law and Economics* 14 (October): 109–48.
———. 1976. "Toward a More General Theory of Regulation." *Journal of Law and Economics* 19 (August): 211–40.
———. 1984. "Constituent Interest and Congressional Voting." *Journal of Law and Economics* 27 (April): 181–210.
Silberman, J., and G. Yochua. 1978. "The Role of Money in Determining Election Outcomes." *Social Science Quarterly* 58: 671–82.

Thomas, S. 1986. "Do Incumbent Campaign Expenditures Matter?" Department of Economics, University of California, Irvine. Manuscript.

Welch, W. P. 1981. "Money and Votes: A Simultaneous Equation Model." *Public Choice* 36, no 2: 290–34.

Zardkoohi, A. 1977. "The Economics of Public Enterprise." Ph.D. diss. Virginia Polytechnic Institute and State University.

Part 8
Institutions and Attenuated
Property Rights

Constitutional Constraints and the Size of Legislatures

Gary M. Anderson and Robert D. Tollison

1. Introduction

Constitutional economics maintains that constitutional constraints which limit the discretion of political actors can have significant effects on government behavior. Much attention has been given to the potential effects of a balanced budget amendment to the U.S. Constitution on the spending and taxing behavior of the Federal government (Rowley 1987; Tollison and Wagner 1987). Many public choice theorists have argued that such a constitutional restriction would be equivalent to a kind of brake on the propensity of the legislature in a democracy to expand government spending and public debt beyond levels citizens consider optimal.

While most of the wrangling has taken place at the Federal level, most of the empirical evidence relevant to the debate is found among the states. Most states have some form of balanced budget requirement, either in the state constitution or enacted in the form of statute. Similarly, most states grant their governors line-item veto authority, and some states have various other constraints on the ability of state government to tax and spend. Recent research suggests that these constitutional constraints on state fiscal behavior may have a significant effect on restraining the taxing and spending of state governments (ACIR 1987).

However, the constitutional economics literature has hitherto remained essentially uninterested in the implications of constitutional constraints for problems involving another area of rapid growth in public choice, the economics of legislatures. How would a constitutional balanced budget amendment (for example) affect the organization and structure of the legislature as a firm?

Given the existing body of data at the state level concerning a number of different constitutional constraints, this question is not simply theoretical but

Thanks to James M. Buchanan, Mark Crain, and William Shughart for useful comments on an earlier draft. The usual caveat applies.

can be addressed empirically as well. Our purpose in the present essay is to consider the empirical evidence of the effects on legislative structure and organization of various different constitutional constraints at the state level. To the extent that constitutional constraints increase the cost of legislative transfers to interest groups, we expect to observe a reduction in the scale of the legislative plant as well, as the legislature shifts leftward along its long-run average cost curve. Stated simply, legislatures facing more constitutional restrictions should tend to be smaller, ceteris paribus.

The essay is organized as follows. Section 2 outlines the theoretical argument for a relationship between constitutional constraints and legislative size, and considers the possible relationships between legislative structure and particular forms of constitutional constraints in more detail. Section 3 presents an empirical model and econometric results. Finally, section 4 provides a summary of the preceding argument, and suggests some implications and possible extensions of the basic analysis.

2. Constitutional Constraints and Legislative Structure

The extension of economic theory to the behavior of democratic legislatures as organizations has been the subject of a large and growing literature (McCormick and Tollison 1981). One of the most obvious differences across state legislatures in the United States (which constitute a rich empirical source) is the variation across states in the size of the legislature. Legislative size is, in fact, typically taken into account in models of legislative behavior. However, relatively little attention has been devoted to the problem of the determinants of legislative size.[1] Our intention here is to consider the possible effects that constitutional regulations limiting the ability of legislatures to supply transfers to favored interest groups might have on legislative size.

Assume that a device like a constitutional balanced budget requirement is actually effective, and restricts the ability of a legislature to supply wealth transfers to favored pressure groups. Such a restriction would result now from higher political costs associated with deficit spending, and the consequent reduction in the ability of the legislature to lever higher rates of expenditure than voters would most prefer. This would imply that the costs of supplying wealth transfers through the legislature was higher, and the total quantity of such transfers provided to interest groups would be reduced.

Empirically, it is difficult to distinguish simple wealth transfers from

---

1. A noteworthy exception is the article by Stigler (1976) devoted to this problem. Stigler found that state legislative size was correlated with the size of the state's population and its growth rate—states with larger populations had bigger legislatures, but the size of the legislature tended to lag population growth. Stigler did not directly consider factors that might affect the productivity of legislatures or their costs of doing business across states.

other forms of government spending (for example, spending necessary to provide public goods demanded by voters), and, in general, to measure the magnitude of wealth transfers to organized interest groups. "Pork" is hard to measure precisely. But one of the predictable effects of the reduction in levels of "pork" may be relatively easy to measure. This is the effect of the market equilibrium level of wealth transfers on the size of the legislative "factory."

If legislatures are operating in the range of economies of scale along their respective long-run cost curves, an increase in the quantity-demanded of wealth transfers (which we assume is the chief "output" of the legislative firm) should tend to cause the legislature to expand the size of its operations in order to enjoy increased economies of scale. Hence, any factor which reduces the efficiency of the legislature as a supplier of wealth transfers (that is, raises its costs) may tend to imply that the legislature will become smaller as well. As firms go, even the largest state legislatures are tiny. All American legislatures should face potential economies of scale from expansion of the size of their "plant." Thus, constitutional constraints like balanced budget amendments, a gubernatorial line-item veto, rules of germaneness, and other measures may tend to produce smaller legislatures in the long run.

One particular constitutional constraint may tend not to redistribute wealth from legislatures to voters, but rather to redistribute wealth from one house of the legislature to the other. The literature on the economics of legislatures has frequently taken note of the structural and organizational similarities between state legislatures and the U.S. Congress. The features shared in common include bicameralism, the (typically) longer length of the elective term in the Senate, and the independence of the legislative from the other two branches of government, to mention only three of the most striking similarities. However, there is an important procedural dissimilarity that has heretofore received little attention from either economists or political scientists. This is the limitation in the U.S. Constitution of the appropriations process to the House. In only four states (Georgia, Louisiana, Massachusetts, and New Hampshire) are appropriations similarly restricted by the state constitution as the exclusive domain of the House. Both the U.S. Constitution and the constitutions of these states, in effect, prohibit the Senate from involvement in the appropriations bill introduction and construction process although in all cases actual passage requires approval by a majority in the Senate.

Naturally, the role of the Senate in either voting up or down an appropriations measure is crucial to the appropriations process. Because of this, it might be argued that restrictions on the introduction and detailed design of appropriations bills to only one house makes no difference—it has no net effect on either the net output of the legislature or on the relative influence of the House vis-à-vis the Senate. Even though an appropriations measure may be the exclusive preserve of the House, the Senate would seem to be able to hold the bill hostage, and thereby obtain indirect leverage over its contents. There are really three separate issues here that can be analytically distinguished.

The output of the legislative process—the value of the total wealth transfers produced and supplied to competing interests groups—would only be affected in the event that restricting the design and development of appropriations bills to one house of the legislature significantly increased or decreased the efficiency of the wealth-transfer production process. More precisely, we would expect to observe a net effect only if there were for some reason a reduction in that efficiency. If it were more efficient overall for one or the other house to specialize in the construction of appropriations bills, it would be in the interest of both houses to arrange for that specialization, and a rational body of legislators would act without need for a constitutional restriction. So a constitutional restriction of this sort could be a dead letter, having no net effect or even a negative effect.

On the other hand, even if the restriction of the appropriations process to the lower house resulted in no net effect on the total amount of wealth transfers produced by the legislature, it might possibly affect the relative influence of the two houses in the long run. The appropriations restriction is in one sense equivalent to a constitutional entry barrier preventing the competitive entry of the relevant potential entrant—the Senate—into the market for the provision of wealth transfers to interest groups through the appropriations process. Assuming zero information and transactions costs in the market for transfers, this restriction could have no effect because the indirect influence of the Senate would be no less effective than a direct role in the construction of appropriations bills. However, given positive transactions costs, the monopoly status conferred on the House by such restrictions could conceivably generate net rents for that body if the Senate's ability to influence the appropriations process indirectly were reduced.[2]

---

2. Before proceeding to analyze his case in more detail, it is necessary to acknowledge a broader problem. As in the case of numerous examples of "monopoly" (that is, a single firm granted the legal right to supply some good exclusively in a defined geographic area), monopoly *rent* may not necessarily be associated with the restriction granted to the "firm." Assuming (again) zero transactions costs, even state legislative lower houses granted such a restriction would nevertheless be operating in a highly competitive environment in which fifty other legislative "firms" (forty-nine state legislatures and the U.S. Congress) were also available as suppliers of wealth transfers to interest groups. Similarly, the legislative "firm" located in the District of Columbia necessarily competes with the state legislatures in the supply of transfers. Under such conditions any restriction that limited the effective degree to competition between the House and the Senate *within* the individual legislature might have no effect on the behavior of the legislature as a whole, given that the individual legislature was a "price taker."

In fact, the assumption of zero transactions costs cannot be realistically maintained. An interest group will normally face significant costs in any attempt to shift its investments from the

We are therefore interested in the net effects (if any) of appropriations restrictions within the legislature itself, that is, across the two houses. In short, do such restrictions increase the relative productivity of one house at the expense of the other, ceteris paribus?

Because both the House and Senate each provide complementary inputs in the production process (with enacted legislation requiring the approval of a majority in both houses), under certain assumptions it is possible that entry barriers preventing one or the other house from entering into competition directly with respect to the formulation of appropriations bills will have no net effect on the relative productivity of the two branches. Even in the presence of such a restriction, the Senate can still exert detailed influence over the construction of appropriations indirectly by exercising the threat of rejecting bills if they are inconsistent with the goals of its members. In the limit the only appropriations bill that can pass both houses will be one both houses can agree on. If information concerning bills was costless, there were no transactions costs associated with House/Senate exchange, and the House did not benefit from its ability to set the agenda for appropriations, this limiting case would be realized. If, in addition, neither the lower nor the upper house was the low-cost supplier of the technical services (for example, clerical, organizational, and so on) necessary for the actual construction of appropriations bills, it would make no difference which house undertook the task.

Given positive and significant information and transactions costs, the ability of one house to monopolize the process of design and formulation of appropriations might tend to generate significant relative gains for it and its members. The allocation of rents from the legislative process between the House and the Senate will be a bargaining process, but one in which the strategic positions of the relevant actors will vary significantly across states. In a state where both the House and the Senate can propose appropriations measures, and where the Senate can directly intervene in the appropriations process (regardless of whether or not the House customarily constructs appropriations), the House will not enjoy the advantages associated with setting the appropriations agenda. In the opposite case in which one chamber has monop-

---

legislature of one state to that of another. In particular, the cost of securing electoral support for a wealth transfer can be expected to increase rapidly as a firm shifts its efforts to an out-of-state legislature. The option of shifting firm operations to another state with a more amenable legislature will also involve significant costs in many (perhaps most) cases. In some cases, the firm will also have relatively large, highly specific, nonmovable and nonsalvageable investments in a given state, further impeding the available economic opportunities associated with interstate mobility, or "legislature shopping."

Therefore, the transactions costs associated in reality with shifting suppliers of legislative wealth transfers among the states tend to be positive and significant. Hence, state legislatures may tend to be price *searchers* rather than price takers, and normally earn some positive monopoly rent.

oly power to set that agenda, that chamber can restrict the choices available to the relevant voters—the members of the *other* chamber—in such a way that the latter are confronted with an array of take-it-or-leave-it options, forcing them to choose the appropriations bill they least dislike. On the demand side, interest groups will find it more efficient, all else held equal, to make deals with the House in the restricted setting because that body, unlike the Senate, can deliver a custom-built product. Such interests might still find it efficient to lobby the Senate for approval of the package produced by the House. The Senate will be in a position to extract or appropriate quasi-rents from the House (see Klein, Crawford, and Alchian 1978) as the monopsonist in the intralegislative marketplace, but because of time constraints on the legislative process—the Senate must vote to approve *some* appropriations bill passed by the House—the ability of the Senate to extract rents form the House will be limited. In addition, given the time constraints imposed on the process (failure to pass *any* appropriations bill would result in catastrophic consequences in terms of the present and future income of the legislature, and would represent an expected outcome that would be prevented by the gradual defection of rational individual legislators from the bill-impeding coalition anyway), the House as the legal sole supplier of appropriations "construction" will tend to have detailed informational advantages not enjoyed by the Senate, which would further limit the ability of the latter body to manipulate the appropriations process through indirect threat. In sum, in a positive information and transactions cost setting, in which agenda setting is both possible and potentially rent generating for the agenda controller, an appropriations monopoly right assigned to the House may shift both power and economic rents between the two cameral bodies in the favor of the House.

Furthermore, once a restriction of the appropriations process which prevents direct competition between the House and Senate is enacted in the constitution, there is reason to argue that the restriction will not be subsequently altered. If we assume that such a measure benefits one house relative to the other (either benefitting the House by making it more productive and its seats more valuable, or benefitting the Senate by allowing it to shift a portion of its workload onto the other cameral branch—permitting the Senate some margin of shirking), the net beneficiary body of the legislature will not agree to amend the constitution to alter the restriction.[3]

---

3. We are not directly concerned here with the origins of such restrictions, but we note that in the case of the U.S. Constitution the restriction on appropriations to the House originated with the Constitutional Convention and not the Congress. In those states in which a similar restriction exists, it is also the case that the restriction was a part of the original state constitution and has never been changed, and was not initiated by means of amendment. Therefore, the Senate in those cases never had the option to "vote its power away," so what might seem potentially to constitute a paradox is not relevant.

3. Empirical Results

In order to evaluate the empirical evidence from the states in connection with the relationship between constitutional constraints and legislative size, the following model was specified:

$$SIZE = f\,(Population,\ Y/POP,\ Statehood,\ Appropriations$$
$$Restriction,\ Balanced\ Budget,\ Line\ Item\ Veto,$$
$$Germaneness,\ Turnover),$$

where:

$Size$ = size of the House, 1984;
$Population$ = state population, 1984;
Y/POP = state per capita income, 1985;
$Statehood$ = year of statehood;
$Appropriations$
$Restriction$ = dummy variable, 1 if state constitution restricts appropriations process to the House, 0 otherwise;
$Balanced\ Budget$ = dummy variable, 1 if state government is not allowed to engage in deficit spending, 0 otherwise;
$Line\ Item\ Veto$ = dummy variable, 1 if governor has line-item veto authority, 0 otherwise;
$Germaness$ = dummy variable, 1 if state legislature required by constitution to restrict bills to single topic, 0 otherwise; and
$Turnover$ = the percentage of the House who are new this session, 1984.[4]

The dependent variable is the size of the *lower* house (and the ratio of the House to the Senate) rather than the overall size of the legislature for two reasons. First, it is an observed fact that state Senates maintain a stable size for long periods of time. In most states the Senate has not changed a single seat in size in the past seventy-five years. This may reflect the greater cohesiveness of the Senate as an organization, serving to protect the property rights of Senators (and the resulting flows of income to their membership) by limiting outside entry into that chamber. (State Senates tend to have lower turnover rates and longer terms of office than state Houses.) Also, the costs of altering the size of the Senate in response to interest-group demands are

---

4. Data are from Advisory Commission on Intergovernmental Relations (1987); Council of State Governments (various years); and Legislative Drafting Research Fund (1987).

probably significantly higher than those faced by the House, given that state constitutions define Senate size not directly (or indirectly) in relation to the size of population as in the case of the House, but independently—establishing either a fixed number of seats, or seats per county, or some other inflexible limit. Second, the state House is normally the chamber with primary responsibility for the appropriations process. In most states the Senate can introduce appropriations measures and otherwise directly influence the design of appropriations—that is, the House has no exclusive privilege in this regard—but the House normally performs these duties. The larger size of the House and the increased specialization which this implies may tend to make that body the low-cost producer of the technical services required for the construction of appropriation bills. However, as long as the market remains contestable by the other chamber, this allocation of workload would not be a rent-generating property right. Various constitutional constraints affecting the ability of the legislature to supply wealth transfers to interest groups will have a direct effect on that part of the legislative "firm" responsible for producing those transfers, and if that part is generally the House, we expect that is where to look for possible effects on legislative size.

Population represents a proxy for the degree of interest-group pressure in a state. A more populous state will be one in which the number of interest groups demanding transfers and the aggregate level of interest-group demand in the legislature will be greater. States with larger populations can be expected to have larger legislatures as well. Therefore, the sign of *Population* should be positive.

Y/POP is included to control for wealth effects on the level of demand for transfers from the legislature. In the short run, states with higher per capita incomes may tend to have higher, better organized interest groups, which are able to achieve higher levels of transfers from state government. On the other hand, states with higher levels of wealth got that way by having higher economic growth rates, and in such a setting the relative rate of return from rent-seeking investment aimed at achieving legislative transfers may be relatively lower than nonlegislative, ordinary economic investment, suggesting the possibility of a negative relationship. Also, to the extent that increasing levels of transfer activity impede economic efficiency and thereby economic development, more productive (and therefore bigger) legislatures may tend to depress the wealth of the state in the long run and lead to lower levels of per capita income. The sign of *Y/POP* is a priori ambiguous and could be positive or negative.

Statehood is a related variable, in that it is designed to reflect any effect the age of the state might have on the overall level of transfer activity. Olson (1984) argues that over time nations tend to become increasingly encrusted in transfer activity, as interest groups become more and more efficient at lobbying government for regulations and spending which benefit their members at the expense of consumers and taxpayers generally. All else equal, older nations—or states—may be expected to have higher levels of transfers to interest groups that have "accreted" over time.[5] Implicitly in this notion is the idea that interest groups enjoy economies of scale in lobbying, and these economies are only technically feasible (and therefore accessible) in the long run. Effective lobbying requires long-term investment, in part because interest groups can "buy" voter loyalty only indirectly—the necessary votes cannot simply be purchased using enforceable contracts in open markets; interest groups must engage in the painstaking process of convincing voting blocs that the individual interests of those voters are equivalent to those of the interest group per se. In the present case, this would imply that older states tend to have higher levels of governmental wealth-transfer activity because they are older. If there is an "Olson effect" of any significance, we expect the sign of *Statehood* to be positive.

Appropriations Restriction is included because such restrictions should affect the size of the House (or the House relative to the Senate) to the extent that it has any effect on the relative productivity of the two parts of the legislative branch. There are two reasons why a positive effect is likely. First, if the House has sole responsibility for undertaking the construction of complex appropriation bills, its share in the legislative workload may tend to be larger, in turn requiring a larger number of House members. Second, to the extent that the House monopoly on appropriations increases the productivity of that chamber in supplying transfers to interest groups, the scale of plant (that is, the size of the House) will tend to grow in consequence.

Balanced Budget reflects the most stringent of the various balanced budget requirements at the state level. All states but Vermont have some form of a requirement limiting their ability to engage in deficit spending, but most of these limits are extremely loose (for example, Rhode Island's requirement that the governor submit a balanced budget, which the legislature is left free to "unbalance") or readily evaded. However, states which require that no deficit be carried over into the next fiscal year have the most (nominally) stringent form, the same as that in which balanced budget amendments to the U.S. Constitution have been proposed. By reducing the ability of the legislature to employ deficit spending, the transfers potentially available to interest groups are reduced at the margin. This would represent a reduction of the total productivity of the legislature, and could be expected to reduce the efficient size of legislative plant relative to what it would be in the absence of such a

---

5. Older states might therefore be expected to have more powerful, growth-impeding transfer coalitions than younger states, ceteris paribus. Gallaway and Vedder (1986) employ the year of statehood in a model designed to estimate the determinants of differential patterns of state economic growth. They found a statistically significant, negative relationship.

limit. If a balanced budget requirement does in fact have such an effect, the sign of *Balanced Budget* should be negative, reflecting a reduction in the size of the legislature over time.

Germaneness is another constitutional limitation that might have the effect of reducing the productivity of the legislature as a transfer mechanism and therefore have a negative effect on the size of that body. Rules that serve to restrict the ability of individual legislators to enter into contracts with other legislators, in which support for different measures is exchanged (that is, vote trading or logrolling), should tend to reduce the efficiency of the legislature as an aggregate producer of transfers. The ability to place a technically unrelated measure in a bill dealing with another matter (for example, placing a subsidy to raisin producers in a bill providing appropriations to state welfare programs) allows legislators to protect their respective interests by enforceable contracts—the appropriations bill—rather than simply basing them on promises. Given the rather high turnover rate in most state legislatures, the violation of promises between legislators will be imperfectly controlled by reputational human capital considerations. If an individual legislator has a relatively short time horizon (owing to a high expected probability of electoral defeat), it may be a rational strategy for the legislator to break promises in the short run. Logrolling is one way available to control for this problem, the effects of vote trading being combined in one bill. Restrictions on such arrangements may therefore be expected to reduce legislative productivity and, consequently, legislative size. Because the *Germaneness* variable is designed to distinguish those states that have no constitutional restrictions of this nature, the expected sign of this variable is positive.

Naturally, the legislature is a component part of state government, and the legislative "firm" requires inputs from the other branches in its wealth-transfer production process. In the actual enactment of legislation, the governor will necessarily play a complementary role. In all states governors are authorized to veto legislation in whole or in part (veto override by the state legislature requiring some supermajority in both houses). However, in the case of many bills, numerous different distinguishable features will be included in one highly complex piece of legislation (even if all of those features apply to a "single topic" as defined in germaneness rules). For example, the appropriations bill providing funding for state welfare administration might be dozens of pages long and include a highly detailed breakdown of proposed spending activities. In a setting in which the governor can only vote up or down on approving the entire bill (that is, veto or not veto), in many cases vetoing one relatively minor feature of a large bill will entail very large costs. Frequently, the legislature will act to protect features of appropriation bills that it recognizes might be opposed by the executive branch by inserting them in otherwise acceptable bills, thereby holding the overall bill hostage. Some states permit their executives to avoid this problem by authorizing them to employ a line-item veto, which allows the governor to veto only selected portions of legislation. Such authority limits the ability of legislatures to protect particular (and potentially controversial) features of bills, increases the relative power of the governor in the legislative decision-making process, and thereby lowers the expected productivity of the legislature as a supplier of wealth transfers to interest groups. This may or may not have a net effect of reducing the total wealth transfers supplied to interest groups; it may simply transfer rents from the legislature to the executive. But to the extent that the increased power (that is, productivity) of the executive reduces the productivity of the legislature, this should be reflected in a reduction in the size of the legislature. Hence, the sign of *Line Item Veto* should be negative.

If larger legislatures become larger because of the greater productivity associated with increased scale, in long-run equilibrium the marginal product per legislator will be equal before and after full adjustment to any change (for example, an increase in the net demand for legislative transfers). However, Stigler (1976) notes that although the size of state legislatures does grow over time, that growth rate tends to be slow in relation to changes which might tend to increase the effective demand for legislative output. He found that (for example) the elasticity of legislative size was low in relation to changes in state population over time, which he used as a simple proxy for interest-group pressure: state legislatures tend to take a long time (sometimes decades) to adjust fully to sudden population growth. This, in turn, would imply that, all else equal, larger legislatures (those which have historically grown at the highest net rate) will show higher marginal productivity per legislature. States in which population and economic development (and hence interest-group pressures) have been rising the fastest should also be the states in which the scale of the legislative "plant" should be lagging the most relative to the efficient size. Legislatures in which the marginal product per legislator tends to be higher will therefore have more *valuable* seats, and competition for seats should be greater as a result. This higher level of effective competition should be reflected in a higher turnover rate in the legislature, implying greater levels of competitive entry into that body and reduced stability of tenure of seats for present holders. We expect that the sign of *Turnover* will be positive.

Table 1 reports the regression results in the case of *Size* as dependent variable, and table 2 reports the results where *Ratio* is the dependent variable. The variables generally have signs consistent with our expectations. *Statehood* and *Turnover* are each highly significant, the former negative and the latter positive. *Appropriations Restriction, Line Item Veto, Balanced Budget,* and *Germaneness* also all have the anticipated signs. *Appropriations Restriction* and *Germaneness* are each statistically significant at the 1 percent and 5 percent levels, respectively. In other words, state legislatures that are subject

TABLE 1. Dependent Variable: SIZE, OLS

	Model 1	Model 2
Constant	929.369	821.238
	(3.56)	(3.09)
Population	0.0006	0.0009
	(0.43)	(0.66)
Y/POP	−0.0042	−0.0042
	(−1.05)	(−1.07)
Statehood	−0.4169	−0.3758
	(−2.91)***	(−2.64)***
Appropriations Restrictions	81.475	75.275
	(3.46)***	(3.26)***
Balanced Budget	−21.819	−21.034
	(−1.52)	(−1.50)
Line-Item Veto	−27.842	
	(−1.52)	
Germaneness		35.777
		(−2.14)**
Turnover	0.9149	0.9377
	(2.08)**	(2.19)**
R^2	0.54	0.56
F	7.04	7.70
N	50	50

***significant at 1 percent level
**significant at 5 percent level
*significant at 10 percent level

to germaneness restrictions on bill introduction and (more weakly) to balanced budget requirements and a gubernatorial line-item veto tend to be smaller as a result, and the presence of appropriations-bill restrictions that protect the House from appropriations competition from the Senate is associated with larger Houses.

4. Conclusion

Rules that limit the permissible range of behavior by legislatures in their efforts to deliver wealth-transfers to interest groups and those that restrict the process of competition between the two houses in a bicameral legislature appear to have a significant marginal impact on legislative output in a predictable direction. Constitutional constraints matter, whether in the form of a capital "C" (that is, incorporated in the formal state constitutional document) or a small "c" (present in the body of rules and conventions that are not expressly included in the state constitution).

TABLE 2. Dependent Variable: RATIO, OLS

	Model 1	Model 2
Constant	22.417	20.083
	(2.08)	(1.77)
Population	−2.942D—05	−2.901D—05
	(−0.51)	(−0.50)
Y/POP	−7.427D—05	−8.025D—05
	(−0.44)	(−0.47)
Statehood	−0.0098	−0.0094
	(−1.66)*	(−1.55)
Appropriations Restrictions	3.271	2.995
	(3.36)***	(3.05)***
Balanced Budget	−0.8117	−0.8322
	(−1.37)	(−1.40)
Line-Item Veto	−1.616	
	(−2.16)**	
Germaneness		1.427
		(2.01)**
Turnover	0.0446	0.0464
	(2.46)***	(2.54)***
R^2	0.48	0.47
F	5.60	5.44
N	50	50

***significant at 1 percent level
**significant at 5 percent level
*significant at 10 percent level

REFERENCES

Abrams, B. A., and W. R. Dougan. 1986. "The Effects of Constitutional Restraints on Government Spending." *Public Choice* 49: 101–17.
Council of State Governments. Various years. *The Book of States.* Lexington, Ky.: Council of State Governments.
Gallaway, Lowell, and Richard Vedder. 1987. "Rent Seeking, Interest Groups, and State Economic Growth." *Public Choice* 50: 123–38.
Legislative Drafting Research Fund. 1987. *Constitutions of the United States: National and State.* 7 vols. Dobbs Ferry, N.Y.: Oceana Publications.
McCormick, Robert E., and Robert D. Tollison. 1981. *Politicians, Legislation, and the Economy: An Inquiry into the Interest-Group Theory of Government.* Boston: Martinus-Nijhoff.
Olson, Mancur. 1984. *The Rise and Decline of Nations.* New Haven: Yale University Press.
Rowley, Charles K. 1987. "The Constitutional Route to Effective Budgetary Reform."

In *Deficits,* ed. James M. Buchanan, Charles K. Rowley, and Robert D. Tollison, 391–406. New York: Basil Blackwell.

Stigler, George J. 1976. "The Sizes of Legislatures." *Journal of Legal Studies* 5 (January): 17–34.

Tollison, Robert D., and Richard E. Wagner. 1987. "Balanced Budgets and Beyond." In *Deficits,* ed. James M. Buchanan, Charles K. Rowley, and Robert D. Tollison, 374–90. New York: Basil Blackwell.

U.S. Advisory Commission on Intergovernmental Relations. 1987. *Fiscal Discipline in the Federal System.* Washington, D.C.: Advisory Commission on Intergovernmental Relations.

Democracy in the Marketplace

Gary M. Anderson and Robert D. Tollison

1. Introduction

The literature on voting normally assumes that votes represent nonpriced resources. This is a reasonable assumption under conditions where votes have no explicit prices because of strict laws against bribery of voters and the near-universal use of the secret ballot. In the modern "vote market," buyers of votes cannot monitor compliance, and consequently cheating by sellers can be neither detected nor sanctioned. When voting is conducted secretly, contracts between the buyers and sellers of votes are unenforceable. This imposes a severe impediment on the efficient operation of such a market.

Modern voting theory concentrates on the logical problems associated with majority rule decision making (for example, cycling). However, these problems are contingent on a particular kind of electoral institutional setting. The secret ballot is a *necessary* condition for the existence of majority cycling phenomena in the context of large numbers of voters. In the absence of a secret ballot enforceable contracts between voters and vote buyers become feasible. Other factors will influence the efficiency of such a market, such as laws against bribery and legal penalties imposed on detected "corruption." But the existence of secrecy in voting will effectively eliminate the possibility of a functioning vote market. Given contractual enforceability, however, voters will allocate their votes to the most highly valued use. Under most circumstances, voters will act solely as the paid agents of interest-group principals. Individuals will vote to express the preferences of those principals and if voters choose to retain their own votes (that is, "consuming" their votes by casting ballots for candidates they personally prefer), they will bear the full

Thanks to Keith Acheson, Thomas Borcherding, Pamela Brown, James M. Buchanan, Anton Lowenberg, William Niskanen, and Gordon Tullock for helpful comments on earlier drafts. The usual caveat applies.

opportunity cost of doing so by giving up the market price they otherwise would have received.

In such a contractual setting, political outcomes would represent efficient solutions in the market for wealth transfers to interest groups.[1] Democratic decision making would hence become no more paradoxical than decision making across other kinds of open markets.

A free market for votes might also have important consequences for the behavior of government. In a setting where most voters are relatively poor and disorganized and consequently face relatively high costs of effective political activity, the average voter would choose to sell his/her vote in the open market rather than invest it in an effort to achieve redistribution from government. Most lower-income individuals sell their labor to employers rather than market the output produced by that labor directly (that is, self-employment). Similarly, if it were feasible for voters to sell their votes, many would do so.

Assuming that high-income property owners face lower costs of effective political activity, the relatively rich will tend to purchase the votes of the relatively poor. In the absence of a secret ballot, the potential victims of redistribution will thus be the low-cost producers (that is, buyers) of votes for use in the political decision-making process, while the potential beneficiaries of redistribution will tend to be the vote suppliers.

Such a free vote market would still permit rent-seeking interest groups among the rich to attempt to use governmental regulation to their advantage against competing wealth owners as well as against the nonwealthy. But at the same time it would tend to function to constrain the net redistribution of wealth from those with higher incomes to the less affluent. A free market for

---

1. Assuming that such equilibria tend to be fairly stable over time, political outcomes as well would tend to be stable. In any event, political outcomes would tend to be no less stable than the interest-group market equilibria of which they were the expression. In short, the question Why so much stability? becomes as irrelevant when markets for votes are permitted to function as a similar question would be in the case of the market for shoes or soft drinks. The problems associated with democratic instability enter in only when voters are not contractually bound in their voting behavior. The majority of voters may choose A on Monday, B on Tuesday, and C on Wednesday, precisely because they are completely unconstrained by contractual obligations in their voting behavior.

Of course, for a vote market to emerge it is first necessary that there be only a single voting round for candidates, and that the elected offices have fixed terms; otherwise the expected return to potential buyers of votes would be zero. This is another way of saying that in order for exchange to occur, the object of exchange must be scarce. The majority cycling literature often employs elaborate thought experiments in which the electoral process is not truncated (that is, there is no limit on voting rounds), and in such situations a market for votes is impossible. But in the real world of democratic decision making the situation is very different: typically there is only *one* voting round (election), and successful candidates serve fixed terms of office. Since votes are therefore scarce, vote markets are in principle feasible.

votes would act as a kind of competitive cap on majoritarian income redistribution. To the extent that such redistribution is an object of government spending activity, this implies a lower level of governmental wealth transfers, ceteris paribus.

Historically, there may be no case of a completely free and unrestricted market for votes. However, until fairly recently open voting was the norm. A system of open voting is one where the electoral choices of individual voters is either explicitly or implicitly public knowledge. Throughout history a major characteristic of democratic processes was that voting was not conducted in secret. Because votes were not secret, enforceable contracts between voters and vote buyers were feasible. Although overt bribery of voters has seldom been legal, the buying and selling of votes has often been common for long periods. Like gambling or prostitution, vote selling has usually been against the law but normally ignored by the authorities.

Our purpose in the present essay is to analyze the differences between a democratic political system with, and without, secrecy in voting; to examine the historical evidence of the behavior of markets for votes in Great Britain and the United States; and to assess empirically the impact (if any) that the introduction of the secret ballot had on the growth of government in the United States.

2. Votes as Economic Resources

The possibility of a free market in votes has been discussed by previous writers, but has typically been judged to be either inefficient or simply impossible. We briefly consider those objections here.

Buchanan and Tullock (1962, 270ff.) regard the possibility of free exchange of votes in a democracy as feasible but argue that such a market would tend to generate severe external costs and for this reason would be inefficient. They argue that free exchange of votes under conditions of majority rule would increase the ability of majority coalitions to exploit minorities.[2] Although Buchanan and Tullock (1962, 272) admit that, assuming perfect markets, the ability of interest groups to exploit minorities with "purchased majorities" would disappear (because the potential victims would match the investment in vote purchases of the potential exploiters), they claim that in the real world certain minority groups (for example, the poor) are likely to face

---

2. They also argue that rational individuals would agree at the "constitutional" stage to prohibit such markets because they would tend to increase the level of redistributive activity and make society as a whole worse off in the long run (ibid.) Hence, Buchanan and Tullock view the secret ballot as a kind of constitutional protection against rent seeking.

differentially higher transactions costs in vote markets than others (for example, the rich) and will become the victims of income redistribution as a result.

This argument cannot be limited to vote exchange, but applies to government by majority rule more generally. The "external costs" are the result of a system that allows coercive wealth transfers (by definition non-Pareto optimal), regardless of vote-transfer arrangements, and the only relevant question concerns the relative magnitude of coercive transfers likely to result from a majority rule system with, and without, free vote exchange. If we assume that rent-seeking and rent-protecting interests in vote markets face similar transactions costs, and accept the argument that the "randomness" introduced into the electoral process by unpriced votes introduces a positive bias in the growth of government—an assumption implicit in the Buchanan-Tullock account—free markets in votes might operate to *constrain* the magnitude of wealth transfers, ceteris paribus.

Coleman (1986) also considers the theoretical problems associated with free exchange of votes in detail and concludes that votes are not economic goods at all. Specifically, he claims that there are two critical differences between votes and other goods which greatly hamper the prospects for efficient exchange: first, votes are not alienable by voters (171); and second, votes (unlike other goods) cannot be "conserved"—they are either used in the election or lost forever (173). But the nonalienability of votes is simply a reflection of particular institutional arrangements; the vote could be separated from the owner if allowed by law. In fact, voting rights are commonly sold separately from actual shares by corporate shareholders. Nonalienability is irrelevant anyway; labor markets function efficiently despite the fact that an individual's labor is not "alienable." The second objection concerning the "fungibility" of votes is also irrelevant. Tickets to specific sporting events, plays, and other performances also command a zero price the next day, yet efficient markets for these goods exist. Of course, the nonalienability of votes from voters combined with the "fungibility" of votes together imply that a market for votes may be subject to relatively high transactions costs. A predictable transaction-cost-minimizing solution would be the use of long-term contracts for voting, analogous to labor contracts; voters would tend to sell their voting services over several elections rather than just one. If votes are as fungible as tickets to specific sporting events, we would expect something similar to "season tickets" to be a common contractual option.

There are other implications of market prices for votes. "Rational ignorance" will be irrelevant if voters who do not expect their marginal personal benefits to equal the marginal cost of becoming politically informed can sell their votes to political entrepreneurs who face lower costs. Only the preferences of the vote purchaser are important, and this individual or group, being a residual claimant, has an incentive to acquire information about public policy questions efficiently. (If the voter chooses instead to retain his/her vote for personal use, he/she will only do so if the marginal benefit from the exercise of his/her franchise right exceeds price foregone.) If markets for votes operate efficiently, the problem of voters casting ballots (essentially) at random disappears. Voting will reflect the same kind of rational allocation that we expect to find associated with any other form of private investment.

Interestingly, there are well-defined historical examples of political democracy in the absence of the modern secret ballot, where votes were openly exchanged and priced. Two of the most interesting cases have been studied extensively: Great Britain prior to 1873, and the United States prior to about 1890.

3. The History of Open Voting

There is a tendency among modern writers simply to assume that secrecy of the ballot (and the consequent effective elimination of the possibility of an efficient market in votes) is somehow a necessary feature of electoral systems which has always been a part of the democratic process. But the secret ballot is a relatively recent innovation in Western democracies.

In Great Britain prior to the passage of the Ballot Act in 1872 that established the secret ballot, it was common for votes to be openly bought and sold either through explicit bribes or implicit payments of various sorts. Williams (1970) explains that in eighteenth-century England, even the "forty-shilling freeholders" who were legally permitted to exercise the franchise were generally acting as the agents of others in their voting.[3] In eighteenth-century Britain, voting tended to be the electoral expression of the preferences of the voter's landlord or employer.[4]

---

3. He writes:

. . . the elections were arranged by the nobility and gentry meeting in one or other of the country houses or in an inn in the local market town. Once their wishes became known, the forty-shilling freeholders knew how to cast their votes—such were the pressures that the landed classes could exert, as landlords of farmers, as employers of labour, and as customers of tradesmen, on voters not yet protected by the secret ballot. (1970, 498)

If renters were really paying their rent partly in cash and partly by committing their vote to their landlord's use, the institution of the secret ballot—by significantly lowering the effective market price of their votes—would, ceteris paribus, have tended to increase the pecuniary component of the rent demanded by landlords. Such additional "freedom" was probably not welfare-enhancing for such renters, and (given that it restricted their choice set) may have been welfare-reducing in many cases.

4. According to Namier:

[Because] the voting was open and recorded in poll-books, people in dependent positions could seldom exercise a free choice; and as the agricultural interest was dominant in the counties, the result of county elections was determined as a rule by the big landowners—

At times, the amount spent by competing interest groups in bidding for votes was extremely large. For example, in the Oxfordshire Parliamentary election of 1754, the Tory party spent about 40,000 pounds to oust the Whig incumbents (Plumb 1963, 85). The same writer notes that total expenses for both sides in a contest for seats in a large county could total 100,000 pounds or more (Plumb 1963, 37).[5] The most costly election in the eighteenth century occurred in Northhamptonshire in 1768, where the three contestants were said to have spent over 100,000 pounds *apiece* (Morgan 1988, 178). The more-or-less open buying and selling of votes continued to be standard practice throughout the nineteenth century prior to the passage of the Ballot Act.[6] Combinations of potential vote sellers, organized to extract higher vote prices, were common (Morgan 1988, 176–77).

A similar situation existed in the United States. Ostrogorski (1964, 170) explains that electoral bribery became widespread following the Civil War and attributes this development to the rapid growth of cities, which tended to lower the transactions costs associated with vote buying. In many parts of the United States, agents of political parties set up booths at the polling places where they offered cash for votes. This practice was especially widespread in New York (Bryce 1910, 148). As he summarizes, "in the absence of secrecy, [the] voter could be followed by watchful eyes from the moment when he received the party ticket from the party distributer till he dropped it into the box" (Bryce 1910, 147).

Wendt and Kogan (1974) offer numerous examples of the bribery of

---

the territorial magnates and country gentlemen. . . . Neither in counties nor in boroughs was the least attempt made to hide or disguise the methods by which votes were secured. . . . It was taken for granted that the tenants would vote as instructed by their landlord or his agent, and the methods employed were so common that they were seldom named. (1956, 65, 68)

5. In pre–Reform Britain most Parliamentary seats were actually uncontested in most elections. Rather than attempting to wrest a seat from an incumbent by buying sufficient votes to defeat him, it was more common for those with Parliamentary ambitions to purchase seats outright from the patrons who controlled them through their influence over their enfranchised renters. According to Namier, in 1761 the ordinary price of "safe" seats was about 1,500 pounds, although in cases where additional advantages were to be expected, the price could range as high as 2,000 pounds (ibid., 166). Uncontested elections were often preceded by a "spirited contest" that ended just short of the actual election, when one candidate demonstrated to the others that he had acquired sufficient vote commitments to win (Morgan 1988, 175).

6. Even after the Reform Bill of 1832 (which extended the franchise to owners of property worth as little as ten pounds), bribery remained a common practice, although prices for votes tended to vary across boroughs (with smaller boroughs, where each individual vote had a greater weight in the final outcome of an election, commanding higher prices for votes); for example, according to Spearman (1957, 93) in 1841 the price of votes in the large towns of Leicester and York ranged from one to two pounds, whereas in the same year in the smaller town of Ipswich fifteen to twenty pounds were paid per vote.

voters in Chicago in the period prior to the enactment of the secret ballot in Illinois. For example, in the 1896 election for Mayor, in the Nineteenth Ward alone, the ward boss of the Democratic party reputedly paid $10,000 for votes (Wendt and Kogan 1974, 149).

While much is often made of the property qualifications for the franchise in prereform Britain, in reality all but the very poorest were eligible to vote. The qualifications for voting in the counties allowed essentially all citizens not receiving poor relief to vote; moreover, there is evidence that poor voters sometimes refrained from resorting to parochial relief because they calculated that they could make more money selling their votes (Morgan 1988, 178). In America, the franchise extended to between 60 and 90 percent of adult men in the thirteen states by 1789 (Dinkin 1982, 39).

The traditional British system of voting was especially efficient in facilitating such transactions because it was based on *viva voice* (that is, voters called out their votes), or by the show of hands. This system was also in general use in the American colonies, but after Independence the use of ballots became increasingly common in the United States. (The New England and the Middle Eastern states generally abandoned the *viva voice* method by the end of the eighteenth century; its use was abandoned by North Carolina in 1776, Maryland and Georgia in 1799, Arkansas in 1846, Missouri in 1863, Virginia in 1867, and Kentucky in 1890, and was discontinued in the West during the same period [Evans 1917, 3–6].)[7]

However, while the use of ballots may have raised the costs of monitoring compliance for vote purchasers, the "use of the ballot . . . seemed to have been entirely for convenience and with no object of secrecy" (Evans 1917, 3–6). Secrecy was not protected, and in most cases monitoring of electoral choices was greatly simplified by the widespread use of ballots printed in different shapes or colors by the different candidates or parties.[8]

---

7. The ballot was used in South Carolina (1683), Tennessee (1796), Alabama and Louisiana (both 1812), and Florida (1828–1833) either prior to, or since, statehood (Evans 1917, 5n. 11).

8. As Evans explains:

The ticket of each party was separate, and, as a general rule, could be distinguished, even when folded, from all other tickets as far as it could be seen. Frequently the party tickets were of a different color. In a municipal election in Massachusetts the Republicans used a red ticket and the opposition a black one; and in the same state in 1878 the Republican ticket had a flaming pink border which threw out branches toward the center of the back, and had a Republican endorsement in letters half an inch high. . . . The Democrats had a tissue-paper ticket of a pale-blue color. . . . The Democratic ticket used at the polls in Charleston, South Carolina, had a red checked back and was printed with red ink. (Evans 1917, 6–7)

The same author presents numerous similar examples, and notes that the "reason for making the tickets distinguishable was to discover how the elector voted" (ibid., 7).

Colored tickets and other evasions prevented the use of unofficial ballots from providing mandatory secrecy in voting.[9] Functioning in a similar fashion were laws (in seven states) requiring that the voter's ballot number be recorded on the list of voters next to the voter's name, and legal permission (or even requirement, in the case of Rhode Island after 1822) for the voter to sign his/her name to the ballot (Evans 1917, 10). Thus contracts between voters and vote buyers were readily enforceable because the votes cast could easily be monitored.

The "Australian ballot" was a system involving the mandatory use of uniform, officially printed ballots, and was first enacted in Kentucky in 1888. Over the course of the next twenty years, virtually all states enacted some form of "Australian ballot" system (by 1910, only Georgia and South Carolina were still holdouts; see Bryce 1910, 148). The polemical literature at the time presented this as synonymous with the secret ballot, but this was not always the case. An examination of the actual state ballot laws enacted during this period indicates that only a subset of states passed laws explicitly mandating secrecy in voting. This is important because the other features of the "Australian ballot" system would not necessarily serve to protect voter anonymity, but instead merely increase the cost of monitoring compliance on the part of vote purchasers. It is apparent that many states enacted ballot laws not with the express purpose of providing a secret ballot but to reduce electoral *fraud*. In fact, this was a major argument offered by contemporary proponents of the "Australian" system for its introduction, although modern writers (for example, Williamson 1960, 275) tend to ignore this aspect of the reform. Hence, several state laws (for example, Texas 1891) make reference to the goal of detecting and punishing fraud (Ludington 1911, 182) and also maintaining the "purity of the ballot" (Florida, Oklahoma, and Texas; Ludington 1911, 104, 166, 182). Some states (for example, New Mexico and North Carolina; see Ludington 1911, 154 and 160) allowed voters to prepare the official ballot elsewhere and then cast it at the polling place; Oregon and West Virginia (Ludington 1911, 168, 194) either required (the former) or allowed (the latter) voters to give their votes openly. In short, while some "Australian ballot" laws indeed required that secrecy in voting be guaranteed, such a feature was not universal. Even after this period of electoral "reform," the possibility of market exchange of votes (albeit at higher transactions costs) remained, at least for a period, in a number of states.

---

9. After the Civil War, fifteen states enacted "reforms" that prescribed a uniform color and ink to be used in all ballots. But these acts were evaded by the use of different shades of the required color by different parties (for example, in Ohio the Republicans used a very white paper, while the Democrats used cream color), or different sizes of ticket, or even different thicknesses of paper. See Evans 1917, 8–9.

4. Rent Seeking and Secret Voting

The buying and selling of individual shares in the right to influence government policy—that is, votes—presents unusual problems for the analysis of market efficiency. For example, in ordinary market exchange, the price of a good is a function of its expected use value and its perceived scarcity, and such characteristics can be readily estimated by potential purchasers, whereas the price of a vote will be determined by the expected behavior of *other voters,* and elements of uncertainty in the valuational process will be highly significant. Nevertheless, we assume that vote markets will produce efficient outcomes, given these relatively high information costs. However, it is not our purpose here to consider the efficiency characteristics of open vote markets, and/or how those markets differ from those across which other kinds of goods and services are traded.

Instead, we intend to consider the possible effect of vote exchange on the problem of wealth redistribution by government. Open voting allowed vote markets to develop, which permitted the rich to invest in rent protection by purchasing large blocs of the votes from lower-income citizens; the wealthy minority were less vulnerable to the depredations of the nonwealthy majority because the wealthy could buy a (temporary) majority as needed.

Consider the problem in the context of the universal manhood franchise. Wealthier citizens are likely to have higher reservation prices associated with their votes because they are likely to hold more valuable economic assets that they desire to protect from political confiscation and also because they will more often be members of organized interest groups that will function as voting blocs designed to benefit their members. By contrast, the relatively poor—in the late nineteenth century the majority of eligible voters—will have lower reservation prices associated with their votes. They have fewer assets to protect and relatively fewer opportunities to benefit from entry restrictions or other political rent opportunities. Also, the poor have traditionally tended to be relatively disorganized, probably in part because they have few assets and therefore few things to organize. In other words, the poor in their voting, as in other domains of behavior, are less likely to act as independent entrepreneurs but to sell their voting "services" to an "employer" who pays them a wage.[10]

Under a system of open voting, interest groups composed of both the rich and the nonrich will compete with each other for electoral support in the vote market. Even if the high-income interest groups do not have advantages in

---

10. This does not imply that poor individuals necessarily entered into long-term voting "contracts" with vote purchasers—although in Britain prior to the secret ballot such arrangements were common—but only that in voting they were more likely to be acting as agents of someone else to whom they were under contract, whether for the election in question only or for a longer term.

terms of lower costs or greater efficiency in lobbying, the outcome of the election will reflect a competitive market equilibrium. The size of the investment in vote buying, and not size of a group's membership, will determine the electoral outcome.

But if voters are unable to sell their votes, the nature of the problem changes. Assuming that the marginal cost of voting equals the marginal expected benefit, voters will cast their ballots in a manner consistent with their own personal electoral preferences. If individuals are self-interested income maximizers, they will vote in ways that they expect will serve to increase their personal wealth. Lower-income individuals do not have the valuable assets to protect by voting in favor of deregulation and decreased taxes; instead, they will tend to vote for candidates and programs that will transfer wealth to themselves by means of increased regulation and higher levels of government spending. Therefore, a mandatory secret ballot will increase the likelihood that lower-income (that is, nonrich) citizens will vote in favor of income redistribution to themselves.

There are additional reasons which suggest that the wealthy had major advantages in the competition for vote purchase in the period prior to the institution of the secret ballot. The wealthy and those in propertied classes represented relatively small, cohesive groups and faced low costs of organization for defense against redistribution efforts by government directed at themselves. By contrast, lower-income individuals were dispersed and faced high organizational costs. Even today, the poor are notorious for low rates of political participation and the ineffectiveness of their lobbying efforts. (This does *not* imply that lobbying efforts by others on behalf of the poor have been ineffective.) Perhaps most importantly, the wealthy have access to the financial resources necessary to compete effectively in the market for votes. If capital markets were perfect, low-income competitors would not be at a comparative disadvantage because they could borrow against the expected value of redistributed income resulting from the electoral victory. However, in the institutional context of the late nineteenth- and early twentieth-century period, this option was not available. The cost of raising the necessary capital was much higher for lower-income vote buyers than for the wealthy.

In fact, it would appear that the wealthy tended to dominate the markets for votes in practice. In both Great Britain and the United States, the voting services of the poor seem to have been largely purchased by the relatively wealthy. In eighteenth- and nineteenth-century Britain, it is well documented that entire boroughs of voters were essentially the employees of large local landowners and that the rich were the source of most of the bribery of voters. In the United States, the big-city machines were usually controlled by extremely wealthy groups of individuals and purchased a disproportionate share of the votes of the poor. Labor unions, guilds, and other organizations that could be taken to represent the economic interests of those in the middle range of the income distribution were evidently not major participants in the competitive bidding for votes.

After the passage of the secret ballot in 1872 in Britain, the percentage of Commons seats held by the landed interest fell rapidly.[11] Intellectual champions of the secret ballot predicted exactly this outcome.[12] Other factors may also have played a part in this development, but this change is consistent with the hypothesis proposed previously.

Circumstantial evidence suggests the possibility that this important electoral transition may have had some effect on the growth of government in both Britain and America. In the 1880s, the long period of decline in government expenditures as a percentage of national income (27.1 percent in 1811 to 7.4 percent in 1871) came to an end and was reversed.[13] By the first decade of the twentieth century, the basic legislation that formed the basis for the emerging Welfare State was in place in Britain.[14]

According to the U.S. Census (1959), government's share in the Gross Domestic Product fell fairly consistently from the end of the Civil War to the beginning of the twentieth century (dropping from an average of 6 percent per annum for 1869–78, to about 3.8 percent per annum from 1902 to 1906—a

---

11. According to Bentley (1985, 195–96), in 1868, 47.3 percent of Conservative MPs could be classified as representatives of the landed interest, while 30.9 percent represented industrial, commercial, and financial interests. By 1900 these percentages had changed to only 21.2 percent and 50.4 percent, respectively (the Liberal party had throughout the century overwhelmingly represented the latter group in its membership). The expansion of the franchise probably accounted for some of this shift; in the pre–Reform Parliament of 1832, the landed-commercial percentages in the Conservative side of Commons were 58.3 percent and 22.3 percent, respectively, indicating a significant drop between 1832 and 1868 in favor of the latter group. The introduction of the secret ballot may have been a factor in this diminished representation of the landed interests.

12. Although both Gladstone and John Stuart Mill had expressed opposition to the concept of the secret ballot in the first half of the nineteenth century, John Bright—the classical liberal and leader in the fight to repeal the Corn Laws in the early 1840s—was the chief proponent of the secret ballot within the Liberal Cabinet and played an important role in the eventual passage of the Ballot Act. Spearman explains:

The high seriousness of Gladstone and Mill [about the duty of a citizen to be publicly accountable for his vote] was not shared by the new generation; in the boroughs the majority of men were now voters, and the new Liberals were more impressed by the danger of losing elections through bribery and intimidation by their opponents than by the danger of tempting the elector to make a frivolous or selfish [?] choice. (1957, 124–25)

In other words, at least some of the advocates of the secret ballot did so (at least in part) because they openly sought a temporary political advantage over the (primarily Tory) landed interests.

13. Calculated from data in Mitchell and Deane 1962, 366, 389–91, and 396–99. See also Peacock and Wiseman 1961.

14. See Schweinitz 1943, 202, for a detailed summary of these developments.

decline of about 36 percent). Federal government receipts as a percentage of GDP fell by nearly 58 percent over the same period.[15] (Alternative data reported by Kendrick [1961, 296] show that federal government receipts as a percentage of Gross National Product fell by almost 32 percent from 1869 to 1900.)

Although the U.S. Census does not report GNP or GDP numbers for the period prior to 1869, the National Industrial Conference Board calculated the figures for the slightly different concept of realized national income (RNI) for ten-year intervals beginning in 1799 (Martin 1976, 6).[16] Federal revenues as a percentage of RNI fell from 1.11 in 1799 to 0.84 in 1809, rose to 2.80 in 1819, and proceeded to become smaller at each succeeding ten-year interval, reaching 1.24 percent in 1859. The 1859 level was 55.81 percent lower than the 1819 level.[17] (For purposes of comparison with the GNP figures mentioned above, it is useful to calculate the same percentages for the last half of the nineteenth century. Following the Civil War, federal revenues had increased to 5.43 percent of RNI in 1869. But once again, over the next forty years, this percentage fell consistently until in 1909 it equaled only 2.28—a post–Civil War decrease of 57.96 percent.)

During and after World War I, government spending at all levels grew steadily in the United States (allowing for periods of exceptionally rapid growth during, and partial declines following, major wars). Government growth has been as positive and consistent in the twentieth century as it was negative and consistent in the nineteenth.[18]

---

15. During the same period, federal budgetary *surpluses* were both large and persistent, making the percentage of *revenue* to GDP rather than *spending* the more appropriate measure of the relative size of government. Statistics for spending as a percentage of GDP would show a similar drop after the Civil War.

16. Realized national income is defined as realized private production income (including salaries and wages, entrepreneurial income, dividends, interest, and net rents and royalties) and realized income from government (which in the nineteenth century included salaries and wages of government employees, interest payments, and pension disbursements, for all levels of government). RNI is an obsolete national income concept, which is similar to, but tends to underestimate, GNP.

17. Given the fluctuations between deficits and surpluses in the antebellum era, it is not surprising that federal expenditures as a percentage of RNI do not show exactly the same pattern of steady decrease. However, expenditures divided by RNI were still 34.6 percent smaller in 1859 than in 1819—despite the fact that the later year was one in which the deficit was equal to 22.5 percent of expenditures, while in the earlier year there was a surplus equal to 14.6 percent of spending.

18. Higgs (1987, esp. 3–20) offers a detailed outline of the course of twentieth-century government growth in the United States. He argues that World War I was the first in a series of twentieth-century "crises" during and after which most net government expansion occurred, and attributes this shift to ideological changes among the electorate (which he leaves unexplained).

By 1895, thirty-seven states had some form of "Australian ballot" law (Evans 1917, 27–40); by 1910, this number had increased to forty-six (out of forty-eight states). As we explained previously, the "Australian ballot" was not necessarily equivalent to a secret ballot, although the two were commonly associated. Nevertheless, it is an established fact that previous to 1888 all states allowed for the operation of a system of open voting (although restrictions varied); by 1910, approximately 72 percent of the nation's population lived in states where the secret ballot was either a constitutional requirement or in which information about the electoral choices of voters was not publicly available.[19]

5. Empirical Results

If the introduction of the secret ballot acted to relax a previously existing constraint on the growth of governmental wealth transfers, we would expect to find state government spending levels in such states higher than in other states. Total spending by state governments is an appropriate basis for empirical study because all government spending necessarily involves wealth transfers (or redistribution) from taxpayers to tax "recipients." Was government more active in redistribution in secret ballot states?

In order to evaluate the effect of variations in secret ballot requirements across states, we developed and tested the following model:

> *Expenditures* = *f* (*Wealth, Population Density, House, Senate,*
> *Length of Legislative Term, Session Limit, Female*
> *Suffrage, Constitutional Requirement1, Constitution-*
> *al Requirement2*) ,

where

> *Expenditures* = total outlays of state government, per capita, fiscal
> year 1915;
> *Wealth* = total estimated true value of all private property in
> the state, per capita, 1912;
> *Population*
> *Dispersion* = land area of the state divided by state population in
> thousands, 1914;

---

19. This was calculated using *Constitutional Restriction2* (see section 5) as the basis. Alternatively, if the more conservative basis is used of counting only states in which there was an explicit constitutional requirement for secrecy in voting, in 1910 only 36 percent of the total population would be included; the voting age population would be about 45 percent.

House = membership in the state assembly, 1915;

Senate = membership in the state senate, 1915;

Length of
Legislative Term = dummy variable, 1 for states in which the service in the Senate is longer than that in the House, and 0 in cases where the length is the same;

Session Limit = dummy variable, 1 if the state legislature's session is limited in length in the state constitution, 0 otherwise;

Female Suffrage = dummy variable, 1 if state allowed women to vote prior to 1915, 0 otherwise;[20]

Constitutional
Requirement1 = dummy variable, 1 if the state's constitution requires that voting be secret, 0 otherwise;[21] and

Constitutional
Requirement2 = dummy variable, 1 if either the state's constitution requires that voting be secret, or that the use of voting machines is mandatory, 0 otherwise.[22]

The dependent variable is based on Census data for "governmental cost payments," which include all expenses of government operations (for example, the cost of collecting taxes, operating the legislature, interest on debt, and so on) plus the amount of payments made by state government to groups and individuals (for example, pensions). Use of this variable permits us to explore the relationship between the level of state government activity and other factors, most importantly the voting rules in effect in particular states. We chose fiscal year 1915 data even though earlier state-level spending data are available because of data limitations for some of the independent variables.

Wealth is based on Census calculations of the market value of all private property in the state, and serves instead of a per capita annual income variable, which we expect would be very highly correlated with the former if available data permitted a comparison; unfortunately, it does not. However, *Wealth* controls for the value of the tax base in a way that per capita income would not; in fiscal year 1915, approximately 58 percent of state revenue receipts derived from various forms of the property tax. (There were no state

---

20. Data from McDonagh and Price 1985, 417. States permitting female suffrage were Arizona, California, Colorado, Kansas, Idaho, Montana, Nevada, Oregon, Utah, Washington, and Wyoming.

21. This includes California, Colorado, Connecticut, Delaware, Idaho, Kentucky, Louisiana, Missouri, New York, North Dakota, Pennsylvania, Utah, Virginia, Washington, and Wyoming. Data are provided in Ludington 1911.

22. Those states listed in note 21, plus Montana.

income taxes at this time.) Assuming that government spending is a normal good, we expect *Wealth* to be positive.

Population Dispersion is included to control for the higher governmental transactions costs associated with a less highly concentrated population. The greater the dispersion of population, the higher will be the costs of providing any given level of public education, regulation, and other public services. States with a more highly concentrated population will require a lower level of per capita state spending on highways in order to provide a given level of transportation service to the community. Therefore, we expect that a state in which *Population Dispersion* is higher will tend to show a higher level of per capita government spending, ceteris paribus. This effect would imply a positive sign for this variable.[23]

Senate and *House* are intended to isolate the effect if any, of legislative size on state government spending levels, while allowing for the possibility that the size of each house may have a separate and distinct effect. McCormick and Tollison (1981, 29–45) outline a theory that predicts that legislative size should affect the cost faced by interest groups of influencing legislative outcomes. One reason is that larger legislatures imply a higher cost of reaching agreement. Also, as the size of the legislature increases, the marginal influence of (and hence return to) individual legislators will decrease, and hence the incentives for legislative diligence will be lower. Legislators will tend to devote less time and other resources to legislating. While there are various devices that serve to minimize the effects of this free-riding problem in legislatures (for example, the committee system), members of larger legislatures should tend to shirk more. This implies a negative sign for both *Senate* and *House*.

Term and *Limit* should show the effect, if any, of some important structural aspects of the legislature on legislative output (that is, state spending). Legislatures in which the terms of the two houses are not of equal length may experience higher costs of achieving agreement and entering into legislative "contracts" between houses because of this disparity. As the two houses become more similar, special and general interests may face less disparity of opinion and greater coordination between the two and, therefore, lower costs of lobbying for wealth transfers. Therefore, we expect *Term* to have a negative sign. Legislatures face a number of constraints in their production process, but one of the simplest to measure is the time in which they are permitted to enact bills. Most states limit their legislatures to a maximum length of session; in 1915, the most common length was sixty days. It is possible that

---

23. However, the variable also might be interpreted as a proxy for the cost of lobbying facing interest groups seeking transfers from state government. A higher population density, ceteris paribus, tends to lower the cost of political organization, and the cost of exerting effective influence in the state capitol. This in itself implies that greater dispersion of state population might be associated with lower levels of total political transfers (that is, spending).

such constitutional limits actually represent effective constraints on legislative activities. If this is the case, *Limit* should have a negative sign.

Prior to the passage of the nineteenth amendment to the U.S. Constitution, some states permitted women to vote in state and local elections. Women's suffrage was a major aim of the progressive movement, and most prominent advocates of the female vote were also proponents of expanded governmental redistribution. A number of writers (for example, Lichtman 1979) have argued that the increasing political participation of women was associated with shift in electoral outcomes toward a greater role for government in the economy and higher levels of income transfers by government. *Female Suffrage* is included to take into account the possibility that the participation by women in voting affected the level of state government spending. If woman voters tended to favor progressive government programs, we would expect this variable to have a positive sign. We would expect to find the same result if the state's law pertaining to the female franchise served as a metric for "progressivism" among state voters.

The model includes two alternative dummy variables designed to represent the presence of secret ballot requirements at the state level. Unfortunately, detailed information regarding the precise voting procedures used at the state level for earlier than the 1930s is unobtainable. However, the body of law (both constitutional and statutory) affecting voting has been studied extensively, and it is therefore possible to define the broad legal parameters of the voting process. In other words, available information does not permit us to determine the exact details of state voting practices, but we can isolate those states that mandated secrecy in voting. We assume that in states where there were not express mandates for the secret ballot, voting took place in a publicly verifiable manner, as it had traditionally. States in which the secrecy of the ballot was not actually mandated but that required, or allowed, the use of voting machines imposed severe restrictions on the process of vote-selling contracts by increasing the difficulty of monitoring contractual compliance by purchasers. At the same time, the absence of an express mandate for secrecy technically would have permitted vote markets to operate, although probably less efficiently. (Hence, if a state is included in two but not one, it had relatively weaker secret ballot requirements.) If the presence of mandatory secrecy in voting at the state level relaxed a relevant constraint on the growth of state government, we expect that each of these variables should have a positive sign.

Summary statistics for all the data appear in table 1. Table 2 reports the results of four regressions based on alternative specifications of the basic model with, and without, *Female Suffrage* (which was found to be correlated with several other independent variables). The independent variables generally have the predicted signs, with the exception of *House*, which was positive

TABLE 1. Summary Statistics

Variable	Mean	Standard Deviation	Minimum	Maximum
Expenditure	5.414	2.667	$ 1.87	$ 12.17
Wealth	2,080.12	940.66	$748.00	$5,642.00
Population Dispersion	0.0947	0.1925	0.0016	1.112
House	120.18	67.036	35	414
Senate	37.645	10.932	17	67
Length of Term	0.5833	0.4982	0	1
Session Limit	0.6666	0.4763	0	1
Female Suffrage	0.2291	0.4247	0	1
Constitutional Restriction1	0.3958	0.4942	0	1
Constitutional Restriction2	0.3125	0.4684	0	1

TABLE 2. Dependent Variable: EXPENDITURES

	Model 1	Model 2	Model 3	Model 4
Constant	5.221	5.579	5.35	5.61
	(3.16)	(3.42)	(3.33)	(3.51)
Wealth	0.0013	0.0013	0.0010	0.0011
	(2.79***)	(2.86***)	(2.21**)	(2.30**)
Population Dispersion	2.999	2.591	1.743	1.542
	(1.26)	(1.11)	(0.72)	(0.65)
House	0.0004	0.0001	0.0018	0.0015
	(0.08)	(0.02)	(0.34)	(0.28)
Senate	−0.0534	−0.0615	−0.049	−0.056
	(−1.68*)	(−1.98**)	(−1.62)	(−1.85*)
Length of Term	−1.381	−1.480	−1.291	−1.367
	(−1.84*)	(−1.99**)	(−1.76*)	(−1.86*)
Session Limit	−0.8956	−0.9498	−1.098	−1.110
	(−1.15)	(−1.24)	(−1.44)	(−1.46)
Female Suffrage			1.788	1.602
			(1.83*)	(1.61)
Constitutional Restriction1	1.630		1.263	
	(2.33**)		(1.78*)	
Constitutional Restriction2		1.800		1.395
		(2.63***)		(1.95**)
R^2	0.47	0.49	0.52	0.52
F	5.26	5.61	5.29	5.43
N	48	48	48	48

*significant at the 10 percent level
**significant at the 5 percent level
***significant at the 1 percent level

but insignificant throughout. *Wealth* is positive and significant at the 1 percent level in models 1 and 2, and at the 5 percent level in models 3 and 4. *Senate* was also negative and generally significant, at the 10 and 5 percent levels in 1 and 2, below significance in 3, and at 10 percent again in 4. *Term* was negative and significant at the 10 and 5 percent levels in models 1 and 2, and at 10 percent in 3 and 4. *Female Suffrage* was significant at the 10 percent level in 3, but below significance in 4. Most importantly, both *Constitutional Restriction* variables were positive and significant in the four models: at the 1 percent level in model 1, the 5 percent level in 2 and 4, and the 10 percent level in 3. The regressions had R^2's of 0.47, 0.49, 0.52, and 0.52, respectively. Each was significant at the 5 percent level.

Thus, our empirical investigation supports the hypothesis that the introduction of the secret ballot had a positive impact on the growth of government. States with an effective secret ballot by 1915 had significantly higher levels of per capita spending than did other states, holding other important factors constant.

6. Conclusion

Many of the purported "paradoxes of democracy" are in reality paradoxes of nonpriced votes. But modern voting theorists have failed to acknowledge some major changes in electoral institutions in this century. Historically, votes were normally marketed commodities. The recent introduction of the secret ballot is often portrayed as a victory against corruption. However, because vote markets permitted the tax suppliers of revenue for government redistribution to engage in more efficient rent-protection activities, ballot secrecy may have also relaxed a previously important constraint on government growth. The empirical evidence reported here corroborates this hypothesis.

REFERENCES

Bentley, Michael. 1985. *Politics without Democracy: Great Britain 1815–1914.* New York: Barnes and Noble.
Bryce, James. 1910. *The American Commonwealth,* Vol. 2. New York: Macmillan.
Buchanan, James M., and Gordon Tullock. 1962. *The Calculus of Consent.* Ann Arbor: University of Michigan Press.
Coleman, James S. 1986. *Individual Interests and Collective Action.* New York: Cambridge University Press.
de Schweinitz, Karl. 1943. *England's Road to Social Security.* Philadelphia: University of Pennsylvania Press.
Dinkin, Robert J. 1982. *Voting in Revolutionary America: A Study of Elections in the Original Thirteen States, 1776–1789.* Westport, Conn.: Greenwood Press.

Evans, Eldon Cobb. 1917. *A History of the Australian Ballot System in the United States.* Chicago: University of Chicago Press.

Higgs, Robert. 1987. *Crisis and Leviathan: Understanding the Growth of Government in the U.S. Since 1900.* New York: Oxford University Press.

Kendrick, John W. 1961. *Productivity Trends in the United States.* NBER Monograph. Princeton, N.J.: Princeton University Press.

Lichtman, A. J. 1979. *Prejudice and the Old Order: The Presidential Election of 1928.* Chapel Hill, N.C.: University of North Carolina Press.

Ludington, Arthur C. 1911. "American Ballot Laws, 1888–1910." *Education Department Bulletin* (New York), no. 448 (February): 1–207.

Martin, Robert F. 1976. *National Income in the United States, 1799–1938.* New York: Arno Press.

Mathews, John Mabry. 1915. *American State Government.* New York: D. Appleton and Co.

McCormick, Robert E., and Robert D. Tollison. 1981. *Politicians, Legislation, and the Economy.* Boston: Martinus-Nijhoff.

McDonagh, Eileen L., and H. Douglas Price. 1985. "Women Suffrage in the Progressive Era: Patterns of Opposition and Support in Referenda Voting, 1910–1918." *American Political Science Review* 79 (September): 415–35.

Mitchell, B. R., and Phyllis Deane. 1962. *Abstract of British Historical Statistics.* Cambridge: Cambridge University Press.

Morgan, Edmund S. 1988. *Inventing the People: The Rise of Popular Sovereignty in England and America.* New York: W. W. Norton and Co.

Namier, Lewis. 1965. *The Structure of Politics at the Accession of George III.* London: Macmillan.

Ostrogorski, M. 1964. *Democracy and the Organization of Political Parties.* Chicago: Quadrangle Books.

Peacock, Alan T., and Jack Wiseman. 1961. *The Growth of Public Expenditure in the United Kingdom.* Princeton: Princeton University Press.

Plumb, John H. 1963. *England in the Eighteenth Century.* New York: Penguin.

Spearman, Diana. 1957. *Democracy in England.* New York: Macmillan.

U.S. Bureau of the Census. 1916a. *Financial Statistics of States, 1915.* Washington, D.C.: Government Printing Office.

———. 1916b. *Statistical Abstract of the United States, 1915.* Washington, D.C.: Government Printing Office.

———. 1959. *Historical Statistics of the U.S.: Colonial Times to 1957.* Washington, D.C.: Government Printing Office.

Wendt, Lloyd, and Herman Kogan. 1974. *Bosses in Lusty Chicago.* Bloomington, Ind.: Indiana University Press.

Williams, E. N. 1970. *The Ancien Regime in Europe: Government and Society in the Major States 1648–1789.* New York: Penguin Books.

Williamson, Chilton. 1960. *American Suffrage: From Property to Democracy, 1760–1860.* Princeton, N.J.: Princeton University Press.

Contributors

Gary M. Anderson, California State University, Northridge
W. Mark Crain, George Mason University
Margaret N. Davis, Enron Corporation
Roger L. Faith, Arizona State University
Brian L. Goff, Western Kentucky University
Richard S. Higgins, Howrey and Simon
Donald R. Leavens, U.S. Chamber of Commerce
Arleen A. Leibowitz, Rand Corporation
Delores T. Martin, University of Nebraska
William F. Shughart II, University of Mississippi
Scott J. Thomas, University of California, Irvine
Robert D. Tollison, George Mason University

Index

DATE DUE

		MAY 1 4 1993	
~~DEC 19 1991~~			
~~OCT 0 9 1991~~			
~~DEC 27 1991~~	MAY 0 5 2004		
~~DEC 07 1992~~			
~~SEP 1 6 1993~~			
~~DEC 1 5 1998~~			
~~AUG 0 8 2000~~			
~~MAR 2 0 2004~~			